Islam, Authoritarianism, and Underdevelopment

Why do Muslim-majority countries exhibit high levels of authoritarianism and low levels of socioeconomic development in comparison to world averages? Ahmet T. Kuru criticizes explanations which point to Islam as the cause of this disparity, because Muslims were philosophically and socioeconomically more developed than Western Europeans between the ninth and twelfth centuries. Nor was Western colonialism the cause: Muslims had already suffered political and socioeconomic problems when colonization began. Kuru argues that Muslims had influential thinkers and merchants in their early history, when religious orthodoxy and military rule were prevalent in Europe. However, in the eleventh century, an alliance between orthodox Islamic scholars (the ulema) and military states began to emerge. This alliance gradually hindered intellectual and economic creativity by marginalizing intellectual and bourgeois classes in the Muslim world. This important study links its historical explanation to contemporary politics by showing that, to this day, the ulema–state alliance still prevents creativity and competition in Muslim countries.

Ahmet T. Kuru is Professor of Political Science and Director of the Center for Islamic and Arabic Studies at San Diego State University. He is the author of award-winning *Secularism and State Policies toward Religion: The United States, France, and Turkey* (Cambridge 2009) and co-editor (with Alfred Stepan) of *Democracy, Islam, and Secularism in Turkey* (2012). His works have been translated into Arabic, Chinese, French, and Turkish.

Islam, Authoritarianism, and Underdevelopment

A Global and Historical Comparison

AHMET T. KURU

San Diego State University

CAMBRIDGE
UNIVERSITY PRESS

CAMBRIDGE
UNIVERSITY PRESS

University Printing House, Cambridge CB2 8BS, United Kingdom

One Liberty Plaza, 20th Floor, New York, NY 10006, USA

477 Williamstown Road, Port Melbourne, VIC 3207, Australia

314–321, 3rd Floor, Plot 3, Splendor Forum, Jasola District Centre, New Delhi – 110025, India

79 Anson Road, #06–04/06, Singapore 079906

Cambridge University Press is part of the University of Cambridge.

It furthers the University's mission by disseminating knowledge in the pursuit of education, learning, and research at the highest international levels of excellence.

www.cambridge.org
Information on this title: www.cambridge.org/9781108419093
DOI: 10.1017/9781108296892

First published 2019

Printed in the United Kingdom by TJ International Ltd. Padstow Cornwall

A catalogue record for this publication is available from the British Library.

Library of Congress Cataloging-in-Publication Data
NAMES: Kuru, Ahmet T., author.
TITLE: Islam, authoritarianism, and underdevelopment : a global and historical comparison / Ahmet T. Kuru.
DESCRIPTION: New York, NY : Cambridge University Press, 2019. |
    Includes bibliographical references and index.
IDENTIFIERS: LCCN 2019004815 | ISBN 9781108419093 (hardback) |
    ISBN 9781108409476 (paperback)
SUBJECTS: LCSH: Islamic countries–Civilization. | Islamic countries–Economic conditions. |
    Islamic civilization–Economic aspects. | East and West.
CLASSIFICATION: LCC DS35.62 .K87 2019 | DDC 909/.09767–dc23
LC record available at https://lccn.loc.gov/2019004815

ISBN 978-1-108-41909-3 Hardback
ISBN 978-1-108-40947-6 Paperback

To Uğur (1935–2004), who I wish could have read it, and Yusuf and Yunus Ali, who I hope will read it one day.

Contents

Maps

Tables

Preface

As well as I can remember, I was having breakfast with my parents in Iskenderun (Alexandretta), on Turkey's Mediterranean coast, on a hot day in the summer of 1989. My father seemed upset, and when I asked why, my mother replied that he had had a challenging debate the night before. My father then explained to me how a secularist Turkish army general we had hosted for dinner had broached the issue of Muslim backwardness around midnight, after I had gone to sleep. The general argued that it was only Protestant nations who truly contributed to modern civilization, while Muslim nations were mere consumers of it. My father, provincial chairman of then Prime Minister Turgut Özal's right-wing party, defended Muslims' importance in world history by listing their early contributions to mathematics and other fields. The polarized discussion had left my father frustrated. Intrigued by the debate, I read a book in my father's library, the Turkish translation of Walther Kiaulehn's *The Iron Angels: Birth, History and Power of the Machines from Antiquity to the Time of Goethe.* I immediately told my father that by reading that book I came to understand how Western Europeans surpassed Muslims in technology. He smiled at me in a compassionate way and said, "You should read at least ten to fifteen more books to say that." This is how I began and have continued to read on the subject of the present book, and why it is dedicated to my father, Uğur Kuru.

ACKNOWLEDGMENTS

I am thankful to my teachers, colleagues, and friends for their valuable contributions. The late Bernard Weiss taught me Islamic political thought when I was a graduate student about two decades ago. The late Alfred Stepan, Robert Hefner, Reşat Kasaba, Joel Migdal, and Daniel Philpott inspired and encouraged my comparative work on religion–state relations. I have had rewarding intellectual engagements with Gökhan Bacık, Özgür Koca, and Fevzi Bilgin about Islam and politics. Mikhail Alexseev, Ronnee Schreiber, Hisham Foad, and Ranin Kazemi were among my numerous critically engaging colleagues at San Diego State University (SDSU). Several SDSU fellowships, including the UGP and Hostler grants, supported my research. I am grateful to the SDSU librarians, particularly Edward DiBella and Joan Goodwin, for their assistance with my research.

I thank Cambridge University Press's editor Robert Dreesen and content manager Robert Judkins for their patience and professionalism, and the two anonymous referees for their helpful recommendations. I owe thanks to several colleagues for their helpful comments and criticisms on earlier drafts of various chapters, including Aaron Glasserman, Maya Shatzmiller, Timur Kuran, Khaled Abou El Fadl, Michael Cook, Frederick Starr, Daniel Chirot, Randall Collins, Jan Luiten van Zanden, Louise Marlow, Hasan Kayalı, Nader Hashemi, Şürü Hanioğlu, Stephen Dale, Charles Kurzman, Ziauddin Sardar, Burak Eskici, Kristin Fabbe, Kadir Yıldrım, Peter Adamson, Yüksel Sezgin, Etga Uğur, Anas Malik, Rıza Yıldırım, Renat Shaykhutdinov, Mehdi Aminrazavi, Serhan Tanrıverdi, and Naser Ghobadzadeh. I appreciate the hospitality of several friends during my research in Turkey, Qatar, Syria, Egypt, Tunisia, and Kazakhstan in various periods between 2010 and 2013.

I am blessed with the unconditional love and support of my mother Çiçek Kuru, brother Mehmet, and sisters Mine and Lale. My wife Zeynep has always been a source of love, inspiration, and joy. Our sons Yusuf and Yunus Ali have already begun asking comparative questions about the West and the Muslim world – two inextricable parts of their life. They will probably continue to ask many of the questions explored in this book; that is why it is dedicated to them too.

METHODOLOGY, THEORY, AND NORMATIVE CONCERNS

This book employs comparative historical methods while comparing certain periods of Islamic history with each other as well with particular periods of Western European history.[1] One method it uses is "process tracing," which traces the causes of change by dividing a historical process into smaller and analytically comparable periods.[2] The book also uses the methodological tool of "path dependence"[3] to examine how ideational and material conditions in particular historical periods, especially "critical junctures,"[4] shape subsequent conditions by creating a path dependence. For example, in order to examine currently low levels of literacy in Muslim societies, the book traces the historical origins of this problem to these societies' three-century-long delay in establishing printing presses. Muslim societies did not take advantage of the printing

---

[1] See Mahoney and Rueschemeyer 2003; Sartori 1970; Collier 1991.
[2] George and Bennett 2005, 205–32.
[3] North 1990, esp. 93–4,112; Mahoney 2001, esp. 4–11; Pierson 2000; Thelen 2000.
[4] Capoccia and Kelemen 2007; Kuru 2009, esp. 27–8; Lerner 2014.

technology during and even after the critical juncture of the mid-fifteenth century, when first presses were established in Western Europe. This historical experience created a path-dependent literacy gap between Muslim and Western European societies.

There are two main theoretical approaches in the literature on the problems of violence, authoritarianism, and underdevelopment in Muslim countries. The first one is the essentialist approach, which points to Islam as the main source of Muslims' current problems. Several critics of Islam in the West as well as in Muslim countries have adopted various versions of this approach. They define certain "essential" characteristics of Islamic texts or history and then single out these alleged essentials as causes of the problems. The second one is the postcolonial or anti-colonial approach, which is more international in its analysis. It stresses Western colonization of Muslim countries and ongoing Western exploitation of their resources as reasons for Muslim societies' contemporary problems. Many ideological groups in Muslim countries, from Islamists to secularists, have shared this anti-Western perspective.[5]

This book takes issue with both of these approaches. It criticizes essentialism by documenting that between the eighth and twelfth centuries Muslim societies exhibited great philosophical and economic achievements, which indicates Islam's compatibility with progress.[6] The book also criticizes the anti-colonial approach by emphasizing that in the mid-nineteenth century, when the pervasive colonization of Muslim lands by Western powers began, Muslims had already suffered multiple political and socioeconomic crises.

My theoretical approach focuses on the relations between religious, political, intellectual, and economic classes. In both the Muslim world and Western Europe, these class relations have resulted in societies' success or failure in the intellectual and socioeconomic spheres. Early Muslims' intellectual and economic achievements were led by independent intellectual and bourgeois classes. Starting with the eleventh century, however, class relations changed in the Muslim world; the ulema–state alliance emerged and it sidelined intellectuals and the bourgeoisie.

My theoretical approach emphasizes the connections between ideas and material conditions. Historically, the ulema–state alliance was based on some Sasanian-inspired and quasi-Islamic ideas, as well as certain material conditions, including the militarized land revenues and state control over commerce. The

---

[5] In the words of Timur Kuran (2011, 302), the Middle East "region as a whole has not yet come to terms with the reasons why it turned into an economic laggard. The idea that outsiders are somehow responsible for the Middle East's underdevelopment resonates with much of the population, including secularists who consider Islamic law backward and obsolete."

[6] Referring to this early period, Fernand Braudel (1993, 73) writes, "For four or five centuries, Islam was the most brilliant civilization." Braudel (1982, 559) gives credit to Islam for early Muslims' economic development: "Western civilization did not benefit as Islam did from the bonus of a benevolent religion."

links between dominant ideas and material conditions are also visible today; Islamist ideology and rentierism (particularly based on oil rents) are both critical to understanding various authoritarian regimes in the Muslim world.

It is necessary to make some generalizations about Muslim countries in order to find solutions for their common problems. Initially helpful post-structuralist, post-colonial critiques of Orientalist stereotypes[7] have been exaggerated and used by apologists to obscure Muslims' cultural and ideological problems; this has prevented many scholars from critically analyzing Muslim societies. On the one hand, this book criticizes simplistic over-generalizations, especially what I call "statistical Orientalism," which draws sweeping conclusions about Muslims based on mere numerical correlations without any in-depth analysis. On the other hand, the book tries to conduct a comparative and critical analysis of Muslim countries.

In some of my presentations of this book project, critics have claimed that democracy and development were façades for Western imperialism, and that my analysis would therefore serve the Western agenda in Muslim countries. I have had two responses to this challenge. First, I wish Western policy-makers had a consistent policy of promoting democracy and development in Muslim countries, which is generally not the case. Second, surveys show that the overwhelming majority of the people in Muslim societies favor democracy as the best form of government.[8] Most people in Muslim countries see violence, authoritarianism, and underdevelopment as problems; this book is not imposing a Western perspective upon them.

SPELLING, NAMES, AND TRANSLATIONS

This is primarily a book of political science, not history. It analyzes contemporary problems and explores history to understand their origins. That is why it begins with chapters on contemporary issues and then moves to historical chapters.[9] Dates throughout the text, including quotations, are given with reference to the Common Era. In order to reach a broader audience, I use Arabic names and words with their forms in English without using diacritical marks (e.g., sharia, instead of *shari'a*). I italicize words rarely, only if the word is not used in English (e.g., *bay'a*). I use diacritical marks for *'ayn* (') and for *hamza* (') only in italicized words, in direct quotations, and in the Bibliography. Referring to Islamic scholars, I write "ulema," instead of "ulama," because the former better indicates the proper Arabic pronunciation without the diacritical marks.

For Arabic names, I generally do not use the definite article "al." In Ottoman words and names I use the letter "k" instead of "q," the modern Turkish usage.

---

[7] Said 1979. See also Asad 2003, esp. ch. 7.
[8] Pew Research Center 2013, 32; Fish 2011, 245; Inglehart and Norris 2003, 64.
[9] I used the same chapter order, contemporary before historical, in my previous book, Kuru 2009.

For pre-modern persons, I use the most well-known version of their names, which may be one (e.g., Biruni) or two (e.g., Harun al-Rashid) words. If the person is well known by both long and short versions of his or her name (e.g., Ahmad ibn Hanbal/Ibn Hanbal), or if there is more than one person with the same name (e.g., Razi), I use the longer version the first time and whenever it helps with clarification. If a pre-modern person's name has two words (e.g., Yunus Emre), the second word functions like a last name in the Bibliography and Index.

In the Bibliography, the overwhelming majority of translations are from Arabic into English; I specify the translations from languages other than Arabic and into languages other than English. For Arabic sources, I mostly rely on English translations. Unless noted otherwise, translations in the text and footnotes from original Arabic, French, and Turkish sources are mine.

Introduction

In November 2014, the media reported that in a single month, the attacks perpetrated by sixteen different jihadi groups killed more than 5,000 people; most of this bloodshed befell Iraq, followed by Nigeria, Afghanistan, and Syria.[1] At least since September 11, 2001, the world media has frequently covered Muslim perpetrators in terrorism, minor conflicts, and wars. The prominence of Muslims in this coverage cannot entirely be disregarded as journalistic sensationalism or bias. Scholarly data support the disproportionate attention to Muslims in reporting on violence. Two-thirds of all wars and about one-third of all minor military conflicts in 2009 occurred in Muslim-majority countries.[2]

Muslim-majority countries have also experienced disproportionate rates of authoritarianism, which is a major factor leading to violence. In 2013, Freedom House classified less than one-fifth of the forty-nine Muslim-majority countries as electoral democracies, while classifying three-fifths of the 195 countries in the world as electoral democracies. Authoritarianism is also a multifaceted phenomenon; it is associated with several factors, especially socioeconomic underdevelopment. Around 2010, Muslim-majority countries' averages of gross national income per capita (GNIpc), literacy rate, years of schooling, and life expectancy were all below world averages, as Table I.1 indicates. These data lead us to ask: Why are Muslim-majority countries less peaceful, less democratic, less developed?

---

[1] Ian Black, "Jihadi Groups Killed More than 5,000 People in November," *Guardian*, December 10, 2014.
[2] See Table I.1. For the data showing Muslim groups' disproportionate involvement in terrorism, see Chapter 1.

TABLE I.I *Muslim-Majority Countries and the World (around 2010)*

	Muslim-majority countries (49)	All countries (around 195)
Violence (total numbers)	Wars: 4 Minor conflicts: 9	Wars: 6 Minor conflicts: 30
Authoritarianism	Electoral democracies: 14%	Electoral democracies: 60%
Underdevelopment (averages)	GNIpc: $9,000	GNIpc: $14,000
	Literary rate: 73% Schooling: 5.8 years Life expectancy: 66 years	Literary rate: 84% Schooling: 7.5 years Life expectancy: 69 years

Sources: Violence: Uppsala Conflict Data Program's (UCDP) 2009 data quoted in Harborn and Vallensteen 2010, 506–7. UCDP defines conflicts that cause at least 1,000 casualties as wars and those that lead to between 25 and 999 casualties as minor conflicts. Electoral democracies: Freedom House 2013. GNIpc: World Bank 2010. In my calculation, I excluded Qatar's GNIpc ($179,000), which was about three times higher than the second highest in the world, Luxembourg ($61,790). Literacy rates: United Nations Statistics Division 2013. Years of schooling and life expectancy: United Nations Development Programme 2011.

Contemporary problems of Muslim-majority countries[3] are especially puzzling given the scholarly and socioeconomic achievements of their predecessors between the eighth and twelfth centuries. During that period, the Muslim world produced creative polymaths, such as Farabi, Biruni, and Ibn Sina, and played a pivotal role in intercontinental trade,[4] while Western Europe[5] was a marginal corner of the Old World.[6] This historical experience shows that Islam was perfectly compatible with scholarly flourishing and socioeconomic progress.

[3] For the sake of simplicity, from now on, I will refer to "Muslim-majority countries" as "Muslim countries."
[4] During that period, Muslim merchants invented several economic tools, such as the check and the bill of exchange. Braudel 1982, 556; Udovitch 1979, 263, 269; Van Zanden 2009, 61. The "Persian word *sakk* is the origin of our word 'check.'" Bloom and Blair 2002, 114.
[5] In analyzing the Middle Ages, this book generally uses the terms "Western Christians" or "Catholics" when comparing them with another religious/cultural entity, "Muslims." Yet, especially by the Reformation and the Enlightenment, it becomes increasingly difficult to use these terms given the complex religious and secular identities in Western Europe. Thus, for modern periods I use the term "Western Europeans," referring to a cultural/civilizational, rather than simply geographical, entity. By Western European countries, I mean present members of the European Union, excluding Bulgaria, Cyprus, and Greece (which are in Eastern Europe), and adding Switzerland and Norway.
[6] In the late eighth century, Muslim economic influence on Western Europe was so deep that in the English kingdom of Mercia, King Offa minted imitations of the Abbasid gold coin carrying the bungled Arabic inscriptions "There is no deity but God [Allah], who is without associates" and "Muhammad is the Prophet of God [Allah]." Beckett 2003, 58.

In the eleventh and twelfth centuries, however, a gradual process of reversal in terms of comparative levels of scientific and socioeconomic development started between the Muslim world and Western Europe. Especially between the sixteenth and eighteenth centuries, Western Europe experienced multiple progressive transformations, while the Muslim world became stagnant and fell behind. When widespread Western colonization of Muslim lands began in the mid-nineteenth century, Muslims had already faced multiple intellectual, socioeconomic, and political problems.

Hence, contemporary Muslim countries' political and socioeconomic problems have long-term historical origins and cannot simply be explained as the result of either Islam or Western colonialism. The difference between the intellectually and economically dynamic Muslim world during its early history, on the one hand, and the stagnant Muslim world during its later history, on the other, requires more nuanced and sophisticated explanation. What historical factors explain this difference and constitute the roots of Muslims' contemporary problems?

THE ULEMA–STATE ALLIANCE

I argue that the relations between religious, political, intellectual, and economic classes have been the main engine behind the changes in and reversals between the levels of development in the Muslim world, as well as in Western Europe. In early Islamic history, Islamic scholars generally regarded close entanglements with political authorities as corrupting; they preferred to be funded by commerce and maintained close relations with merchants. According to one analysis I will elaborate later, from the eighth to the mid-eleventh century, 72.5 percent of Islamic scholars or their families worked in commerce and/or industry.[7]

Islamic scholars' distance from state authorities went back to the mid-seventh century, when the Umayyads established their dynasty by persecuting the Prophet Muhammad's descendants and violently crushing any opposition to their rule. This violent consolidation of power led to the disenchantment with the political authority in the eyes of many Islamic scholars. These scholars' aloofness with respect to political authorities was reinforced in the late Umayyad and early Abbasid eras, from the mid-eighth to the mid-ninth century. During this period, the four main Sunni schools of jurisprudence (*fiqh*) were founded by independent scholars – Abu Hanifa, Malik, Shafii, and Ahmad ibn Hanbal – all of whom refused to be state servants. Moreover, these founders were imprisoned and persecuted by authorities due to their dissenting opinions. Shii religious leaders faced even more persecution by the political class.

In early Islamic history, Islamic scholars' independence from the state and the economic influence of merchants enabled the freedom of thought enjoyed by

---

[7] Cohen 1970, 36 (table A-I).

philosophers, a diverse group including not only Sunni and Shii Muslims, but also Christians, Jews, and agnostics. These philosophers were funded by both merchants and political authorities. The rulers particularly patronized the translation of ancient works (from Greek, Syriac, Middle Persian, and Sanskrit into Arabic). Yet there were no state-led schools to standardize philosophy. Thus, state patronage of philosophers in early Islamic history was less harmful for intellectual flourishing than what would become the state patronage of Islamic scholars (the ulema; sing. *alim*) following the eleventh century.

What happened in eleventh-century Central Asia, Iran, and Iraq was a multidimensional transformation. Abbasid caliphs in Baghdad, severely weakened by the rising Shii states in North Africa, Egypt, Syria, and even Iraq, called for the unification of Sunni Muslims to meet this threat. In order to unify Sunni sultans, ulema, and masses, two Abbasid caliphs declared a "Sunni creed" in the early eleventh century; those whose views were deemed to contradict this creed, including certain Shiis, rationalist theologians (Mutazilis), and philosophers, were declared to be apostates and faced the threat of execution. This call for the formation of a Sunni orthodoxy coincided with the rise of the Ghaznavids, a Sunni military state in Central Asia. Later, the Seljuk Empire (1040–1194) emerged as an even more powerful Sunni military state that ruled over a large territory including most parts of Central Asia, Iran, Iraq, and Anatolia.

Central to Seljuk rule was the expansion of the *iqta*, an existing system of land revenue assignment and tax farming designed to bring agricultural revenues in particular and the economy in general under military control. This policy weakened the economic capacity and social position of merchants, who had previously provided funding to both the ulema and philosophers. One Seljuk grand vizier (minister) also initiated the foundation of a series of madrasas, the so-called Nizamiyyas, to synthesize competing Sunni schools of jurisprudence and theology and to produce Sunni ulema who could challenge Shiis, Mutazilis, and philosophers. A genius scholar, Ghazali, played a key role in this project, writing multiple influential books criticizing these three "unorthodox" groups.

From the twelfth to the fourteenth century, the Seljuk model of the ulema–state alliance spread to other Sunni states in Andalus, Egypt, and Syria, particularly the Mamluks. The Crusader and Mongol invasions accelerated the spread of this alliance because Muslim communities sought refuge from the chaos of foreign invasion in military and religious authorities. Later, around the sixteenth century, Muslims established three powerful military empires: the Sunni Ottoman, the Shii Safavid, and the Sunni-run (but non-sectarian) Mughal Empires. These empires established versions of the ulema–state alliance in territories extending from the Balkans to Bengal.[8] These empires were militarily

---

[8] Although these three empires dominated the Muslim world, there existed other Muslim political entities, including small states in what we call today Indonesia and Malaysia. Unlike the three empires, several of these Southeast Asian states did not have an ulema–state alliance and they were mainly mercantile. Hefner 2000, 14, 26; Lombard 2000, 120; Reid 1993a, chs. 1 and 2.

very powerful, but they failed to revive early Muslims' intellectual and economic dynamism because they virtually eliminated philosophers and marginalized merchants.[9]

While the Muslim world was losing its intellectual and economic momentum, Western European progress began. In the second half of the eleventh century, three transformations occurred in Western Europe. First, the Catholic Church and royal authorities tried and failed to dominate one another, leading to the institutionalization of the separation between them as a *modus vivendi*. This substantially contributed to decentralization and balance of power among Western European actors and institutions. Second, universities started to be established and provided an institutional basis for the gradual emergence and increasing influence of the intellectual class. Many revolutionary thinkers, from Aquinas to Luther, from Copernicus to Galileo and Newton, would be university graduates and professors. Third, the merchant class, which would be the engine of Western European economic breakthroughs, began to flourish.[10] These new relations among religious, political, intellectual, and economic classes eventually drove various progressive processes, including the Renaissance, the printing revolution, geographical explorations, the Protestant Reformation, the scientific revolution, the American and French Revolutions, and the Industrial Revolution. As a result of these processes, Western Europe surpassed its once-superior competitors, the Muslim world and China.

After nearly a century of Western colonialism, Muslims began to establish independent states in the 1920s and 1930s. These states inherited deep political and socioeconomic problems as a result of centuries of intellectual and economic stagnation followed by colonial exploitation. In order to address the problems of violence, authoritarianism, and socioeconomic underdevelopment, Muslim countries needed creative intellectuals (i.e., thinkers who criticize established perspectives and produce original alternatives) and independent bourgeoisie (i.e., economic entrepreneurs, such as merchants, bankers, and

---

These states, however, could not provide an alternative model of class relations to the Muslim world for two main reasons. First, even as late as the sixteenth century, Islam co-existed with local religious beliefs and practices in these states. According to Anthony Reid (1993b, 156), "no Islamic texts in Southeast Asian languages which date before 1590 have come to light." See also Reid 1993a, ch. 3. Second, European colonization began as early as the seventeenth century in this region. Hence, the period between Islamization and colonization was too short to establish a Southeast Asian model. Moreover, in the nineteenth and twentieth centuries, Middle Eastern interpretations of Islam influenced Southeast Asian Muslims, rather than vice versa. Hefner 2009, 15–23.

[9] After Ibn Khaldun (d. 1406) in history, Ali Kushji (d. 1474) in astronomy, and Taftazani (d. 1390) and Jurjani (d. 1414) in theology, the Muslim world very rarely produced scholars in that caliber, with few exceptions such as Takiyuddin (d. 1585) in astronomy and Mulla Sadra (d. 1640) in philosophy.

[10] European universities taught translations of several works of Muslim polymaths, such as Ibn Sina, until the sixteenth century.

industrialists).[11] Yet these two classes did not emerge in most Muslim countries, an absence I attribute to the historical (post-eleventh-century) dominance of the ulema–state alliance. Nonetheless, starting with Turkey and Iran in the 1920s, new states that were formed in the Muslim world – with few exceptions such as Saudi Arabia – did away with the ulema–state alliance and embraced more secular arrangements of political power. But why, even in these cases of political secularization, did independent intellectual and bourgeois classes not emerge in an influential manner?

SECULARISTS AND ISLAMIC ACTORS

Despite their century-long struggles against each other, secularists and Islamic actors have both contributed to the enduring marginalization of intellectuals and the bourgeoisie in their societies. There are three main explanations for the secularists' contribution. First, most twentieth-century secularist leaders in such cases as Turkey, Iran, Egypt, Iraq, Syria, Algeria, Tunisia, Pakistan, and Indonesia were former military officers. By training and socialization, they were unlikely to truly appreciate the importance of intellectuals and the bourgeoisie for the political and economic development of their countries. Second, these secularist leaders were generally under the influence of socialist and fascist ideologies, in particular, and authoritarian modernist ideas, in general. Thus, they imposed ideological views to society and established state control over the economy by restricting the intellectual and bourgeois classes. Third, many secularist rulers have arbitrarily tried to use Islam to legitimize their regimes. Such cooptation has eventually promoted the established ulema at the expense of independent Islamic scholars and intellectuals.

Though they were founded by secularist leaders, many modern states in the Muslim world experienced Islamization of public life as a result of policy failures of the secularists and general conservatism of Muslim societies. Islamization has elevated the status of three groups of Islamic actors, who have shared negative attitudes toward intellectuals and the bourgeoisie. One group is the ulema, who are trained in madrasas or their more modernized equivalents (such as Turkey's departments of theologies) in Islamic disciplines, including jurisprudence, the hadith, and Quranic exegesis. Another group is the Islamists, who engage in electoral or other types of politics through political parties and movements. The third group is the Sufi shaykhs, who are mystical and social leaders of Sufi orders (*tariqa*s).

Despite their internal disagreements, these Islamic actors have shared negative attitudes toward the independent bourgeoisie, given their statist and hierarchical outlook, according to which religious and political authorities are

---

[11] According to Eric Hobsbawm (1987, 170), the definition of the bourgeoisie is "notoriously difficult" and various Western languages include such "shifting and imprecise categories" as "big bourgeoisie" or "petty bourgeoisie."

supposed to hold the highest social status. These Islamic actors have also had a common anti-intellectual attitude. This attitude follows the ulema's epistemology, which is based on four hierarchical sources: the Quran, hadiths (the records of the Prophet's words and actions), consensus of the ulema (*ijma*), and analogical reasoning (*qiyas*).[12] Two characteristics of this epistemology discourage new interpretations of Islam, particularly by Muslim intellectuals. First, it restricts reason to making analogies on points where the literal meanings of the Quran and hadiths offer no clear ruling, and where there is a lack of consensus among the scholars.[13] Second, and relatedly, it establishes the consensus of the ulema as an entrenched authority, which weakens alternative views.

In fact, the basis of consensus as a jurisprudential concept is a hadith: "My community will never agree upon an error." The term "community" here referred to Muslim people at large. If it had continued to be understood in this broad manner, this concept could have provided opportunities for participation and change. However, the ulema have monopolized the concept of consensus by exclusively interpreting it with reference to themselves, turning it into "a bulwark of conservatism."[14]

Early Muslims actually assigned a more significant and emancipatory role to reason. Abu Hanifa (699–767), the founder of earliest Sunni school of jurisprudence, acknowledged a jurist's reason-based judgment as an important source of jurisprudential authority. Two generations later, however, Shafii developed the jurisprudential method that prioritized the literal understanding of the Qur'an and hadiths followed by the consensus of the ulema, limiting the role of reason to mere analogy. Moreover, with the works of such eminent ulema as Ghazali, Shafii's jurisprudential method influenced other fields of Islamic knowledge such as theology and Sufism.[15] At first, Shafii's method was one of the many alternative jurisprudential approaches. By the establishment of the ulema–state alliance starting in the eleventh century, however, it gradually became the main pillar of Sunni orthodoxy. Ultimately, Hanafis adopted this methodology, as did Malikis and Hanbalis.[16]

---

[12] The way the Muslim Brothers led the drafting of a new Egyptian constitution in November 2012 reflects Islamists' acknowledgment of the ulema's authority to interpret Islamic law. In this drafting, Islamist Brothers constitutionally empowered Al-Azhar's senior ulema with a consultative authority "in matters relating to" Islamic law (article 4), which was "the principle source of legislation" in Egypt (article 2). See also Euben and Zaman 2009, 19; Roy 1996, x.

[13] The Shii ulema's epistemology is similar, though for them consensus is less authoritative, and they put more emphasis on reason. Weiss 1998, 36. The overwhelming majority (87–90%) of Muslims in the world are Sunni and the rest (10–13%) are Shii. Pew Research Center 2009, 1. Among Muslim countries, forty-five are Sunni-majority, while the remaining four (Iran, Iraq, Azerbaijan, and Bahrain) are Shii-majority.

[14] Lambton 1981, 10, 12.   [15] Al-Ghazali 2015 [c. 1097].

[16] Lambton 1981, 4; McAuliffe 2015, 196; Abou El Fadl 2014, xxxiv–vii.

Consequently, Shafii's jurisprudential method became a dominant episte-mology that came to order other aspects of knowledge in the Muslim world. "If it were admissible to name Islamic culture according to one of its products," wrote Mohammed Abed al-Jabri in the 1980s, "then we would call it 'the culture of *fiqh* (jurisprudence)' in the same sense that applies to Greek culture when we call it a 'culture of philosophy' and contemporary European culture as a 'culture of science and technology.'" For Jabri, the rules of jurisprudence established by Shafii "are no less important in forming Arab-Islamic reason than the 'rules of methodology' posited by Descartes about the formation of French reason."[17]

There have been some attempts to include additional sources of knowledge into this jurisprudential epistemology. Although Ghazali was a leading pro-moter of this epistemology, particularly its sidelining of reason, he was also a sophisticated scholar with complex, if not always consistent, ideas. He pro-moted the idea of the five "higher objectives" of Islamic law. About three centuries later, the Andalusian jurist Shatibi elaborated these five objectives – the protection of religion, of life, of intellect, of progeny, and of property – as a way of making jurisprudence more flexible.[18] Sufi shaykhs' promotion of mystical knowledge was another attempt to relax the epistemological con-straints on Muslim intellectual life.[19] Nonetheless, these efforts have mostly remained inconsequential in comparison to the dominant epistemology origin-ally formulated by Shafii, which assigns a marginal role to reason and no role to empirical experience. This epistemology has been a source of the anti-intellectualism among the ulema, Islamists, and Sufi shaykhs.

From the 1980s onward, many Muslim countries experienced Islamization of the public life,[20] as part of the global rise of religious movements.[21] The ulema, Islamists, and Sufis gained more public influence and reinforced the marginalization of the intellectual and bourgeois classes. The secularists by and large have been similarly anti-intellectual and anti-bourgeois in implementing their authoritarian secularist ideologies and policies. Under these class condi-tions, Muslim countries have mostly failed to solve their multifaceted and historically rooted problems.

---

[17] Al-Jabri 2011 [1984], 109, 114.
[18] Opwis 2010; Masud 1995; al-Raysuni 2005; Zaman 2012, ch. 4.
[19] Ghazali also played a role in promoting mystical knowledge. He depicted the emphasis on *fiqh* as an exaggeration and tried to balance it with Sufism. Ghazali (2015 [c. 1097], 87–90) noted that the word *fiqh* mentioned in the Quran and hadiths does not mean jurisprudence (in terms of knowing the details of legal issues) but rather implies such broader things as understanding, piety, and mystical insight. For more on Ghazali, see Chapter 4.
[20] A recent survey conducted in fifteen Middle Eastern and North African countries between 2002 and 2010 shows that 70 percent of respondents define themselves Muslim above all national or other identities. Tessler 2015, 81.
[21] Casanova 1994; Berger 1999; Juergensmeyer 2007.

Those who see Islam as inherently rejecting religion–state separation may regard my explanation as pessimistic. For them, if the ulema–state alliance is the source of Muslims' problems, then there is no way to solve them, because the alliance is based on Islam's essentially non-separationist approach to religion–state relations. However, my analysis actually explains that the ulema–state alliance is neither an essential part of the Quran and hadiths nor a permanent feature of Islamic history. Early Islamic history includes examples of religion–state separation, and it is a mistake to see Islam as inherently rejecting such separation. But what might be the cause of this widespread and by now conventional misunderstanding?

RELIGION AND THE STATE (*DIN WA DAWLA*)

There are two main sources of the conventional view about Islam's relationship with the state. One source is the body of work by Western (i.e., North American and Western European) scholars who have taken the ulema's quasi-Islamic political views written during and after the eleventh century as the definition of what is essentially Islamic. In his well-known book, *Political Thought in Medieval Islam*, Erwin Rosenthal falsely attributes a saying to the Prophet Muhammad: "[R]eligion and ('secular') power are twins."[22] Rosenthal claims that it is Ghazali who quotes this "hadith."[23] In *Moderation in Belief* – cited by Rosenthal – Ghazali does indeed define religion and the state as twins: "[I]t has been said that religion and sultan are twins, and also that religion is a foundation and the sultan is a guard: that which has no foundation collapses and that which has no guard is lost."[24] Yet, when Ghazali wrote, "it has been said," he was not referring to a hadith. In fact, the maxim "religion and royal authority are twins" was a well-known saying, not of Prophetic but of Sasanian origin.[25]

A century and a half before Ghazali, the historian Masudi quoted an Arabic translation of a Sasanian text in his book. In Masudi's narrative, the founder of the Sasanian Empire, Ardashir I (r. 224–42), provided the following advice in his testament: "Religion and royal authority are twins, who cannot exist without each other; because, religion is the foundation of royal authority and royal authority is the guard of religion. Any structure that does not repose on a foundation collapses, and any structure that is not guarded perishes."[26] Before Masudi, the Testament of Ardashir had been translated from Middle Persian into Arabic several times, the first of which was completed as early as the eighth century.[27] In sum, the origin of the idea of religion–state

---

[22] Rosenthal 1958, 8. For a similar perspective, see Lambton 1981, xv.

[23] A "[h]adith he [Ghazali] quotes ...: 'Religion and (temporal) power are twins.'" Rosenthal 1958, 39.

[24] Al-Ghazali 2013 [1095], 231.   [25] Bagley 1964, xlii; Abbès 2015, 56.

[26] Quoted in Maçoudi 1863 [947], 162. See also "Le Testament d'Ardasir" 1966 [n.a.], 49, 62.

[27] Askari 2016, 155; Boyce 1968, 14.

brotherhood in the Muslim world is a Sasanian, not an Islamic, text. I elaborate more on this issue in Chapter 4.

In various episodes of his life, Ghazali (1058–1111) had inconsistent relations with state authorities – another indication that Islam–state relations have never been straightforward. Early in his career, Ghazali taught in a state-controlled madrasa and was subject to direct influence from the rulers. Later on, Ghazali renounced all affiliation with the state to become an independent Sufi and scholar, by declaring his regret for previous entanglements with state authorities.[28] Things changed again toward the end of Ghazali's life, when he briefly returned to teaching in a public madrasa. Ghazali's writings reflect this inconsistent relationship with the state. In his magnum opus, *The Revival of Religious Sciences*, which promotes Sufism, Ghazali reiterated his lines about religion–state brotherhood[29] but also urged the ulema to avoid close connections with rulers, defining the latter as generally corrupt and repressive.[30] Thus, despite the construction of the ulema–state alliance in the eleventh century, the earlier ulema's ideas about the necessary distance between scholars and political authorities partially survived in Muslim lands.

Islamist propaganda is the second source of the misperception of Islam as inherently opposed to religion–state separation. Although Islamists have gained power in only a few countries, they have helped drive the Islamization of the public sphere across the Muslim world and informed perceptions of Islam around the globe. Throughout the twentieth century, Islamist leaders, including Hassan al-Banna (the founder of the Muslim Brothers in Egypt), Abul Ala Maududi (the founder of Jamaat-i Islami in the Indian subcontinent), and Ruhollah Khomeini (the founder of the Islamic Republic of Iran), rejected the notion of a secular state and championed the integration of religion and state, going beyond the pre-modern notion of a religion–state alliance.

Al-Banna (1906–43) popularized the idea that Islam is both religion and the state, "*al-Islam din wa dawla.*"[31] Khomeini (1902–89) was both a prominent member of the Shii ulema and an Islamist revolutionary leader.[32] For Khomeini, the "slogan of the separation of religion and politics and the demand that Islamic scholars not intervene in social and political affairs" are

---

[28] Griffel 2009, 43–4.

[29] "[T]he state and religion are twins. Religion is the foundation whiles the state is the guard. That which has no foundation will certainly crumble and that which has no guard is lost." Al-Ghazali 1962 [c. 1097], 33–4. See also Gazali 1974a [c. 1097], 51.

[30] Al-Ghazali 1962 [c. 1097], 172–6; al-Ghazali 2015 [c. 1097], 199–203; Gazali 1974b [c. 1097], 344.

[31] Al-Banna 1979 [1938–45], 179; also 18, 317–18, 356. The Muslim Brothers, according to Banna, are calling people to Islam and "government is part of it." If the critics say, "This is politics!" they should reply: "This is Islam, and we do not recognize such divisions." Al-Banna 1978 [1938–45], 36. See al-Banna 1979 [1938–45], 110.

[32] Maududi also had a madrasa education but concealed that fact. Nasr 1996, 19; Moosa 2015, 24.

propagated by the imperialists, and "it is only the irreligious who repeat them."[33] Khomeini's idea of the guardianship of the jurist (*velayat-e faqih*), which entailed the ulema's domination of both judicial and executive powers in an unprecedented manner, became the basis of the post-revolutionary politico-legal system in Iran.

In the twentieth and early twenty-first centuries, there have also been Western scholars and Muslim thinkers who argued that Islam did not inherently reject religion–state separation. Historian Ira Lapidus argued in several publications that a certain level of Islam–state separation existed in early Islamic history. For him, the ulema–state alliance emerged during and after the eleventh century.[34]

Three Muslim thinkers have similarly and compellingly argued that religion–state separation is integral to Islamic thought and practice. One Muslim thinker who advocated a certain level of separation between Islam and the state was Seyyid Bey, an Islamic jurist and member of the Ottoman ulema. After the founding of the Turkish Republic, he became the minister of justice. Seyyid Bey gave the famous speech in the Turkish Parliament in 1924 that convinced many deputies to abolish the caliphate. The speech argued for the necessity and reality of a certain level of Islam–state separation by claiming that (1) Islam did not require a political institution such as the caliphate and that it allowed people to determine their own political institutions; (2) the caliphate had been based on the representation of the people, and the new and true representative of the people was the parliament; (3) the Prophet Muhammad stated that the true caliphate would last only thirty years after him and then would be followed by the corrupt sultanate; and (4) many Arabs chose to ally with Britain against the Ottoman caliph during World War I.[35]

A year later, Ali Abdel Razek, an Egyptian Islamic jurist and judge, wrote an influential treatise against the idea of an Islamic caliphate. He argues that (1) there is no evidence in the Qur'an or hadiths about the necessity of an Islamic political authority (caliph); (2) the Prophet Muhammad's political acts were results of mundane needs, not a part of his main religious mission; (3) the Prophet left behind neither a political successor nor a political system; and (4) the history of the Umayyad and Abbasid caliphates was full of rebellions and oppression, which showed the corrupt nature of politics.[36]

About a century later, another Egyptian, Gamal al-Banna, defended a similar thesis. He was a self-made Muslim thinker, a left-wing author, as well as the youngest brother of Hassan al-Banna. In *Al-Islam Din wa Ummah wa Laysa Dinan wa Dawlah (Islam Is Religion and Community, Not Religion and the*

---

[33] Khomeini 1981 [1970], 38. See also Maududi 1960, esp. 202–4.
[34] Lapidus 1975; Lapidus 1996.   [35] Bey 1969 [1924], 40–61; Bey 1942 [1924].
[36] Abdel Razek 2012 [1925], esp. 36–56, 71–4, 87–96, 104–7. For proponents and opponents of Abdel Razek's thesis, see Filali-Ansary 2002, esp. 47–77; Filali-Ansary 2003, 95–114; Radhan 2014, 22–4, 112–25; Ali 2009.

State), Gamal argues that state power inherently and inevitably corrupts any religion, including Islam. He lists the Quranic verses that stress that the Prophet Muhammad was a messenger, not a ruler; that putting the faith in people's hearts is up to God, not a human authority, even the Prophet; that believing or not believing is a personal choice; that there is no worldly punishment for apostasy; and that Islam emphasizes the community, not the state. Gamal held that the Prophet's political authority should not be taken as a model today, because his governance was very different from the modern state, in terms of the latter's institutionalized coercive and other capacities.[37]

Unlike Hassan al-Banna, Maududi, and Khomeini, these Muslim thinkers who endorsed religion–state separation had only a marginal impact on Muslim politics. Although Seyyid Bey was not an Islamist, he was too Islamically conservative for the taste of Mustafa Kemal (later, Atatürk). Immediately after Seyyid Bey helped to abolish the caliphate, Mustafa Kemal replaced him with a new, staunchly secularist minister of justice. Abdel Razek also faced a similar dismissal, which came from the ulema, who unlike their counterpart in secularizing Turkey, were still influential in Egypt. In response to Abdel Razek's book criticizing the idea of the caliphate, the ulema council of Al-Azhar – the famous madrasa from which he graduated – condemned him, revoked his license, and thus made him unable to serve as a judge. More recently, the influence of Gamal al-Banna did not even come close to that of his Islamist older brother.

There are two reasons for the limited influence of these Muslim thinkers. First, their middle-way position between Islamists and secularists won support from neither of these two polarized groups. Second, the idea of an Islam–state alliance, or more specifically the ulema–state alliance, was so well established in Turkish, Egyptian, and many other Muslim societies that whoever criticized it was likely to be marginalized, if not persecuted.

Part I of this book will examine how the ulema, the authoritarian state, and various alliances between them have substantially contributed to problems of violence, authoritarianism, and underdevelopment in many Muslim countries today. Part II will analyze how the ulema–state alliance began to emerge in the eleventh century – a critical juncture before which Muslims had achieved scholarly and socioeconomic progress and after which they started to experience intellectual and socioeconomic stagnation.

[37] Al-Banna 2003, 3–4, 12–18, 38–9. See also al-Banna 2001.

PART I

PRESENT

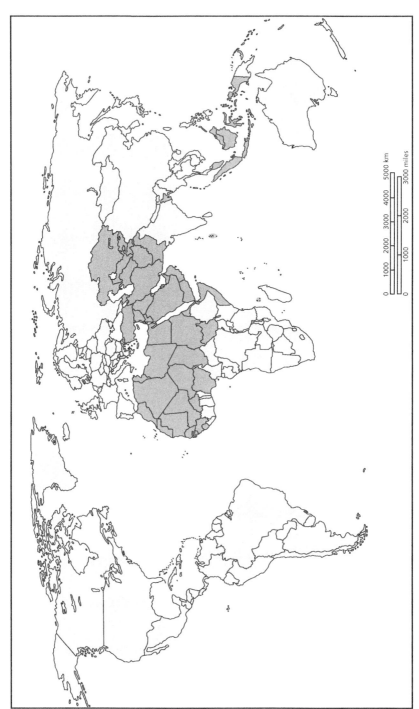

MAP 1 Forty-Nine Muslim-Majority Countries (2018)

I

Violence and Peace

Followers of world affairs frequently see news about terrorist attacks and military conflicts in which Muslims took part. From 1994 to 2008, Islamist groups perpetrated three-fifths of the 204 high-casualty terrorist bombings that occurred throughout the world.[1] In 2009, there were six wars and thirty-one minor conflicts in the world (each having two main sides). Two-thirds of the sides in the wars (8 out of 12) and two-fifths of the sides in the minor conflicts (24 out of 60) were Muslim-majority states or Muslim groups.[2] These rates of participation are disproportionate, as Muslims constitute only one-quarter of the world's population and Muslim-majority countries make up only one-quarter of the world's countries (see Map 1).

Muslims' association with violence is disproportionate only in terms of political violence (including war, minor conflict, and terrorism). That association is also a recent phenomenon. When it comes to homicide (measured as homicides per 100,000 people in a year), the average rate of Muslim-majority countries is lower (2.4) than that of non-Muslim countries (7.5).[3] Even regarding political violence, Muslims did not have a disproportionately high involvement until the late twentieth century.[4] They played a very limited role in the World War I and World War II. Until the 1980s, Muslims generally experienced less state violence domestically in comparison to several communist and fascist regimes in the Soviet Union, China, Southeast Asia, and Latin America. From the 1940s to the 1980s, the major terrorist organizations were also primarily socialist, not Islamist. Thus, the disproportionate Muslim

---

[1] Fish 2011, 151.   [2] Harborn and Vallensteen, 2010, 506–7.   [3] Fish 2011, 9, 120.
[4] "Are Muslim countries more war-prone? Not necessarily, if we look at data for the whole period after World War II. But in the post–Cold War era, most wars are civil wars and Muslim countries have a disproportionate share of these." Gleditsch and Rudolfsen 2016, 1.

participation in political violence is mostly a phenomenon of the last three decades.[5] If this is the case, what explains the recent surge of Muslim involvement in political violence?[6]

The chapter begins by critically reviewing the impact of Western colonization and occupation on Muslims' relations with violence. It then critically explores the complex relations between Islam and violence. Next, the chapter examines the role of the ulema in the problem of violence. Finally, it analyzes how authoritarian rule has been a major factor for terrorism, civil wars, and interstate wars in the Muslim world.

WESTERN COLONIZATION AND OCCUPATION

Several analysts have blamed Western colonialism for the rise of violence in various Muslim societies. For Frantz Fanon, French colonialism in Algeria did not leave many options to the Algerian people other than using violence against the colonizer to regain not only their independence, but also their dignity.[7] More recently, Mohammed Ayoob has presented Western colonialism as a cause of the popularity of radical Islamists at the expense of quietist ulema in the eyes of many young Muslims, who have seen the former as more resistant and compelling in their responses to Western colonialism and occupation.[8]

Western interventions in the Middle East have not been confined to direct colonization and occupation, but have taken various forms.[9] The history of Saudi Arabia provides an example. Saudi Arabia has unapologetically been a leading force in spreading Salafi ideas around the world. Salafism is a Sunni reform movement that claims to purify Muslim thought and practice of what it takes to be corrupt traditions.[10] It received its name from the word *salaf* (predecessors), because Salafis regard the earliest (three) generations of Muslims as the exemplars of true Islam and criticize the traditions established by the ulema, with such exceptions as the works of Ahmad ibn Hanbal and Ibn Taymiyya. Notwithstanding their general criticism of the ulema's authority, Salafis have their own ulema today in Saudi Arabia and elsewhere.[11]

Salafis take the Quran and hadiths very literally and reject any innovative interpretation. Salafis' literalism is a source of their opposition to Sufis' mystical understanding of Islam. Moreover, given their rejection of any spiritual

---

[5] Some scholars make a distinction between "religious" and "non-religious" conflicts. Fox 2004; Toft 2007. I do not use such categories because most conflicts are multifaceted, with religious, ethnic, economic, and other dimensions. See Cavanaugh 2009.

[6] For the sake of simplicity, from now on, I will simply use the term "violence," instead of "political violence."

[7] Fanon 2004 [1961], 1–43.   [8] Ayoob 2007, esp. 27.   [9] Salt 2009; Khalidi 2004.

[10] For a comparison between Protestant and Salafi puritanism, see Goldberg 1991.

[11] The Saudi ulema "have arguably unrestricted capacity to educate the Saudi public about religious matters." Ismail 2016, 3. See also Mouline 2014.

mediator between man and God, Salafis have strongly opposed Sufis (who venerate both living and dead shaykhs) and Shiis (who venerate both living and dead imams).[12]

A particular version of Salafism, so-called Wahhabism, has been the official religious doctrine of Saudi Arabia.[13] Wahhabi control of Mecca and Medina (which enables them to preach millions of pilgrims) and of nearly 20 percent of the world's oil reserves has been crucial for the spread of Salafism around the globe. The recent destruction of Sufi shrines by Salafis in Mali and of various historical buildings by the Islamic State of Iraq and Syria (ISIS) is reminiscent of Saudi Wahhabis' demolition of Sufi shrines and historical buildings in the Arabian Peninsula in the nineteenth and twentieth centuries. Particularly following their conquest of Mecca and Medina, the Saudi Wahhabis destroyed historical sites, including the tombs of the Prophet Muhammad's companions,[14] as well as certain historical texts.[15]

A Western observer can hold Muslims responsible for letting a puritanical interpretation of Islam dominate in the two holy cities of Islam. Yet it was not Muslims but Britain that let this happen. The Ottoman Empire, with its mainstream Sunni understanding of Islam, ruled the two cities for four centuries until the World War I. At that time, Britain and its Arab allies led by Sharif Hussein forced the Ottomans out. Britain was deeply concerned about the Ottoman caliph's influence in its colonies, especially India.[16] The removal of Ottomans from the Arabian Peninsula and the abolishment of the caliphate by the new Turkish Republic suited British interests in this regard. Yet Britain's ally Sharif Hussein, who was also a mainstream Sunni, declared his own caliphate to fill the vacuum left by the Turks. There was, however, another British ally in the Arabian Peninsula – the Saudi tribe defending Wahhabism. At least for some British diplomats, Saudis were preferable partners, since Ibn Saud had assured them that he had no interest in becoming a caliph and theologically "his Wahhabi sect did not recognize any caliphs after the

---

[12] Sufism generally seems to have provided a peaceful understanding of Islam. Nonetheless, various examples, including the anti-colonial armed struggles of Abd al-Qadir in Algeria against France, Omar Mukhtar in Libya against Italy, Muhammad al-Mahdi in Sudan against Britain, and Shaykh Shamil in Northern Caucasus against Russia, show that Sufis can be violent as well. Green 2012, 191–205; Trimingham 1971, 239–41.

[13] Some observers define the nineteenth-century modernist thinker Muhammad Abduh of Egypt as the historical founder of Salafism. This definition is confusing because today's Salafi movement is far from being modernist. It is more instructive to trace the roots of today's Salafism to the eighteenth-century scholar Muhammad Abdul-Wahhab of the Arabian Peninsula; Wahhabism is named after him. See Brown 2013, 25–9; Afsaruddin 2008, 148–51; Lauzière 2016. One reason for the perceived blurry boundary between Abduh and Wahhabism was that a prominent student of the former, Rashid Rida, ultimately became a propagandist of the latter. Hourani 1983, 231–2; Abu Zaid [Zayd] 2006, 45–6; Zaman 2012, 4–15.

[14] Sardar 2014, esp. 4, 346.   [15] Abou El Fadl 2014, 229, 251.

[16] Fromkin 2001, 97, 106, 327, 426.

first four."[17] Ibn Saud defeated Sharif Hussein and eventually established the Kingdom of Saudi Arabia.[18]

In fact, Saudi Arabia, together with Turkey and Iran, is one of the exceptional Muslim countries that were never directly colonized. Western impact on colonized Muslim countries has been much deeper. In the Muslim world and elsewhere, the colonialist "divide and rule" policy exacerbated ethnic and religious tensions. Even at the end of their colonial rule, Western policy-makers drew borders of many countries based on their interests and caused border disputes. A well-known example of these sorts of colonial effects has been the Arab-Israeli conflict; British colonial rule left behind disputed borders and contributed to this ethno-religious conflict.

The overwhelming majority of Muslim countries are young, post-colonial states. Young states tend to be weak in terms of the Weberian criterion of monopolizing the legitimate use of force and need time to establish stable institutions. State weakness is directly linked to civil wars and terrorism, while post-colonial border disputes have led to several interstate wars.

The Algerian War (1954–62) was a landmark event for colonized Muslims. Algerian independence after a bloody war against French colonialism demonstrated the effectiveness of violence as a means of resisting and removing the colonizer. The Soviet invasion of Afghanistan in 1979 marked a turning point, particularly in the rise of Islamist violence.[19] With the support of the United States, Saudi Arabia, and Pakistan, Afghan *mujahideen* (those who engaged in jihad) fought against the Soviet Union for about a decade. US support was so enthusiastic that President Ronald Reagan dedicated the launch of the Space Shuttle Columbia to "the people of Afghanistan" in 1982 and met with representatives of the Afghan *mujahideen* in the Oval Office a year later.[20] Osama bin Laden was one of the Arab participants in this anti-Soviet jihad in Afghanistan.[21] Later, especially following 9/11, when jihad gained a totally pejorative meaning, the old, positive term *mujahideen* was replaced by a new, derogatory term – jihadists.[22]

[17] Fromkin 2001, 108. See also Abou El Fadl 2014, 237–9.
[18] "Britain played a crucial role in Ibn Sa'ud's expansion" by providing him with subsidies and weapons and by abandoning Sharif Hussein. Al-Rasheed 2002, 42–9, esp. 47. See also Provence 2017, 154–5. Additionally, Britain helped House of Saud to crush the rebellious Ikhwan – religious zealots who initially provided strong support to the Saudis. Alatas 2014, 132–5, 137; Salame 1990, 34–8, 44–5.
[19] Gerges 2005, esp. ch. 5.
[20] In the online archive of the Ronald Reagan Presidential Foundation and Library, a photo with *mujahideen* is recorded as "President Reagan meeting with Afghan Freedom Fighters to discuss Soviet atrocities in Afghanistan, 2/2/83": https://reaganlibrary.archives.gov/archives/photographs/large/c12820–32.jpg, accessed on March 30, 2016.
[21] See Robert Fisk's interview with and depiction of Osama bin Laden: "Anti-Soviet Warrior Puts His Army on the Road to Peace: The Saudi Businessman Who Recruited Mujahedin Now Uses Them for Large-Scale Building Projects in Sudan," *Independent*, December 5, 1993.
[22] Mamdani 2005, 119–77; Ayoob 2007, 144–66.

In the Middle East, particularly between the Iranian Revolution in 1979 and the collapse of the Soviet Union in 1991, Islamism gradually replaced socialism as the ideology of violent anti-Western groups. This is visible in the rise of Islamist Hezbollah as an alternative to the secularist and older Amal movement among Shii Arabs in Lebanon, and in the emergence of Islamist Hamas against the secularist and older Fatah among Palestinians. Their fight against the Israeli occupation of southern Lebanon and Palestinian lands helped Hezbollah and Hamas, respectively, gain popularity among their communities.[23]

A more recent foreign occupation was the US invasion of Iraq in 2003. Right after the invasion, the United States abolished two pillars of the Iraqi state – the Baath Party and the military. Amid the political chaos, most Iraqis turned to their ethnic and sectarian identities for survival.[24] The rise of ISIS through radicalization of local Sunnis and the influx of jihadists from neighboring countries and Europe cannot be explained without reference to the chaos created by the occupation of Iraq.

The anti-colonial approach has some power in explaining the problem of violence in certain Muslim countries. But Western colonization/occupation is neither a necessary nor a sufficient condition for violence. It is not sufficient, as there have been non-Muslim and Muslim countries that were colonized or occupied but where many influential agents did not choose to use violence. Such leading figures as Syed Ahmad Khan (1817–98)[25] and Mahatma Gandhi (1869–1948), for example, adopted a position of non-violence against British colonization in India. Western colonization/occupation is not a necessary condition either, because several non-Western countries and groups have fought each other for various reasons. The long list includes the Iran-Iraq War and recent civil wars in several Arab countries. In Turkey, violence has continued between the Turkish state and the PKK (Kurdistan Workers' Party) for more than three decades, regardless of whether Turkey was ruled by secularists or Islamists, and regardless of whether the PKK defended or renounced Marxist-Leninist ideology.[26]

The anti-colonial approach overemphasizes the impact of Western countries' policies toward other parts of the world while downplaying the role of non-Western countries' own domestic and regional dynamics.[27] Hence, it cannot explain why Muslims have experienced interstate wars, civil wars, and terrorism by and against other Muslims, rather than simply fighting against Western colonial powers and occupiers. In the last decade or so, jihadists have killed more Muslims than non-Muslims. According to one official US report, "In

---

[23] Robinson 2004, 124–5; Ayoob 2007, ch. 6. [24] See Hashemi and Postel 2017.
[25] See Chapter 7. [26] Gürbüz 2016; Tezcür 2016; Şahin 2011.
[27] The US invasions of Germany and Japan at the end of the World War II led to political order, while its recent occupation of Afghanistan and Iraq produced political disorder. The difference cannot be explained by disregarding country-specific characteristics.

cases where the religious affiliation of terrorism casualties could be determined, Muslims suffered between 82 and 97 percent of terrorism-related fatalities" between 2007 and 2011. According to the report, the top five countries having the greatest numbers of attacks involving ten or more deaths in 2011 were all Muslim-majority – Afghanistan, Iraq, Pakistan, Somalia, and Nigeria.[28]

Various weaknesses of the anti-colonial approach in explaining violence are related to its preoccupation with material and international factors. This problem points to the need to analyze the roles of ideas and states. The following sections undertake such analyses.

THE ROLE OF ISLAM

Some scholars have argued that – based on its texts or history – Islam has some essential characteristics that are associated with violence. Referring to its history, Max Weber defined Islam as originally a "warrior religion."[29] Focusing on contemporary Muslims, Bernard Lewis claimed the existence of a general "Muslim rage." For Lewis, Muslims are angry and anti-Western because they cannot accept the fact that they lost their historical supremacy and fell behind the West.[30] In a similar vein, Samuel Huntington defined Islamic civilization as in a position of clash against Western civilization and asserted that "Islam has bloody borders."[31]

A more recent example of an essentialist explanation is the Arab poet Adonis's *Violence and Islam*. Adonis depicts Islam as a religion of violence and tries to prove that by quoting several Quranic verses. In his words, the Quran is "an extraordinarily violent text."[32] He seems to ignore the role of human actors in interpreting religious texts. Adonis also alleges that Arabs are somehow perpetually violent: "For fifteen centuries, the war between Arabs has not ceased ... The history of Arabs is a perpetual war."[33] He overemphasizes the history of intra-Arab wars and virtually ignores the Crusader and Mongol invaders; the Turkish, Circassian, and Berber rulers; and Western colonizers in the last millennium of the Arab world.

---

[28] The National Counterterrorism Center 2012, 14.
[29] In Weber's (1978 [1922], 626) words, "The ideal personality type in the religion of Islam was not the scholarly scribe (*Literat*), but the warrior." See also Weber 1978 [1922], 623–7. According to Bryan Turner (1974, 143), "Weber completely overstated the social role of the Muslim warrior and was probably unaware of the importance of merchants in shaping the values of early Islam."
[30] Lewis (1990) developed this claim as an alternative to the argument that anti-Westernism in Muslim societies has been caused by Western support of Israeli policies against Palestinians.
[31] Huntington 1993, 135. There have been persecuted Muslim minorities in Chechnya (Russia), Kashmir (India), Moro (the Philippines), Palestine (Israel), Rakhine (Myanmar), and Xinjiang (China). The blood on "Islam's borders," as claimed by Huntington, is mostly Muslims' blood.
[32] Adonis 2015, 48; also 49–58. [33] Adonis 2015, 28, 30; also 25–41, 60–74.

The essentialist explanations have several shortcomings. By singling out Islam as the cause of violence, they disregard the fact that violence is a general human problem.[34] Millions were killed in historical atrocities perpetrated by various ethno-religious groups, from the Mongol massacres to the colonization of the Americas,[35] from the Taiping and Dungan rebellions in China,[36] to the two world wars.

More specifically, for the last two centuries, it is Western powers, not Muslim countries, who have militarily dominated the world. The British Empire has "invaded, had some control over or fought conflicts in the territory of something like 171 out of 193 UN member states in the world today."[37] In 2006, the United States had 833 military installations in more than a hundred countries and territories (766 in other countries and 77 in US territories).[38] In 2012, the US military expenditure was $682 billion, which constituted 39 percent of world's entire military expenditure.[39]

Individuals justify violence in many ways, including by invoking religion.[40] In the words of Alfred Stepan, all religions are "multivocal"[41] and thus can be interpreted to promote peace or violence.[42] In other words, religions do not have unchanging "essences" regarding violence. Critics of this view have pointed to Buddhism as essentially peaceful, unlike Islam and Christianity. Yet recently Buddhist monks' participation in massacres against the Muslim minority in Myanmar revealed that Buddhism is no different from other religions, as far as the potential for violence is concerned.[43] Similar incidents have also occurred in Sri Lanka and Thailand: "It's a faith famous for its pacifism and tolerance. But in several of Asia's Buddhist-majority nations, monks are inciting bigotry and violence – mostly against Muslims."[44]

---

[34] Anger is a human faculty (together with appetite and reason); thus each human being has a potential to commit violence. Plato 1945 [c. 380 BCE], 120–9; Aristotle 1996a [c. 350 BCE], 268–71, 437; Sloterdijk 2012.

[35] In Hispaniola, one of the Caribbean islands Columbus reached and where the first Spanish colonial settlement was established, the population was estimated to be more than a million in 1492. The native population continued to decline until it became extinct by 1535. Levene 2005, 10. For Mongol massacres, see Chapter 5.

[36] In China, the population declined "from around 410 million in 1850 to 350 million in 1873" due to the brutal conflicts during the Taiping, Dungan, and other uprisings. Millions of Muslims were among those who died. Levene 2005, 286. See also Davis 2001, 113; Maddison 2006, 244.

[37] Laycock 2012, 7.   [38] Cooley 2008, xii, 6.   [39] Perlo-Freeman et al. 2013.

[40] Armstrong 2014.

[41] Stepan 2001, 234. For diverse political strategies of the Catholic Church in different political contexts, see Gill 1998; Kalyvas 1996.

[42] For different Muslim views on peace and violence, see Denny 2004. For Jewish and Christian violent fundamentalism, see Perliger 2015.

[43] Juergensmeyer 2017, ch. 6. Human Rights Watch (2012, 2) notes that in Myanmar "local Buddhist monks have initiated a campaign of exclusion, calling on the local Buddhist population to neither befriend nor do business with Muslims."

[44] Hannah Beech, "The Face of Buddhist Terror," *Time*, July 1, 2013, 42.

Particularly following 9/11, some pundits have held Islam solely responsible for suicide bombings and asserted that terrorists seek to be martyrs. Robert Pape emphasizes that suicide bombing is a strategic tool through which terrorists fight against regimes they see as occupiers. He defines suicide bombing as a tactic pioneered by socialist Tamil Tigers and only later adopted by Islamist groups. Thus suicide bombing is not "Islamic" in logic or origin.[45] Nevertheless, the perceived linkage between suicide bombing and Islam has been, at least partially, based on some irresponsible fatwas, in which certain ulema have legitimized violence. In an infamous fatwa in 2003, Yusuf al-Qaradawi endorsed suicide bombing attacks by Palestinians:

The martyrdom operations carried out by the Palestinian factions to resist the Zionist occupation are not in any way included in the framework of prohibited terrorism, even if the victims include some civilians … What weapon can harm the enemy, can prevent him from sleeping, and can strip him of a sense of security and stability, except for these human bombs – a young man or woman who blows himself or herself up amongst their enemy?[46]

Violence is a multicausal phenomenon that cannot be explained by simply referring to religious texts. Moreover, religious texts are open to multiple interpretations. The Bible, for example, includes numerous passages about violence.[47] It is the interpretations of these passages, rather than their sheer existence, which really matter.[48] Khaled Abou El Fadl explains that the Quran is understood differently due to the diversity of human readers. For pro-violent interpretations of the Quran, he points to the problem of puritanical readers, who disregard the text's historical and moral contexts. Instead, Abou El Fadl interprets the Quran as a text promoting peace and tolerance.[49] Yaser Ellethy also interprets the Quran prohibiting wars of aggression; for him, jihad is only permissible either for a defensive purpose or for offense against an oppressive regime.[50]

Despite Quranic discouragement, Muslims have killed each other in many cases. The Quran says: "Whoever slays a believer willfully, his recompense is Hell, abiding therein. God is wroth with him, and curses him, and prepares for

---

[45] Pape 2003.
[46] Al-Qaradawi 2007 [2003], 469–70. Like Shii Khomeini, Sunni Qaradawi is both an Islamic scholar and an Islamist. Egypt's Muslim Brothers invited him to serve as their supreme leader, which he declined. For an analysis of Qaradawi's views on jihad, see Zaman 2012, 261–81, 304–8.
[47] According to Eberhard Bons and Erik Eynikel (2011, 17), depending on the definition, the number of biblical passages about acts of violence varies between 600 and 1,700.
[48] "Terms for killing and destruction were in 2.1 percent of the Qur'an, 2.8 percent of the New Testament, and 5.3 percent of the Old Testament." Tim Barger, "Bible, Qur'an, and Violence Computerized Software Uses Scripture to Show What Text Analytics Can Do," *The Blade*, February 6, 2016.
[49] Abou El Fadl 2003. See also Abou El Fadl 2004.   [50] Ellethy 2011, 35–42.

him a mighty punishment" (4:93).[51] The subsequent verse prevents believers from declaring those who greet them with peace as infidels and further restricts the possibility of Muslims killing each other: "O you who believe! When you go forth in the way of God, be discerning, and say not unto him who offers you peace, 'You are not a believer,' seeking the ephemeralities of the life of this world" (4:94). Notwithstanding these verses, there have existed Muslims who killed their co-religionists in interstate conflicts, civil wars, terrorist attacks, and government persecutions. This further problematizes the alleged links between the Quran and violence committed by Muslims. Hence, we should analyze how human actors, particularly the ulema, have interpreted the Quran and hadiths regarding the issue of violence.

THE ULEMA

The previous section has examined both pro-peace and pro-violence interpretations of Islam. Pro-violence interpretations reflect the political conditions of not only modern Muslim societies (under occupation) but also medieval Muslim societies. The latter is problematic because in the Middle Ages the perception and experience of violence had differences from what we perceive and experience today. There was no international law or international institutions at that time, nor were there concepts of war crimes, human rights, or domestic violence. The contemporary ulema generally aim to protect the Islamic tradition rather than produce new Islamic perspectives. The tradition includes various medieval perspectives, some of which contradict our modern notion of peaceful relations.

According to medieval and early modern interpretations, Muslims would be beaten, imprisoned, or even executed for not performing daily prayers. Apostasy was a capital offense. This judgment was typical of the age; apostates were to be killed in the medieval and early modern Christian tradition too.[52] As a result of the persistently traditionalist preaching of the contemporary ulema in mosques, Islamists in party gatherings, and shaykhs in Sufi orders, medieval conceptions of physical punishment have not only survived but also spread throughout the Muslim world. Recent polls indicate vast acceptance of the idea of killing apostates in contemporary Muslim societies. According to Pew Research Center's 2013 survey, the median percentages of Muslims who favor

---

[51] A similar verse with a broader implication (i.e., not limited to the killing of Muslims) is the following: "whosoever slays a soul – unless it be for another soul or spreading corruption upon the earth – it is as though he slew mankind altogether, and whosoever saves the life of one, it is as though he saved the life of mankind altogether" (5:32). The translations of Quranic verses in this book are generally from Nasr et al. 2015.

[52] For the medieval and early modern executions of alleged apostates in Catholic and Protestant societies, see Angenendt 2011, 53–9. For the Orthodox Byzantine society, see Mez 1937, 32. For the executions with apostasy charges in the late fifteenth- and the early sixteenth-century Ottoman Empire, see İnalcık 2000 [1973], 178, 182.

making sharia (Islamic law) the law of the land in various regions is as follows: South Asia, 84 percent; Southeast Asia, 77 percent; Middle East and North Africa (MENA), 74 percent; Sub-Saharan Africa, 64 percent; Southern and Eastern Europe, 18 percent; and Central Asia, 12 percent. Among those who support sharia, the median percentages of those who favor "executing those who leave Islam" are: South Asia, 76 percent; Southeast Asia, 27 percent; MENA, 56 percent; Sub-Saharan Africa, no data; Southern and Eastern Europe, 13 percent; and Central Asia, 16 percent.[53] In the last three decades, public acceptance of capital punishment for apostasy seems to have muted reactions to certain executions and assassinations of public figures declared to be apostates in some Muslim countries.[54]

There have been many Muslims who oppose the punishment of apostasy, even when facing the risk of being declared as apostates themselves because of this opposition.[55] Some Muslim intellectuals have offered Islamic criticisms of the punishment of apostasy,[56] but such criticism could not become mainstream, since the ulema have claimed a monopoly over interpreting Islam, and Muslim masses have largely upheld the ulema's claim. In Shii Islam, the ulema's authority is based on a clergy–laity dichotomy largely similar to that in Catholicism.[57] Theoretically, there is no such a dichotomy in Sunni Islam, but in practice, the Sunni ulema have also enjoyed something resembling clerical authority in matters of religious interpretation.

The ulema have raised the bar for making a new interpretation (*ijtihad*) very high,[58] even for its junior members – requiring years of studying Arabic grammar, memorizing hadiths, etc. The long processes of memorization and socialization generally lead the junior ulema to eventually lose their creativity. If some exceptionally creative junior ulema still produce new interpretations – as

---

[53] Pew Research Center 2013, 16, 23.

[54] Mahmoud Mohammed Taha, a reformist Muslim thinker and activist, was defined as an apostate by a sharia court and later, in 1985, executed by the Sudanese state. Taha 1987; Mahmoud 2000; Packer 2006; El-Affendi 2014. In Egypt, in 1992, some Al-Azhar scholars declared Farag Foda, a reformist Muslim scholar and activist, to be an apostate. A few days later, he was assassinated by two Islamists. Radhan 2014, 234–61; Kassab 2009, 221–4.

[55] In Pakistan, a Christian woman was sentenced to death for blasphemy against Islam. In 2011, the governor of Punjab, Salman Taseer (a Muslim), and the federal minister of minority affairs, Shahbaz Bhatti (a Catholic), were both assassinated due to their opposition to her sentence and Pakistan's blasphemy law.

[56] Barakat Ahmad (1989) writes that capital punishment for apostasy historically emerged as a political choice and is not a part of Islam as a religion. Abdullah Saeed and Hassan Saeed (2004) argue that the punishment of apostasy by death contradicts the Quran and hadiths. Mohsen Kadivar (2006) develops a similar argument from a Shii perspective. See also Moosa 2014, 169–88; Kurucan 2006, esp. 123–142, 153.

[57] Momen 1985, esp. 189–207, 246–9. In Iran, the Shiia ulema have referred "themselves as 'clergymen' (*ruhaniyyan*)." Halm 1997, 106.

[58] See Abou El Fadl 2014, 210–14; Weiss 1998, 127–34; Hallaq 2009, 110–13.

happened in the previously mentioned case of Abdel Razek – the senior ulema discourage and even punish them. This conservatism is the main reason why Muslim thought has been stagnant for centuries and recently caught unprepared to respond the jihadist claims of Al-Qaeda and ISIS.[59]

Many terrorists have adopted Jihadi-Salafism, a strand of Salafism, as their ideology.[60] A basis for radical interpretations of Islam for Jihadi-Salafis and others is the idea that the so-called sword verse (9:5) about attacking the polytheists abrogated a large number of other Quranic verses, up to 140, which encourage peace, patience, tolerance, forgiveness, and freedom of conscience.[61] This verse says, "Then, when the sacred months have passed, slay the idolaters wherever you find them, capture them, besiege them, and lie in wait for them at every place of ambush. But if they repent, and perform the prayer, and give the alms, then let them go their way. Truly, God is Forgiving and Merciful" (9:5). For those who accept this particular idea of abrogation, there remains almost no textual basis for a peaceful relationship with non-Muslims, or even with various Muslims.

An influential defender of this radical idea was Sayyid Qutb (1906–66). In his *Milestones*, Qutb extensively quotes Ibn Qayyim al-Jawziyya (1292–1350) to explain that Islam's relationship with violence experienced various stages during the Prophet's lifetime. Qutb argues that the Quran initially ordered Muslims to preach Islam peacefully, that later it allowed them to engage in defensive war, and that ultimately it enjoined Muslims to use force offensively "for abolishing the organizations and authorities of the *jahili* [ignorant] system."[62] For Qutb, contemporary Muslims should read all Quranic verses through the lens of this last, offensive stage and not confine jihad to defensive war.[63]

According to Qutb, contemporary Muslims are supposed to use force world-wide to affirm that sovereignty belongs to God, to liberate people from servitude to their own desires, and to enforce sharia by abolishing man-made laws. Qutb equates all modern societies to the pagan society of pre-Islamic Arabia, in terms of being in the state of ignorance (*jahiliyya*), as if international law and even domestic legal systems do not matter.[64] For him, there should be two options for non-Muslims: submission (in the form of special taxes) to Muslims or war against

---

[59] Even worse, according to Muhammad Qasim Zaman (2005, 67–8), in Pakistan, most of the ulema reject the idea of equal citizenship, while many leading ulema regard jihad against unbelievers as "a continuing obligation" and "maintain varied links with the radical sectarian militants."

[60] Wiktorowicz 2010, 270–1; Esposito 2015, 1071–5.

[61] See Qadhi 1999, 252–4; Ellethy 2015, 117–18.   [62] Qutb 2002 [1964], 55; also 53–76.

[63] "When God restrained Muslims from *jihad* for a certain period, it was a question of strategy rather than of principle ... Only in the light of this explanation can we understand ... the Holy Qur'an." Qutb 2002 [1964], 76.

[64] Qutb 2002 [1964], 57–8, 61–3, 69–70, 80–4, 93, 110.

them.[65] By defining all existing Muslim societies as *jahili*, Qutb also legitimizes the use of violence against Muslim political leaders and their supporters.[66]

Qutb's radical ideas and selective reading of Quranic verses were shaped by his personal views and experiences, including his anti-Americanism[67] and the torture he and other Muslim Brothers endured in Egyptian prisons for about a decade. Similarly, his main reference, Jawziyya, reflected a particular understanding of jihad in the context of anti-Crusader and anti-Mongol sentiments of the late thirteenth- and early fourteenth-century Mamluk Empire. This context was also influential on Jawziyya's teacher Ibn Taymiyya (1263–1328), one of the most prominent Islamic scholars ever.[68] Ibn Taymiyya had such deep animosity against the Mongols that he endorsed jihad against the Mongol rulers in the Middle East (the Ilkhanids), even after they converted to Islam, with the justification that they did not implement sharia.[69]

Although Qutb's perspective has influenced several radical groups, it is far from becoming the mainstream Muslim approach. The idea of the abrogation of certain Quranic verses on peace and other issues has remained controversial.[70] Some argue that there is no such thing as abrogation, while others disagree on its particular application. The defenders of peaceful interpretations of Islam propose that the meaning of the so-called sword verse (9:5) is limited by its historical context, that it does not abrogate any Quranic verse at all, and/or that the verse itself is abrogated by the subsequent verse (9:6) – "And if any one of the idolaters seeks asylum with thee, grant him asylum until he hears the Word of God. Then convey him to his place of safety. That is because they are a people who know not."[71] In fact, the designation "sword verse" was a late construction: no commentator "before Ibn Kathir (d. 1373)" referred to the

---

[65] Qutb 2002 [1964], 63–4, 70, 73. On Muslims' relations with non-Muslims, Qutb's views depend on his interpretation of the Quranic verse 9:29. Muhammad Asad (1984, 261–2) interprets this verse more peacefully by arguing that the general message of the Quran is based on defensive, not aggressive, war. Yet Asad also interprets the verse as rejecting the idea of equal citizenship.

[66] Qutb 2002 [1964], 82.   [67] Jackson 2002a, 21–5. See also Abu-Rabi' 1995, chs. 4 and 5.

[68] Laoust 1939, 45, 60–5, 117–20. Ibn Taymiyya's hostile views against the Nusayris (today's Alawites) in Syria were also shaped by their political tension with Sunni Mamluk rule. Laoust 1939, 59–60, 124–5; Laoust 1971, 951–5. For more on Ibn Taymiyya, see Chapter 5.

[69] "In modern times the position known as 'accusing the ruler of unbelief' is inspired by a *fatwa* of Ibn Taymiyya that was directed against the Ilkhanid rulers of this time. Since the 1980s, this argument has been used to legitimise militant political actions of radical Islamic groups." Griffel 2007, 133. See also Kadri 2012, 144–78; Ahmad 1989, 13–14.

[70] According to Jane McAuliffe (1990, 114), while commenting on the so-called sword verse 9:5, the eminent scholar Fakhr al-Din al-Razi "did not even raise the possibility of abrogation" of the verse 2:256. ("Let there be no compulsion in (the) religion. Right has been distinguished from wrong, so whoever disbelieves in idols and believes in God has grasped a firm, unbreakable handle.")

[71] Burton 1990, 184–5; Badawi 2014, 303; Ellethy 2015, 119–22; Dagli 2015, 1808–9.

verse with this name.[72] In fact, the word "sword" does not exist in this verse or any other verse in the Quran.[73]

Several Muslim scholars have emphasized peace as a general objective of Islam.[74] According to Sherman Jackson, peace treaties are sanctified in the Quran. For him, the Quranic verses endorsing and even encouraging armed struggle should be understood in the context of the state of war that existed in the Arabian peninsula before and during the revelation of the Quran. Today, however, the development of international law and institutions necessitates an overall rethinking of the concept of jihad, which was historically interpreted in terms of offensive military actions.[75]

Pre-modern jurists divided the world into the *dar al-Islam* (abode of Islam) and the *dar al-harb* (abode of war). These concepts contradict the modern ideals of the establishment of equal citizenship in Muslim countries, integration of Muslims into Western societies, and development of a more peaceful international system.[76] This contradiction is so deep that it makes a new interpretation of these two concepts impossible. Jackson, for example, interprets Mawardi's definition of *dar al-Islam* "as *any* land in which a Muslim enjoys security."[77] Yet in fact Mawardi encouraged Muslims to remain in lands "[w]here a Muslim is able to protect and isolate himself, even if he is not able to proselytize and engage in combat."[78] He did not legitimize Muslims' residence under non-Muslim rule as a normal condition. Rather, he legitimized their residence as contingent on the idea that they would gradually foster the necessary conditions to convert these lands into a genuine *dar al-Islam* ruled by Muslims. Hence, even a sincere and clever attempt to reinterpret these medieval concepts seems ultimately ineffective.

As the previous section has elaborated, essentialist explanations exaggerate possible links between Islam and Muslims' violent actions. Yet a particular interpretation of Islam, Jihadi-Salafism, has been associated with terrorist activity. The ulema share responsibility for this problem, because their monopolization of the interpretation of Islam has led to the stagnation of Muslim intellectual life. As a result, Muslim societies have not been intellectually dynamic enough to produce effective counterarguments against Jihadi-Salafi propaganda.

Terrorism and other types of violence are complex phenomena; they are not simply caused by religious or secular ideas alone.[79] Other factors, especially political and socioeconomic conditions, also lead to violence. Moreover,

---

[72] Afsaruddin 2015, 128; also 123–7.   [73] Fatoohi 2013, 121; also 114–20.

[74] See Shaltut 2005 [1948].

[75] Jackson 2002a, 15, 25–6. See also Donner 1991, 34. Jackson (2002a, 18) argues that even after the establishment of Muslim states, a sense of insecurity continued, because "throughout the Middle Ages, while one could live as a Jew in Morocco, a Christian in Cairo, or even a Zoroastrian in Shiraz, one could not live as a Muslim in Paris [or] London."

[76] See Ramadan 2003, 65–77; Mayer 1995, 196.   [77] Jackson 2011, 174 (emphasis in original).

[78] Quoted in Jackson 2011, 187n13. For more on Mawardi, see Chapter 4.

[79] Philpott 2007, esp. 522; Kuru 2011, 173–4.

pro-violence or pro-peace interpretations of religions do not emerge in isolation, but rather are formed within a political context. The next section will examine how the authoritarian state has provided conditions conducive for both religious radicalism and violence in many Muslim countries.

THE AUTHORITARIAN STATE

Democratic peace theory argues that democracies are not likely to wage wars against each other. This theory helps us understand possible mechanisms linking authoritarianism and war. The theory argues that democratic norms and institutions strengthen mutual understanding between societies. In contrast, authoritarian norms and institutions might promote mutual distrust. Another mechanism for maintaining peace is that democratic institutions and open public conversations constrain decision-makers.[80] Authoritarian rulers, on the contrary, are neither checked by representative institutions nor held accountable by open public debate. Thus authoritarian regimes are more likely to wage war due to their rulers' unaccountable decisions.[81]

When we compare the Middle East and East Asia, we find some historical commonalities. Both regions had a colonial experience, faced Western interventions since decolonization, and consisted mostly of authoritarian states until the late 1980s. During the last three decades, however, East Asia has achieved a process of democratization; currently, half of the countries (nine of eighteen) in the region are electoral democracies. Eten Solingen has also noted an important divergence between the two regions in terms of war and peace. She observes that in the aftermath of World War II, both regions encountered multiple military conflicts. From 1965 to 2007, however, "the incidence of interstate wars and militarized conflicts has been nearly five times higher in the Middle East, as was their severity ... By contrast, declining militarized conflict and rising intraregional cooperation has replaced earlier patterns in East Asia."[82] Solingen explains these two diverging trajectories with opposite models of governance in these two regions: "Leaders in most East Asian states pivoted their political control on economic performance and integration into the global economy, whereas most Middle East leaders relied on inward-looking self-sufficiency, state and military entrepreneurship, and a related brand of nationalism." In other words, while in East Asia, export-oriented economies have led to regional trade and peace, in the Middle East, a particular version of authoritarianism, which is based on inward-looking model of governance, has exacerbated militarization and regional conflict.[83]

---

[80] Doyle 1983; Russett 1993. For a critique, see Layne 1994.
[81] For the association among authoritarianism, corruption, and violence in Afghanistan, Uzbekistan, Egypt, and Nigeria, see Chayes 2015.
[82] Solingen 2007, 757–8.   [83] Solingen 2007, 761.

Authoritarianism also leads to terrorism and civil conflicts by blocking peaceful power transition and radicalizing dissenting groups. Ideas and money support government as well as opposition in a democracy. When the system is authoritarian, violence is more likely to be used by both the government and the opposition.[84] In many Muslim countries, authoritarian regimes have survived by suppressing the opposition, leading the latter to turn to the use of force in order to capture the power.[85] In this condition of mutual violence, peaceful groups have had much less opportunity to survive than they would have had in democratic conditions.

The historical and socioeconomic roots of the authoritarian state have been so strong in most Muslim countries that it has persisted regardless of whether the official ideology is Islamism or secularism. In the twentieth century, secularist leaders, including Atatürk of Turkey, Reza Shah of Iran, Gamel Abdel Nasser of Egypt, and Habib Bourguiba of Tunisia, established authoritarian regimes, which led to the radicalization of various Islamist and socialist groups. After the Iranian Revolution led by Khomeini, Islamists have shaped politics in many Muslim countries by becoming either a part of the government or an influential opposition.[86] Additionally, other Islamic actors, the ulema and Sufi shaykhs, have also gained more political influence in these countries. The increasing political influence of Islamic actors has not helped Muslim countries solve the problems of authoritarianism and violence; in fact, these Islamic actors have made these problems even more complicated. In short, the authoritarian state, regardless of whether it is dominated by secularists or Islamic actors, has been associated with terrorism, civil conflict, and war in many Muslim countries.

Recently, Sunni and Shii ulema have contributed to the escalation of violent sectarianism in the Middle East.[87] Sectarian tension has in turn fueled civil wars and terrorism in such cases as Iraq and Syria. The civil wars and the rise of ISIS in these two countries cannot be fully grasped without also exploring the roles of secularist and Islamist authoritarian regimes. Syria has been ruled by the Arab Socialist Baath Party controlled by the Alawite minority for half a century. Hafez al-Assad and later his son Bashar al-Assad conducted massacres against various Sunni insurgent groups, including Islamist Muslim Brothers, which ultimately helped ignite the current civil war. Political chaos engendered a safe haven for thousands of jihadists coming from Europe, MENA, and elsewhere, who formed various groups, including ISIS.

---

[84] Regan and Greed 2005, 334; Hegre et al. 2001.

[85] Hafez 2003; Wiktorowicz 2004; Khalid 2007, chs. 6 and 7; Rashid 2002, 144–55.

[86] Lust 2011; Akyol 2011, esp. 201.

[87] "The positions of the Saudi *ulama'* in relation to the Shi'a are explicable first and foremost by their theological and doctrinal opposition to Shi'a beliefs and practices." Ismail 2016, 199. Muslim sectarianism is not limited to the Middle East. In Pakistan, there has been a sectarian conflict between Sunnis and Shiis since the 1980s, in which many Sunni ulema are "hostile to the Shi'a." Zaman 2005, 67.

In Iraq, the Arab Socialist Baath Party was controlled by the Sunni minority and ruled the country from 1968 to 2003. Saddam Hussein waged a decade-long war with Iran, invaded Kuwait, and massacred thousands of Shii Arabs and Kurds. After the US invasion, the Shii Islamist politicians dominated Iraqi politics. The Shii-dominated regime became so sectarian that many Sunnis joined Al-Qaeda and later ISIS.[88] In short, the Iraqi and Syrian civil wars and the rise of ISIS in these two countries had a complex background, including secularist and Islamist regimes, both of which were authoritarian.

This section has summarized how authoritarian states have caused wars, civil conflicts, and terrorism. Needless to say, authoritarian rulers are not the only cause of these problems. Violence is characteristically a multicausal phenomenon.[89] Previous sections revealed the roles of the colonial legacy, Jihadi-Salafism, and the ulema. There are also several socioeconomic factors, such as urban poverty[90] and the "youth bulge,"[91] which affect the authoritarian state, violence, and the relationship between the two. Muslim countries have generally suffered from these socioeconomic problems,[92] as elaborated in the subsequent two chapters.

CONCLUSION

During the last three decades, Muslims have participated in violence at a disproportionately high level. This cannot be explained by referring simply to some "essential characteristics" of Islam, because religions are open to diverse and contradictory interpretations. Beyond the diversity of theological views, there is also a gap between theology and human practice. The former is supposed to be based on religious texts, whereas the latter depends on human choices affected by structural conditions. Violence is a particularly complex phenomenon that is not confined to religious or secular ideas. Western colonialism has been a major condition for Muslims' engagement with violence. Yet Western colonialism has been neither a sufficient nor a necessary condition for non-Western actors' engagement in violence.

---

[88] The pro-Iranian Prime Minister Nouri al-Maliki discriminated against Sunnis in Iraq. He made a court sentence Sunni Vice-President Tariq al-Hashimi to death in absentia. When ISIS occupied Mosul few years later, Hashimi was among those who declared it better than Maliki's rule in the city.

[89] Dixon 2009; Fearon and Laitin 2003; Gupta 2008; Collier and Hoeffler 2004.

[90] Mousseau 2011; Collier 2007, ch. 2; Fish et al. 2010, 1337.

[91] Urdal 2004; Cammett et al. 2015, ch. 4. See also Shaykhutdinov 2011.

[92] Süveyda Karakaya (2013, 8) notes that "Muslim-plurality states are indeed disproportionally involved in domestic armed conflicts, but these states are also characterized by lower GDP per capita, oil dependency, state repression, autocracy, and youth bulges, all of which correlate strongly with domestic armed conflict." See also Sorli et al. 2005.

Although depicting Islam as an essentially pro-violence religion is inaccurate, there is a particular interpretation of Islam, Jihadi-Salafism, which has been associated with terrorism. Muslim societies have largely been unable to counter the propaganda of ISIS and other jihadist groups. This inability has to do with the ulema's ambition to monopolize the interpretation of Islam and the resulting intellectual stagnation among Muslims. The ulema themselves could not produce effective counterarguments either, due to their focus on protecting the tradition rather than producing new ideas. The fact that Salafis, who have confronted the traditional authority of the mainstream ulema and Sufi shaykhs, ended up producing even more radical interpretations of Islam, has paradoxically made some Muslims more cautious about questioning the ulema and shaykhs.

The problem of violence cannot be understood without analyzing the problem of authoritarianism in many Muslim societies. Regardless of whether they are ruled by secularists or Islamists, most states in the Muslim world have continued to be authoritarian. These states have pursued oppressive policies and thus led to war, civil conflict, and terrorism. Chapter 2 will analyze why the overwhelming majority of Muslim-majority states have been authoritarian.

2

Authoritarianism and Democracy

Muslim countries have a disproportionately high rate of authoritarian rule. In 2018, although three-fifths of all countries in the world were classified as electoral democracies, less than one-fifth of Muslim countries were classified in this category.[1] Analyzing Freedom House's democracy scores for other years also reflects a long-lasting disparity between Muslim countries and the rest of the world.[2] What explains the problem of authoritarianism in Muslim countries?

The chapter begins with a critical analysis of Western colonialism and occupation as contributing factors for authoritarianism. It then critically examines the arguments about the influence of Islam, particularly in relation to the issues of patriarchy and secularism, in sustaining authoritarianism. Next, it elaborates the role of the ulema, in terms of their alliances with authoritarian rulers and their promulgation of authoritarian ideas regarding gender relations, public order, and Muslims' relations with non-Muslims. It also explains the impact of rentierism (particularly oil rents) in fostering authoritarianism in the Muslim world. Finally, the chapter explicates how the connections between rentierism and authoritarianism in Muslim countries are effects of not only rich oil reserves but also economic underdevelopment in these countries.

---

[1] Freedom House 2018. Polity (2010) data also indicate a big gap between the democracy rate of Muslim countries and that of the rest of the world.

[2] Freedom House 1973–2018. According to Freedom House (2013), 39 percent of all countries were liberal democracies, while only 6 percent of Muslim countries were in that category. For the sake of readability, the rest of the chapter uses the term "democracy" instead of "electoral democracy," except when I want to emphasize the difference between liberal and electoral democracies.

WESTERN COLONIZATION AND OCCUPATION

It is difficult for recently decolonized countries with young political institutions to establish democratic polities. With modern borders often drawn by former colonizers, decolonized countries also face challenges forming national identities, which further inhibits democratization. As Anthony Marx writes, "National unity is a necessary precondition to democracy, for it establishes the boundaries of the community to which citizenship and rights are then accorded, without which democracy is impossible."[3]

More than fourth-fifths (42/49) of Muslim countries became independent after the end of the World War II; therefore, their democratic deficit has often been attributed to the legacy of colonialism. However, my analysis of all countries (with populations greater than 200,000) indicates that many decolonized countries have achieved democratization. About half (68 out of 125) of all non-Muslim countries gained independence after the end of the World War II, and about three-fifths (40 out of 68) of these decolonized countries have democratized. The democracy rate of these non-Muslim, decolonized countries is much higher than the democracy rate of Muslim countries, which is less than one-fifth.[4] Thus, colonization alone does not explain why Muslim countries appear to be disproportionately authoritarian when we compare them with the rest of the world.

Western occupations or interventions in Muslim countries have continued into the post-colonial era. In the 1980s and 1990s, the United States and Western European countries largely supported democratization in Latin America and Eastern Europe,[5] whereas they have preferred to work with authoritarian rulers in most Muslim countries, especially in MENA.[6] For long time, this preference was perceived to fit US priorities in MENA – protecting the state of Israel, stabilizing the oil supply, and preventing new Islamist regimes.[7]

Recently, the Bush and Obama administrations briefly and inconsistently pursued pro-democratic agendas in the region. In 2004 and 2005, the Bush administration encouraged democratic elections in Iraq, Lebanon, and Palestine, while also urging Jordan, Egypt, and Saudi Arabia to embrace political reforms.[8] This policy, however, did not endure. The Obama administration's emphasis on democratization in MENA was also ephemeral. Barack Obama's

---

[3] Marx 2003, 31.
[4] I calculated these figures using primarily data from Freedom House (2013) and the Central Intelligence Agency (2014).
[5] Levitsky and Way 2010, chs. 3 and 4.
[6] Bellin 2004, 149; Brownlee 2012; Yom 2015, chs. 5 and 6.
[7] See Migdal 2014; Hudson 2009; Quandt 2005; Mearsheimer and Walt 2007; Carter 2006.
[8] George H. Bush signaled this policy shift as the following: "Sixty years of Western nations excusing and accommodating the lack of freedom in the Middle East did nothing to make us safe." "Bush Asks Lands in Mideast to Try Democratic Ways," *New York Times*, November 7, 2003.

2009 Cairo speech, in which he called for political liberalization across the region, created expectations for a new, pro-democratic US policy. When the Arab Spring broke out one and half years later, the administration cautiously supported the transformation. The NATO operation against the Qaddafi regime in 2011 gave momentum to the Arab uprisings. Unlike in Algeria in 1992, Western countries tolerated the electoral victories of Islamists in Egypt and Tunisia.[9] Nevertheless, this trend was halted by a series of events, including the killing of the US ambassador to Libya (Christopher Stevens), the rise of ISIS, and internal conflicts in many MENA countries. In 2013 the Egyptian military staged a coup and designated the Muslim Brothers as a terrorist organization. The Obama administration did not even define the incident as a "military coup," signaling return to the old policy patterns.

Although Western interventions have contributed to authoritarianism in Muslim countries, on their own they are insufficient to explain the democratic deficiency. Explanations that look only at Western interventions overemphasize foreign actors' impact on Muslim societies, while downplaying the role of these societies' internal dynamics, including their ideologies, class relations, and economic conditions. The following sections will explore these internal aspects.

THE ROLE OF ISLAM

Essentialist explanations point to Islam as the cause of authoritarianism in most Muslim countries. Islam, however, is not exceptional; like other religions, it has both pro-democratic and pro-authoritarian interpretations.[10] One example of such essentialism can be found in an article by Charles Rowley and Nathanael Smith, who argue that democracy deficits in Muslim countries "appear to have something to do with the nature of Islam itself." These authors define a "heartland" of the Muslim world, including countries in MENA and Central Asia, which became part of Muslim lands by the year 750. In these countries, the authors argue, "Islam has the deepest historical roots, has had the most time to shape and to transform culture."[11] It is, however, problematic to present Islam as influential in territories where it dominated by 750, but not in those where it dominated or was prominent from some later point over the last 1,269 years. Moreover, this claimed "heartland" includes Central Asian countries, which experienced Russian colonization followed by atheistic Soviet rule. By focusing on Islam as the cause of authoritarianism in these countries, Rowley

---

[9] See Diamond 2010; Jamal 2012, ch. 8; Hamid 2014.
[10] See Khalaf-Allah 1998 [1973]; Kurzman 1998; Soroush 2000; Madjid 2003; Abou El Fadl 2004; Hashemi 2009; March 2011, 163–258; Bilgin 2011; Osman 2011; Kubicek 2015; Esposito et al. 2016.
[11] Rowley and Smith 2009, 298, 273, 284, 287, respectively.

and Smith disregard their recent history of Russian/Soviet rule and secularist dictators today.[12]

A historical analysis of Muslims' problems should trace change and continuity by dividing a long historical process into smaller periods, rather than simply showing some statistical correlation between today and circumstances a millennium ago. Additionally, in contrast to what Rowley and Smith claim, a religion's long history in a territory does not necessarily make its followers there more pro-authoritarian than those in a territory where the religion has a shorter history. Several Western European converts to Islam, for example, have embraced authoritarian interpretations as Jihadi-Salafism, despite the fact that Western Europe is not a place with a long Islamic history.

Many other scholars have analyzed the role of Islam in contributing to authoritarianism based on contemporary observations. They have generally developed arguments about two main themes in the Muslim world: the presence of patriarchy and the absence of secular states.

Patriarchy

Muslim countries' problem of patriarchy becomes more visible when they are compared with Western countries. Based on World Values Survey in 1995–6 and 2000–2, Ronald Inglehart and Pippa Norris write, "On the matter of equal rights and opportunities for women – measured by such questions as whether men make better political leaders than women or whether university education is more important for boys than for girls – Western and Muslim countries score 82 percent and 55 percent, respectively."[13]

Steven Fish argues that patriarchy has led to authoritarianism in Muslim countries.[14] Fish documents gender inequality in Muslim countries with some convincing data. Nonetheless, I have two main criticisms of his analysis. First, the causal mechanism between patriarchy and authoritarianism is controversial. Western history has shown us that democracy and patriarchy can coexist. Even today, there are democracies coexistent with patriarchy, such as India. Moreover, gender equality can be seen as an effect, rather than a cause or necessary condition of, democratization. For example, women became chief executives in four Muslim countries – Pakistan, Bangladesh, Turkey, and Indonesia – when these countries held democratic elections.

Second, I find Fish's data about the sex ratio (of men to women) questionable. Fish argues that the average sex ratio of Muslim countries is very high,

---

[12] See Kuru 2014, 404–5; Khalid 2007; Kuru 2002. Eric Chaney (2012) also argues that being conquered by Arab armies before the year 1100 explains authoritarianism in Muslim countries. Unlike Rowley and Smith, Chaney points to historical institutions, rather than Islam, as the source of authoritarianism. Chaney, however, shares some of their problems, such as neglecting what has happened in the last 919 years and ignoring the Russian/Soviet legacy.

[13] Inglehart and Norris 2003, 67.   [14] Fish 2002.

especially in comparison to Catholic countries. For him, "[a] higher sex ratio often reflects lower status for and poorer treatment of women and girls" and "the imbalance cannot be explained without reference to neglect of girls' health care and nutrition and sex-selective abortion."[15] I double-checked the numbers by using Fish's data source – United States Census Bureau. In 2010, the sex ratio of aggregated populations of non-Muslim countries (101.3) appeared to be almost the same as the sex ratio of the aggregated populations of Muslim countries (101.5).[16]

Fish's calculation was inflated by data from four countries that had exceptionally high sex ratios due to extensive employment of foreign male workers.[17] Muslim countries do have a patriarchy problem, but they do not have exceptional sex ratios. Patriarchy is not sufficient to explain why most Muslim countries have failed to democratize.

Michael Ross explains the problems of patriarchy and authoritarianism in Muslim countries as a symptom of oil rents.[18] He compares some Middle Eastern and East Asian societies (especially South Korea) that were once similarly patriarchal. In the 1960s, South Korea started to become less patriarchal because women participated into the labor force of manufacturing industries, such as textiles, and eventually gained political influence. In the oil-rich Middle Eastern societies, by contrast, oil has weakened the export-oriented manufacturing sector (due to appreciation of the national currencies) and thus limited the job opportunities for women in this sector, while also maximizing unearned household income through state allocations, thereby reducing women's incentive to work.[19]

Ross's explanation is insightful. But patriarchy exists in most Muslim countries with various degrees; it is not limited to those whose economies are dominated by oil.[20] Moreover, Ross's analysis is too materialist; it overlooks the role of ideas[21] in the complex problem of patriarchy.[22] There has been a doctrinal struggle between supporters and opponents of women's rights in the Muslim world since the late nineteenth century. Supporters have included

---

[15] Fish 2002, 26, 31.
[16] United States Census Bureau 2010. There is a small difference between these ratios, because the younger a society, the higher its sex ratio; Muslim societies have a lower median age (23) than the rest of the world (30).
[17] Kuru 2014, 407–9.
[18] Instead of repeating "oil and gas" every time, Ross only writes "oil." I will do the same in most passages.
[19] Ross 2008; Ross 2012, ch. 4.
[20] See Alexander and Welzel 2011, esp. 66; Moghadem and Mitra 2013.
[21] For the role of ideas and ideologies in sociopolitical life, see Scott 1998; Hanson 2010.
[22] Salafism has promoted patriarchy in the Gulf countries, which are crucial cases in Ross's analysis. Tribalism has also been an important aspect of patriarchy in these countries. See the 2009 special issue of *Politics and Gender* (5, 4: 545–82) for a critique of Ross's focus on the Gulf. For an alternative explanation, see Angrist 2012. For tribalism, Islamic law, and patriarchy in Algeria, Morocco, and Tunisia, see Charrad 2001.

reformist officials and Western-educated intellectuals, whereas the opponents have consisted largely of socially conservative officials and Islamic actors (ulema, Islamists, and Sufi shaykhs). Islamic actors have generally preached patriarchal understandings of Islam, which present men as more suitable for leadership positions from the state to family, require women to have male guardianship during long trips, and undermine women's positions in marriage, divorce, inheritance, and testimony.[23] The consequences of Islamic actors' patriarchal preaching can be seen in a recent (2002–10) survey conducted in fifteen MENA countries, which shows that two-thirds of respondents disagree with the statement that "a woman can travel abroad by herself if she wishes" and two-fifths agree with the statement that "it is a violation [of the precepts of] Islam for male and female university students to attend class together."[24] There have been Muslim women thinkers promoting women's rights,[25] but their resources and access to the wider Muslim public have been limited in comparison to those of Islamic actors.

In the first half of the twentieth century, Muslim supporters of women's rights took important steps forward. But these supporters were largely associated with authoritarian secularist ideologies and state practices. Several secularist regimes, including those in Turkey and Tunisia, imposed headscarf bans,[26] in addition to other restrictions on pious women and men. These authoritarian policies, together with secularist regimes' socioeconomic and foreign policy failures, helped Islamic actors gain popularity. In the second half of the century, Islamic actors have pushed Muslim-majority states and societies toward more conservative lines, which has resulted in the Islamization of constitutions and certain laws in several countries. This legal Islamization has negatively affected women's rights. I analyze the Islamization of state laws in several Muslim countries below.

Secular and Islamic States

For scholars who have explained authoritarianism in the Muslim world as a result of the close entanglement between Islam and the state, Lewis has been the main source of inspiration. In numerous publications, Lewis repeatedly argued that Islam, unlike Christianity, rejects constitutional secularism, in terms of religion–state separation, and that this rejection leads to authoritarianism. In his words, "For believing Muslims, legitimate authority comes from God

---

[23] "In 2007, the Mufti [jurist] of Egypt, ʿAli Jumʿa, issued a *fatwa* declaring that it was forbidden for a woman to assume the presidency." Masoud et al. 2016, 1566.
[24] Carnegie Middle East Governance and Islam Dataset. Quoted and analyzed in Tessler 2015, 116, 94.
[25] Ahmed-Ghosh 2015; Mernissi 1993; al-Hibri 1997; Wadud 1999; Mir-Hosseini 2006; Ali 2006; Hassan 2009, 175–7.
[26] Göle 1996; Akbulut 2015a; Akbulut 2015b; Barras 2014.

alone, and the ruler derives his power not from the people, nor yet from his ancestors, but from God and the holy law."[27] Lewis presents Turkey as the exception that proves the rule: "[T]hose who see in Islam an obstacle to democratic development, point to secularism as the crucial difference between Turkey and the rest of the Muslim world."[28] On this issue, Huntington's views are almost identical. He writes, "In Islam ... no distinction exists between religion and politics or between the spiritual and the secular, and political participation was historically an alien concept." Thus, "Islam ... has not been hospitable to democracy."[29]

Lewis's and Huntington's claims have many problems. Part II of this book will make the case that a certain level of separation between religious and political authorities existed in early Islamic history. The way dominant Islamic discourses today reject religion–state separation began to be constructed in the eleventh century. Moreover, the problem of authoritarianism in the Muslim world cannot be explained by the asserted absence of secular states. In fact, many secular states have existed in the Muslim world. However, most of these secular states have been authoritarian, like their non-secular counterparts.

As summarized in Table 2.1, out of 49 Muslim countries, 22 have constitutionally secular states.[30] Fourteen of these 22 Muslim countries have constitutions that define their states (or republics) as explicitly "secular."[31] I collected the original terms from these countries' constitutions in their official languages, including the vernacular, Arabic, English, French, Portuguese, Russian, and Serbian, as the following: Azerbaijan (*dünyevi*), Burkina Faso (*laïc*), Chad (*laïque, almaniyya*), Gambia (*secular*), Guinea (*laïque*), Guinea-Bissau (*laica*), Kazakhstan (*zayirli, svetskiy*), Kosovo (*laik, sekularna*), Kyrgyzstan (*dinden tyshkary, svetskiy*), Mali (*laïcité de l'Etat*), Senegal (*laïque*), Tajikistan (*dunyavi, svetskoe*), Turkey (*laik*), and Turkmenistan (*dünyewi, svetskoe*).

The remaining eight secular constitutions in Muslim countries do not use the term "secular," but they do not recognize Islam as the official religion either; thus, they implicitly define their states as secular. Among them the legal systems of three cases (Albania, Niger, and Uzbekistan) are fully secular. In one case (Sierra Leone), Islamic family law is considered as customary law and is under the jurisdiction of local courts. In two cases (Eritrea and Lebanon) there are sharia courts for family law matters, including marriage, divorce, and inheritance. In the remaining two cases (Indonesia and especially Nigeria), some provinces' legal systems, including both family and criminal law, are based on sharia.

---

[27] Lewis 2010, 66. See also Lewis 2003, 96–116.   [28] Lewis 1994, 45.

[29] Huntington 1984, 208. See also Huntington 1991, 307.

[30] Among these twenty-two cases, the constitution of Gambia alone refers to sharia courts, and does so only for matters of family law.

[31] Among these fourteen cases, only in Gambia and Senegal does Islamic family law have a role in the legal system. In Senegal, its role is limited and under the jurisdiction of local courts.

TABLE 2.1 *Secularism and Sharia in Forty-Nine Muslim Countries' Constitutions*

Constitutions explicitly or implicitly defining states as secular (22)	Constitutions recognizing Islam as the official religion (8)	Constitutions referring to sharia as a (or the) legal source or compatibility requirement (19)
Explicitly defining the state as secular (14)	1. Algeria	1. Afghanistan
1. Azerbaijan	2. Bangladesh	2. Bahrain
2. Burkina Faso	**3. Comoros**	3. Brunei
3. Chad	4. Djibouti	4. Egypt
4. Gambia	5. Jordan	5. Iran
5. Guinea	6. Malaysia*	6. Iraq
6. Guinea-Bissau	7. Morocco	7. Kuwait
7. Kazakhstan	**8. Tunisia**	8. Libya
8. Kosovo		9. Maldives
9. Kyrgyzstan		10. Mauritania
10. Mali		11. Oman
11. Senegal		12. Pakistan
12. Tajikistan		13. Qatar
13. Turkey		14. Saudi Arabia
14. Turkmenistan		15. Somalia
Implicitly defining the state as secular (8)		16. Syria
15. Albania		17. Sudan
16. Eritrea		18. UAE
17. Indonesia*		19. Yemen
18. Lebanon		
19. Niger		
20. Nigeria*		
21. Sierra Leone		
22. Uzbekistan		

Note: Bold indicates electoral democracies.
* Federal systems where some provinces implement Islamic criminal law.
Sources: Constitutions of these countries; US Department of State 2015; Grote and Röder 2012; Kuru 2009, 247–54.

In short, almost half of Muslim countries have secular constitutions, which indicates that the essentialist claim about the inherent incompatibility between Islam and constitutional secularism is not based on empirical data.[32] Some essentialists could respond by arguing that secular states in the Muslim world are a legacy of colonialism. In fact, with few exceptions – Iran, Saudi Arabia,

[32] On the compatibility of Islam and the secular state, see Filali-Ansary 2002; An-Na'im 2008; Ghobadzadeh 2014; Rahim 2013.

and Turkey – all Muslim countries were colonized by European countries, and while some of them became secular states, some did not.[33] Hence, secular states in the Muslim world are not simply a product of colonialism.[34]

As of 2018, 17 of these 22 Muslim countries with secular constitutions have authoritarian regimes. The five democracies are Albania, Burkina Faso, Indonesia, Senegal, and Sierra Leone.[35] This proportion indicates that secularism is not a sufficient condition for democracy and that the problem of authoritarianism in the Muslim world cannot be explained simply by its absence. Authoritarianism in these secular states can be explained by three factors. First, as Part II of this book will explain, authoritarianism in Muslim countries has deep historical roots based on the marginalization of the intellectual and bourgeois classes by the ulema–state alliance, which began in the eleventh century. Second, the colonial legacy has further inhibited democratization in many Muslim countries. In the cases where the colonizer itself was authoritarian in its mainland, the colonial effect was particularly pro-authoritarian, as seen in the Soviet legacy in Central Asia's authoritarian secular states.[36] These two explanations are not unique to secular states in the Muslim world; they also apply to Islamic states. The third explanation, however, is unique to secular states. In many cases, the secularists have embraced authoritarian ideologies of sociopolitical transformation, including socialism and fascism, and opposed democratization as a barrier to their top-down modernization projects.

Table 2.1 classifies constitutions in Muslim countries in three categories: secular constitutions, constitutions that recognize Islam as the official religion without referring to sharia, and constitutions that recognize some legal status for sharia. The second category includes eight cases: Algeria, Bangladesh, Comoros, Djibouti, Jordan, Malaysia, Morocco, and Tunisia.[37] In these countries, the family law is based on various interpretations of Islamic law. In 2013, six of these eight countries were ruled by authoritarian regimes (the only democracies were Comoros and Tunisia). This category is a transition between the first and the third, and the countries it includes thus have some overlap with those in the other two categories in terms of the causes of authoritarianism.

In countries in the third and last category, constitutions refer to sharia as a (or the) legal source or specify a compatibility requirement with sharia for laws to be constitutional: nineteen countries (Afghanistan, Bahrain, Brunei, Egypt,

---

[33] The French colonial impact was more pro-secular than the British alternative. Yet there is still a variation among the former French colonies in the Muslim world; some (Burkina Faso, Chad, Guinea, Lebanon, Niger, Mali, and Senegal) are secular states, while others (Algeria, Comoros, Djibouti, Mauritania, Morocco, Syria, and Tunisia) are not. See Kuru and Stepan 2012; Özbudun 2012.

[34] British colonial rulers codified and implemented sharia in certain cases, such as India and Malaysia. Hussin 2016; Yılmaz 2005, 126–8.

[35] Freedom House 2018.   [36] Boix and Stokes 2003, 535–7.

[37] As an exception in this category, in Malaysia, some provinces have declared that they will fully implement sharia, including criminal law matters such as corporal punishment.

Iran, Iraq, Kuwait, Libya, Maldives, Mauritania, Oman, Pakistan, Qatar, Saudi Arabia, Somalia, Syria, Sudan, the United Arab Emirates [UAE], and Yemen) are in this category. These countries have sharia courts with jurisdiction over family law matters. Moreover, in many of these cases, sharia courts deal with criminal law matters. All of these countries are currently ruled by authoritarian regimes. These data show that the constitutional status of sharia is associated with authoritarianism.

In the last four decades, several Muslim countries have adopted less secular constitutions and legal systems. This transformation has generally followed two complementary courses. The first one has been top-down Islamization by rulers. In several cases, authoritarian rulers have put sharia into the constitutions to legitimize their regimes, in the eyes of religiously conservative masses, and to counter the rising Islamist opposition.[38] In this context, legal Islamization might be seen to have legitimized regimes that were already authoritarian. The second course has been a more bottom-up Islamization through sociopolitical mobilization. A combination of various factors, such as the global trend of religious revivalism, authoritarian and ineffective policies of secularist regimes, and political efforts of Islamists, led to this mobilization.

We have seen either or both of these courses of Islamization in different cases.[39] Iran officially became an Islamic state, as did Afghanistan, Sudan, and (unified) Yemen. In Egypt and Pakistan, articles about sharia were put into the constitution, and the legal roles of the ulema and sharia courts expanded. More recently, certain provinces of Indonesia, Malaysia, and Nigeria adopted sharia laws. The ruler of Brunei declared the Islamization of the legal system. In four cases of civil wars, in Iraq, Libya, Somalia, and Syria, there occurred a sharp move toward legal Islamization via new constitutional articles referring to sharia.[40] In all these cases, legal Islamization has been associated with further authoritarianism of the political regime. Of course, the relations between Islamic mobilization and democracy are complex. In cases where Islamic actors have not focused on legal Islamization, such as certain ulema in Indonesia, Sufis in Senegal, and Islamists in Tunisia, they have contributed to the democratization processes of their countries.[41]

Although in various cases Islamists captured power, the class which most expanded its legislative and judicial influence was the ulema, who claimed the authority to interpret sharia. The constitutional designation of a legal status to sharia in a country at least partially means that the law is regarded as something to be formed by the ulema. This arrangement is almost the opposite of the democratic notion of law-making by parliamentarians based on changing conditions and public opinion. In other words, the way the ulema produce

---

[38] Hibbard 2010, chs. 2 and 3; Buehler 2016.   [39] Bayat 2007, chs. 2–5.

[40] Hefner 2011; Hefner 2016; Sezgin 2013, ch. 5; Stahnke and Blitt 2005; Fox 2008; Barro and McCleary 2005.

[41] Hefner 2000; Künkler and Stepan 2013; Menchik 2016; Stepan 2012; Diouf 2013; Marks 2018.

Islamic law excludes the people's participation in the legal process; therefore, it inherently contradicts democratic processes and ideals.

There are two conclusions. First, the essentialist arguments about Islam overlook the historical as well as the contemporary complexity of Islam's relations with the state. There have existed many secular states in the Muslim world, yet authoritarianism remains widespread. Second, for the last four decades, the role of the ulema in both law-making and the judiciary has expanded throughout the Muslim world. In many cases this expansion has contributed to the persistence of authoritarianism. The ulema's position is worth analyzing in detail.

THE ULEMA

Ulema–State Alliances

In countries where there have existed or emerged constitutional references to sharia, the ulema have functioned as an undemocratic legislative authority. Even in various secular states, the ulema have cooperated with or been coopted by authoritarian rulers. Although these rulers initially planned to use the ulema strategically, in the long run, the ulema seems to have benefited more from this relationship by Islamizing public discourse and ultimately promoting their own political and legal positions.

In many Muslim countries, governments have controlled mosques to regulate the ulema and legitimize their rule. Even the secularist governments in Turkey controlled mosques through a governmental agency, the Directorate of Religious Affairs (Diyanet), founded in 1924.[42] Since then, all imams in Turkish mosques have been state servants, and the government has controlled the content of preaching there. In essence, the secularists established the Diyanet to maintain their oversight of Islamic activities.[43] Recently, however, when Tayyip Erdoğan began to establish a populist Islamist regime, he was able to exploit the Diyanet as a centralized institution under government control. In about 100,000 mosques nationwide, state servant imams continue to recite Friday sermons composed by the central Diyanet office; at critical times, such as prior to elections, these sermons propagandize the Erdoğan regime's views.[44]

Erdoğan has adopted a long list of authoritarian measures, including the confiscation of thousands of citizens' private property and the jailing of tens of thousands under terror charges. Yet he continues to receive the support of most

[42] For ulema–state relations in the early Turkish Republic, see Başkan 2014, ch. 3; Bein 2011, chs. 6 and 7.
[43] Kuru 2009, 166–227. Military rule in the early 1980s was Kemalist and secularist. Yet it promoted Islamic schools and discourses as ways of containing socialism. See Kaplan 2002.
[44] See Kılınç 2019, chs. 6, 9; Öztürk 2016; Cizre 2017.

Islamic actors, including prominent ulema and Sufi shaykhs.[45] The leading Turkish scholar of Islamic law, Hayrettin Karaman, has played a key role in maintaining the alliance between Erdoğan and the ulema. For decades, Karaman has bridged the Turkish ulema and Islamist ideology. He famously argues that "each and every Muslim should be an Islamist; even if he does not use this term, he should accept the meaning and content of this concept."[46] As early as 1990, Karaman characterized secular legal systems as antithetical to Islam and claimed that "an individual or a society cannot avoid polytheism, unless they base all of their behaviors on the divine will either through the revelation or its interpretations."[47] In 2013, when Erdoğan attempted in vain to ban the mixed-sex student residence, Karaman wrote: "If there is an unmarried couple or mixed-sex students who are living together in a house ... the state inspects and raids such houses in order to hinder illegitimate behaviors, and punishes these perpetrators." For Karaman, Islam is incompatible with both secularism and democracy, because "according to philosophical basis of democracy, human being is equal to, superior to, or independent of the Creator." Muslims, for him, ought to ask whether democratic institutions have a divine origin, or whether they are productions of human reason and ego. Karaman justifies Erdoğan's and other Islamists' usage of secularism, democracy, and pluralism only as temporary instruments: "If our conditions require the usage of some means while we are marching toward Islam step-by-step, we would use such means ... Necessity justifies the means."[48]

The Arab Republic of Egypt is another example of a polity that was founded as a secular state and experienced a gradual process of legal Islamization. Like his Turkish counterparts, Nasser aimed to put Islamic institutions, particularly Al-Azhar, the famous center of Sunni learning, administratively and financially under his control. He was powerful enough to bring "the ulema to heel."[49] The following presidents continued to expand governmental supervision of Islamic institutions in Egypt. The proportion of state-controlled mosques increased from less than one-fifth in 1962 to more than three-fifths in 1994, while the total number of mosques also enlarged from fewer than 20,000 to around 70,000. A bureaucratic council has decided the topics to be covered in these state-controlled mosques, particularly in Friday sermons.[50] Obviously, the Egyptian state could not monopolize the Islamic sphere; there appeared

---

[45] Elsewhere I have examined the changing relationship between Erdoğan and the Gülen movement, critically examining both sides over the course of Erdoğan's initial alliance and subsequent conflict with and current persecution of this movement. Kuru 2017. See also Kuru 2015.

[46] Hayrettin Karaman, "Müslüman Sıfatı Yetmemiş," *Yeni Şafak*, August 30, 2012.

[47] Karaman 1990, 22.

[48] Karaman's articles in the order of these three quotes: "Hangi Eve Girilemez," *Yeni Şafak*, November 10, 2013; "İslam, Demokrasi ve Medine Vesikası," *Yeni Şafak*, May 29, 2014; "Demokrasi Çoğulculuk Laiklik ve İslam," *Yeni Şafak*, May 25, 2014.

[49] Zeghal 1999, 372.   [50] Moustafa 2000, 8.

alternative religious authorities, and even Al-Azhar made certain challenges to the government.[51] Yet overall, not only Nasser but also subsequent presidents Anwar Sadat[52] and Hosni Mubarak "all benefited from this dominance over Al-Azhar by securing fatwas legitimating their policies."[53]

In January 2013, when Mohammed Morsi was the Egyptian president, I conducted interviews in Cairo with politicians and bureaucrats affiliated with the Muslim Brothers. Answering my questions about the state control over mosques, they generally expressed willingness to increase this state control.[54] The Kemalist and Nasserist policies to put mosques under state oversight were secularist projects. Islamists in Turkey and Egypt have not been different; they are equally eager to keep mosques under state control. Part II of this book will analyze the deep historical roots of this eagerness.

Iran has also followed a similar trajectory by moving from secularism to Islamism. In contrast to the Egyptian and Turkish cases, however, the transformation in Iran was revolutionary.[55] Khomeini articulated his vision of post-revolutionary Iran in his concept of the guardianship of the jurist (*velayat-e faqih*), according to which the ulema would hold not only legislative and judicial but also executive power. Again, unlike Turkey and Egypt, the trajectory Iran followed has gone beyond an ulema–state alliance, becoming a semi-theocratic regime in which the ulema are supreme. Khomeini held that the ulema, particularly the jurists, are vested by God with the authority to implement sharia.[56] His understanding of governance is simply reduced into the implementation of sharia. From this perspective, humans have very little efficacy: even if the Prophet Muhammad and (Imam) Ali were alive today, Khomeini asserts, they would have had no more agency than a regular jurist in governance. He explains this assertion with an example: "Now the penalty for the fornicator is one hundred lashes. If the Prophet applies the penalty, is he to inflict one hundred fifty lashes, [Imam Ali] ... one hundred, and the *faqih* [jurist] fifty?"[57] Of course, after capturing power, Khomeini and other ulema

---

[51] Zeghal 1999, 380–96; Zeghal 1996, chs. 6–8; Moustafa 2000, 10–18.

[52] Under Sadat, in 1971, the reference to sharia as a source of legislation was added to the Egyptian Constitution, and its stipulation as the principal source of legislation was added in 1980. Moustafa 2007, 107, 110.

[53] Moustafa 2000, 3.

[54] Author's interview in the Supreme Council of Islamic Affairs, Cairo, January 22, 2013. I also conducted interviews with politicians in Tunisia in April 2013. The views of the Islamist Ennahda, particularly its leader Rachid Ghannouchi, were more moderate than those of Egyptian Muslim Brothers, regarding state–Islam relations.

[55] Arjomand 1988; Kurzman 1996.

[56] To justify his Islamist project, Khomeini (1981 [1970], 29) claims, "The ratio of Qur'anic verses concerned with the affairs of society to those concerned with ritual worship is greater than a hundred to one." The reality, however, is different: several scholars have emphasized that the proportion of Quranic verses that address legal matters is only around 5–10 percent. Vikor 2005, 33; Kamali 2003, 25–7; Hallaq 1997, 10.

[57] Khomeini 1981 [1970], 63.

governed Iran with certain levels of pragmatism and realpolitik, but the idea of the guardianship of the jurist is still the basis of the Iranian regime.[58]

In the Indian subcontinent, Pakistan is an important Muslim country, given its large population, nuclear power, and influence over worldwide Islamist groups. The Islamization of the Pakistani legal system was mostly done in the late 1970s and the 1980s by Zia ul Haq, who came to power with a military coup. In 1979, Zia promulgated a series of Islamic criminal laws and took steps to Islamize the education system and economy.[59] Zia's short-term alliance with the Islamist Jamaat-i Islami reflected a tradition with deep historical roots. In the words of Mumtaz Ahmad, Zia "embodied the classic formulation of Islamic polity: a good and pious Muslim who was committed to the enforcement of the Shari'a in consultation with the ulama and the Jamaat-i-Islami." Again, similar to "the medieval Muslim political tradition, no questions were asked about the mode of his coming into power or the methods he chose for Islamizing the society."[60] Zia empowered the ulema by establishing a federal sharia court to review legislation. But he did not let this court take progressive steps. In 1981, when the court declared stoning as un-Islamic in a case of adultery, Zia packed the court with new judges, who overruled the decision.[61] From the era of Zia to the present, certain Islamic actors in Pakistan have promoted authoritarianism and restricted religious freedom of non-Sunni and non-Muslim minorities, as well as restricting women's rights.[62]

The processes of political and legal Islamization seen in these four major Muslim countries reflect a broader trend in the Muslim world. Different forms of alliance between the rulers and the ulema have helped entrench authoritarian regimes. Disappointed by modernist authoritarian regimes, Muslim masses have shown support for Islamist authoritarian regimes in several cases. This transformation has been inspired by certain authoritarian ideas, whose historical origins generally go back to the eleventh century.

Medieval Ideas, Modern Authoritarianism

It is very difficult to challenge the statist and conservative discourses of the ulema and interpret Islam in an individualist and progressive manner. The ulema's authority to interpret Islam based on their rigid epistemology has been very well established in Muslim societies. There is also a hierarchy within the ranks of the ulema that prevents younger ulema from devising new and creative ideas. As a result, the ulema have preserved Islamic legal texts' illiberal content, including those related to corporal punishment, one-man rule, patriarchy, violating privacy, and discriminating against non-Muslims.

---

[58] For some of the Iranian ulema's criticism of the "guardianship of the jurist," see Kadivar 2013, 357–61; Ghobadzadeh 2014, 30–72, 96–170.
[59] Zaman 2011, 216.   [60] Ahmad 1991, 481.   [61] Kadri 2012, 229.
[62] Saeed 2016; Haqqani 2005, chs. 4–7; Ispahani 2017, chs. 5–7; Quraishi 1997.

Whenever they find convenient conditions, these ideas have moved from madrasa textbooks to political systems.

As analyzed in Chapter 4, Ghazali was an influential scholar of the eleventh century. His *Revival* is still widely read, mostly by Sunnis but also by Shiis.[63] This influential text includes misogynistic statements that promote patriarchy.[64] Another eleventh-century scholar, Mawardi, is still regarded as the leading theoretician of the caliphate. Like Ghazali's *Revival*, Mawardi's *Ordinances of Government* has been widely read. Both books emphasize the duty of "commanding right and forbidding wrong" in ordering public life. These medieval texts' influence on the present can be seen in the contemporary institution of the religious police, which has been established with different forms in several countries, including Saudi Arabia, Iran, and Malaysia.

Mawardi emphasizes that the caliph authorizes some individuals to act as public morality officers, while volunteers can also maintain public morality to a certain extent.[65] This duty includes a broad list of issues such as forcing men to fulfill the Friday prayer, preventing men and women from speaking together in public, pouring out alcohol, destroying most musical instruments, policing financial frauds, and even forbidding men from "dying grey hair black unless as a preliminary to participating in a holy war" and punishing "anyone who dyes his hair black in order to win favour with ladies."[66] By contrast, there is no emphasis on the state authority in the writings of Ghazali; for him each Muslim should command right and forbid wrong. A child can pour out his father's alcohol depending the level of the latter's possible anger and retribution. Ghazali defines several steps of "commanding right and forbidding wrong," including providing information, giving polite advice, then threatening advice, physical intervention, and finally coercion. While following these steps, individuals do not need permission from political authorities; they can even use violence if necessary. Ghazali also emphasizes other aspects of "commanding right and forbidding wrong," which sound more positive for a modern reader, such as intervening whenever there is an injustice and speaking truth to power in the face of oppressive ruler.[67]

To put these ideas into practice in contemporary societies would be to establish either an authoritarian state with a religious police (à la Mawardi) or an anarchy in which citizens constantly intervene in each other's daily lives,

[63] In the seventeenth century Fayd al-Kashani paraphrased Ghazali's *Revival* with a Twelver Shii approach, which is "still used by scholars in Iran today." Moosa 2005, 13.

[64] Al-Ghazali 1984 [c. 1097], 57, 62–5, 90–105, 115–26; Gazali 1974a [c. 1097], 376–82; Gazali 1974b [c. 1097], 71, 77–81, 106–27, 141–56; 738, 789. See also Kınalızade 2012 [1565], 350–3.

[65] Al-Mawardi 1996 [1045–58], 260.   [66] Al-Mawardi 1996 [1045–58], 280; also 263–79.

[67] Passages against privacy: Gazali 1974b [c. 1097], 753–834, esp. 782, 788, 792, 815–16. Passages against injustice: Gazali 1974b [c. 1097], 835–65. These passages have an abridged translation with very poor English: al-Ghazali 1963 [c. 1097], 224–43 and 243–58. It is better to read their extended summary in Michael Cook's book (2000, 427–46).

even by force (à la Ghazali). In short, the central Islamic concept of "commanding right and forbidding wrong" needs a modern interpretation to become compatible with democracy and individual freedom.[68]

Similarly, medieval interpretations of Islam regarding Muslims' relations with non-Muslims are not compatible with democracy. Medieval Muslim states designed their relations with non-Muslim subjects through the concepts of protected people (*dhimmi*) and poll tax (*jizya*). Although these states' treatments of Christian and Jewish subjects were much better than Christian states' treatments of Muslims and Jews,[69] their concepts and policies are incompatible with today's democratic and human rights standards. Abdulaziz Sachedina quotes the leading ninth-century jurist Shafii, who argued that Muslim rulers should prohibit their Christian subjects from building new churches, riding horses, and wearing dress similar or equal to that of Muslims. Sachedina concludes, "Most of the past juridical decisions treating non-Muslim minorities have become irrelevant in the context of contemporary religious pluralism, a cornerstone of interhuman relations."[70]

Even in the mid-nineteenth century, Ottoman rulers left aside the medieval conceptions of Islamic law regarding Muslims' relations with non-Muslims and initiated a series of legal reforms.[71] The Ottoman ulema did not have sufficient power to publicly resist these reforms; however, like the ulema of other countries, they kept medieval interpretations on these subjects in textbooks taught in madrasas.

In order to solve contemporary problems of authoritarianism, patriarchy, and religious discrimination, Muslim countries need creative intellectuals. These countries, however, have had various barriers to the flourishing of intellectuals. Many Muslim countries have passed blasphemy and apostasy laws,[72] which have further restricted freedom of conscience and intellectual life. These laws have been applied against a small number of individuals, but this limited application was enough to create a general atmosphere hostile to critical thinking. In 1995, a sharia court declared Egyptian intellectual Nasr Abu Zayd to be an apostate and his marriage to be null because he proposed some reformist approaches to interpreting the Quran.[73] Throughout the Muslim world, intellectuals who criticize orthodox views have faced various threats, including being labeled as apostates, native Orientalists, or lackeys of Western agenda.[74]

---

[68] See Cook 2000, 3–11; Asad 1993, 233–4. [69] Goddard 2000, 68.
[70] Sachedina 2001, 68; also 65–7. [71] See Chapter 7. [72] See Pew Research Center 2012.
[73] Abu Zaid 2004; Abu Zaid 2000; Radhan 2014, 179–205.
[74] Saba Mahmood (2006, 329, 332–47) accuses three critical Muslim intellectuals, Abu Zayd, Hasan Hanafi, and Abdul Karim Soroush, for echoing the US agenda as expressed in a report by Rand Corporation (*Civil and Democratic Islam*). The report was published in 2003, while these intellectuals' works cited by Mahmood were published in the 1980s and 1990s. The source of inspiration for the Rand report may be these intellectuals, rather than vice versa. See also Jansen 2011, 983–8.

Islamists have also disseminated certain ideas that are incompatible with democratic participation and separation of powers. They generally present Islam as a comprehensive doctrine that, unlike Christianity, covers every aspect of life. As Part II of this book will elaborate, this claim is inaccurate – Islam has played an important but limited role in Muslims' political history for more than a millennium, and it is no different from Christianity in terms of recognizing a differentiation between religion and politics, as well as between religion and such other spheres of life such as science and economy, although Islamists' well-known slogan, "Islam is the solution!" denies it.[75]

Theoretically, Sufi shaykhs could have provided a more spiritual alternative to Islamists' top-down utopian projects and the ulema's formal legalism. Practically, they did not. Instead, the Sufi shaykhs have generally contributed to authoritarianism with their hierarchical teachings as articulated in such widespread sayings of Kadiri and Nakşibendi Sufi orders in Turkey as "Whoever does not have a shaykh, his shaykh is Satan" and "When Satan will approach a Muslim's death-bed to steal his faith, his shaykh will save his faith." This kind of hierarchical Sufi preaching blocks individual freedom, which is necessary to make democracy work.

In sum, the ulema have generally enabled authoritarianism in many Muslim countries through its alliances with authoritarian rulers and its promotion of certain medieval and anti-democratic ideas. Especially if sharia is declared to be the law of the land in a country, it becomes almost impossible to challenge the ulema's authority to interpret Islam. Through their rigid epistemology, control over madrasas and equivalent institutions, societal prestige, and state support, the senior ulema have marginalized intellectuals, as well as some dissenting junior ulema. On the issue of blocking critical thinking, the secularists have also made a major contribution in the Muslim world. The secularist rulers have pursued top-down modernization projects and regarded independent intellectuals as largely useless and even inconvenient.

Obviously, the ideas of Islamic actors and the secularists are not sufficient to explain the complex problem of authoritarianism in the Muslim world. Regardless of whether they are Islamist or secularist, authoritarian regimes need financial resources. In most Muslim countries, authoritarian rulers have used rents, especially oil revenues, to sustain their regimes.

OIL AND THE RENTIER STATE

A rent is a geological gift that does not need labor-intensive production. The revenues from rents, such as those from oil and gas, make the economy rentier.

---

[75] This Islamist perspective rejects the differentiation between religion and other spheres of life, and thus hinders the development of division of labor, specialization, and meritocracy. For differentiation and spheres of life, see Casanova 1994; Walzer 1983.

A state is defined as "rentier" if rents constitute over 40 percent of its revenues.[76] The state control over rents maintains the rulers with incentive,[77] as well as power to reject people's participation in governance. Rulers of rentier states do not financially depend on taxation; therefore, the people cannot use taxation as leverage to hold rulers accountable.[78] On the contrary, the people in rentier states are dependent on governmental allocation of rents; the rentier state allocates rents to the people in the form of money, jobs, and social services.[79] This creates a patron–client relationship between the rulers and people, as well as a lack of independent political, economic, and civil society. Without independent political parties, a bourgeois class, and civic associations, democracy becomes impossible.[80]

In a non-rentier system of extraction, taxpayers constitute a very large number of citizens who are relatively mobile in terms of their capital and even production. If the government loses legitimacy, it becomes very hard for it to monitor and coerce all taxpayers. Oil production, however, is geographically static and controlled by a small number of elites. Therefore, its rents are much easier to monitor and extract, if not monopolize, by a government, than other types of production.[81] An oil-dependent economy, in short, is unlikely to have either an autonomous bourgeoisie, because of the government monopoly over oil, or an organized labor, due to the fact that oil production is not labor-intensive.[82] Moreover, rents provide authoritarian regimes with the financial capacity to expand their despotic security apparatuses and to use state-owned media and other propaganda mechanisms against opposition.

To analyze the relationship between rentier states and authoritarianism, I prepared a global index of rent and tax rates as a percentage of government revenue.[83] Table 2.2 summarizes the index's conclusions about rentier states.

[76] Luciani 1987, 70; Herb 2005, 299.
[77] According to Adam Przeworski and Fernando Limongi (1997, 167), the "struggle for dictator-ship is more attractive in poorer countries," because "the gain from getting all rather than a part of total income" is bigger. Similarly, the struggle for dictatorship is very attractive in a rentier state, where maximizing one's share of rent revenues is a big gain. See also Boix 2003, 12, 237.
[78] The rulers of rentier states could say, "no representation without taxation." Luciani 1987, 75.
[79] Around 2009, in Kuwait, Qatar, and the UAE, around 90 percent of citizens who held jobs were employed "by the state (or in a state-owned enterprise)." Herb 2009, 382.
[80] Ross 2001; Beblawi and Luciani 1987; Ulfelder 2007; Tsui 2011.
[81] According to Stanley Engerman and Kenneth Sokoloff (2012, 66), diffusion of property owner-ship is associated with democratization. In around 1900, the proportion of household heads who owned land was only 3 percent in authoritarian Mexico, whereas it was much higher in its relatively democratic neighbors: 75 percent in the United States and 87 percent in Canada.
[82] In Saudi Arabia, oil production constitutes about half of the GDP, but it employs less than 2 percent of the labor force. Ross 2012, 45.
[83] Kuru 2014, 414–16 (tables 6 and 7). I calculated the percentages of oil, gas, and mineral rents; non-rentier taxes; and other revenues in the total revenues of governments. My primary sources were the International Monetary Fund's (2007–11) country reports. I completed and

TABLE 2.2 *Rents, Taxes, and Rentier States (around 2010)*

#	Country	Rent %	Tax %	#	Country	Rent %	Tax %
1	East Timor	0.93	0.05	15	**Yemen**	0.75	0.18
2	**Brunei**	0.92	0.03	16	**UAE**	0.74	0.18
3	**Equatorial Guinea**	0.91	0.03	17	**Qatar**	0.66	0.13
4	**Libya**	0.90	0.05	18	**Algeria**	0.66	0.31
5	**Iraq**	0.88	0.05	19	**Sudan**	0.61	0.34
6	**Saudi Arabia**	0.85	0.04	20	**Azerbaijan**	0.61	0.35
7	**Republic of Congo**	0.85	0.14	21	Gabon	0.59	0.40
8	**Kuwait**	0.82	0.02	22	**Iran**	0.55	0.28
9	**Bahrain**	0.80	0.15	23	Trinidad and Tobago	0.52	0.31
10	Angola	0.80	0.13	24	Venezuela	0.51	0.42
11	**Chad**	0.79	0.20	25	**Kazakhstan**	0.50	0.50
12	**Oman**	0.77	0.11	26	**Mauritania**	0.42	0.30
13	**Nigeria**	0.75	0.23	27	Bolivia	0.41	0.52
14	**Turkmenistan**	0.75	0.20	28	**Malaysia**	0.41	0.53

Notes: Bold indicates Muslim countries. The combination of rent and tax rates is not equal to 100 percent because government revenues include other items, especially international loans. Sources: International Monetary Fund 2007–11; Economist Intelligence Unit 2011; Revenue Watch 2011.

It shows that Muslim countries constitute between two-thirds and three-quarters (20 out of 28) of all rentier states, although they comprise only over a quarter (48 out of 170) of all countries in this analysis. The high rate of Muslim rentier states is linked to Muslim countries' rich natural resources; they have two-thirds of the world's oil reserves, and those in MENA have about three-fifths of the world's reserves. Additionally, Muslim countries have three-fifths of the world's gas reserves, and those in MENA have about half of the world's reserves.[84]

All Muslim countries listed in the table are authoritarian, as are five of the eight non-Muslim countries listed. The fact that the Muslim world includes a disproportionate number of rentier states helps us understand the disproportionately high rate of authoritarian rule in Muslim countries. Two questions, however, still need to be addressed. First, three non-Muslim rentier states in the table – East Timor, Trinidad and Tobago, and Bolivia – are democratic.

cross-checked data with various sources, including Economist Intelligence Unit (2011) and Revenue Watch (2011) reports.

[84] BP 2011.

Second, there exist twenty-nine non-rentier Muslim states, most of which (22 out of 29) are also authoritarian.[85]

Elsewhere, I explained these issues by referring to the concept of "regional diffusion," which implies that political regimes in a region affect each other through various mechanisms, including military intervention, regional diplomacy, economic policy, and sociocultural exchange. Regional diffusion explains democratization in East Timor, with the influence of its democratic neighbor Australia, and in Bolivia and Trinidad and Tobago, with the impact of their democratic neighbors in Latin America. By contrast, oil-poor countries in the MENA region and Central Asia have been under the political and economic influence of their oil-rich and authoritarian neighbors, such as Iran, Saudi Arabia, and Kazakhstan.[86] MENA is the only region in the world where countries' average rent rate (55%) is higher than the average tax rate (32%) as a percentage of government revenue.[87] Thus oil rents appear to have a region-wide impact in MENA. Many oil-poor countries in this region, including Egypt, have sought international loans, which is similar to rent.[88]

There is another weakness of an oil-based explanation of authoritarianism in the Muslim world: the impact of oil on political regimes is not absolute but relative to the size of a country's or a region's economy.[89] Norway, for example, has more oil income per capita than Brunei, but oil rents constitute only 36 percent of government revenues and 18 percent of the gross domestic product (GDP) in Norway, whereas they account for 92 percent of government revenues and 65 percent of GDP in Brunei.[90] If the economy and the total governmental revenue of Norway were smaller, its economy would be much more dependent on rents and its state would be a rentier state.

Consequently, if Muslim economies were larger, then oil rents would not dominate them so overwhelmingly. However, in 2014, the total GNI of Muslim

---

[85] Freedom House 2018. In five cases, the rents/government revenue rate is between 31 and 40 percent. Among these "semi-rentier" states, Egypt and Russia are authoritarian, while Ecuador, Norway, and Mexico are democratic. I counted Suez and Panama Canal fees as rents.

[86] Kuru 2014, 420–5. See also Linz and Stepan 1996, 72–6; Kopstein and Reilly 2000; Bellin 2012, 141–4.

[87] In all regions, except MENA, the average rent rate is lower than the average tax rate: Europe (1% vs. 85%), Americas (12% vs. 73%), Asia-Pacific (13% vs. 68%), Sub-Saharan Africa (18% vs. 62%), and former Soviet Republics (21% vs. 66%). Kuru 2014, 416.

[88] See Morrison 2009. Egypt shares many characteristics with its rentier neighbors, such as patron–client relations between the state and the people. See Masoud 2014, esp. part I.

[89] Thad Dunning (2008, 10–20) argues that oil has a pro-democratic effect in Latin America and pro-authoritarian effect in Arab Gulf countries largely due to the different oil rents/GDP ratios in these two regions. In Latin America, where the oil rents/GDP ratios are lower, elected governments can allocate oil rents to the people and minimize elites' concern about democracy's redistribution of their non-oil wealth through taxation. In the Gulf, however, oil rents/GDP ratios are much higher, and thus the elites do not want to share oil rents and oppose democratization.

[90] Ross 2012, 21; Kuru 2014, 416.

countries constituted only 9 percent of the world's GNI, and it was less than the combined GNI of Germany and the United Kingdom.[91] The limited size of economies in the Middle East is particularly important to assess the economic and political impact of oil in this leading oil-exporter region. As Charles Boix writes, "Once we exclude oil production, total output in the Middle East is similar to that of Finland."[92]

One may argue that oil revenues have inhibited Muslim countries' economic growth. It is true that high oil exports lead to the appreciation of the national currency and thus make exporting other products more difficult. Nonetheless, as Ross documents, oil does not hinder overall GNI growth.[93] In fact, Muslim countries' economic conditions were even worse in the early 1970s, when they began to receive large oil revenues.[94] In 1970, the rate of the total GNI of Muslim countries in the world's GNI was smaller (only 4 percent) than it is today.[95] The next section will briefly assess Muslim countries' economic underdevelopment and its connection to authoritarianism.

ECONOMIC UNDERDEVELOPMENT

Scholars have extensively studied and debated the association between economic development and democracy. For some, the former causes the latter,[96] while others are skeptical about such a direct causal relationship.[97] In a recent work, Boix and Susan Stokes argue that "economic development both causes democracy and sustains it."[98] Elsewhere, Boix reiterates: "Whereas 94% of the countries with a per capita income above $10,000 ... held free and competitive elections in 1999, only 18% with a per capita income below $2,000 did so."[99]

With regard to the Muslim world, Alfred Stepan and Graeme Robertson developed an important argument about the association among economic underdevelopment, Arab/non-Arab identity, and authoritarianism. If a country becomes democratic despite having a GNI per capita less than $3,500, Stepan and Robertson call it an "overachiever."[100] If a country is authoritarian

---

[91] In 2014, the total GNI of Muslim countries was $6.7 trillion, and that of the world was $77.6 trillion. United Nations 2016.

[92] Boix 2003, 237.   [93] Ross 2012, 189, 221.

[94] The total oil exports of Saudi Arabia, Kuwait, the UAE, Qatar, and Bahrain increased from $5 billion in 1970 to $48 billion in 1975. Their oil production also increased from 0.35 billion barrels in 1950 to 1.2 billion barrels in 1960, 3 billion barrels in 1970, and 5 billion barrels in 1980. Owen and Pamuk 1999, 266–7.

[95] In 1970, the total GNI of Muslim countries was $141 billion, while that of the world was $3.4 trillion. United Nations 2016.

[96] Lipset 1959.

[97] Linz and Stepan 1996, 76–81; Przeworski et al. 2000; Acemoglu and Robinson 2009, 51–8.

[98] Boix and Stokes 2003, 545.   [99] Boix 2011, 809.

[100] My calculation based on Freedom House (2013) and World Bank (2010) shows that 72 percent of all countries and 79 percent of Muslim countries, which are below the threshold of $3,500 GNI per capita, are authoritarian.

notwithstanding its GNI per capita of more than $5,500, they call it an "underachiever." For the authors, if a country's GNI per capita is between $3,500 and $5,500, then it is theoretically indeterminate whether it is likely to be democratic or authoritarian.[101]

With data from 2004, Stepan and Robertson categorized eight Arab countries as underachievers and found not a single non-Arab Muslim underachiever. By contrast, five non-Arab Muslim countries were overachievers, whereas no Arab country was in that category. As a group, non-Arab Muslim countries exceeded their predicted level of democratization based on their level of GNI per capita, while Arab Muslim countries failed to reach their expected level. In conclusion, Stepan and Robertson argue that while there is no Muslim democratic deficiency, there is an Arab democratic deficiency.[102]

Using 2010 and 2013 data, I retested Stepan and Robertson's thesis.[103] The updated data had three results supporting their argument: there was still no Arab overachiever; the number of Arab underachievers increased from eight to ten (Qatar, Kuwait, the UAE, Oman, Bahrain, Saudi Arabia, Lebanon, Algeria, Egypt, and Jordan, in the order of highest to lowest GNI per capita); and the number of non-Arab overachievers was still five (Senegal, Bangladesh, Comoros, Sierra Leone, and Niger). Yet the fourth result substantially weakened their argument: there were eight, instead of zero, non-Arab underachievers. During the period between the two analyses, eight non-Arab countries (Brunei, Malaysia, Iran, Kazakhstan, Azerbaijan, Maldives, Turkmenistan, and Kosovo) experienced a substantial increase in GNI per capita without corresponding democratization.[104]

Among these eight non-Arab underachievers, six (Brunei, Malaysia, Iran, Kazakhstan, Azerbaijan, and Turkmenistan) are rentier states. Their GNI per capita became inflated given the sharp increase in oil prices after the US invasion of Iraq in 2003. Among ten non-Arab underachievers, seven are also rentier states. GNI per capita is not a good predictor of democratization for oil-rich countries where oil revenues inflate GNI.[105] These countries earn money without establishing a complex economy, which would include industrial production, technological sophistication, division of labor, specialization, and skilled labor. Such a complex economy would require a complex political system governed by democratic principles and institutions. Oil-rich Muslim countries, on the contrary, have reached high levels of GNI without having a complex economy; therefore, their GNI levels are not correlated with their political systems. The next chapter will explore how and why Muslim countries lack complex economies.

---

[101] Stepan and Robertson 2003.   [102] Stepan and Robertson 2004.
[103] Freedom House 2013; World Bank 2010.   [104] Kuru 2014, 410–12.
[105] Boix and Stokes 2003, 535–7.

CONCLUSION

Authoritarianism in the Muslim world is a phenomenon with multiple causes. Although Western policies such as support for reliable authoritarian rulers have worsened conditions for democratization in Muslim countries, these foreign policies can be seen more as effects than as causes of Muslims' own ideological, political, and socioeconomic conditions. It would also be misleading to explain the complex problem of authoritarianism by simply referring to Islam's alleged rejection of secularism. Rather than making sweeping generalizations about Islam, it would be more effective to focus on the specific roles of Islamic actors – the ulema, Islamists, and Sufi shaykhs.

These Islamic actors have generally contributed to the problems of patriarchy and authoritarianism in many Muslim countries, though in some cases their contributions have been more progressive and democratic. Whether these Islamic actors ultimately strengthen authoritarianism or support democracy derives from their religious and political ideas. This chapter has provided a selection of some illiberal ideas, originally articulated by some eleventh-century ulema, on patriarchy, commanding right and forbidding wrong, and Muslim rule over non-Muslims. Certain Islamic actors still spread these illiberal ideas in mosques, party meetings, and Sufi lodges. It is not an "Orientalist generalization" to analyze the association between these ideas and the problem of authoritarianism in many Muslim countries.

Islamic actors' preaching and political activism have driven the recent trend of political and legal Islamization in many Muslim countries. From the 1920s to the 1970s, the dominant political and legal trend in the Muslim world was secular. In the last four decades, however, Islamization has gradually gained salience in the politics and legal systems of many countries. In several crucial cases, ulema–state alliances were created or revived. Nonetheless, the struggle between secularist and Islamic forces still continues. This chapter has documented the existence of secular constitutions in a large number of Muslim countries. These data indicate that the claim about the inherent incompatibility between Islam and the secular state has no empirical basis. Most of these secular states, however, are authoritarian. Thus, the problem of authoritarianism in the Muslim world cannot be explained by the absence of secular states. The fact that both secular and Islamic states are mostly authoritarian signals the deeper historical and socioeconomic roots of authoritarianism in the Muslim world.

In addition to their shared responsibility for authoritarianism, secularist and Islamic actors have also been similarly anti-intellectual. For Islamic actors, intellectuals are too critical of religion and too Western-minded; therefore, their ideas are potentially un-Islamic, if not anti-Islamic. Secularist politicians have generally regarded intellectuals as obstacles to their top-down and authoritarian modernization projects. The common anti-intellectualism of secularists and Islamic actors suggests that this problem too has deeper historical and socioeconomic causes.

A major economic problem in the Muslim world has been rentierism. Both secularist and Islamist regimes have been financially dependent on rents, particularly oil rents. Democratic polities are normally based on a mutual relationship between the rulers and the people: the latter pay taxes and thus hold the former accountable. In rentier states, however, the rulers are not financially dependent on the people's taxes; instead, the people are dependent on the rulers' allocation of rents. Muslim countries have about three-fifths of world's oil reserves; thus, there are many rentier and authoritarian states in the Muslim world.

The oil-based explanation helps us better understand not only authoritarianism but also violence in Muslim countries. Scholars have emphasized that oil-rich countries are more likely to have interstate and intrastate military conflicts, largely because potential rents are incentives for groups to fight to capture resources.[106] Especially in MENA, oil rents have led to authoritarianism, which in turn has increased the probability of violence.

Oil rents have also contributed to the dominance of ulema–state alliance and the marginalization of the bourgeoisie in many cases. The bourgeois class was already peripheral in Muslim countries when the mass oil revenues began in the early 1970s. Since then, Muslim-majority rentier states have controlled oil rents and made the emergence of an independent bourgeoisie almost impossible in their territories. The business elites in various Muslim rentier states have been too entangled with the government to become an independent bourgeoisie. Without an independent bourgeoisie that can check the power of the ruling class, democracy cannot work. In the words of Barrington Moore, "no bourgeois, no democracy."[107]

Through mechanisms of regional diffusion, the impact of oil rents has gone beyond state borders and affected even oil-poor countries, particularly in MENA. The regional diffusion approach suits my comparative framework too. Several chapters of this book explore Muslim and Western European cases as two region-like entities, both of which exhibit internal mechanisms of diffusion. Intellectual, economic, and political characteristics of some parts of the Muslim world (or Western Europe) have eventually diffused to other parts, creating a certain level of region-wide resemblance.

If Muslim countries had had more developed economies, oil revenues would not have dominated their economies and polities in such a profound manner. In this regard, economic underdevelopment has been a major cause of authoritarianism in many Muslim countries. Oil-rich countries have boosted their GNI, but this growth has not provided a basis for democratization. Democratization might be fostered by a complex economy, which has been absent in most Muslim countries. Chapter 3 will analyze this absence.

---

[106] Ross 2012, ch. 5; Humphreys 2005; Elbadawi et al. 2010.

[107] Moore 1966, 418. Stephens et al. (1992) instead point to the working class as the main pro-democratic social class. But Muslim rentier states do not have an organized working class either.

3

Socioeconomic Underdevelopment and Development

For multiple measures of socioeconomic development, forty-nine Muslim countries' average scores are lower than those of Western countries; they are even lower than the world averages. These criteria evaluate economic (GNI per capita),[1] educational (literacy and years of schooling),[2] and health-related (life expectancy and minimized infant mortality)[3] levels of development. Comparative analyses also show that Muslim countries[4] have not done well in scientific research.[5] What explains socioeconomic underdevelopment in Muslim countries?

This chapter critically evaluates explanations that identify Western colonization/exploitation or Islam as the key factor for underdevelopment. It then

---

[1] Around 2010, the average GNI per capita of Muslim countries (despite their substantial oil revenues) was $9,000, whereas that of the world was $14,000. World Bank 2010. (I excluded the outlier Qatar.)

[2] Muslim countries' average life expectancy is 66 years, while the world average is 69 years. United Nations Development Programme 2011. Regarding infant mortality (under 5 years old, per 1,000 live births), Muslim countries' average (49) is also worse than the world average (34). World Bank 2014a.

[3] Muslim countries' average literacy rate is 73 percent and years of schooling is 5.8. The world's average literacy rate is 84 percent and years of schooling is 7.5. United Nations Statistics Division 2013; United Nations Development Programme 2011.

[4] Members of the Organization of Islamic Cooperation (OIC) spend, on average, less than 1 percent of their GDP on research and development, which is about a third of the world average. "Islam and Science: The Road to Renewal," *Economist*, January 26, 2013. For OIC, see Kayaoğlu 2015.

[5] Out of 4 million biomedical articles indexed in 1994–2003, the contributions from twenty-three Arab countries constituted less than 1 percent. Falagas et al. 2006, 1585. An analysis based on Thomson Scientific reveals that in 2007 the combined number of scientific papers by seven of the most productive Muslim countries was less than that of India, less than half of that of China, and less than 10 percent of that of the United States. Hoodbhoy 2007, 52. See also Yalpani and Heydari 2005, 732.

explores the roles of the ulema's anti-progressive ideas and political authoritarianism in contributing to socioeconomic underdevelopment in Muslim countries. The chapter uses the term "vicious circle" to highlight the interactivity of these problems. Next, the chapter examines the impact of history and institutions. It stresses that exclusionary institutions in the Muslim world have been produced by authoritarian rulers, who hold political power, and the ulema, who provide the ideological legitimation. The chapter concludes with an explanation of why it is necessary to analyze the history of Muslim societies and polities in order to assess their contemporary problems, linking Part I of the book to Part II.

WESTERN COLONIZATION AND EXPLOITATION

Almost all Muslim countries experienced colonial subordination and exploitation between the mid-nineteenth and mid-twentieth centuries, if not longer. Western interventions in and exploitation of certain Muslim countries have largely continued even after the decolonization process. Charles Issawi provides a balanced perspective on this subject. He explains that British colonial rule in Egypt did not invest sufficiently in education because it aimed to minimize expenses and because it feared that education could produce a class of nationalists who would seek independence, as had already happened in India. Nonetheless, Issawi also criticizes Egypt's own educational system before and after British colonization. He sees pre-colonial schools, particularly madrasas, as ineffective and obsolete. He also notes that after decolonization Egypt did not take necessary steps to reform its education system.[6]

Dependency theory has explained Western countries' political hegemony over and economic exploitation of non-Western countries, particularly in Latin America.[7] From this perspective, in the capitalist world system, the core (mostly Western) countries have used other peripheral countries as sources of raw materials and markets for their manufactured exports.[8] Many sociopolitical movements in Muslim countries, from Islamists to secular leftists, have shared dependency theory's perspective in their anti-Western stance and blamed the West for the socioeconomic problems of the Muslim world.

Dependency theory has received two main criticisms, both of which are relevant for my analysis of Muslim countries. First, several scholars have criticized dependency theory for downplaying the role of the state. Scholars have explained how effective state policies in East Asian countries led to socioeconomic development, while ineffective state policies in several Latin American and African countries have created the opposite result. Similarly,

---

[6] Issawi 1968, 390, 398n41; Issawi 1983, 291.

[7] Galeano 1973; Amin 1976; Cardoso and Faletto 1979.

[8] Immanuel Wallerstein's (2004) world system theory has many similarities with dependency theory.

58 Present

without analyzing the roles of state actors, it is not possible to understand Muslim countries' socioeconomic problems.[9]

Second, certain scholars have also criticized dependency theory for exaggerating the role of foreigners while undermining that of local people. Lawrence Harrison has articulated the political implications of this perspective: "Dependency theory implies that Latin America is impotent, the course of its history determined by outside forces. Dependency theory both patronizes and paralyzes Latin America."[10] Likewise, singling out Western exploitation as *the* cause of socioeconomic underdevelopment in Muslim countries may be not only analytically wrong but also normatively counterproductive.

THE ROLES OF ISLAM AND THE ULEMA

Since Weber, several scholars have defined some characteristics of Islam or Muslim culture and then pointed to them as reasons for Muslims' socioeconomic underdevelopment.[11] In *Lost in the Sacred: Why the Muslim World Stood Still*, Dan Diner argues that Muslims have historically been skeptical of written culture: "It was part of the culture of early Islam that before dying, one destroyed everything one had written during one's lifetime."[12] Diner's anecdotal evidence does not reflect the general attitude of Muslims.[13] In Part II, I will explain that early Muslims had a written culture manifested in large libraries that dwarfed their Western European counterparts. Moreover, from that time to the present, if Muslims have taken their religious texts seriously, as Diner himself argues, then they must have known the reference to "the pen" in the chronologically earliest Quranic verses: "Read! Thy Lord is most noble. Who taught by the pen; taught man that which he knew not" (96:3–5) and the order about writing contracts as part of the longest Quranic verse (2:282): "Believers, when you contract a debt for a fixed period, put it in writing."[14]

Additionally, Diner points to the usage of classical Arabic (which is linked to the Quran) rather than local vernaculars as the standard written language as a major reason for Arab countries' socioeconomic stagnation.[15] His stress on the

---

[9] Bates 1981; Evans et al. 1985; Migdal 1988; Evans 1995; Migdal 2001; Kohli 2004.
[10] Harrison 1985, 162; also 151–61.
[11] Weber 1964 [1920], 262–6. Maxime Rodinson (2004 [1966]) criticizes the Weberian depiction of Islam as incompatible with capitalism and rationality. See also Turner 1974, 143; Turner 2013a, 12; Hall 1992, 17.
[12] Diner 2009, 75.
[13] Diner cites Cook's long article (1997) on the oral tradition. Cook's article, however, is limited to the debates on transmitting the hadiths. Moreover, it discusses not only the opponents but also proponents of the writing of the hadiths, though its title emphasizes only the former.
[14] For the verse 2:282, see also Chapter 6.
[15] Diner 2009, 20–22, 88–95, 125. For a more nuanced critique of the usage of classical Arabic as written language, see Nusseibeh 2016, 229–33.

pedagogical problems of memorization at the expense of creativity is a point well taken. Yet he overemphasizes some negative aspects of classical Arabic and ignores its potential positive impacts. Having a common written language might help economic and sociocultural exchanges among two dozen Arabic-speaking countries. Moreover, non-Arab Muslims do not have a similar linguistic dichotomy, but they still have similar socioeconomic problems. [16]

Neither Islam nor putative "Muslim culture" is monolithic; both religion and culture are complex phenomena open to multiple and divergent interpretations. Therefore, it is much more useful to analyze the role of particular actors, such as the ulema, while exploring the ideological background of Muslims' socioeconomic problems. The main problem of the ulema, regardless of whether they are Sunni or Shii, is their conservatism and opposition to the idea of progress. According to the ulema's worldview, religious knowledge represents all that is good in a perfect and permanent way; change means deviation and corruption. Salafi ulema have gone even beyond mainstream Sunni ulema in their hostility toward change and progress. Among thousands of hadiths, Salafis have taken one as their favorite and repeatedly invoked it: "Every innovation is misguidance and every misguidance is in the Hellfire."

Ebrahim Moosa stresses this problem: due to conservative religious teachings, Muslims always feel the need to justify their views on any subject with reference to the Quran, hadiths, or "some of the learned savants (imams) of the past." This "suggests that Muslims can act confidently in the present only if the matter in question was already prefigured in the past." In other words, "Muslims discredit the legitimacy of their experience in the present and refuse to allow this experience to be the grounds of innovation, change, and adaptation." [17]

Similarly, according to Fazlur Rahman, Muslims' skepticism toward the idea of progress has to do with the literalist and formalist religious interpretations. The solution he proposes is to concentrate on the Quran's higher objectives, rather than particular verses, and to prioritize the *sunna* (the Prophet's way of life), rather than particular hadiths. [18] In addition to the ulema, Fazlur Rahman also criticizes Sufi shaykhs and claims that these two groups share certain ideas that deny the individual free will. For Fazlur Rahman, the dominant school of theology, Ashari theology, is fatalistic, while the most influential Sufi thinker, Ibn Arabi, defended a monistic denial of reality except God. In his own words,

[16] For a discussion about the connection between the usage of classical Arabic as written language and authoritarianism in Arab countries, see Safaouan 2010, esp. 9–10, 44–56, 63–5; Lahlali 2010, 240–1.

[17] Moosa 2003, 122. See also Iqbal 2013 [1930], 112–13; Lakhdhar 2013, 21; Laroui 1974, 7–18, 55–8.

[18] Rahman 1965, 75, 141; Rahman 1982, 1–11, 141–62. See also Mazrui 2007; Charfi 2004.

Asharis "taught that only God can act and that the application of this term to other beings was metaphorical" due to their occasionalism, while Ibn Arabi and his disciples similarly "taught that only God exists in reality and the application of this term to others is metaphorical."[19]

The ulema's and Sufis' ideas would not hinder progress if there were alternative ideas challenging them. But there have been very few Muslim intellectuals who could pose such a challenge. In a broader sense, to solve their socioeconomic problems, Muslim countries need influential intellectuals and an independent bourgeoisie. Presently in most Muslim countries, there are few influential intellectuals, and businesspeople rely too much on political patronage to constitute an independent bourgeoisie. The ulema have contributed to the weakening of these two classes by imposing certain religious restrictions that discourage conservative Muslim youth from pursuing careers in intellectual and financial sectors. For the ulema, there are hardly any issues that do not eventually become jurisprudential questions. Hence, the ulema categorize issues related to professional careers as permissible or impermissible. The religious restrictions they have constructed against philosophy, certain arts,[20] and interest-related financial activities have discouraged conservative Muslim youth from studying philosophy, performing certain arts, and working in the financial sector (with the exception of Islamic finance). Additionally, religious restrictions on women's public visibility and interaction with men have also limited Muslim women's career advancement.[21]

To impose these prohibitions and restrictions, the ulema have always needed state support. This reliance has made the ulema willing to cooperate with and legitimize authoritarian rulers. In this regard, the main problem with the ulema's ideas is not simply their illiberal content but their role in maintaining authoritarian regimes. In a democratic setting with open public debates, the ulema's views could be challenged and transformed. In fact, both Islamist and secularist regimes in the Muslim world have been mostly authoritarian, as explained in Chapter 2. Regardless of whether it is justified by an Islamist or a secularist ideology, the authoritarian state has played an important role in the marginalization of intellectuals and the bourgeoisie and thus hindered socioeconomic progress in the Muslim world.

---

[19] Rahman 2000, 86. For a similar perspective, see al-Jabri 2011 [1984], esp. 432–3. For a sharply different perspective, see Chittick 1989, 205–11. See also Chapters 4 and 5.

[20] For the ongoing debates on the permissibility of music, see Abou El Fadl 2014, 42, 230.

[21] The tension between religious morality and professional careers is not unique to Islam and exists in many other religious contexts. In the United States, in the late nineteenth and early twentieth centuries, professionals with progressive ideals, including academic and literary intellectuals, journalists, teachers, lawyers, and businesspeople, regarded Protestant cultural domination and restrictions as an impediment to their career advancement. They engaged in politico-legal activism to effectively secularize American public institutions. Smith 2003, esp. 36–7, 48–53.

AUTHORITARIANISM AND THE VICIOUS CIRCLE

Chapter 2 explained how economic underdevelopment has been a cause of authoritarianism in many Muslim countries. Socioeconomic underdevelopment is a more complex phenomenon; it is measured by not only economic but also social criteria, including education and health. In some cases, socioeconomic underdevelopment is associated with authoritarianism, and these two phenomena constitute a vicious circle.

Corruption and mistrust are two important elements of the vicious circle as conceptualized by Robert Putnam in analyzing southern Italy's interconnected socioeconomic and governmental problems.[22] Most Muslim countries exhibit a high level of corruption and a low level of trust. Transparency International measures the perceived levels of public sector corruption worldwide using a scale of 0–100, where 0 is highly corrupt and 100 is very "clean." Muslim countries' average score (31) shows a higher level of corruption than the world average (42) in 2013.[23] Similarly, the World Values Survey evaluated interpersonal trust in forty-five non-Muslim societies and ten Muslim societies between 2004 and 2008. To the question of whether "most people can be trusted," the average rate of positive responses is 27 percent in all cases and only 20 percent in Muslim cases.[24] In general, a corrupt government and its authoritarian interferences in the economy corrode a country's economic productivity.[25]

Amartya Sen is a leading defender of the idea that freedom and development are mutually constitutive. For him the expansion of freedom is both the primary end and the principal means of development.[26] He explains this relationship with the example of democracy's contribution to the prevention of famines:

[N]o famine has ever taken place in the history of the world in a functioning democracy – be it economically rich (as in contemporary Europe or North America) or relatively poor (as in postindependence India, or Botswana, or Zimbabwe). Famines have tended to occur in colonial territories governed by rulers from elsewhere (as in British India or in an Ireland administered by alienated English rulers), or in one-party states

---

[22] Putnam 1993. See also Banfield 1958; Fukuyama 1995; Acemoglu and Robinson 2012, chs. 11 and 12.
[23] Transparency International 2013.   [24] World Values Survey 2004–8.
[25] Hall and Jones 1999, 86. There are other factors such as technological differences that affect levels of productivity. As an example of the productivity gap between a Western and a Muslim African case: "In 1988 output per worker in the United States was more than 35 times higher than output per worker in Niger." Hall and Jones 1999, 83.
[26] Sen 1999, xii. Mancur Olson (1993, 567) sees a similar relationship: "The conditions necessary for a lasting democracy are the same necessary for the security of property and contract rights that generates economic growth." Olson (1993, 572) adds: "Not surprisingly, then, capital often flees from countries with continuing or episodic dictatorships."

(as in the Ukraine in the 1930s, or China during 1958–1961, or Cambodia in the 1970s), or in military dictatorships (as in Ethiopia, or Somalia, or some of the Sahel countries in the near past).[27]

There has been a debate over whether the developmental successes of East Asian authoritarian states, including China, have discredited the emphasis on democracy in development.[28] Three points in these debates are directly relevant to the analysis of Muslim countries. First, as Chapters 1 and 2 explained, Muslim and East Asian countries currently have different types of authoritarianism. In the Muslim world, authoritarian states to various and changing degrees have been rentier, militaristic, and/or religious. In contrast, in East Asia, most authoritarian states have focused on export-oriented production, not rentierism; have concentrated on developmentalist policies and economically expansionist goals, rather than military policies and goals;[29] and have embraced secular, not religious, ideologies and discourses. Thus, the developmental success of the East Asian type of authoritarianism does not necessarily bear on criticisms of other forms of authoritarianism dominant in Muslim countries.

Second, authoritarian regimes in East Asia have had effective states based on relatively meritocratic bureaucracies while achieving development.[30] In most authoritarian states in the Muslim world, however, there has been a problem of governance. The World Bank Institute annually ranks all countries in terms of six indicators of governance quality, with percentile scores ranging from 0 (worst governance) to 100 (best governance). In 2014, all average rankings of Muslim countries were lower than 50 (the world average for each): government effectiveness (33), regulatory quality (34), rule of law (32), control of corruption (31), political stability and absence of violence (27), and voice and accountability (23). The scores of South Korea and Taiwan, which have been democracies since the early 1990s, are much higher. Even authoritarian China has better scores of governance – government effectiveness (66), regulatory quality (45), rule of law (43), control of corruption (47), and political stability and absence of violence (30) – except voice and accountability (5).[31] Muslim countries' low scores reflect negative conditions for socioeconomic development, because "there is a strong causal relationship from good governance to better development outcomes such as higher per capita incomes, lower infant mortality, and higher literacy."[32]

Third and finally, authoritarian states in East Asia grew their human capital by effectively investing in mass education, which became a basis of their

---

[27] Sen 1999, 16. Sen (1999, 170) explains that exploitative policies are primarily responsible for famines and that "the coexistence of hunger and food exports is a common phenomenon in many famines."

[28] Glaeser et al. 2004, esp. 298; Hung 2015, ch. 3; Acemoglu and Robinson 2012, 437–43.

[29] Solingen 2007.   [30] Evans 1995; Kohli 2004, part I; Fukuyama 2014, esp. 291.

[31] World Bank 2014b.   [32] Kauffman et al. 1999, 1.

economic growth.[33] Sen points to education to explain why China's economy grew faster than India's in the 1990s: "When China turned to marketization in 1979, it already had a highly literate people." India, in contrast, "had a half-literate adult population when it turned to marketization in 1991." India, according to Sen, has the problem of "social backwardness" due to "its elitist concentration on higher education and massive negligence of school education, and its substantial neglect of basic health care," which made it "poorly prepared for a widely shared economic expansion."[34] Analyses of other parts of the world also show that education and the cultivation of human capital lead to economic growth by improving labor productivity, expanding innovative capacity, and facilitating the diffusion of new technological knowledge.[35]

Muslim countries have performed worse than East Asian and Western countries in terms of improving their education systems and human capital. The Program for International Student Assessment (PISA) has assessed fifteen-year-old students' mathematics, reading, and science literacy in coordination with the Organization for Economic Cooperation and Development (OECD). In 2012, among sixty-five participant countries and economies, Shanghai–China, Singapore, Hong Kong–China, Taiwan, South Korea, Macao–China, and Japan were the top seven in mean scores in mathematics. The rankings of nine participating Muslim countries, however, were all toward the bottom of the list: Turkey, 44; the UAE, 48; Kazakhstan, 49; Malaysia, 52; Albania, 57; Tunisia, 60; Jordan, 61; Qatar, 63, and Indonesia, 64. In the other two categories, these nine Muslim countries' rankings were similarly very low.[36]

In short, developmentally successful authoritarian states in East Asia have had different characteristics (regarding rentierism, militarism, and religious ideology), better governing bureaucracies, and better educational policies than authoritarian states in the Muslim world. The vicious circle of underdevelopment and authoritarianism in Muslim countries is reflected in their low governance and educational scores.

A vicious or virtuous circle does not develop overnight; it is a result of a complex, long-term process. Change is possible, but continuity is likely. Understanding and solving Muslim' socioeconomic problems thus requires a historical analysis.

HISTORY AND INSTITUTIONS

East Asian countries' rapid socioeconomic development over the last fifty years is a global exception. For the last two centuries or so, North Atlantic and European countries have had higher levels of development than the rest of the

---

[33] Glaeser et al. 2004, esp. 298; Sen 1999, 143.   [34] Sen 1999, 42.
[35] Hanushek and Woessmann 2008; Goldin and Katz 2009.   [36] OECD 2012.

world – East Asia has only recently appeared as the challenger.[37] In fact, East Asian development also has historical roots.[38] The historical background of this regional change can be extended back to the Japanese modernization project in the second half of the nineteenth century, or even to China's older history of commercial and technological progress.

Several scholars have emphasized the importance of analyzing history to understand current levels of economic development. Joel Mokyr highlights this point while noting that the present-day level of national income is generally "determined by its past."[39] In his recent book, Thomas Piketty also states, "Once constituted, capital reproduces itself faster than output increases. The past devours the future."[40]

Scholars of the new institutionalist school have employed a historical perspective in their analysis of economic success and failure.[41] According to Douglass North, a leading scholar of this theoretical approach, "the present and the future are connected to the past by the continuity of a society's institutions. Today's and tomorrow's choices are shaped by the past."[42] Institutions, in the words of North, are a "set of rules." They are the "humanly devised constraints that structure political, economic and social interaction."[43] From the new institutionalist perspective, the protection of property rights plays a key role in socioeconomic progress – an argument that goes back at least as far as Adam Smith.[44]

A recent example of new institutionalist analysis is Daron Acemoglu and James Robinson's *Why Nations Fail*. Acemoglu and Robinson argue that inclusive economic institutions, such as laws protecting property rights and patents, provide incentives to invest and innovate, which ultimately lead to economic development. Extractive economic and political institutions, however, serve only the interests of a small group of elites and thus cause economic failure.[45]

My approach diverges from new institutionalism by directly analyzing the actors who create institutions. In the Muslim world, the exclusionary and ineffective institutions have been created by state authorities and the ulema, who did not allow the bourgeois and intellectual classes to be influential in crafting institutions. My analysis emphasizes that this class domination is based on certain religious and political ideas. By contrast, new institutionalism,

---

[37] In 1850, the estimated primary school enrollment rates for the total population were the following in some Western countries: United States (18%), Germany (16%), United Kingdom (10%), France (8%), and Spain (5%). More than a century later, in 1960, Egypt (10%), Turkey (10%), and Iran (7%) finally attained those rates. Easterlin 1981, 18–19.

[38] Kohli 2004, ch. 1.   [39] Mokyr 1990, 3.   [40] Piketty 2014, 571.   [41] See also Chapter 6.

[42] North 1990, vii.   [43] North 1991, 97. See also North 1990, 3–6.

[44] "Commerce and manufactures can seldom flourish long in any state which does not enjoy a regular administration of justice, in which the people do not feel themselves secure in the possession of their property." Smith 1993 [1776], 209.

[45] Acemoglu and Robinson 2012.

especially its rational choice version, underestimates the role of ideas.[46] Institutions, however, do not inherently have legitimacy; they need to be legitimized by ideologies. Exclusionary institutions in many Muslim countries have been legitimized by politically hierarchical and economically ineffective ideas (promoted by the ulema) and enforced by certain power relations (controlled by authoritarian state actors). Part II will explain the historical origin of these ideas and power relations.

CONCLUSION

Muslim countries currently exhibit low levels of economic, educational, academic, and health-related development, particularly in comparison to Western and East Asian countries. Explanations that single out Western colonization/exploitation or Islam are insufficient to explain Muslims' complex socioeconomic problems. Further deepening that complexity, authoritarianism and socioeconomic problems have constituted a vicious circle in many Muslim countries. It is true that an absence of inclusive institutions characterizes many Muslim countries. Nonetheless, institutional inefficiencies are more effects of authoritarian rulers legitimized by the ulema than causes of Muslims' long-term problems.

In certain periods of Islamic history, the ulema and rulers allied to marginalize intellectuals and the bourgeoisie. Hence, the current weakness of the intellectual and bourgeois classes – a weakness that has further complicated socioeconomic underdevelopment in the Muslim world – has deep historical roots. In this regard, Muslim countries' contemporary problems cannot be understood without analyzing the historical origins of the dominant ideas and power relations in these countries. Part II will explore the history of the ulema–state alliance, which began to emerge in the eleventh century and came to dominate Muslims' intellectual and economic life.

While there clearly exist educational and scientific problems in Muslim countries, one should be cautious about relying on misleading data and drawing faulty comparisons. The 2002 volume of *Arab Human Development Report*, for example, includes the following comparison: "The Arab world translates about 330 books annually, one-fifth of the number that Greece translates. The cumulative total of translated books since the Caliph Maa'moun's time (the ninth

---

[46] In an exemplary rational choice institutionalist analysis, David Waldner (1999, esp. 14, 88, 126) explains economic stagnation in Turkey and Syria as a product of elite division (which led to clientelist policies), and economic growth in South Korea and Taiwan as a product of elite cohesion (which resulted in developmental policies) in 1965–80. He underestimates the roles of (1) the secularist ideology of the Kemalist state elite in Turkey and the socialist ideology of the ruling Baath Party in Syria, (2) religious ideas and conflicts that are associated with elite division in both countries, and (3) the export-oriented regional model led by Japan and adopted by South Korea and Taiwan.

century) is about 100,000, almost the average that Spain translates in one year."[47] This comparison has been cited and quoted by scholarly publications,[48] as well as the *New York Times* and the *Economist*.[49] Leaving the absurdity of its contemporary data to other critics,[50] I want to focus on the historical dimension of this comparison. By equating the translations in the Arab world over a millennium to those in modern Spain in a single year, this comparison under-mines the historical achievement of Arab translators. It contributes to the false notion that Arabs' and Muslims' low levels of literacy and scholarship today represent their entire history, particularly in comparison to Western Europe.

Part II will examine early Muslims' scholarly achievements and analyze how translators and polymaths in various parts of the Muslim world, including Iraq, Egypt, and Spain itself, taught philosophy and natural sciences to Western Europeans for centuries. Part II will also explore how later Muslims experi-enced an intellectual and economic stagnation, which constituted the historical origin of their current vicious circle of authoritarianism and socioeconomic underdevelopment.

---

[47] United Nations Development Programme 2002, 78.
[48] Lewis 2004, 115–16; Hoodbhoy 2007, 53.
[49] Thomas L. Friedman, "Arabs at the Crossroads," *New York Times*, July 3, 2002; "Arab Development: Self-Doomed to Failure," *Economist*, July 4, 2002.
[50] Rogan 2004, 68–70.

PART II

HISTORY

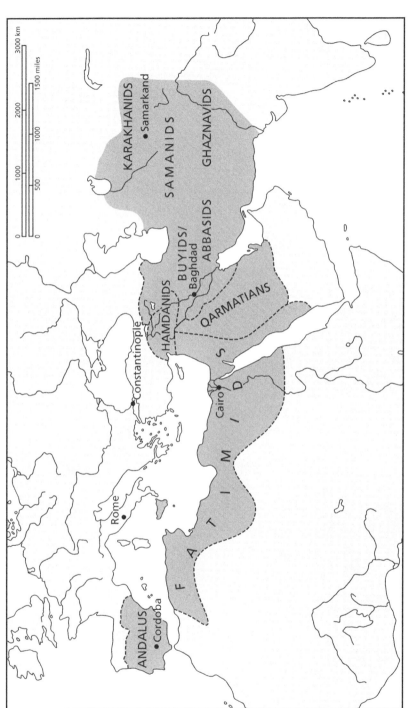

MAP 2 The Muslim World (c. 1000)

4

Progress

Scholars and Merchants (Seventh to Eleventh Centuries)

Part I had several references to the historical roots of current problems of authoritarianism and underdevelopment in the Muslim world. This and subsequent chapters in Part II will emphasize the ulema, the military state, and the alliance between them as the historical root cause of these problems. In early Islamic history, Muslims were scientifically and economically superior to Western Christians because they ascribed high status to scholars and merchants, whereas Europe was mostly under the hegemony of the clergy and the military elite. Later on, the positions eventually became reversed. In Muslim lands, the ulema and the military elite became dominant, while in Western Europe, scholars and merchants became increasingly important. In a nutshell, this reversal explains the rise of Western Europe and the decline of the Muslim world.

This chapter begins by examining Muslims' military, commercial, and intellectual achievements between the seventh and eleventh centuries. At that time, most of Islamic scholars (ulema) were funded by commerce, while only few of them served the state. The merchants flourished as an influential class. The chapter then addresses two opposing arguments about the role of Islam in Muslims' achievements. The first one is the claim that the intellectual dynamism in the lands under Muslim rule was a product of non-Muslims, so no credit can be given to Islam. This argument is associated with the modern assertion that Islam and science are incompatible. The second argument is the polar opposite of the previous one: it claims that Muslims had scholarly achievement in their early history precisely because they followed Islam. It is linked to the contemporary Islamist cliché that Muslim countries are undeveloped because they deviated from true Islam and that Islam is the solution for the future. The chapter explains the problems of both of these arguments. It also critically reviews some assertions that Western Europe was always more developed than Muslim lands.

The chapter goes on to analyze the beginning of the intellectual and economic stagnation in Muslim lands in the eleventh century. It explains how, gradually, the ulema became a state-servant class and the military state came to dominate the economy. The alliance between the ulema and the military state diminished the influence of philosophers and merchants. This changing distribution of authority led to the long-term stagnation, if not the decline, of Muslim intellectual and economic life. This gradual process began in the eleventh century and continued for centuries, as subsequent chapters will elaborate.

ISLAM IN ASIA, AFRICA, AND EUROPE

After the fall of the Western Roman Empire in 476, Western Europe experienced political disorder and economic problems for centuries. At the time when the Prophet Muhammad (570–632) was spreading the message of Islam in the Arabian Peninsula, there were two powerful empires in the neighborhood: the Byzantine and Sasanian.[1] During the era of the Four Caliphs (Abu Bakr, Umar, Uthman, and Ali) (632–61), Muslims conquered the latter and occupied all of the former's Middle Eastern territories (except Anatolia). During the Umayyad dynasty (661–750), Muslim lands were expanded to Transoxiana in the east and the Iberian Peninsula in the west. Given their central geographical location, Muslims took control of main trade routes between China, India, and Europe.

The Abbasid dynasty (750–1258) replaced the Umayyads everywhere except Andalus in Iberia, where the Umayyads ruled as an independent state (756–929) and then an independent caliphate (929–1031).[2] In other territories, the Abbasids gradually lost control, and various alternative sovereigns emerged. In 945, the Abbasid caliphs lost sovereignty even in Baghdad (to the Shii Buyids). Alternative authorities included the Sunni Samanids (from the ninth to the tenth century), who recognized the Abbasid Caliphate, and the Fatimids (from the tenth to the twelfth century), who established an alternative caliphate (see Map 2).[3]

This political decentralization did not hinder intellectual or economic progress. On the contrary, the existence of multiple political entities and the balance of power between them contributed to intellectual and economic flourishing. Baghdad in particular experienced an intellectually productive era under the coexistence of Shii Buyid rulers and Abbasid caliphs from the mid-tenth to the mid-eleventh century.[4]

---

[1] Long and exhausting wars between the Byzantine and Sasanian Empires weakened both and thus facilitated later Muslim conquests. Kennedy 2007, 367–8. Muslims generally regarded the Byzantines as friendlier than the Sasanians. This opinion is visible in Muslims' understanding of the Quranic verse 30:2–4 about the war between these two empires. Beate Dignas and Engelbert Winter (2007, 231) report that certain "Persian Christians fought alongside the conquerors" during the Muslim conquest of Persia because "they felt their religion had greater affinity to that of the Arab tribes."

[2] Lewis 2009, esp. 324.   [3] Mez 1937, 1–2.

[4] Mez 1937; Kraemer 1992; Hourani 1991, 38–58.

ISLAMIC SCHOLARS, THE STATE, AND RELIGIOUS DIVERSITY

A decisive event for Islam–state relations was the civil war between Ali, the fourth caliph and the son-in-law of the Prophet, and Muawiya, the governor of Damascus. It resulted in the death of thousands and was followed by a series of tragic events including the assassination of Ali. Muawiya established the Umayyad dynasty and consolidated the state as an institution.[5] He and subsequent Umayyad caliphs prioritized the *raison d'état*.[6] The Umayyads had the Prophet's grandson and Ali's son Hussein murdered and perpetrated a long-lasting harassment of the Prophet's descendants through his daughter Fatima and Ali.[7]

By persecuting the Prophet's family members, the Umayyads lost their legitimacy in the eyes of the Shiis. This persecution was problematic for Sunnis too. As a result, Umayyad rulers, with one exception,[8] lacked religious stature, even though they continued to use the title "caliph."[9] Umayyad and Abbasid caliphs generally claimed both political and religious authority; but their religious authority remained mostly symbolic. Sunni legal schools regarded only the Four Caliphs as combining political and religious authority, and thus they "denied the Caliphs after the *Rashidun* [Four Caliphs] authority in the elaboration of the law."[10] Another related result of the civil war and its aftermath was the emergence of various alternative interpretations of Islam. The contemporary depiction of Islam as a religion inherently inseparable from the state – promoted by Islamophobes and Islamist alike – fails to capture this historical complexity.

A certain level of Islam–state separation during the Umayyads and the Abbasids was reflected not only in the Shiis' resistance to the Sunni state authorities, but also in the politically dissenting attitudes of various Sunni

---

[5] Lapidus 2002, 47–9. "The first to use a throne in Islam was Mu'awiyah." Ibn Khaldun 2005 [1377], 216. "[T]he first real royal bodyguard was established by Mu'awiya at Damascus." Morony 1984, 93.

[6] According to Hichem Djaït (1989, 411), Muawiya promoted a sort of secularization in Muslims' conception of political power, because he showed that power belonged to those who knew how to capture and hold it. Fazlur Rahman (1968, xx) also notes that "the Umayyads ... were largely lay rulers who exercised political authority but lost a large measure of religious prestige."

[7] Al-Tabari 1996 [c. 915]; Morony 1984, 467–506; Hodgson 1974a, 212–23; Spellberg 1994, ch. 4.

[8] Umar ibn Abd al-Aziz (r. 717–20) is the exception that proves the rule. He is the only Umayyad caliph who has been respected by various Muslim groups because of his piety. Dawani 1839 [c. 1477], 407; Kınalızade 2012 [1565], 461–2. It is reported that a member of the Umayyad dynasty poisoned him to death. Afsaruddin 2008, 92; Anjum 2012, 67–70.

[9] Patricia Crone and Martin Hinds (1986) give too much credit to the Umayyad and subsequent caliphs' official propaganda of defining themselves as "God's caliphs" as if this self-image was accepted by other Muslims. For a critique of the Crone–Hinds thesis, see Anjum 2012, 42–8.

[10] Lapidus 1975, 369. With few exceptions, Umayyad and Abbasid caliphs are not "cited in legal hornbooks or in the *fatawa* literature." Abou El Fadl 2009, 94–5.

jurists, theologians, hadith folk, and Sufis.[11] Further complicating Islam–state relations, each of Shii and Sunni groups had multiple internal divisions. In his famous book, Shahristani (1076–1153) analyzed religions that existed in his time. His book categorizes and analyzes seventy-three sects within Islam.[12]

This diversity engendered an intellectual vibrancy in religious thought. As Wael Hallaq puts it, Islamic law was originally formed by "private, highly individualistic legal experts."[13] Many prominent religious figures of the eighth and ninth centuries, including the founders of four Sunni schools of law – Abu Hanifa, Malik, Shafii, and Ahmad ibn Hanbal[14] – as well as Shii imams, such as Jafar al-Sadiq, refused to serve the state.[15] They did not concede to the rulers' political demands despite being threatened and persecuted. Abu Hanifa died in prison, Malik was whipped, Shafii was detained and chained, Ibn Hanbal was beaten in prison, and Jafar al-Sadiq was poisoned to death (according to his followers), all for their dissenting views.[16]

Abu Hanifa's story represents the insistence of the early ulema on remaining independent from state authorities notwithstanding threats of punishment and even death. Abu Hanifa rejected the Abbasid Caliph Mansur's personal offer of judgeship with the excuse that he was not qualified for the post. "Mansur became angry and called him a liar." In response, Abu Hanifa said that "if that was so, he could not be fit for the post as a liar cannot be appointed as a judge." Mansur swore an oath that he would make him accept the post. Abu Hanifa similarly declared on oath that he would never accept it. As a result, Abu Hanifa was imprisoned and then poisoned to death.[17]

It is true that some Sunni ulema, such as the two prominent students of Abu Hanifa – Abu Yusuf and Shaybani – served the state as judges (qadis).[18] Yet they did not represent the mainstream approach to the ulema–state relationship in early Islamic history. Let alone serving the state, some ulema refused to make even gestures. The provincial ruler of Khurasan asked Bukhari – who would become the most famous hadith scholar – to teach his children in his palace. Bukhari refused and replied that the ruler "was welcome to send his children to

---

[11] Hodgson 1974a, 359–443.

[12] Shahrastani 1984 [c. 1127–8]; Shahrastani 1986 [c. 1127–8], 105–585. Ahmed Hilmi's (2011 [1911], 347–72) categorization of sects in Islam is a summary of Shahrastani's book but fails to give him credit.

[13] Hallaq 2009, 18. See also Schacht 1964, 4–5, 209.

[14] Although Ibn Hanbal was originally a hadith scholar, later he became regarded as a founder of a legal school. Hallaq 2009, 67; McAuliffe 2015, 205.

[15] As an exception, Shafii served as a judge in his youth. Fadel 2011, 117. State–religion relations have always and everywhere been a matter of degree. The existence of certain entanglements between some ulema and caliphs in the early Abbasid period (Zaman 1997, esp. 208) does not disprove that many other ulema put a distance between themselves and caliphs.

[16] Afsaruddin 2008, 96–105, 137–41. For Malik, see al-Nadim 1970 [987], 494; al-Ghazali 2015 [c. 1097], 72.

[17] Nadwi 2010, 39. See also al-Ghazali 2015 [c. 1097], 75–6.

[18] Fadel 2011, 117; Lambton 1981, 55–8.

his hadith circle." In reaction, the ruler forced Bukhari into exile in a village, where he died.[19]

The early ulema also attached importance to their financial independence from political authorities. Analyzing the ulema between the eighth and eleventh centuries, Munir-ud Din Ahmed writes, "An exceedingly large number of scholars are reported to have rejected all financial help from authorities. This was done by the scholars in the first place to keep themselves free of governmental pressure."[20] Many ulema, including certain Hanafi scholars, Ibn Hanbal, and Sufyan al-Thawri, declared that it was forbidden for Islamic scholars to take money from public authorities.[21] Moreover, the ulema of the time generally depicted those in the company of the rulers as unreliable "in matters of knowledge" and thus untrustworthy in their hadith reports.[22]

Hayyim Cohen analyzes biographies of about 3,900 Islamic scholars living between the eighth and mid-eleventh centuries, from Egypt eastward. He concludes that at that time the ulema were very different from the Christian clergy, in the sense that the ulema, except the judges and few other scholars, "functioned in an entirely private capacity, unappointed either by the authorities or by any religious institution ..., received no emoluments and had to support themselves, which they did in a variety of ways."[23] Most scholars or their families worked in commerce and industry – as merchants or artisans in the textile industry (22%); those processing or dealing with food (13%); miscellaneous merchants (11%); those who sold or made leather, metals, wood, or clay (9%); those who dealt with ornaments (e.g., jewelers) and/or perfumes (8%); bankers, money-changers,[24] and middlemen (5%); and booksellers, book copiers, and paper sellers (4.5%). Some worked as teachers (especially tutors) (8%), or investigators of witnesses (3%). Only a small portion (8.5%) worked as officials.[25]

Eliyahu Ashtor also emphasizes that in the early Abbasid era, "[m]any merchants became ... interested in the sciences of Islam," and that in some cases "their sons devoted themselves entirely to the scholarly life." Thus, "it can

[19] Abdul-Jabbar 2007, 19. See also Ahmed 1968, 135, 232.   [20] Ahmed 1968, 229.

[21] Mez 1937, 184. Sufyan al-Thawri had a "stringent refusal to serve in the judicial administration, and in fact to have anything at all to do with the caliphs – even to give them moral and religious advice." Zaman 1997, 79.

[22] Ahmed 1968, 228–9. "The first impression, which every reader of the biographies of Muslim scholars gains, is that the attitude of a very large number of scholars was everything but friendly towards those in power." Ahmed 1968, 224.

[23] Cohen 1970, 16. The biographies of these scholars and their families reveal 410 different occupations, only 56 of which (less than 15%) were "connected with official services." Cohen 1970, 17; also 45–61.

[24] According to Cohen (1970, 33), Muslims were engaged in professions about banking starting with the seventh century; there were Muslims who "took deposits, lent money for interest and paid money for cheques."

[25] Other occupations, such as physicians, lawyers, porters, mule drivers, and hair-dressers, constitute the remaining 8 percent. Cohen 1970, 36 (table A-I).

be seen from the study of the Arabic collections of biographies that most theologians of this period belonged to the bourgeois class, i.e. were merchants or sons of merchants."[26] Analyzing parts of Iraq and Iran under the Buyid rule from the mid-tenth to the mid-eleventh century, Roy Mottahedeh makes two observations about the ulema. First, the ulema wanted to distance themselves from the government. This aim was one reason why "families whose ancestors had exercised *riyasah* [leadership] in the bureaucracy or the army of the central government did not produce many leading men of religious learning." Second, at that time the ulema were a "vaguely defined body of men" who had "little internal structure" and held multiple identities and occupations.[27]

Another dimension of religious diversity during both the Umayyad and Abbasid eras was the coexistence of Muslims with other religious groups, especially Christians and Jews.[28] In *The Renaissance of Islam*, Adam Mez notes that during the tenth century, there were many Christian and Jewish bureaucrats in the Abbasid state.[29] He also stresses that at that time in Baghdad Muslims participated in Christian celebrations.[30] In the ninth century, some caliphs ordered the protected subjects (mostly Christians and Jews) to show their lower social status in certain dress codes and vehicles, such as riding on mules and donkeys instead of horses. In practice, however, these measures were not always effectively implemented. According to Mez, throughout the tenth century these rules remained "dormant. With the ascendancy of orthodoxy in the 11th century they were once again taken more seriously."[31] This diversity and relative toleration was not limited to Baghdad. According to Shelomo Goitein, the Geniza documents (which were found in a synagogue in Old Cairo and provide information primarily about Jewish merchants in Muslim lands) reveal that in Cairo, Damascus, and Jerusalem, "Jewish houses often bordered on those of Muslims or Christians or both. There was no ghetto, but, on the contrary, much opportunity for daily intercourse. Neither was there an occupational ghetto."[32]

In fact, a certain level of religious toleration was an important dimension of Muslims' rule in vast lands, where they did not constitute a majority for centuries. According to Richard Bulliet's estimates, at the end of the Umayyad period, less than 10 percent of the native populations converted to Islam in all territories except the Arabian Peninsula. A century later, around 850, the converts probably made up more than half of the native population only in Iran, whereas they still constituted less than a third of the native populations in

---

[26] Ashtor 1976, 111.   [27] Mottahedeh 1980, 135–7.

[28] The case of John of Damascus (675–753) shows how a Christian could become a world-renowned theologian under Muslim Umayyad rule. As a similar case, in Baghdad, under the Abbasids, Yahya ibn Adi (893–974) became a famous Christian theologian, philosopher, and translator. Fakhry 2004, 197–207.

[29] Mez 1937, 51.   [30] Mez 1937, 418.

[31] Mez 1937, 50; also 48–9. See also Wood 2015, 43–5.   [32] Goitein 1966b, 247.

Iraq, Syria,[33] Egypt, and Tunisia, and an even lower percentage in late-conquered Andalus. Around 950, the converts probably constituted three-fourths of the native population in Iran, and they constituted a majority of the native population in other regions, except Andalus.[34]

Diversity did not mean harmony or even lasting peace. For example, hadith folk, who stressed the literal interpretation of hadiths, occasionally came into physical conflict with other groups.[35] An infamous example of state intervention in religious diversity was the *mihna* (inquisition) incident, which took place between 833 and 848. Caliph Mamun initiated it among state servants and the ulema in order to confirm his authority in religious affairs and in response to religious opposition to his rule. Mamun's interrogations, which continued during two subsequent caliphs, imposed the rationalist Mutazili idea that the Quran was God's creation, rather than his eternal, uncreated speech.[36] Some leading scholars such as Ibn Hanbal refused to obey, despite threats of punishment and even execution.[37] Caliph Mutawakkil (r. 847–61) ended the *mihna* and allowed Hanbali hadith folk to persecute alternative groups – Mutazilis, Shiis, Christians, and Jews received their shares of this vengeful backlash.[38]

As these examples indicate, there were many limitations on religious diversity during the Abbasid era. Nonetheless, it was a period of dynamism and creativity, which provided crucial opportunities for the flowering of philosophy and the natural sciences.

THE PHILOSOPHERS

In the eighth century, Muslims imported paper production techniques from China and began producing paper, first in some Central Asian towns and then in Baghdad.[39] In the late ninth century, Baghdad was reported to have more than a hundred booksellers.[40] In the late tenth century, Nadim wrote a multivolume annotated bibliography, the *Index of the Sciences (Fihrist al-Ulum)*, on

---

[33] Historically, the term "Syria" was used to mean a greater area that included today's Syria, Lebanon, and Jordan, and, sometimes, even Israel and Palestine.

[34] Bulliet 1979, 43–7, 81–3, 97, 102–3, 108–11, 124. Bulliet (1979, 43–4) guesses that around 20 percent of native populations remained non-Muslim in the late eleventh century in most territories.

[35] Melchert 2006, 80.

[36] According to Mutazilis, to depict the Quran as timeless and not created was similar to how the Christians depicted Jesus. Corbin 1986, 160; Melchert 2006, 10.

[37] "[The] sources list a total of forty-eight persons who were subject to official interrogation." Lapidus 1975, 379. See also Nawas 2013, 18–22; Zaman 1997, 106–14.

[38] Hodgson 1974a, 486. Ironically, Mutawakkil was a heavy alcohol drinker. Masudi 1989 [947], 260.

[39] Bloom 2001, 45–9; Kennedy 2005, 36.   [40] Wellisch 1986, 6; Harris 1995, 79.

Arabic authors and books of his era.[41] His title represents the pre-modern use of the term "science," which encompassed Islamic scholarship and philosophy as well as the natural sciences.[42] According to Frederick Kilgour, the *Index* includes an estimated 9,620 titles: "This figure falls not far short of the 15,000 titles in Konrad Gesner's *Bibliotheca Universalis*, published five and half centuries later and a century after the invention of printing from cast type, which attempted to list all existing titles in Latin, Greek, and Hebrew."[43]

Although Islamic scholars valued independence from rulers, political patronage was crucial for philosophers. Some Umayyad caliphs patronized Arabic translations of ancient texts on various fields.[44] In the early Abbasid period, Jabir, the famous polymath of the eighth century, was supported by the rich and politically powerful Barmakid family.[45] Jabir produced foundational scholarship on chemistry and alchemy, though he wrote on numerous other fields as well. He was known as Geber in Europe, and several of his writings were translated into Latin.[46]

A major example of institutionalized patronage was the House of Wisdom, a library in Baghdad inaugurated by Caliph Harun al-Rashid (r. 786–809) and developed by the above-mentioned Mamun (r. 813–33).[47] The House of Wisdom was a key node in a larger translation movement spanning many cities across the Muslim world. Ancient Greek, Syriac, Middle Persian, and Sanskrit works on philosophy, psychology, mathematics, medicine, physics, geology, and other subjects were translated into Arabic.[48] Besides translations, original works also proliferated. For example, a world map commissioned by Mamun featured a spherical shape and represented "a continuous ocean surrounding the landmasses, showing Africa as a continent which can be circumnavigated

---

[41] Al-Nadim 1970 [987]. In the introduction to his translation of the *Index*, Bayard Dodge (1970, xv–xvii) explains why he uses the name "al-Nadim," rather than the commonly used alternative, "Ibn al-Nadim." Hans Wellisch (1986, 7) also prefers to call him "al-Nadim."

[42] In pre-modern times, the term "natural philosophy" was used instead of the "natural sciences." I prefer to use the latter to avoid any confusion with other branches of philosophy.

[43] Kilgour 1998, 58.   [44] Sezgin 2011a, 2–4.   [45] Starr 2013, 136, 162–3.

[46] Al-Nadim 1970 [987], 853–62; Kraus 1986 [1942].

[47] Nadim (1970 [987], 583) reported Mamun's narration of a dream. Mamun said: I saw a man and asked: "'Who are you?' He replied, 'I am Aristotle.' Then I was delighted with him and said, 'Oh sage, may I ask you a question?' He said, 'Ask it.' Then I asked, 'What is good?' He replied, 'What is good in the mind [reason].' I said again, 'Then what is next?' He replied, 'What is good in the law.' I said, 'Then what next?' He replied, 'What is good with the public.' I said, 'Then what more?' He answered, 'More? There is no more.'" This narration and Nadim's report of it seem to reflect that Muslim intellectuals integrated Aristotle into their worldview and probably expressed this inclusion to the general public in the form of a dream. See also Gutas 1998, 95–104.

[48] Gutas 1998, chs. 1 and 2; Swain 2013, 57–68; Fakhry 2004, 4–19; Pormann and Savage-Smith 2007, 24–37; Haque 2004; Ülken 2016 [1935], 43–83, 95–123. Ibn Khaldun (2005 [1377], 374) reports that Mansur and then Mamun received books of Greek philosophy by sending ambassadors to Byzantine emperors.

and the Indian Ocean – in contrast to its Ptolemaic representation as an inland sea – as an open sea."[49]

Baghdad was the center of learning, but there were many other important Muslim cities with large libraries and important scholars, such as Damascus and Aleppo in Syria; Basra in Iraq; Nishapur, Rayy, and Tus in northeastern Iran; and Balkh, Bukhara, Gurganj, and Merv in Central Asia.[50] The Fatimid dynasty, centered in Egypt, also developed significant libraries. In the late tenth century, Caliph Aziz had a library in Cairo with a collection of books estimated between 200,000 and more than one million.[51] In comparison, Western European monasteries and cathedral libraries between the ninth and eleventh centuries were generally reported to have fewer than 500 books.[52] Another Muslim center of learning was Andalus. In order to promote education, Caliph Hakam II (r. 961–76) funded several schools and libraries in his capital, Cordoba. Hakam's main library in Cordoba had around 400,000 volumes.[53] These estimated book numbers in Muslim libraries are probably exaggerations, but they still show that early Muslims deeply appreciated books and had better access to knowledge than Western Christians.[54]

Prominent philosophers and scientists emerged in this atmosphere of intellectual appreciation. In the ninth century, Khwarazmi studied mathematics, geography, and astronomy. The translation of his work into Latin played a major role in the introduction to Europe of "Arabic" numerals, which were in turn based on the Hindu system. Elements of this numeric system, including the number zero and decimal place values, make it more efficient than Roman numerals for large calculations. The terms "algorism" and "algorithm" stem from Khwarazmi's Latinized name, Algoritmi, and the term "algebra" comes from "*al-jabr*," a word in the title of one of his books.[55] Another scholar from ninth-century Baghdad was Kindi, a polymath known in particular as a pioneer of philosophy among Muslims.[56]

[49] Sezgin 2011c, 9; also 10–11.
[50] Starr 2013, esp. 192–3. In historical terminology, Nishapur, Rayy, Tus, Balkh, and Merv were in Khurasan, Gurganj was in Khwarazm, and Bukhara was in Transoxiana.
[51] Bloom 2001, 122. Also under Aziz, Al-Azhar mosque developed as an educational institution. Aziz's successor, Caliph Hakim, founded the Abode of Knowledge as a library and center of education, again in Cairo. Mackensen 1935a, 97–102.
[52] Mez 1937, 172; Bloom 2001, 116.
[53] Menocal 2002, 32–5; Mackensen 1935a, 108–9; Prince 2002, esp. 80.
[54] Albin 2007, 169–70; Hirschler 2016, 2, 33. Western Christians were still writing on "animal skins (parchment)" which required "a dozen sheep to produce the material for a book." In this regard, "the largest library in northern Europe at that time, at the monastery of St Gall in Switzerland, had some 800 volumes ... Europe did not have paper until its manufacture came to Italy from the Muslim world in the twelfth century." Goody 2010, 90.
[55] Joseph 2000, 311–28; al-Khalili 2011, 93–123.
[56] Al-Nadim 1970 [987], 615–26; Fakhry 2004, 67–95; Corbin 1986, 220–4; Adamson 2016, 26–32.

Again in Baghdad, Banu (sons of) Musa bin Shakir, or the Banu Musa brothers, were three innovative scholars. In 850, they wrote an illustrated text on mechanical devices – *Book of Ingenious Devices*.[57] It included about a hundred devices, three-fourths of which were the Banu Musa brothers' own designs.[58] Donald Hill describes most of their devices as "trick vessels of various kinds," with others including "fountains, lamps, a 'gas mask' for use in polluted wells and a clamshell grab." Hill highlights Ahmad among the brothers, whose "mastery of aerostatic and hydrostatic pressures and … use of automatic controls and switching systems places him well in advance of his Hellenistic predecessors."[59]

Abu Bakr al-Razi (c. 854–925), who worked both in his native Rayy and in Baghdad, was a prominent physician. His medical treatises included groundbreaking work on the distinction between smallpox and measles. Translations of Razi's medical treatises were taught in Western Europe as late as the sixteenth century.[60] His philosophical writings were reported to include severe criticisms of religions, indicating the intellectual openness of the time.[61] Aziz al-Azmeh defines Razi and some other philosophers as "Abbasid freethinkers" and sees "the cosmopolitan era of the Abbasids" as comparable to the European Radical Enlightenment.[62]

Another philosopher who was able to articulate unorthodox views was Farabi (c. 878–950). He lived in various cities, including Baghdad, Damascus, and Aleppo. Farabi wrote on politics, logic, psychology, and music. In philosophical circles he was called the "second teacher" (after Aristotle).[63] Seeking happiness is an important purpose of life in Farabi's philosophy. He writes, "Happiness is the good without qualification."[64] The political chapters of Farabi's *Virtuous City* were inspired by Plato's *Republic* and became an important reference for subsequent Muslim political philosophers.[65]

In the tenth century, Ikhwan al-Safa (the Brethren of Purity), a secret intellectual society based in Basra and Baghdad, produced an encyclopedia, *The Epistles of the Brethren of Purity*. It was a collection of fifty-two letters providing synoptic explanations on subjects such as mathematics, logic, and

[57] Banu Musa bin Shakir 1979 [850]. See also al-Nadim 1970 [987], 645–6.
[58] Al-Hassan and Hill 1986, 14.   [59] Hill 1994, 27.
[60] Pormann and Savage-Smith 2007, esp. 169; Dallal 1999, 201–3; al-Nadim 1970 [987], 701–9.
[61] Fakhry 2004, 97–109; Adamson 2016, 48–54; Starr 2013, 516; Adıvar 1969, 131–2.
[62] Al-Azmeh 2014, esp. 83–8. See also Israel 2006, 633–8.
[63] Al-Farabi 2005 [c. 930]; al-Nadim 1970 [987], 629. See also Mahdi 1987; Fakhry 2004, 111–32.
[64] Farabi lists alternative and misleading ends as "what is useful, what is pleasant, domination, what is honorable, and the like." For him, "when man … makes something other than happiness the end that he desires in his life, and uses all his faculties to attain that end, then everything that originates from him is evil." Al-Farabi 1963 [c. 941–49], 34–5.
[65] Al-Farabi 1985 [c. 940], chs. 15–9; Tusi 1964 [c. 1235], esp. 187. See also Rosenthal 1958, 122–42; Parens 1995.

metaphysics.[66] Around the same time, Miskawayh (c. 930–1030) was another polymath who lived in Baghdad and other cities. He was distinguished as a historian and philosopher. His book on ethics (*The Refinement of Character*), which drew primarily on Aristotle's *Nicomachean Ethics*, among other sources, inspired subsequent Muslim works on ethics.[67]

Later, Ibn al-Haytham (Alhazen) (965–1040) emerged as an eminent mathematician and astronomer. Working primarily in Cairo, Ibn al-Haytham made particularly noteworthy contributions to the field of optics. He pioneered the use of the experimental method of controlled testing. He built the first version of a *camera obscura*, which was an important early step toward the development of photography. According to David Lindberg, "Alhazen was undoubtedly the most significant figure in the history of optics between antiquity and the seventeenth century."[68]

Last but certainly not least, two Central Asian contemporaries, Biruni (973–1048) and Ibn Sina (980–1037), became intellectual giants in the Muslim world. Biruni studied a broad range of subjects, such as astronomy, mathematical geography, history, and religion.[69] His anthropological book on India was translated into English with the subtitle, *An Account of the Religion, Philosophy, Literature, Geography, Chronology, Astronomy, Customs, Laws and Astrology of India.*[70] A twentieth-century book published by the Indian National Science Academy notes, "It is needless to emphasize the importance of al-Biruni's works as a source of inestimable value for the study of the history of science in India."[71] Biruni and Ibn Sina had a famous correspondence in which the former questioned Aristotelian physics, particularly concerning astronomy, while the latter defended it. Biruni, who was more empiricist, argued "against Aristotle, the possibility of other worlds, either ones that have different natures or ones that have the same nature as our world," while Ibn Sina, who preserved the consistency of Aristotelian philosophy, claimed that "multiple worlds are impossible."[72]

Among the scholars I have covered so far, Ibn Sina had the most enduring impact on Muslim philosophy.[73] According to Dimitri Gutas, Ibn Sina's philosophical work was continually challenged and countered given "the penetration of his philosophy in all Islamic intellectual life."[74] Translations of

[66] El-Bizri 2008; Fakhry 2004, 167–85.
[67] Miskawayh 1968 [c. 1030]. See also Leaman 1996; Kraemer 1992, 222–33; Goodman 2003, 101–12, 199–201.
[68] Lindberg 1976, 58. See also Belting 2011, ch. 3.   [69] Lawrence 2014, esp. 63–8.
[70] Al-Biruni 1964 [1030]. His translator, Ainslie Embree (1971, v) claims, "Not for over eight hundred years would any other writer examine India with such thoroughness and understanding."
[71] Sen 1971a, 49.
[72] Dallal 2010, 74; also 75–80. See also Lawrence 2014, 63–4; Starr 2013, 1–4.
[73] Ibn Sina 1974 [c. 1037]; Ibn Sina 2005 [c. 1020]; McAuliffe 2015, 265–76; Rosenthal 1958, 143–57; Corbin 1986, 238–47.
[74] Gutas 2014, XIV: 89.

Ibn Sina's philosophical as well as medical works were also influential in Europe from the twelfth to sixteenth century.[75] Versions of the translation of his *Canon of Medicine* were printed in Europe "at least sixty times between 1500 and 1674."[76]

Philosophical and scientific achievements summarized in this section were not isolated from other aspects of early Muslim societies. Instead, they were directly associated with Muslims' commercial and agricultural developments. The next two sections will explore these developments.

THE MERCHANTS

Ruling over major cities in Iberia, North Africa, the Middle East, northern India, and Central Asia, Muslims were able to control trade routes between Europe, India, and China.[77] Moreover, they had a common language (Arabic), a shared set of laws, and a religious motivation to travel (the pilgrimage to Mecca). All of these factors contributed to Muslims' intercontinental trade. According to Maya Shatzmiller, between the seventh and eleventh centuries, Muslim economic achievement included an expanding division of labor, increasing money circulation, the formation of credit institutions, and the creation of legal institutions to uphold property rights.[78]

Merchants as a class gained a crucial position in early Muslims' socioeconomic structure.[79] They enjoyed religious legitimacy, given that the Prophet Muhammad and many of his close companions themselves were merchants. Cohen's previously mentioned analysis of the ulema shows that, from the eighth to the mid-eleventh century, 72.5 percent of Islamic scholars or their families worked in commerce and/or industry.[80] Bulliet supports Cohen's findings with additional data from four Iranian cities, especially Nishapur, indicating the ulema's strong connection to booming (cotton) trade in the ninth and tenth centuries.[81] An important example of the early ulema's relations with commerce was Abu Hanifa, who was a silk merchant.[82] In the same vein, his prominent student Shaybani, a founding figure in Hanafi jurisprudence,

[75] Marenbon 1996, 1001–6; Irwin 2006, 29–30; Ülken 2016 [1935], 183–6, 203–4.
[76] Pormann and Savage-Smith 2007, 169.
[77] Findlay and O'Rourke 2007, 43–61. Muslims had strong commercial interactions between their own cities as well. Cities in various regions exported the following items in the ninth century: Azerbaijan (wood, minerals, and petroleum), Iran (cotton products, perfumes, and non-perishable food), and Central Asia (skins, silk products, carpets, and soap). Shatzmiller 2000, 470.
[78] Shatzmiller 2011, 176.
[79] According to Ann Lambton (1962, 121), in Iran and parts of Central Asia, Islam replaced "Zoroastrian religion [which] held the merchant in contempt." Moreover, "the anti-ascetic attitude of Islam contributed to the growth of the merchant community and helped to raise the status of the merchant."
[80] Cohen 1970, 36 (table A-I).   [81] Bulliet 2009, 1–5, 43–4, 131.
[82] Cohen 1970, 26. Ibn Hanbal also worked in private textile industry as "at least at one time a weaver of cords for under trousers." Cohen 1970, 28.

emphasized that "the profession of the honest merchant, or indeed any trade, pleases God more than Government service."[83] At that period, merchants were both funders of and participants in religious learning: "[I]t was predominantly merchants who were engaged in the development of the religious sciences of Islam."[84]

The famous ninth-century litterateur Jahiz compared merchants with state servants in his letter entitled "A Praise of Merchants and Condemnation of Officials." For him, even senior officials admitted that merchants "are always the most scrupulous, the happiest and the most secure of men," whereas it is "quite otherwise with men close to the government and in its service. Officials wear the mantle of servility and the badge of flattery, and their hearts are filled [with awe] of their superiors; fear dwells in them, servility never leaves them, and dread of poverty is their constant companion." Jahiz also reminds the reader that "the Prophet is known to have been a trader; and the very name [of his tribe] Quraish is derived from trade (*taqrish*)."[85]

In addition to Islamic scholarship, merchants were supporters of philosophy and the arts. As Bryan Turner points out, merchants accumulated wealth with "the expansion of trade under *pax Islamica* from the eighth to the eleventh century" and patronized scholarship. There was a particular connection between Muslim merchants' economic mentality and their support of mathematics: "Because merchants had special needs relating to book-keeping, accounting and price determination, they were also associated with the patronage of arithmetic."[86] Patronage by rulers and patronage by merchants were not mutually exclusive. Ibn Sina, who served several state authorities in his professional life, notes the following about his childhood education in his autobiography: "[My father] sent me to a vegetable seller who used Indian calculation [and algebra] and so I studied with him."[87] Additionally, Muslim merchants' patronage of artists, in the words of Oleg Grabar, was unprecedented: "[E]arly Islam is the first medieval illustration of the phenomenon of an art of the bourgeoisie in contrast to the art of the church or of an aristocracy."[88]

Kitab al-Ishara ila Mahasin al-Tijara (*Book of Advice on the Merits of Commerce*) was written around the eleventh century by an educated merchant of Damascus, Dimashqi. It is related to our analysis in three respects. First, Dimashqi uses a very limited number of religious references. Instead, he praises commerce on the basis of its own significance for human life: "If we compare trade with all other sources of income, we would find it as the best in terms of

---

[83] Paraphrased by Goitein 1966a, 223. See also Essid 1995, 225–8; Cahen 1962, 170–1.
[84] Goitein 1966a, 219. See also Zubaida 1972, 322.   [85] Jahiz 1969 [c. 862], 272.
[86] Turner 2013b, 64. "Like their Puritan counterparts, the [Muslim] merchants created a calling in the world which held business motives in the highest regard." Turner 1974, 143.
[87] Ibn Sina 1974 [c. 1037], 21.   [88] Grabar 1987, 176.

bringing happiness to the people in the world."[89] Second, chapters of Dimashqi's book on division of labor, monetary exchange, and the preservation and
expenditure of wealth are based on the treatise by the first-century Greco-
Roman author Bryson.[90] This can be seen as another example of the connection
between philosophy and Muslim merchants.

Finally, Dimashqi reveals contemporary Muslim merchants' consciousness
to pursue their commercial interests above politics. Among his recommendations to merchants, Dimashqi emphasizes that they "should consider the
characteristics of the ruling authority, which are the strength or weakness of
its state [structure], its justice or injustice, and its richness or poverty." A just
ruling authority with weak enemies and abundant tax revenues and properties
are the perfect conditions for trade. If the ruling authority is just but weak
vis-à-vis its enemies, then merchants should avoid big and risky purchases. If
the ruling authority is unjust but strong, then merchants should stop doing
business; they should behave like poor people who cannot buy anything. Last,
if the ruling authority "combines injustice, poverty, and weakness," then
merchants should "leave the country."[91]

Merchants in early Islamic history were not as politically powerful as
the Dutch or British bourgeoisie in the seventeenth century. Nonetheless, there
were "very powerful merchants, people of influence involved in court intrigue
and forming a link between the palace milieu and the wealthy city circles."
These merchants, "together with the scribes of the civil service and the court,"
were "the main agents of economic activity in the Muslim World, the mainstay
and the vehicle of its most brilliant civilization, from the eighth to eleventh
centuries."[92] In the mid-tenth century, under Abbasid rule, great merchants
"constituted an international credit community that the government could
abuse only at considerable risk."[93]

Early Muslim rulers did not allow foreigners or even non-Muslim subjects
to dominate trade. They favored Muslim merchants with special tax rates.
According to Goitein, the Geniza documents of Old Cairo "clearly indicate
that the great merchants of the eleventh and twelfth centuries were mostly
Muslims." Goitein also refers to a tenth-century writer who argued that
"[m]erchants are more powerful than viziers" because "a bill of exchange
was accepted with greater readiness than an allocation of income from
taxes."[94] Goitein even characterizes the situation as a "bourgeois revolution."

---

[89] Al-Dimashqi 1995a [c. 11th century], 38. French translation: al-Dimashqi 1995b [c. 11th
century], 55.
[90] Al-Dimashqi 1995a [c. 11th century], 7–9, 46–8, 56; al-Dimashqi 1995b [c. 11th century], 21–3,
64–6, 74; Bryson 2013 [c. 1st century], 5–11. See also Swain 2013, 103–4, 252–4; Cahen 1962,
160–70.
[91] Al-Dimashqi 1995a [c. 11th century], 41; al-Dimashqi 1995b [c. 11th century], 58–9. For an
English summary, see Essid 1995, 223.
[92] Lombard 1975, 150.   [93] Mottahedeh 1980, 118.   [94] Goitein 1966a, 238–9; also 232.

He writes, "The 'bourgeois revolution' of the Middle East during the early centuries of Islam had many repercussions on world history. To mention just one: through it the Jews, who up to that time had been engaged mainly in agriculture and other manual occupations, were converted into a predominantly commercial people."[95] Maristella Botticini and Zvi Eckstein explain in greater detail that the "full-fledged transition of the Jews from farming to crafts and trade took place" roughly between 750 and 900, under Umayyad, Abbasid, and Fatimid rule, where "Jews were legally permitted to own land ... and to engage in any occupation they wished."[96]

In addition to the development of trade, Muslims' central geographical location linked to Africa, India, and China also helped them achieve agricultural innovation and growth. According to Andrew Watson, between 700 and 1100, Muslims developed numerous farming techniques and cultivated a variety of crops – Old World cotton, Asiatic rice, sorghum, and sugar cane, as well as artichoke, colocasia, eggplant, spinach, watermelon, banana, coconut palm, mango, lemon, lime, sour orange, and shaddock. Muslims adopted most of these crops from India and China, and some from sub-Saharan Africa. Gradually, many of these crops spread from Muslim lands to Europe too.[97]

Watson stresses three factors besides the adoption of diverse techniques and cultivars that contributed to Muslims' agricultural achievement. The first factor was the laws and policies of land ownership. By maintaining "full individual ownership over several categories of land," these laws and policies provided individuals with incentives to innovate agricultural techniques. Although there were "state lands" administered by the ruler and "conquered lands" owned by the Muslim community, in practice both of these categories "appeared quickly to have reverted to what was in effect private ownership." In other words, "virtually all cultivated land was owned by an individual who had the right to sell, mortgage or will it, and could farm it or have it farmed."[98]

Second, Watson argues that tax policy encouraged effective and innovative agricultural production: "Light rates of taxation were one factor helping to keep alive a class of smaller, independent landowners and a relatively prosperous peasantry." For him, "in the early centuries of Islam increased profits could not easily be scooped off by capricious tax collectors or a greedy State."[99] Third, Watson points to population growth as a contributing factor for agricultural development in early Muslim societies.[100]

Between 700 and 1100, the virtuous circle of agricultural productivity, demographic growth, and commercial expansion contributed to the development of Muslim urban life. Muslims generally lived in lands with limited rainfall, so they built dams, canals, and kanats (underground channels) to sustain complex irrigation systems for agriculture and drinking water systems

---

[95] Goitein 1966a, 241.   [96] Botticini and Eckstein 2012, 55–6.   [97] Watson 1983.
[98] Watson 1983, 112–13.   [99] Watson 1983, 115.   [100] Watson 1983, 129, 132.

for cities.[101] Muslims had large cities that required communication systems. Thus they developed a "commercial post" used by the general population, in addition to "the governmental courier and intelligence service" (*barid*).[102] Early Muslims' urban development and intellectual productivity complemented each other. There has been a modern debate about the role of Islam in these achievements, to be analyzed in the next section.

NEITHER IMITATION, NOR ORTHODOXY

In his well-known 1883 lecture, Ernest Renan argued that the scholars behind the intellectual flourishing of early Islamic history were in fact "Zoroastrians, Christians, Jews, those from Harran, Ismailis, Muslims with internal revolts against their own religion."[103] Since then, several others have repeated similar claims. Recently, for example, Adonis argued that the "Mutazilas were not part of the recognized Muslim 'body' – neither the mystics, nor the philosophers, nor the poets."[104] According to this view, Islam is incompatible with intellectual progress. Philosophical works in early Islamic history were either imitations of Greek civilization[105] or achievements of freethinkers. In contrast, modern Islamists have presented development in early Islamic history as the direct products of Islam. Later, according to Islamists, Muslims deviated from "true Islam" and as a result experienced multiple crises. Islamists have, at least implicitly, presented early Muslim scientists as "orthodox Muslims." I will elaborate on the weaknesses of these two arguments, starting with the first one.

Renan's and his followers' assertions ignore several Sunni and Shii (other than Ismaili) Muslim scholars in the intellectually productive era. In fact, it is not easy to determine whether a medieval philosopher was a Sunni or a Shii, or an observant Muslim or not. Gutas argues that defining Ibn Sina as an Ismaili is a "misunderstanding" and characterizes him as a Hanafi instead.[106] Moreover, Gutas notes that biographical information about Ibn Sina (Avicenna) in particular and philosophers in general was manipulated by their rivals in order to

---

[101] For Iran, Iraq, Egypt, and Tunisia: al-Hassan and Hill 1986, 80–7. For Central Asia and Iran: Starr 2013, 37–40, 175, 198. For Iran: Hodgson 1974a, 295–6. For Andalus: Butzer et al. 1985.

[102] Goitein 1964, 118. See also Mez 1937, 78.

[103] Renan 1883, 16. The translation of Afghani's rebuttal – "Réponse à Renan," *Journal des Débats*, May 18, 1883 – is in Keddie 1968, 181–7. For Turkish critics of Renan, see Kemal 1962 [1910]; Meriç 1996, 66–77.

[104] Adonis 2015, 25.

[105] Renan (1882 [1852], vii–viii) wrote in his dissertation: "We cannot ask lessons of philosophy from the Semitic race ... Philosophy among the Semites has always been purely ... an imitation of Greek philosophy."

[106] Gutas 2014, I: 5; Gutas 2014, II: 323–34.

depict them as irreligious and immoral:[107] "More seriously is the tendency, apparently initiated by al-Ghazali[108] ... to counter Avicenna's influence by *ad hominem* attacks (Avicenna's drinking and sexual activities) that were sophistically elevated to the general level of impugning the allegedly irreligious behavior of all philosophers."[109]

Presenting Muslim intellectuals as merely transmitters of the accomplishments of Greek and other civilizations is also misleading. Muslims' translations from Greek, Syriac, Middle Persian, and Sanskrit were "not just a matter of transmission of texts but a process of the appropriation and transformation of scientific knowledge in an intercultural context."[110] Muslims reconstructed earlier scholarly traditions and made original contributions to them.[111] They offered criticism on the works of their Greek predecessors (such as Galen and Ptolemy) while carrying on their legacy in various fields.[112] Even if one focuses on the influence of earlier traditions and non-Muslim scholars in achievements of early Islamic history, such a perspective would have to admit the remarkable success of early Islamic civilization in bringing together various traditions in an inclusive manner, similar to other multicultural cases such as the Hellenistic period and the recent history of the United States.

A multiculturalist position is very different from that of Renan, who had a particular distaste for Arabs. Renan said that, except for Kindi, scholars of early Islamic history were "Persians, the Transoxians, the Spaniards ... Not only they were not Arab by blood, but also they had no Arab spirit."[113] This assertion echoes Ibn Khaldun, who himself was a Sunni Arab: "It is a remarkable fact that, with few exceptions, most Muslim scholars both in the religious and in the intellectual sciences have been non-Arabs. When a scholar is of Arab origin, he is non-Arab in language and upbringing and has non-Arab teachers."[114] Ibn Khaldun offers two explanations for this observation: (1) Arabs were originally mostly nomadic people from the desert, and thus traditionally sedentary Persians dominated scholarship, and (2) many sedentary Arabs in the Abbasid Empire took up government positions and "considered it

---

[107] In reality, Farabi "lived in the greatest possible simplicity and worn Sufi dress. He was characteristically contemplative, and stayed away from social life." Corbin 1986, 226.

[108] An example of Ghazali's attacks: "Ibn Sina actually writes in his *Testament* that he swore to God ... that he would praise what the sacred Law prescribed, that he would not be lax in taking part in the public worship of God, and that he would not drink for pleasure but only as a tonic or medicine. Thus the net result of his purity of faith and observance of the obligations of worship was that he made an exception of drinking wine for medical purposes! Such is the faith of those philosophers who profess religious faith." Al-Ghazali 1953 [c. 1108], 73. See also al-Ghazali 1999 [c. 1108], 90.

[109] Gutas 2014, XV: 25. See also Adamson 2016, 115.   [110] Abattouy et al. 2001, 2.

[111] Sabra 1987, 224–8, 242; Collins 2000, 833.   [112] Dallal 2010, 31–43.

[113] Renan 1883, 15. Renan (1882 [1852], 90–1) saw Indo-European Persians as superior to Semitic Arabs. He appreciated Afghani for being an Aryan Persian. Keddie 1968, 85, 92.

[114] Ibn Khaldun 2005 [1377], 428.

a lowly thing to be a scholar, because scholarship is a craft, and political leaders are always contemptuous of the crafts and professions."[115] These arguments do not explain the situation in Egypt and Andalus, where many astronomers, physicians, and philosophers such as Ibn Yunus, Ibn al-Haytham, and Ibn al-Nafis (in Egypt) and Ibn Zuhr, Ibn Tufayl, and Ibn Rushd (in Andalus) could be defined as Arab.

While defining Muslim achievements as imitations or exclusive products of freethinkers is misleading, the opposite argument – which claims the centrality of "Islamic orthodoxy" or "religiosity" in these achievements – is also problematic.[116] Contemporary Islamists generally explain Muslims' failures by pointing to their alleged deviation from (orthodox) Islam, while defining their early historical achievements as a result of their religiosity.[117] On the contrary, early Muslim achievements were products of a very diverse people with different religious affiliations. Scholars, merchants, and even bureaucrats of the Abbasid Empire and other Muslim countries included Sunnis, Shiis, heterodox Muslims, and freethinkers, as well as Christians, Jews, and followers of some other religions.[118] In fact, most eminent philosophers of early Islamic history would have experienced accusations of being apostates and been persecuted if they had lived in countries ruled or dominated by contemporary Islamists.

A balanced approach between Renan-type arguments and Islamist clichés is to acknowledge both Muslims' original works and their debts to non-Muslim predecessors and contemporaries. The Dome of the Rock in Jerusalem and Umayyad Mosque in Damascus are architectural examples of such a synthesis. They are Muslim monuments that reflect the legacy of Byzantine, Sasanian, and pagan traditions.[119] According to Michael Morony, pluralist explanations of Islamic civilization "probably go back to Mas'udi (d. 965)," who saw it as "the

---

[115] Ibn Khaldun 2005 [1377], 430; also 428–9.
[116] Said Nursi (1996 [1929–34], 558) defends this argument: "History witnesses that whenever followers of Islam strongly held their religion, they progressed; whenever their religiosity weakened, they became backward. It was the opposite with Christianity." For a critique, see Bacık and Kuru 2017.
[117] Qutb (2002 [1964], 111) argues that Europe learned scientific methods from "Islamic universities of Andalusia and of the East," while "the Muslim world gradually drifted away from Islam, as a consequence of which the scientific movement first became inert and later ended completely."
[118] Starr 2013, esp. 91–9, 120–4; Menocal 2002, 3–90; Corbin 1986, ch. 4. Hodgson (1974a, 58–9) uses the term "Islamicate" to define sociocultural entities that are not necessarily Islamic but belong to lands dominated by Muslims. Nonetheless, as Clifford Geertz (1975, 18) predicted, this term has not been widely used.
[119] Grabar 1987, 9–10, 167–8, 209–10; Briggs 2005 [1931], 161. In general, "medieval Islamic civilization ... incorporated, without destroying, many different cultures which continued to maintain their religious and social practices together with their art and material culture." Ettinghausen et al. 2001, 291; also 7–26, 43–9.

heir to the cultural contributions of Persians, Chaldaeans, Greeks, Egyptians, Turks, Indians, Chinese, and Arabs."[120]

ISLAMIC CIVILIZING PROCESS

Muslims borrowed certain ideas and institutions but had their own original dynamics as well. The organization of the lunar calendar is important for demarcating months, including Ramadan (the month of fasting). Khwarazmi "in the early ninth century compiled a table showing the minimum distances between the sun and moon (measured on the ecliptic) to ensure crescent visibility throughout the year."[121] Daily prayer requires knowledge of the direction to Mecca as well as precise timing (five times a day) and thus incentivized Muslims to learn about geography, cartography, astronomy, and mathematics. In the eleventh century, Biruni wrote a treatise to determine the *qibla* (direction to Mecca) in Afghanistan, which became, according to David King, the "most important Muslim contribution to mathematical geography."[122] Muslims used astrolabes, quadrants, and sundials for these calculations. By the thirteenth century, major mosques began to hire *muwaqqit*s (time keepers).[123]

These time-sensitive requirements may have provided discipline to early Muslims at a time when there were no clocks or other modern tools of time management. Similarly, Islamic rules on washing, including toilet hygiene, brushing the teeth (with miswak tree roots), daily ablutions before prayer, and bathing after sexual intercourse, may have maintained both discipline and hygiene under pre-modern conditions. At that time, Western Europeans generally paid less attention to manners and hygiene. According to Paulina Lewicka, major etiquette books on eating were generally written between the tenth and fifteenth centuries in Muslim lands, whereas they were written in a later period – between the thirteenth and eighteenth centuries – in Western Europe.[124]

In the eleventh century, Ghazali wrote an influential manners book. His guidelines include the following: check whether the food is lawful and lawfully acquired; wash your hands; place the food on a cover on the floor (following the Prophet, but you can also eat on a table); sit properly; be content with what is available; avoid eating alone and do not be silent over the food; keep each mouthful small and chew well; eat what is closest to you from the common dish; do not blow on hot food; if you take something out of your mouth, move

---

[120] Morony 1984, 6. Early Islamic civilization "was above all a synthesis. Its art also bore witness to the most varied origins: Persian, Mesopotamian, Byzantine, and even Visigothic. Islam's great achievement was to fuse all these elements into one single civilization." Lombard 1975, 97–8.

[121] King 1993, I: 248.   [122] King 1993, I: 257. See also King 1999.

[123] King 1993, I: 252–3. See also King 2004; Sezgin 2011b, 78–202.

[124] Lewicka 2003, 96–105. According to her, European manners books represented the evolution of people's attitudes and everyday activities, while their Muslim counterparts generally emphasized the continuation of the tradition. Lewicka 2003, 106–7, 107n33. See also Kınalızade 2012 [1565], 374–6.

your face away from the food; do not dip into the common dish a piece of bread, etc. you already cut with your teeth; stop eating before your stomach is full; and, at the end, wash your hands and clean your mouth and teeth.[125]

In *The Civilizing Process*, Norbert Elias outlines the evolution in social manners and subsequently self-restraint and discipline in Western Europe from the twelfth to the eighteenth century and especially in the sixteenth and seventeenth centuries. Etiquette books instructed how to wash hands and take baths, to not blow one's nose on clothing, to avoid bad odors such as the smell of garlic, and to dress appropriately while sleeping.[126] Elias points to the role-modeling of the courtly aristocracy and, later, the bourgeoisie as important factors in this progress. He does not recognize any positive contributions of Christianity or interactions with Muslims in this process.[127]

In addition to discipline and manners, Islamic civilization initially provided a certain level of egalitarianism. The fact that the Prophet Muhammad's close companion Bilal al-Habashi was an African and former slave[128] indicates some level of racial equality in early Muslims' outlook.[129] Islamic law also maintained private property for both men and women. Lewis, who is critical of the status of slaves, women, and non-Muslims in Islam,[130] still acknowledges that if we compare Muslim rule "at the time of its advent with the societies that surrounded it – the stratified feudalism of Iran and the caste system of India to the east, the privileged aristocracies of both Byzantine and Latin Europe to the West," then the Islamic alternative "does indeed bring a message of equality. Not only does Islam not endorse such systems of social differentiation; it explicitly and resolutely rejects them."[131]

---

[125] Additionally, Ghazali lists instructions about invitations and hospitality, including not preferring the rich to the poor in terms of accepting or offering an invitation. Al-Ghazali 2000 [c. 1097], 1–17, 31–32; Gazali 1974b [c. 1097], 12–23, 35–6.

[126] Elias 2000 [1939], 62, 108, 114–17, 122, 138–9. See also Braudel 1981, 206–7.

[127] "Religion, the belief in the punishing or rewarding omnipotence of God, never has in itself a 'civilizing' or affect-subduing effect. On the contrary, religion is always exactly as 'civilized' as the society or class which upholds." Elias 2000 [1939], 169. According to Jack Goody (2006, 174), "earlier Christians in Europe had often destroyed Roman baths," considering them to be associated with pagan, Jewish, and Muslim practices. Later, their gradual "revival in the medieval period may have been connected with the Crusades and with Muslim influence."

[128] Jahiz (1969 [c. 862], 195–7), a famous litterateur and Mutazili theologian of African descent, wrote on the "Superiority of the Blacks to the Whites." See Masudi 1989 [947], 309–10; al-Nadim 1970 [987], 397–409.

[129] Rose Wilder Lane (2014 [1943], 82–108, 114) argues that early Islam's iconoclastic characteristic created the necessary human energy for its worldwide influence. See also Weaver 2014 [1947].

[130] See Cole 2002.

[131] Lewis 2003, 82. "[T]he Arabs won support in Roman territories and probably in the Iraq and even parts of Iran by curbing a persecuting ecclesiastic rule." Hodgson 1974a, 241; also 199. For a similar observation in Syria and Egypt, see Wiet 1953, 64.

According to Michael Cook, the political ethos of the time of the Prophet Muhammad and the Four Caliphs had three main characteristics that had affinities with republicanism. First, the ethos was "strongly antithetical to patrimonialism – to the kind of political culture in which the king regards his kingdom as his property."[132] The Prophet had a humble life with public access. The Four Caliphs followed him in terms of refusing to have palaces or guardians. The "second feature is rejection of despotism." Both the Prophet and Four Caliphs received the political allegiance of followers (*bay'a*), based on handshaking similar to a commercial transaction. The third feature of the early Islamic political ethos is "a strong commitment to the rule of law."[133] Robert Bellah also notes that under the leadership of the Prophet and then the Four Caliphs, Arabs attempted to institutionalize a nonhereditary system of governance. Yet this progressive attempt failed and relapsed "into pre-Islamic principles of social organization" because it did not have the necessary social infrastructure in the rapidly expanding state. The traditional Muslim suspicion of Umayyad kingship "must be taken seriously as … another indication that something precious was lost with the collapse of the early experiment."[134]

In *Hierarchy and Egalitarianism in Islamic Thought*, Louise Marlow stresses that "the Islamic tradition of classical times may be said to be strikingly egalitarian." In early Islamic history, "neither a church nor a priesthood had developed, and classical Islamic law, with the significant exception of marriage equality, overwhelmingly assumed the equality of free male believers."[135] Marlow points to elitist Greek and Sasanian ideas as promoters of social hierarchy among Muslims;[136] she also emphasizes the role of the ulema in this doctrinal transformation: "Once scholars were engaged not only in accepting but also in justifying the existence of unofficial social hierarchies in Islamic terms, the realisation of the egalitarian ideal was increasingly postponed to the next world."[137]

As an example to support Marlow's argument, we can look to Mawardi, the influential eleventh-century jurist, who recommended the establishment of an office that would record family/clan genealogies. This office would protect the privileges of those of noble lineage. Among the duties Mawardi proposed for this office was the prevention of women with higher lineages from marrying men of lower ones.[138]

In short, Islam promoted some good characteristics in early Muslim societies, such as time discipline, manners, and relatively egalitarian social

---

[132] Cook 2014, 319; also 322–3.   [133] Cook 2014, 320–1.   [134] Bellah 1991, 150–1.
[135] Marlow 1997, 1–2. Marlow (1997, esp. 99) analyzes various interpretations of the Quranic verse 49:13, "O men! We have created you from male and female, and have made you into people and tribes that you may know one another. The most noble among you in the sight of God is the most pious."
[136] Marlow 1997, chs. 2 and 3.   [137] Marlow 1997, 174.
[138] Al-Mawardi 1996 [1045–58], 107–8.

relations. On these characteristics, Muslims were largely ahead of Western Christians at that time.

MUSLIMS AND WESTERN CHRISTIANS

In 922, when Ibn Fadlan traveled to Volga Bulgaria (north of the Caspian Sea) as an emissary of the Abbasid caliph, Muslim rule stretched from Transoxiana to Iberia, whereas Western Christians were mostly limited between northern Iberia and eastern Germany and from the British Isles to Italy. Ibn Fadlan reported on various Scandinavian, Slavic, and Turkic groups who were neither Christian nor Muslim.[139] His account betrays a clear sense of Muslim superiority, which makes his reflections "similar to the attitudes of many European travelers of the nineteenth century in Africa and Asia."[140]

From the ninth to the twelfth century, if not a longer period, the Muslim world overall enjoyed intellectual and socioeconomic conditions superior to those of Western Europe.[141] Marc Bloch writes, "Until the twelfth century the Moslem world, along with the Byzantine world, exercised a true economic hegemony over the West: the only gold coinage ... [in Western] Europe came from Greek or Arab mints, or at least ... were copies of their productions." He adds that for "a long period neither Gaul nor Italy, among their poor cities, had anything to offer which approached the splendour of Baghdad or Cordova."[142]

Between 800 and 1000, Baghdad, with an estimated population between 300,000 and 1 million, was much larger than any Western European city.[143] According to Tertius Chandler, in the year 1000, Muslim Cordova had the largest population (450,000) in Europe, including Constantinople (300,000), whereas the largest Western Christian city, Palermo, had only 75,000 people.[144] Comparing Europe and the Arab Middle East, Maarten Bosker, Eltjo Buringh, and Jan van Zanden notice that around the year 800 in these two regions Iraq was "by far the most urbanized 'country' with a 25 to 30 percent share of people living in cities with more than 10,000 inhabitants."[145] In 800, the estimated total population of such cities was 1,325,000 in Arab

---

[139] Ibn Fadlan 2005 [922]; Ibn Fadlan 1995 [922].   [140] Frye 2005, 106.

[141] See Southern 1970, 27; Landes 1998, 29.

[142] Bloch 2014 [1940], 6. "In the eleventh and twelfth centuries, Muslim countries were the only ones to mint gold coins." Maddison 2004, 73. Around 1000, Western Europe "was undeniably backward when compared to the flourishing societies of Sung China and the Arab world." Van Zanden 2009, 32.

[143] Watson 1983, 133; Chandler 1987, 70, 467–8; Lapidus 2002, 56. Between 800 and 1000, the largest city in Transoxiana was Samarkand. Barthold (1977 [1900], 83, 88) estimates its population at 500,000, though Janet Abu-Lughod (1989, 184n12) considers this figure an "exaggeration." For the same period, Bulliet (1995a, 136) depicts Nishapur as the largest city in Khurasan and estimates its population at around 150,000.

[144] Chandler 1987, 14–15, 467–9. See also Bairoch 1988, 118, 372.   [145] Bosker et al. 2008, 9.

lands, whereas it was only 407,000 in Christian Western Europe, and 390,000 in Byzantium.[146] This trend mostly continued during the following three centuries, thus in "Western Europe ... before 1100 levels of urbanization are very low, with the exception of (Islamic) Spain."[147]

Some scholars reject this comparative data and depict Western Europe as consistently ahead of the Muslim world. The appeal of historical revisionism plays a role in their depictions. Moreover, these scholars' understanding of history may be based on continuity, rather than cyclical or random "rise and fall" experiences. From this point of view, the "rise of the West" was not a rupture but rather a continuation of long-term improvements even over the course of the Early Middle Ages (500–1000). Therefore, by this account, whatever happened in medieval Western Europe must have contributed to later European progress. The main problem of this teleological view is that it denies basic causality. It presents various behaviors and events (each of which actually had its own causes and effects) as parts of a single consequence – the rise of the West. In addition, some of these authors seek to challenge the explanations of the rise of the West as a result of secularization or the Protestant Reformation. In order to credit Catholicism with modern European successes, they may choose to portray medieval Europe as a place of continuous, if gradual, progress.[148]

I will briefly review two examples of exponents of this position. One is Lynn White, Jr., whose "work helped to create the field of the history of medieval technology."[149] White's influential publications are important for understanding the gradual development of agriculture in Western Europe, covering such new techniques as the heavy plough[150] and the three-field system of crop rotation.[151] White, however, is too quick to move from this development to democracy and capitalism: "The increased returns from the labour of the northern peasant ... provided surplus food which, from the tenth century on, permitted rapid urbanization. In the new cities there arose a class of skilled artisans and merchants, the burghers who ... created a novel and characteristic

---

[146] In 900, Arabs also had a larger urban population (1,671,000 in MENA and 361,000 in Iberia) than Christian Western Europe (625,000) and Byzantium (495,000). Bosker et al. 2008, 33. See also Botticini and Eckstein 2012, 33.

[147] Bosker et al. 2008, 9.

[148] If Catholicism led to progress in Europe, David Cosandey (1997, 120–1) rightly asks, why had it not done so for centuries before the Renaissance? See also Van Zanden 2009, 66.

[149] Worthen 2009, 1201.

[150] "The agricultural revolution of the early Middle Ages was limited to the northern plains where the heavy plough was appropriate to the rich soils, where the summer rains permitted a large spring planting, and where the oats of the summer crops supported the horses to pull the heavy plough." White 1962, 78.

[151] Douglass North and Robert Thomas (1973, 41) note that the three-field system slowly diffused; its spread "throughout Western Europe took several centuries. Not until the twelfth century was triannual rotation even introduced into England." See also Lewis 1988, 73–5.

way of life, democratic capitalism."[152] White makes broader claims, which undermine the position of not only Islamic but also Chinese civilization, without providing any comparative data. He asserts that "the West seized the initiative in agricultural systems in the sixth century, in military methods in the eighth, and in industrial production in the eleventh."[153] For him, certain aspects of Christian theology, as well as Catholic monks' emphasis on scholarship and manual labor, played an important, if not leading, role in European technological development.[154]

Another example is Rodney Stark, who has recently repeated several of White's arguments.[155] In *The Victory of Reason: How Christianity Led to Freedom, Capitalism, and Western Success*, Stark argues that Christianity is a uniquely rational religion that spurred the rise of the West: "I demonstrate the absolutely essential role of rational theology for the rise of science, showing the religious reasons why science arose in Europe but failed to do so in China, ancient Greece, or in Islam."[156] According to Stark, Catholicism did not have a problem with science in the Middle Ages: "The success of the West, including the rise of science, rested entirely on religious foundations, and the people who brought it about were devout Christians." He criticizes Weber and others stressing the Protestant Reformation for reflecting "academic anti-Catholicism" and writing "as if the previous fifteen hundred years of Christianity either were of little matter or were harmful."[157] Despite its bold claims, his book provides no systemically comparative data on various periods of Western history, nor on the Muslim or Chinese cases.

In reality, in the Early Middle Ages, while scholars and merchants enjoyed a relatively high social status in Muslim lands, the clergymen and the military elite dominated Western Europe. In the words of Elias, until the mid-eleventh century, "there were, essentially, only two classes of free people" in Western Europe, "the warriors or nobles and the clergy; below them existed only bondsmen and serfs." He defines these two dominant classes as "those who pray [and] those who fight." This structure began to change, according to Elias, around 1050, with the development of European cities; merchants,

---

[152]   White 1962, 78. For a critique of White's argument about the stirrup (that its introduction led to the mounted chivalry and feudalism), see Homans 1962. For a recent review essay on White's book, see Worthen 2009.

[153]   White 1963, 280.

[154]   White 1963, 283–90. For similar assertions, see Landes 1998, 54–9.

[155]   According to Mokyr (2006, 14), "Stark reproduces in some form many of White's arguments, but oddly enough this is nowhere acknowledged in the text of his books." See also Goldstone 2006.

[156]   Stark 2005, xiv. This argument is paradoxical given that Stark was a leading scholar of the rational choice approach to the sociology of religion, which stresses that each and every human being is a rational actor regardless of his or her religion.

[157]   Stark 2005, xi. For an opposite view, see Freeman 2005, esp. chs. 19 and 20.

artisans, and other groups in towns start to gradually constitute a third class of free people.[158]

Bloch's account is slightly different; he acknowledges that various classes of free people, particularly "isolated nuclei of merchants and craftsmen," had always existed in Western Europe. Nonetheless, like Elias, Bloch regards 1050 as a turning point. Until that time, he emphasizes, townspeople were marginal because they depended on commerce, which was peripheral in Western European societies. The legality of commercial (or financial) profit "was denied by the theologians and its nature ill-understood by knightly society." Thus, commercial activity was "in flagrant conflict with prevailing moral notions." It was hindered by feudal restrictions on property, archaic judicial processes, fragmented political authority, and various privileges of ecclesiastical and knightly classes.[159]

Like merchants, scholars were marginal in Western Europe. In comparison to antiquity and the modern period, early medieval Europe suffered intellectual stagnation. For example, *Great Books of the Western World*, the sixty-volume set published by Britannica (second edition in 1990), includes around 130 authors from the antiquity to modern times. It does not include even a single author from the period between Augustine (354–430) and Thomas Aquinas (1224–74). [160]

Nevertheless, the eleventh and twelfth centuries experienced various transformations in both the Muslim world and Western Europe, narrowing the intellectual and socioeconomic gap between them. The transformation in Western Europe will be analyzed in Chapter 5. Here we will now turn to transformations in the Muslim world.

DIN WA DAWLA (RELIGION AND THE STATE)

A major transformation in the eleventh century was the beginning of the formation of the *din wa dawla* (religion and the state) alliance, which basically implies an alliance between the ulema and the military state. This process included the transformation of Islamic scholars into state servants through state-led madrasas, the militarization of the economy through the *iqta* system of land tenure and tax farming, and the marginalization of philosophers and merchants.

---

[158] Elias 2000 [1939], 221. See also Bartlett 1993, esp. 308. According to Georges Duby (1980, 5), the three orders – "men of prayer, men of war, and farmers" – were important to understand late medieval and early modern French society where "some pray, others fight, still others work."

[159] Bloch 2014 [1940], 372–3; also 307.

[160] Britannica 2018. A summary of forty-four other great books lists shows similar results. Except for a few epic tales and religious writings, they do not include authors or books from early medieval Europe. Kau 2018.

The ulema–state alliance was not an essential part of Islam; instead, it began to be constructed as late as the eleventh century. It is true that unlike Jesus, Muhammad commanded armies and administered public money. Similarly, the Four Caliphs were regarded as both religious and political authorities. However, the foundational era of Islam differed in two main ways from the post-eleventh-century period, which was characterized by the ulema–state alliance. First, the religious authority of the Prophet was believed to come directly from God, and that of the Four Caliphs was believed to derive from their personal connections to the Prophet.[161] The ulema, by contrast, lacked such religious authority in this personal sense. Second, the political authority of the Prophet and the Four Caliphs was charismatic, not institutional. In other words, political power was based on their personalities, rather than any institutions that could be called a state in the full sense of the term. By contrast, the ulema–state alliance included a fairly institutionalized notion of the state.

Sunni Orthodoxy

A major component of the ulema–state alliance was the orthodox Sunni ulema. The epistemology of the orthodox ulema was mostly formed in the ninth century. Shafii (767–820) played a leading role in the formation of orthodox jurisprudence. Before Shafii, the two leading ulema of jurisprudence were Abu Hanifa (699–767), who promoted the use of reason, and Malik (711–795), who took as normative the Medinan practice of Islam. In other words, the Hanafi school was reason-based, and the Maliki school was tradition-based. Shafii, by contrast, promoted a text-based approach. In his methodology, Islamic legal rules should be determined based on the Quran, hadiths (reports about the sayings and actions of the Prophet), consensus of the ulema, and analogical reasoning, in that order. This formula empha- sizes texts at the expense of reason. Another leading supporter of the text- based approach was Ibn Hanbal (780–855), who strongly defended literalism and formalism. He rejected reason-based interpretations and reading Quranic verses and hadiths metaphorically. Through a gradual process that started in the eleventh century, Shafii's and Ibn Hanbal's text-based approaches became dominant, even among Hanafis and Malikis. The Shii ulema's position remained somewhat different because they attached particular importance to the "infallible" imams who lived between the seventh and ninth centuries. The Shii ulema similarly regarded the Quran and hadiths as the main sources of law; however, their views about consensus remained

---

[161] Gamal al-Banna (2003, 4, 7–9) stresses that the political leadership of the Prophet Muhammad was a "unique historical experience" with extraordinary characteristics and thus "cannot be repeated." See also Barani 1961 [c. 1358–9], 33–4; An-Na'im 2008, 54–62.

largely ambiguous, and, instead of analogical reasoning, they explicitly referred to reason. [162]

The codification of hadiths further empowered text-based understandings of Islam. Six main hadith collections have gained canonical status among Sunnis. Eventually, two of these collections, those of Bukhari (810–70) and Muslim (815–75), particularly became sacred texts for Sunnis; today, they are virtually immune from criticism. [163] A significant contribution to the formation of the Sunni orthodoxy came from Ashari (873–935), the most influential scholar of theology (*kalam*) to date. [164] Ashari was initially a Mutazili. Later, he declared his rejection of the Mutazilis' rationalist ideas that the Quran is a creation of God, that certain Quranic verses (e.g., the human vision of God in the hereafter) are metaphorical, and that human beings are makers of their deeds. Instead, he adopted the view that the Quran is God's eternal speech, beyond time; that (debated) Quranic verses should be taken literally; and that God creates everything, including humans' deeds and intentions. [165] Ashari's new perspective reflects not only literalism but also determinism and a denial of causality.

The formation of Sunni orthodoxy took a few more centuries because various schools had internal disagreements. For example, Bukhari's collection "achieved canonical status among Sunnis only in the tenth century." [166] Moreover, according to Montgomery Watt, "even at the death of al-Ash'ari in 935," though Hanafis, Hanbalis, and Asharis "were moving closer together doctrinally, they were not prepared to recognize one another" as fellow-Sunnis. There has been a debate whether the term "orthodox" may be used for Islam. Watt acknowledges the fact that "Islam has had no machinery comparable to the Ecumenical Councils of the Christian Church which could say authoritatively what constitutes 'right doctrine.'" Nonetheless, he rightly concludes that "by the typically Islamic process of *ijma* or consensus a wide area of agreement was eventually reached (after the year 1000), and to this the term 'orthodoxy' might be applied." [167]

Struggles between followers of various jurisprudential and theological Sunni schools continued in the eleventh century and even afterward. [168] To minimize

---

[162] Weiss 1998, 36; McAuliffe 2015, 196, 205; Abou El Fadl 2014, xxxiv–vii. See also Hallaq 2009, ch. 2.

[163] See Abou El Fadl 2014, 36.

[164] The other influential Sunni theologian was Maturidi (870–944). The two theologians differed in terms of their jurisprudential schools: Imam Maturidi was a Hanafi, and Imam Ashari was a Shafi. Watt 1973, 312–16. I will briefly discuss their differences in Chapter 5.

[165] Al-Ashari 1953 [c. 935], 20–32, 45–52, 53–75, respectively. For the Mutazili theological school and Ashari's departure from it, see Fakhry 2004, 43–66, 209–15; Watt 1973, 303–12; Corbin 1986, 165–72.

[166] McAuliffe 2015, 166.

[167] Watt 1973, 5–6. See also Makdisi 1981, 280; Jackson 2002b, 30; Aslan 2005, 146.

[168] In Nishapur, in 1158, the Hanafis and the Shafis began waging a civil war, which continued for a few years. Bulliet 1995a, 140–1.

disagreements and to contain conflicts between Sunni schools took centuries. It was much easier and earlier for Sunnis to define their "others" – Shiis, Mutazilis, and philosophers – as elaborated in the next section.

The Qadiri Creed and Mawardi

Every action creates a reaction. In the early eleventh century, a Sunni reaction against the domination of Shii rulers was taking shape. A century prior, an Ismaili Shii dynasty, the Fatimid caliphate (909–1171), emerged as a rival to the Abbasids. The Fatimids established their rule in North Africa, made Egypt their center, and expanded their rule to such lands as Sicily, both coasts of the Red Sea (including Mecca and Medina), and the southern parts of Syria (including Jerusalem and Damascus). Another Shii force in the tenth century was the Twelver Shii Buyids (934–1062), who ruled most major cities in Iraq and southwestern Iran. They even invaded Baghdad in 945 and took control of the Abbasid caliph. Another Shii dynasty at the time was the Hamdanids, who controlled southeastern Anatolia and the northern parts of both Syria and Iraq. Meantime, the Qarmatians, a Shii political entity, ruled Bahrain and the eastern Arabian Peninsula.

The Abbasid Caliph Qadir (r. 991–1031) played a leading role in driving the Sunni reaction. By attacking Shii theology, he tried to constitute a bloc with Sunni sultans, such as Mahmud of Ghazni, against the Buyids in Baghdad and the Fatimid caliphate in Cairo. In 1017, Qadir issued a decree against heterodox groups, including the Mutazilis, forbidding them from teaching views "at variance with the orthodox Islam on pain of punishment."[169] Mahmud supported this decree by persecuting Mutazilis and various Shii groups.[170]

In 1029, in Baghdad, Qadir was joined by several ulema and issued a broader decree, which intended to put an end to theological debates by establishing a Sunni orthodoxy and threatening those who rejected it. Three points in the creed established a framework for an inquisition. The creed declared that (1) those who depict the Quran in any sense as "created" (i.e., the Mutazilis) are infidels and may be killed; (2) the religious ranking of each of the Four Caliphs follows their chronological ranking (i.e., Abu Bakr, Umar, and Uthman are religiously superior to Ali – the opposite of the Shii belief), and those who slander the Prophet's wife Aisha (i.e., the Shiis) have nothing to do with Islam; and (3) those who do not perform daily prayers become infidels.

---

[169] Mez 1937, 206. See also Bulliet 1995a, 145–56.
[170] Makdisi 1981, 137; Hanne 2007, 68, 70. Mahmud destroyed libraries in Rayy by labeling the books of Ismailis, Mutazilis, and philosophers. Yet he carried some of the books into his capital to build a library. Mackensen 1935a, 93–5. According to Barthold (1977 [1900], 291), under Mahmud, the "persecution of heretics is ... explained by the political motives ...; sometimes the accusation of heresy was but the pretext for seizing the property of the suspected person."

Two years later, Qadir's son Qaim (r. 1031–75) became the caliph. In 1041, Qaim reiterated his father's creed and reemphasized its role in the consolidation of orthodox Sunni theology.[171]

In this context, Mawardi (972–1058), a prominent Shafi jurist and judge, served both Qadir and Qaim in different positions. His most important contribution was his book *The Ordinances of Government*, on the subject of the Islamic caliphate. This book has been influential in linking Islamic law with political thought and in promoting a state-centric Islamic outlook. Arguably, it has been the most influential and systematic book ever written on the caliphate theory. Mawardi argues that the political authority exclusively belongs to the caliph, who delegates his authority by appointing viziers, governors, commanders, judges, prayer leaders, and public morality overseers.[172] These officeholders' powers direct flow from the caliph, who is a man from the Quraysh tribe.[173]

At the time when the book was written, the Abbasid caliph lived under Buyid rule in Baghdad. Mawardi tried to reclaim the caliph's authority as a source of religious legitimacy. Hence, he claimed that even if a sultan captured political authority by force, the approval of the caliph would be both necessary and sufficient for him to gain legitimacy.[174] In the words of Ingrid Mattson, Mawardi was "constrained by his historical situation, as well as by the sensitivities of the Caliph who commissioned the [book]."[175] Therefore, Mawardi seemed to focus, at least partially, on political circumstances more than principles.[176]

Mawardi's book provided a convenient framework for the Abbasid caliph's collaboration with sultans. This dynamic would become particularly relevant under Seljuk rule. Similarly, Qadir's creed maintained a basis for future alliances among Sunni caliphs, sultans, and ulema. Qaim married a Seljuk princess, facilitated the Seljuks' conquest of Baghdad, and materialized his father's vision of reinstituting Sunni political domination in the city.

[171] Mez 1937, 206–9. According to Eric Hanne (2007, 71), Mez and others quote the full text of Qadir's 1029 creed from its reiteration by Qaim.

[172] Al-Mawardi 1996 [1045–58], 9, 23–120, 260.

[173] For him, women should not even become viziers. Al-Mawardi 1996 [1045–58], 4–5, 29.

[174] Al-Mawardi 1996 [1045–58], esp. 3–5, 15–16, 20–7, 36–7.

[175] Mattson 2000–1, 401. See also Rosenthal 1958, 27–8; Lambton 1981, 88–93; Ibrahim 1994, 53, 69n1.

[176] On the one hand, Mawardi diverges from Shii notion of imamate and Umayyad/Abbasid hereditary monarchy by insisting "on the election of the *imam* [caliph] by the proper body of qualified electors." On the other hand, "he makes the curious compromise that the electorate could be reduced to a single individual," which legitimizes the (Abbasid) caliph's designation of his son. Wahba 1996, xiv. Al-Mawardi 1996 [1045–58], 5–16. A similar contradiction exists in Mawardi's (1996 [1045–58], 6–9) depiction of the caliphate as a contract-based position and his top-down notion of caliphal authority.

The *Iqta* System

The weakening of the old economic regime, which depended on the monetary economy, was an important factor in the emergence of the ulema–state alliance. The newly emerging economic regime, by contrast, was based on the *iqta* system of land revenue assignments and agricultural tax distribution to (primarily military) officials. In the words of Goitein, by the early eleventh century, "the monetary and mercantile economy of the Middle East gave way to an economy in which feudalistic trends became dominant."[177] This transformation shrank private financial sources for Islamic scholars and made many of them accept, if not seek, public funding in the service of the state.

The weakening of the old economic system began with the gradual decline of the state revenues from crucial Sawad (central and southern Iraq) fields,[178] which suffered from, among other problems, salinization due to intensive irrigation and poor drainage.[179] Another reason for the Abbasids' financial problems was "lavish expenditure of the court and the inflated bureaucracy."[180] Beyond public finance, economic difficulties were reflected in the declining population and famines in Baghdad in the eleventh century.[181] According to Bulliet, Baghdad's problems were part of a broader crisis. Throughout the eleventh century, a chilling of the climate in Iraq, Iran, and Central Asia resulted in agricultural decline (affecting grain directly and cotton indirectly), famine, and urban disorder. It also motivated Turkmen nomads led by the Seljuk dynasty to migrate from Central Asia to the Middle East.[182]

In response to these financial problems, Abbasid rulers began distributing *iqta*s to officials.[183] The *iqta* grantees either collect taxes or more directly

---

[177] Goitein 1966a, 218.
[178] Michael Bonner (2010, 354) calculates that the Abbasid state's agricultural revenues from Sawad declined from 112,416,000 dirhams in 819 to 22,500,000 dirhams in 915. See also Ashtor 1976, 63; Waines 1977.
[179] Hodgson 1974a, 483–5. Peter Christensen (1993) argues that agricultural production declined in various parts of "greater Iran" throughout the Middle Ages. For critiques of his book and counterarguments, see Morony 1999; Bulliet 1995b.
[180] Lewis 1970, 103. "[I]n no century and at no period was so much spent as during the reign of Mutawakkil [d. 861] ... He had, they say, 4,000 concubines and slept with each one of them." Masudi 1989 [947], 263.
[181] Bosker et al. 2008, 45; Wiet 1971, 106–7.
[182] Bulliet 2009. See also Bulliet 1995a, ch. 8. Similarly, Ronnie Ellenblum (2012) argues that between 950 and 1072, there occurred periods of freeze in (parts of) Iraq, Iran, and Central Asia, which led to such problems as nomadic movements and the weakening of state authority. Meanwhile, Western Europe, Andalus, and Morocco went through a period of warmer climate. For a critique, see Shatzmiller 2013.
[183] Lambton 1962, 129.

extract revenues from granted lands.[184] Abbasid rulers used *iqta*s as a solution in cases when the military personnel demanded payments and the treasury did not have sufficient funds. These early *iqta*s emerged out of "crisis mode improvisation" and were unsystematic. Yet they still paved the way for the militarization of the land regime. Certain lands, which were previously owned by civilians and traded by civilian contracts, "became open to domination of military landholders."[185]

The *iqta* system became more widespread under the Buyids, who were, at least initially, dependent on Dailami soldiers, while ruling most of Iraq and Iran.[186] In contrast to comparable privileges in feudal Europe, *iqta*s were not subject to inheritance or sale.[187] *Iqta*s were generally not even granted for life. These characteristics led to various negative consequences, as Claude Cahen summarizes:

> The soldier, who does not live in the land of *iqta* and has no training as a rural farmer, does not consider himself as its landlord: he sends his steward to collect royalties from peasants, with the mission of pressing them at maximum. The land could be under the risk of being ruined. But who cares? [If so, the soldier] would turn to the state – the guarantor of his income. [The state] would verify that his *iqta* no longer provides revenue, and then either supplement or replace it. These are the reasons that Miskawayh ... delineates the Buyid regime economically catastrophic.[188]

Watson points to the *iqta* system as a major reason for the end of the innovative and productive era of Muslim agriculture around the year 1000. For him, this system restricted private property and entrepreneurship and thus diminished agricultural productivity.[189] Despite its negative consequences, the *iqta* system was further institutionalized under the Seljuks, because it already created a path dependence and suited the Seljuks' military state structure. According to Ann Lambton, *iqta* was an important component of "the increased militarisation of the state in the 11th and 12th centuries," which was directly associated with the decline in "the position and status of the merchants."[190] In addition to *iqta*, another major feature of the militarization of the economic system was the increasing emphasis on conquest.

---

[184] *Iqta*s had two main types: *iqta al-istighlal* (revenue assignment) and *iqta al-tamlik* (land assignment). In both types, the real owner of the land was the central state. Cahen 1953, 30–3; Lambton 1991, 29.

[185] Bonner 2010, 353.   [186] See al-Mawardi 1996 [1045–58], 208–16.

[187] Unlike European serfdom, in the *iqta* system, the *iqta* holders are "only allowed to take a specified sum from the inhabitants, and have no right beyond this to the persons, property, wives, and children of the population." Barthold 1977 [1900], 307.

[188] Cahen 1953, 33.   [189] Watson 1983, 142–4.

[190] Lambton 1962, 129–30. Ashtor (1976, 114) argues that until the mid-eleventh century, the Muslim "bourgeoisie tried to resist the feudal lords and that the struggle between these two classes was one of the leitmotifs" of Middle Eastern history. For Goitein (1966b, 254) the Muslim bourgeoisie's "failure to achieve political power was its undoing."

The Military State and Conquests

An economic characteristic of the military state structure was its focus on rent-seeking through conquest. A major early example of a military state that focused on conquests was the sultanate founded by Mahmud of Ghazni (r. 998–1030). Mahmud continually waged wars of conquest in the southern Central Asia, eastern Iran, and northern India. Mahmud's military state, according to Frederick Starr, differed from trade-based rule, which had been the norm in Central Asia. In contrast, the economy of Mahmud's sultanate was based on the extraction of wealth mostly from conquered lands. The Abbasids, the Fatimids, and several other Muslim rulers had used slave soldiers before,[191] but Mahmud's army was the first to consist exclusively of slaves and mercenaries.[192]

According to Wilhelm Barthold, under Mahmud, the "concept of the state was brought to its extreme expression."[193] Mahmud prevented the civilian subjects from using violence for even defensive and patriotic purposes. It was seen in the example of Balkh, where residents resisted the Karakhanid occupation, and in response the Karakhanids pillaged the city and burned the bazaar. After retaking the city, Mahmud did not praise the resistance but rather admonished the people:

> What have subjects to do with war? It is natural that your town was destroyed and that they burnt the property belonging to me, which had brought in such revenues. You should have been required to pay an indemnity for the losses, but we pardoned you; (only) see to it that it does not happen again: if any king (at a given moment) proves himself the stronger, and requires taxes from you and protects you, you must pay taxes and thereby save yourselves.[194]

Mahmud's speech aimed to destroy any notion of belonging to a political community independent of a sultan. This mentality of the military rulers weakened the people's political solidarity or group feeling – *asabiyya*, as Ibn Khaldun would later call it. Barthold regards the Ghaznavid case as the beginning of a new political model: "From this time evidently begins the division of the nation into an army to whom the king pays grants, requiring in return faithful service, and subjects whom the king defends ..., requiring from them unconditional obedience and the unmurmuring payment of taxes."[195]

Mahmud's relations with scholars were complex. On the one hand, he provided patronage to such important scholars as Biruni. Moreover, Mahmud, a Sunni Turk, was open-minded enough to patronize the Persian poet Firdawsi

---

[191] In addition to the army, slaves were also employed in harems, as well as being used as workers under these Muslim dynasties. Shatzmiller 2011, 151–5.

[192] Starr 2013, 332, 335.   [193] Barthold 1977 [1900], xxx.

[194] Barthold 1977 [1900], 291; also 272. See also Crone 2004, 154–5.

[195] Barthold 1977 [1900], 291–2.

to complete his epic poem *Book of Kings* (*Shahnama*), one of the most important sources on the pre-Islamic, Zoroastrian culture of Iran.[196] On the other
hand, Mahmud obsessively forced Biruni and some other scholars to join his
court. Ibn Sina refused and thus had to flee westward for years.[197]

Immediately after Mahmud's death, the Seljuk Turks, who were generally
regarded as "a more magnanimous alternative" to the Ghaznavids,[198] founded
even a bigger empire. Theirs was not exclusively based on a slave army and
mercenaries, but still gave the military a pivotal role. At the beginning of the
Seljuk period, four main conditions for an ulema–state alliance were available.
The Sunni orthodoxy formation process was at least partially complete. Sunni
religious and military forces tended to unite against a common enemy – the
Shiis. The rise of the *iqta* system weakened the merchants and made Islamic
scholars more likely to accept state patronage. The state structure already
became militarized. In political science terminology, this moment in history
was a critical juncture, when the structural conditions were ready for a substantial change, which could leave a long-lasting legacy of path dependence.
For such a change, however, structural conditions are not sufficient; an effective
agency is also necessary. Agents came in the forms of Seljuk rulers and
Sunni ulema.

THE SELJUKS AND THE ULEMA

The Seljuk dynasty was founded in Central Asia and conquered Iran and most
of both Iraq and Syria. It was the first Seljuk sultan, Tughrul Bey (r. 1037–63),
who ended the Buyid rule in Baghdad in 1055. The Seljuks had hostile relations
with the Fatimids and the Ismaili Assassins. In 1071, the second sultan, Alp
Arslan (r. 1063–72) won a historic victory at Manzikert against the Byzantine
Empire. This victory enabled Turkish conquest in most parts of Anatolia.

Both Tughrul Bey and his last grand vizier Kunduri (1055–64) were Hanafi.
With the sultan's support, Kunduri attacked Asharis and Shafis. Juwayni,
a leading Ashari/Shafi scholar, fled to the Hejaz (Mecca and Medina). Subsequently, Nizam al-Mulk became grand vizier (1064–92) and ended this
persecution, though the Seljuk dynasty's Hanafi favoritism continued.[199]
Nizam al-Mulk ("Order of the Realm") served under Alp Arslan and then
Malikshah.

Nizam al-Mulk patronized the establishment of a madrasa in Baghdad,
which was called Nizamiyya. He also led the opening of a series of Sunni
madrasas in Iraq (Baghdad, Basra, and Mosul), Iran (Isfahan and Nishapur),

---

[196] Ultimately, Firdawsi found Mahmud's reward insufficient. Askari 2016, 7–8, 79–81.
[197] Starr 2013, 284, 295–6.   [198] Starr 2013, 386.
[199] Madelung 1985, 126–37; Bosworth 1968, 46, 73; Laoust 1970, 27; Köprülü 1976
[1919], 18n16.

and Central Asia (Balkh, Herat, and Merv).[200] These madrasas have been collectively referred to Nizamiyyas. Such eminent professors as Juwayni promoted Ashari theology in these madrasas, which were funded by waqfs (pious foundations). Nevertheless, this financial arrangement did not insulate the schools from state influence; officials and their family members often became the founders of the waqf–madrasa complexes. Daphna Ephrat examines twenty-four madrasas endowed in Baghdad between 1066 and 1193. Many of these madrasas' founders, according to Ephrat's data, were rulers and officials, or their wives. Elites competed in founding madrasas to support their respective favored school of jurisprudence. Members of the Seljuk dynasty founded madrasas with Hanafi beneficiaries, whereas leading bureaucrats partnered with Shafi beneficiaries and the Abbasid caliph's household partnered with Hanbali beneficiaries. Initially, the Hanafis and the Shafis were more influential, while later the Hanbalis and the Shafis gained more prominence.[201]

Through Nizamiyya madrasas, the Seljuk state authorities went beyond receiving the support of the ulema; they began to systematically affect the formation of the ulema. State authorities influenced the waqf–madrasa deeds and beneficiaries, and intervened in the appointment of professors. For Seljuk rulers these madrasas were largely instruments "to control or supervise the religious milieu."[202] State patronage of the ulema through Nizamiyyas entailed much deeper political intervention than the previous state patronage of philosophers. Ibn Sina and many other philosophers received patronage as professionals, but they were not educated and socialized in public institutions as students.

Additionally, Nizam al-Mulk systematized the *iqta* system and allocated an unprecedentedly large number of land revenue assignments in order to maintain a strong army.[203] The prevalence of *iqta* substantially weakened the landowner class and militarized both the economy and the state structure.[204] Subsequent dynasties, such as the Ayyubids, Mamluks, Ottomans, and Safavids, largely followed the Seljuk model of the *iqta* system.[205]

Under the Seljuks, while the military personnel controlled certain lands through the *iqta* system, the ulema, who taught in madrasas, began to benefit from some other lands through the waqf system. Moreover, a number of ulema served and were paid as state servants. These material incentives encouraged

---

[200] Arjomand 1999, 270; Bulliet 1972, 73–4.

[201] Ephrat 2000, esp. 28–9 (figure 1.1). See also Ahmed 2003, 179–81; El-Hibri 2002, 737–8.

[202] Shatzmiller 1993, 312.

[203] Cahen 1953, 40. Under the Seljuk Empire, *iqta*s were granted not only to military personnel but also to some royal family members, court bureaucrats, and other civil servants. Lambton 1988, 103–11; Lambton 1965, 369–73. See also Safi 2006, 87–90.

[204] For Hodgson (1974b, 49), the assignment of land revenues directly to military officers reflected the military characteristic of Buyid rule and then Seljuk rule. In the same vein, Lambton (1965, 373) observes the "militarization of the fiscal administration" in the Seljuk period.

[205] Cahen 1953, 44–8; Lambton 1965, 373–6.

the ulema to legitimize the new economic order based on *iqta*s. Through Nizam al-Mulk's policies on madrasas, waqfs, and *iqta*s, the ulema and the Seljuk military state formed an alliance.[206]

According to Lapidus, the formation of the ulema–state alliance in the Seljuk period had a long-lasting impact on the Muslim world: "The Saljuq system of relations between '*ulama*' and the state worked out in Baghdad and Iran, was carried westward by the Saljuq conquests to Syria and Egypt, and was later adopted by the Ottoman Empire in Anatolia, the Balkans and the western parts of the Fertile Crescent. A similar system was constructed by the Safavids in Iran."[207] The long-lasting Seljuk impact on Muslims in subsequent centuries also had an ideational dimension, manifested most powerfully in the work of Ghazali.

GHAZALI AND THE DECLINE THESIS

Ghazali's (1058–1111) relations with Seljuk authorities were complex and inconsistent. At first, he established strong personal and political connections with Seljuk viziers, members of the Seljuk dynasty, and Abbasid caliphs. Ghazali was educated in Nishapur as a student of Juwayni. Later, he spent several years in Nizam al-Mulk's court. In 1091, Nizam al-Mulk appointed him to a prestigious teaching position in Baghdad.[208] There, Caliph Mustazhir asked Ghazali to criticize the Ismaili Shii notion of the infallible imam. As Ghazali revealed in his autobiography: "I received a definite command from His Majesty the Caliph to write a book showing what their [Ismaili] religious system really is."[209] In response, he wrote *The Infamies of the Batinites and the Virtues of the Mustazhirites*, which refers to the caliph's name in its title.[210]

In late 1095, the second period of his life began: Ghazali resigned from the madrasa position, adopted a Sufi lifestyle, and traveled through many cities. Ghazali regretted his services to state authorities during this "mid-life crisis." He visited the tomb of Abraham in Hebron and vowed there never again "to go to any ruler, to take a ruler's money, or to engage in one of his public disputations."[211] In *The Revival of the Religious Sciences*, Ghazali urged the ulema to avoid close connections with rulers and emphasized that rulers mostly gained wealth unlawfully through unjust taxes, confiscated properties, and bribes.[212] He demanded that the ulema and all other Muslims refrain

---

[206] Hodgson 1974b, 46, 51–2; Safi 2006, 90.   [207] Lapidus 1996, 16.

[208] Laoust, 1970, ch. 1; Ormsby 2007, ch. 1; Garden 2014, 17–29.

[209] Al-Ghazali 1953 [c. 1108], 44. See also al-Ghazali 1999 [c. 1108], 71.

[210] Al-Ghazali 1999 [1095]. See also Mitha 2001.   [211] Quoted in Griffel 2009, 44.

[212] Al-Ghazali 2015 [c. 1097], 199–203; al-Ghazali 1962 [c. 1097], 172–6; al-Ghazali 2014 [c. 1097], 189.

from social interactions with despotic rulers.[213] Ghazali's journeys included Damascus, Jerusalem, and Mecca-Medina and took about one and a half years. Then he moved to his birthplace, Tus, in eastern Iran, where he founded and taught in a private madrasa and a Sufi lodge (*khanqah*) for about nine more years.[214]

Toward the end of his life, however, Ghazali ended his mystical seclusion and returned to teaching in a Nizamiyya madrasa in Nishapur. Again in his autobiography, Ghazali explains that a major incentive for his decision to return to public life came from a vizier. He writes, "God most high determined Himself to stir up the impulse of the sovereign of the time ... [who] gave me strict orders to hasten to Nishapur."[215] Ghazali taught there for few years.[216] The ups and downs of Ghazali's relations with political authorities support my argument that the ulema–state alliance was based on a historical construction and was not an essential principle of Islam.

Ghazali made the most influential contribution to the formation of Sunni orthodoxy by effectively attacking the "outsiders" of the orthodoxy (Shiis, Mutazilis, and philosophers),[217] as well as helping unite the "insiders" (Asharis, Shafis, Hanbalis, Hanafis, and Malikis). Moreover, his decision to become a Sufi and his related writings brought Sufism from the periphery to the center of Sunni Islam. Thus, Ghazali played a leading role in the eleventh-century construction of Sunni Islam and its persistence until the present. Some scholars have even defined him as the most influential figure in Islam after the Prophet Muhammad.[218]

The Decline Thesis

Since the late nineteenth century, there has been a debate about the intellectual decline in Muslim lands and Ghazali's role in it. One group of scholars accepts that Muslims have experienced an intellectual decline since the eleventh century.[219] These scholars generally identify Nizamiyya madrasas, in terms of their focus on Islamic scholarship and exclusion of philosophy, as the reason for this decline.[220] Although I agree with this group of scholars that the eleventh century was a critical juncture in Muslims' intellectual slowdown and that the

[213] Al-Ghazali 2014 [c. 1097], 201–37; Gazali 1974b [c. 1097], 351–76.
[214] Griffel 2009, xii, 51.
[215] Al-Ghazali 1953 [c. 1108], 74. See also al-Ghazali 1999 [c. 1108], 91.
[216] Hourani 1984, 290–1.
[217] In *The Incoherence of the Philosophers*, Ghazali (2000 [1095]) criticizes twenty main ideas of philosophers and Mutazili theologians by categorizing seventeen of them as heretical innovations and three of them as apostasy.
[218] Watt 1953, 14; McCarthy 1999, 12; Yaqub 2013, xvii; Güngör 1982, 79.
[219] Sarton 1927, 738; Meyerhof 2005 [1932], 311, 337, 345.
[220] Makdisi 1981, 10, 283; Starr 2013, 404–7, 532.

madrasas' prioritization of Islamic studies within the "epistemological hierarchy" led to serious problems, I still have two main disagreements with them.

First, I present the madrasa curricula as a reflection of the ideational and
institutional hegemony of the ulema–state alliance, rather than as an independent cause of Muslim intellectual decline. Second, despite the transformations
in the eleventh century, Muslim scientific and philosophical productions
continued until the mid-seventeenth century, albeit with a slowing pace.
Neither the ulema–state alliance nor its anti-philosophical attitude quickly
dominated all Muslim lands; there were episodes of crisis for this alliance, as
well as exceptional rulers who patronized scientists and philosophers.

In contrast, a second group of scholars has criticized the decline thesis,
pointing to examples of Muslims' scientific and philosophical works after the
eleventh century.[221] Sonja Brentjes demonstrates that books on astronomy and
medicine were taught in some madrasas and existed in libraries in such cities as
Baghdad, Cairo, Damascus, and Sivas in the fourteenth century and even
later.[222] Ahmed Dallal is also critical of the decline thesis. He raises a normative
concern: "The fundamental assumption of histories of decline is that the
eventual waning of scientific activity resulted from the intrinsic, culturally
predetermined disposition of the Islamic sciences, not from specific historical
developments."[223] I agree with Brentjes and will show in the following chapters
the continuing Muslim scholarly production in their observatories and
hospitals. Additionally, in the same vein as Dallal, this chapter has already
documented that there was no cultural predetermination for the decline of
Muslims' scholarly achievement. Far from being essential elements of Islam,
anti-scientific and anti-philosophical attitudes among Muslims were historically
constructed.[224]

Beyond these two points, however, I find the second group's rejection of
the decline thesis unconvincing. In fact, their own data generally show a
slowing of Muslim scholarship. While showing that philosophy and the
natural sciences were not removed from madrasas, Brentjes still acknowledges that madrasa scholars who studied philosophy and the natural sciences adopted "the teaching methods and values of the religious disciplines –
memorizing, authority-centered learning versus disciplinary study, and fitting
into teachers' chains." She also stresses that this shift entailed a weakening
of specialization and "a decrease in complexity."[225] These phrases

---

[221] Saliba 2007, 20–5, 237–9; Endress 2006, 382–3; Adamson 2016, 301, 421. For my critique of
Gutas (1998, 2014) and El-Rouayheb (2010, 2015), see Chapter 6.

[222] Brentjes 2011, 141. See also Hirschler 2016, 2, 27, 106.   [223] Dallal 2010, 151.

[224] Thus, I disagree with John Saunders's (1963, 719) essentialist explanation: "Islam, from the
first an essentially religious culture, turned back to its origins; the Hellenic element was
gradually extruded ... and profane science, which had always operated on the fringe and had
never really cleared itself of the charge of impiety, was quietly abandoned as 'un-Muslim.'"

[225] Brentjes 2011, 142–4.

unintentionally imply the gradual waning of scientific creativity in the post-eleventh-century Muslim world. Similarly, Henry Corbin's *History of Islamic Philosophy*, which argues that a decline in Muslim philosophy did not occur, inadvertently confirms that early Islamic history was much more intellectually vibrant. In the first 350 pages, his book elaborates how philosophy flourished in Muslim lands between the seventh and twelfth centuries. In contrast, it devotes only 150 pages to philosophical production between the thirteenth and nineteenth centuries.[226] One normally would expect the opposite, because after 1200, Muslims substantially expanded their lands and population through both conquests and conversion, and had better research opportunities provided by their ancestors and rising European competitors.

Abdelhamid Sabra – who does not fit neatly into either group of scholars – is more explicit on this point. For him, although the natural sciences were excluded from the official madrasa curriculum, some members of the ulema continued to study them. After the eleventh century, the natural sciences did not disappear, but "the philosopher-physician (represented by Razi [d. 925]) was replaced by the jurist-physician (represented by Ibn al-Nafis [d. 1288]) ... and the astronomer-astrologer by the *muwaqqit* [mosque's timekeeper]."[227] Nonetheless, Sabra still regards this transformation as detrimental for the long-term status of the natural sciences. He holds the orthodox ideas, especially those of Ghazali, responsible for trivializing non-religious scholarship. The orthodox approach, according to Sabra, granted only a limited space to logic, mathematics, astronomy, and medicine.[228] In short, as Sabra rightly stresses, the slowing pace of Muslim intellectual production was due not to a sudden exclusion of the natural sciences but rather to their long-term marginalization.[229]

The decline in creativity was also visible in Islamic scholarship. Most great scholars of Islamic theology and jurisprudence lived before the end of the eleventh century. Some of them lived between the twelfth and fourteenth centuries. From the fifteenth century to the present, it has truly been rare to see an Islamic scholar make original contributions to these fields.[230]

George Sarton's three-volume analysis is helpful for understanding the historical status of Muslim scholarship in relative terms. "From the second half of the eighth to the end of the eleventh century," according to Sarton, "Arabic was the scientific, the progressive language of mankind."[231] He categorizes

---

[226] Corbin 1986.   [227] Sabra 1987, 237. For Ibn al Nafis, see Chapter 5.
[228] Sabra 1987, 238–42.
[229] In addition to Sabra, I also find Aydın Sayılı's (1960, 408–12) nuanced approach persuasive. Sayılı explains how astronomical scholarship continued in Muslim lands after the eleventh century; however, he also stresses that scientific development gradually faded during that period.
[230] See Chapters 5–7.   [231] Sarton 1927, 17; also 543. See also Sarton 1931, 1.

pre-modern science history by giving the name of an eminent scholar of the world to each half-century. From the second half of the eighth century to the second half of the eleventh, the names he chose – Jabir, Khwarazmi, Razi, Masudi, Abu al-Wafa, Biruni, and Omar Khayyam, respectively – are all from Muslim lands.[232] Later, in Sarton's words, Muslims' "golden age" of and "monopoly" on sciences ended.[233]

If so, the question would be: Why did Muslims begin to lose intellectual dynamism and creativity starting with the end of the eleventh century? One answer has to do with the rise of the Turkish dynasties, especially the Seljuks, as the defenders of Sunni orthodoxy. This answer has two main problems. First, although the Seljuk rulers were Turkish, many other promoters of Sunni orthodoxy were non-Turks, such as caliphs Qadir and Qaim, who were Arab, and Nizam al-Mulk and Ghazali, who were Persian.[234] It is also possible to find many Turks who defended Shii Islam and philosophy. The Safavids, who established Twelver Shiism in Iran in the sixteenth century, were a Turkish dynasty. Farabi arguably was a Turk as well.[235] Second, the Seljuk sultans, in various cases, supported philosophers and scientists. With the help of Nizam al-Mulk, Malikshah (r. 1072–92) got "the most important observatory of the eleventh century" built in Isfahan.[236] The distinguished astronomers who worked there included Omar Khayyam (1048–1131), who was a leading mathematician and a renowned poet. Following Malikshah's request, Omar Khayyam and his team reformed the solar calendar; their product "was extraordinarily accurate, probably more so than our own [Gregorian] calendar."[237] In sum, it is unconvincing to attribute the fading of Muslims' intellectual dynamism to simply the rise of Turks.

---

[232] Sarton 1927, x–xi.

[233] Sarton 1927, 738. Sarton (1931, xvi, xxviii; 1947, xvii, xxvi) characterizes each half-century in the twelfth, thirteenth, and fourteenth centuries with the names of three scholars: one Muslim, one Jewish, and one Christian. The Muslim scholars are Ibn Zuhr, Ibn Rushd, Ibn Baitar, Qutb al-din al-Shirazi, Abu al-Fida, and Ibn Khaldun, respectively. The Jewish scholars are Abraham Ibn Ezra, Maimonides, Jacob Anatoli, Jacob ben Machir ibn Tibbon, Levi ben Gerson, and Hasdai Crescas – the first and second lived in Muslim lands, while the third and fourth translated Arabic works to Hebrew. The Christian scholars are William of Conches, Gerard Cremona, Robert Grosseteste, Roger Bacon, William of Occam, and Geoffrey Chaucer.

[234] Qaim was a Hanbali supporter. He asked Tughrul Bey to fight dissenting groups, including Shiis, Mutazilis, Asharis, and "the well-to-do merchants who used to encourage philosophic learning." Schwarz 2002, 595.

[235] Ali 2012 [1902], 427–8; Hodgson 1974a, 433; Khalidi 2005, xiv; Rosenthal 1958, 271n1. For Gutas (2012), "we do not have sufficient evidence to decide" Farabi's ethnic origin. Some important eleventh-century Karakhanid litterateurs were uncontestably Turkish. Mahmud of Kashgar (1986 [1077]) wrote the first Turkish-Arabic dictionary, which includes proverbs, poems, and a map of Turkic peoples. The map unprecedentedly shows Japan. Tekeli 1985. Yusuf Has Hacib of Balasagun (1974 [1070]) wrote an early example of the Muslim advice literature.

[236] Sayılı 1960, 160–1. See also Dallal 2010, 24.   [237] Sarton 1927, 740; also 759–61.

Ghazali and the Decline

A more widespread explanation of Muslim intellectual fading refers to the negative role of Ghazali.[238] In *Lost Enlightenment*, Starr argues that Ghazali contributed to the intellectual decline of Central Asia (and eastern Iran) by attacking philosophers and promoting Sufism.[239] Ghazali, according to Starr, enforced an epistemological hierarchy that reduced "the rational intellect ... to a subordinate status from which it was neither able nor allowed to challenge knowledge gained through mystical intuition and tradition."[240]

Going beyond Central Asia, Ziauddin Sardar points his finger at Ghazali for a broader negative influence: "[T]here is little doubt that al-Ghazzali made a major contribution to the downward spiral of Muslim civilization."[241] Randall Collins also holds Ghazali responsible for the marginalization of philosophy. For him, Ghazali combined theology, scriptural tradition, logic, and Sufism, and this combination became the "orthodox culture of Islam." This combination particularly influenced madrasas: "Only logic, split off from philosophy, is allowed into the *madrasas'* curriculum; but on its own it survives only as a stagnant scholasticism."[242]

On the one hand, I agree with Ghazali's critics on two main issues. First, Ghazali's Ashari occasionalism, which argues that God creates everything at every moment, has had many problematic implications.[243] In *The Incoherence of the Philosophers*, Ghazali discusses the burning of cotton in contact with fire. He accepts the possibility of both (1) the contact of cotton with fire without the end-result of burning and (2) the cotton's burning without contact with fire. He concludes: "The one who enacts the burning by creating blackness in the cotton ... is God, either through the mediation of His angels or without mediation."[244] Ontologically, to accept or reject this approach is a personal choice. Yet epistemologically, if this becomes the dominant approach, it would definitely hinder scientific development. Moreover, if it becomes the dominant religious perspective, it could also make people fatalistic and unable to understand cause-and-effect relations in their daily lives. In addition to his rejection of causality, Ghazali presents non-religious sciences as a potential threat to faith and philosophers as almost categorically irreligious: "[E]very student of mathematics admires its precision ... This leads him to believe in the philosophers ... [and] he becomes an unbeliever merely by accepting them as authorities." Such a student could say: "If religion were true, it would not have escaped the notice of these men since they are so precise in this

[238] Ali 2012 [1902], 428–9; al-Jabri 2011 [1984], 393–403.
[239] Starr 2013, 512, 522. See also Starr 2009, 41.   [240] Starr 2013, 534.
[241] Sardar 2013, 17.   [242] Collins 2000, 452–3 (see figure 9.1).
[243] According to Fazlur Rahman (1982, 27), Ghazali's support for Ashari theology was "crucial for its spread and ultimate dominance as the creed of the vast majority of Sunni Islam."
[244] Al-Ghazali 2000 [1095], 167; also 166–77.

science."[245] These ideas would discourage those who take them seriously from studying non-religious sciences.

Second, Ghazali's Sufi epistemology has also had complicated effects. Both in his multivolume *Revival* (which has been one of the most widely read works on Islam) and in his much shorter but famous autobiography – *Deliverance from Error* – Ghazali upholds mystical insights and undermines observation as a source of knowledge.[246] In the *Deliverance*, Ghazali explains two reasons why he ended his ascetic isolation and returned to teach in Nishapur. One reason was the order of a vizier as already noted, while the other one was purely mystical: "numerous visions of good men" assured him that his return was determined by God, who "promised to revive His religion at the beginning of each century."[247] Based on some dreams of others, Ghazali portrays himself as the "centennial renewer" of Islam in the sixth Muslim century. This mystical emphasis in Ghazali's ideas and life story could have hindered the rationality of his followers.

On the other hand, the argument that Ghazali was the main cause of Muslims' intellectual stagnation has many weaknesses. Ghazali was a genius with complex and sometimes inconsistent ideas. His *The Niche of Lights* includes certain ideas, such as the recognition of intermediary causes, which contradict Ashari occasionalism.[248] Similarly, his attitude toward the natural sciences is not always negative. Following the previously quoted passage about mathematics, Ghazali warns against a kind of Muslim who "thinks that religion must be defended by rejecting every science connected with the philosophers." Such Muslims would misrepresent Islam as if it "is based on ignorance."[249] In the same vein, despite his emphasis on mysticism, Ghazali strongly appreciates human intellect as the first thing created by and the most honorable creation of God.[250]

Ghazali's views on jurisprudence are also complex. Despite upholding orthodox Sunni jurisprudence, Ghazali also promoted the idea of the five "higher objectives" of Islamic law, which has been a major source of legal creativity.[251] Moreover, Ghazali's Sufi perspective in the *Revival* and elsewhere contains a

---

[245] Al-Ghazali 1953 [c. 1108], 33; also 40. See also al-Ghazali 1999 [c. 1108], 63; also 68.

[246] Gazali 1974a [c. 1097]; al-Ghazali 1953 [c. 1108].

[247] Al-Ghazali 1953 [c. 1108], 75. See also al-Ghazali 1999 [c. 1108], 92.

[248] Al-Ghazali 1998 [c. 1098–1105], 44–54. For an analysis of the *Niche*, see Griffel 2009, 179, 264–74. For another alternative interpretation of Ghazali's views on causality, see Ormsby 2007, 80–6.

[249] Al-Ghazali 1953 [c. 1108], 34. See also al-Ghazali 1999 [c. 1108], 64.

[250] Al-Ghazali 2015 [c. 1097], 249, 256; al-Ghazali 1962 [c. 1097], 214, 227; Gazali 1974a [c. 1097], 211, 224.

[251] According to Hamza Yusuf Hanson (2015, xxiv), defenders of a literalist understanding of Islamic law criticize Ghazali, because he promoted Sufism, logic as a pedagogical tool, and a spirit-of-the-law approach by emphasizing the five higher objectives of Islamic law. For these objectives, see the Introduction and Chapter 5.

significant critique of legal formalism.[252] In short, Ghazali could have been interpreted in a different way on various issues.[253]

The question is then: Why have more orthodox interpretations of Ghazali, rather than the alternative interpretations, become dominant? Moreover, we should ask: Why did the ideas of Ghazali become so influential, instead of those of others who were more sympathetic to philosophy and the natural sciences? Answering both questions requires an analysis of power relations. Ghazali and the Nizamiyya madrasas were part of a powerful, broad coalition, which included various other actors and institutions. I call this coalition the alliance between the orthodox Sunni ulema and the military state. Ghazali both contributed to this alliance and received its support.

The main contribution of Ghazali to the ulema–state alliance was his theoretical role in the formation of Sunni orthodoxy. By declaring philosophers with certain views apostates to be killed, Ghazali made the "orthodox views" almost unquestionable. Ghazali was not an inventor of the idea of declaring a self-avowed Muslim as apostate, but as a leading scholar, he helped legitimize it. Ghazali presents his views on this issue with a hypothetical question at the very beginning of the *Incoherence*'s conclusion:

> If someone says: "You have explained the doctrines of these [philosophers]; do you then say conclusively that they are *infidels* and that *the killing of those who uphold their beliefs is obligatory*?" we say: Pronouncing them infidels is necessary in three questions. One of them is the question of the world's pre-eternity and their statement that all substances are pre-eternal. The second is their statement that God's knowledge does not encompass the temporal particulars among individual [existents]. The third is their denial of the resurrection of bodies and their assembly at the day of judgment.[254]

This passage pronounces the philosophers (and their followers) who hold certain ideas (defining the world as eternal, arguing that God's knowledge encompasses only the universals, and/or describing the hereafter as only a spiritual life) infidels punishable by death. In the *Moderation*, Ghazali elaborated the issue of infidelity by stating that an infidel would face not only execution but also confiscation of properties. Because an infidel's "life and property are not inviolable," other persons "may spill his blood and take his property."[255] In the *Infamies*, he declared Ismaili Shiis infidels and specified similar punishments for them.[256]

Toward the end of his life, Ghazali himself was accused of being an apostate for "calling God the 'true light'" in his *Niche* and for certain views in his Sufi-oriented *Revival*.[257] In this context, Ghazali wrote *The Decisive*

[252] Al-Ghazali 2015 [c. 1097], esp. 87–90. For Ghazali's contradictory statements about the value of jurisprudence, see Rahman 2000, 119–24.
[253] See Moosa 2005, esp. 138, 182–9.
[254] Al-Ghazali 2000 [1095], 226 (emphases added). See also Gazali 2014 [1095], 225.
[255] Al-Ghazali 2013 [1095], 241.   [256] Al-Ghazali 1999 [1095], 228–31.
[257] Griffel 2009, 54, 105.

Criterion for Distinguishing Islam from Masked Infidelity, where he revised some of his previous views and asked Muslims to be very careful before declaring someone apostate.[258] Nonetheless, he continued to define "most of the philosophers" as unbelievers.[259] Later, in his autobiography, Ghazali explicitly referred to Ibn Sina and Farabi as such: "We must ... reckon as unbelievers both these philosophers [Socrates, Plato, and Aristotle] themselves and their followers among the Islamic philosophers, such as Ibn Sina, al-Farabi, and others."[260]

At the beginning of the eleventh century, caliphs Qadir and Qaim declared various groups, including Mutazilis and Shiis, apostates to be killed. At the end of the century, Ghazali deployed this approach against some philosophers and Ismaili Shii, but not Mutazilis.[261] Frank Griffel explains that the idea of killing self-defined Muslims based on the charge of apostasy became established during the eleventh century.[262] Previously, the prevailing legal view was that a Muslim would not be killed as long as he did not explicitly and publicly renounce Islam.[263]

Ghazali's views on apostasy had practical consequences. Omid Safi holds Ghazali's intellectual legacy responsible for the execution of Ayn al-Qudat (1098–1131), a scholar and Sufi poet.[264] Ayn al-Qudat was charged with defending the Ismaili creed and two heterodox philosophical views, all of which Ghazali defined as apostasy and punishable by death. Ayn al-Qudat denied these charges but was still executed.[265] This episode is an example of "the persecuting spirit that al-Ghazali created by adding a legal judgment to his epistemological discussion."[266]

In sum, Ghazali's main negative role in Muslims' intellectual life concerns not the details of his particular views but his contributions to the consolidation of the ulema–state alliance. Particularly, the establishment of the idea of declaring those having heterodox views apostates became a crucial pillar of the

---

[258] Al-Ghazali 2002 [c. 1105], 89, 115. In this book, Ghazali (2002 [c. 1105], 126) also makes a tolerant statement about the salvation of Byzantine Christians: "God willing, most of the Christians of Byzantium ... will be covered by God's mercy." He elaborates that there were those who "knew the name 'Muhammad,' but nothing of his character and attributes. Instead, all they heard since childhood was that some arch-liar carrying the name 'Muhammad' claimed to be a prophet ... This group, in my opinion, is [excused] ... Even though they heard his name, they heard the opposite of what his true attributes were. And this does not provide enough incentive to compel them to investigate (his true status)."

[259] Al-Ghazali 2002 [c. 1105], 110.

[260] Al-Ghazali 1953 [c. 1108], 32. See also al-Ghazali 1999 [c. 1108], 62–3.

[261] Ghazali defined Mutazilis as "heretical innovators," but not infidels. Al-Ghazali 2000 [1095], 226–7; al-Ghazali 2013 [1095], 245–6; al-Ghazali 2002 [c. 1105], 111, 114.

[262] "During the middle of the eleventh century, scholars from all schools of law argued that in the case of the political agents of the Isma'ili counter-caliphate, no *istitaba* [invitation to repent] should be granted and they could be killed as apostates." Griffel 2007, 132.

[263] Griffel 2009, 104.   [264] Safi 2006, 196.   [265] Safi 2006, ch. 6; Griffel 2009, 81–7.

[266] Griffel 2009, 86.

ulema–state alliance, in terms of suppressing religious and political opponents. This factor worsened the conditions of intellectual creativity. Ghazali himself was a product of an era of Muslim intellectual dynamism. Later on, critical thinking on religious and metaphysical issues was so discouraged that Islamic civilization rarely produced Islamic scholars and philosophers of the caliber of Ghazali and Ibn Sina again.

As I explained previously, Ghazali's relations with political authorities were inconsistent. Nevertheless, Ghazali consistently defended the idea of the religion-state alliance. As a politically engaged scholar in Baghdad, he wrote in the *Moderation*:[267] "[I]t has been said that religion and sultan are twins, and also that religion is a foundation and the sultan is a guard: that which has no foundation collapses and that which has no guard is lost."[268] After having avoided politics and becoming a Sufi, he repeated the same idea in the *Revival*: "[T]he state and religion are twins. Religion is the foundation while the state is the guard. That which has no foundation will certainly crumble and that which has no guard is lost."[269] Ghazali's views about religion-state alliance were part of the general trend of his time. This trend will be explored in the next section.

THE SASANIAN INFLUENCE ON MUSLIM POLITICAL THOUGHT

On ethical and political philosophy, translations of works by Greek philosophers, especially Aristotle (e.g., the *Nicomachean Ethics*) and Plato (e.g., the *Republic*), deeply influenced Muslim philosophers. On household management, Muslim philosophers referred to a short treatise by Bryson – a Greek author living in first-century Rome.[270] Bryson's ideas on the economy, a wife's role in running the household, and ways of educating boys were quoted by Miskawayh, Ibn Sina, Dimasqhi, and, later, Tusi.[271]

The Sasanian political tradition had even a deeper impact on Muslim political thought for three main reasons. First, Muslims conquered only some parts of the Byzantine lands, whereas they conquered the entire Sasanian Empire. While the Greek elite left Syria and Egypt, the Persian elite did not have "an empire to go to,"[272] and thus they mostly integrated into and influenced Muslim societies. Second, in comparison to Persians, the populations of Syria and Egypt had more linguistic and sectarian diversity; therefore,

---

[267] Unlike Mawardi and Ibn Taymiyya, Ghazali did not write a specific book on the caliphate (or sharia politics). Ghazali revealed his views on this subject primarily in some chapters of the *Infamies* (1999 [1095], 234–44) and the *Moderation* (2013 [1095], 229–40). See also Laoust, 1970, ch. 2; Said 2013, ch. 6; Hillenbrand 1988.
[268] Al-Ghazali 2013 [1095], 231.
[269] Al-Ghazali 1962 [c. 1097], 33–4. See also Gazali 1974a [c. 1097], 51.
[270] Bryson 2013 [c. 1st century], 5–24.
[271] Swain 2013, esp. 83–108, 246–56, 349–63, 402–11; Miskawayh 1968 [c. 1030], 50–5; Tusi 1964 [c. 1235], 155.
[272] Crone 2004, 165.

while the former effectively handed down the Sasanian political tradition to Muslims, the latter did not do the same for the Byzantine political tradition.[273]

Third, Islamic scholars who attacked Greek philosophy were more open to embracing Sasanian ideas, probably because the former had a strong metaphysical component, while the latter focused on Iranian experience in governance. Especially on matters of religion-state relations, the ulema quoted Sasanian maxims. The origin of Ghazali's above-quoted statement about religion–state brotherhood was a Sasanian text[274] – the so-called Testament of Ardashir I (r. 224–42), the founding Sasanian king. Ardashir advises his followers: "Know that royal authority and religion are twins, one of which can not exist without the other, because religion is the foundation of royal authority and royal authority is the guard of religion ... Anything that is not guarded perishes and anything that does not have a foundation collapses."[275]

Living a century after Ghazali, Fakhr al-Din al-Razi has been regarded as the most prominent Islamic scholar of his time. According to Nasrin Askari, Razi quotes "the maxim 'kingship and religion are twin brothers' and attributes it to the prophet Muhammad." This is "yet another example of attributing ancient Persian maxims to Muslim religious figures, thereby granting them credibility."[276]

In early Islamic history, "Ardashir's testament was a well-known Arabic work on statecraft," which was cited by many authors.[277] In addition to the Testament, similar advice could also be found in another Sasanian text – the Letter of Tansar (who was a Zoroastrian priest and advisor to Ardashir). The Letter stresses, "Church and State were born of the one womb, joined together and never to be sundered."[278] Both the Testament and the Letter[279] were translated into Arabic several times, beginning probably as early as the late Umayyad period.[280]

---

[273] Wiet 1953, 64; Marlow 1997, 65.

[274] Sasanian texts were written in Pahlavi scripts and Middle Persian language.

[275] "Le Testament d'Ardasir" 1966 [n.a.], 49, 62. See also Maçoudi 1863 [947], 162.

[276] Askari 2016, 208, 208n178. Askari cites Fakhr al-Din al-Razi, *Jami'al-'ulum: Sittini*, ed. Sayyid 'Ali Al-i Daud (Tehran, 2003), 489–90.

[277] Askari 2016, 153.   [278] *The Letter of Tansar* 1968 [n.a.], 33–4.

[279] Scholars have disagreed over whether the Testament and the Letter were originally written in the early (i.e., third-century) Sasanian period and then revised three centuries later, or whether they were fabricated in the late (i.e., sixth-century) Sasanian period. Boyce 1968, 11–23; Bier 1993, 178–85; Askari 2016, 85, 159–60; Dignas and Winter 2007, 55n13, 211. It is possible that the idea of state–religion brotherhood was more propaganda or an idealization of earlier times than a true reflection of the Sasanian history. However, such qualifications would not weaken the concept's impact on Muslim political thought.

[280] These translations had "a considerable circulation." Marlow 1997, 73. Ibn al-Muqaffa (c. 723–760) translated the Letter into Arabic. Boyce 1968, 2. He was "a convert from Zoroastrianism" and "the best known early advocate of caesaropapism." Bulliet 1979, 38.

Early Muslim governmental institutions were influenced by both Byzantine and Sasanian precedents.[281] Muslims minted imitations of Byzantine coins in Syria[282] and Sasanian coins in Iraq[283] until the Umayyads began minting fully original coins at the end of the seventh century.[284] Under the Abbasids, the capital moved from Damascus to Bagdad (which was founded near the former Sasanian capital), and the Sasanian influence strengthened.[285]

Unlike the Umayyads, who had favored Arabs, the Abbasids worked to integrate non-Arabs, especially Persians, into the administration.[286] Bulliet estimates the percentage of Iran's indigenous population converting to Islam as only 8 percent at the end of the ninety-year Umayyad rule, whereas it increased to 40 percent in the first seventy years of the Abbasid rule and then to 80 percent under the Iranian dynasties of Tahirids, Saffarids, Samanids, and Buyids.[287] While Greek philosophy had been influential only through translations into Arabic, under these dynasties Persian gradually gained the status of a dominant language of literature and bureaucracy.[288] Subsequently, the Ghaznavids and the Seljuks used Persian as an official language and employed Persian bureaucrats in their governments.[289]

In the eleventh century, a symbol of the rising status of the Persian language was Firdawsi's (c. 935–1020) *Book of Kings*, which narrates the history of the Persian kings. It quotes the Testament of Ardashir, especially its "most prominent theme . . ., the idea of the union of kingship and religion":[290]

> No religion survives without the royal throne,
> Nor any kingship lasts without religion.
> When the king is the protector of religion,
> Do not call these two other than brothers.[291]

In the eleventh century and afterward, a major source of Sasanian political tradition's influence on Muslim political thought was the advice literature

---

[281] Lapidus 2002, 51, 76.   [282] Grabar 1987, 89–90.

[283] These Muslim imitation coins included the Sasanian pattern of the crescent and star, and even profiles of Sasanian kings. Morony 1984, 38–51, esp. 44–5. See also al-Azmeh 1997, 68.

[284] In around 697, the Umayyads began minting fully novel (Calip Abd al-Malik's) silver and gold coins, which included Quranic phrases, instead of images of leaders. Grabar 1987, 90–1, figure 20. See also Morony 1984, 50.

[285] Wiet 1953, 64–70.

[286] Ibrahim 1994, 63–6. According to Bulliet (1979, 39), the Sasanian tradition of religious hierarchy could be a reason for Persian converts' appeal to Shii Islam "with its rigid authority structure based upon the theory of the Imamate" or to the orthodox hierarchy based upon "the later emergence of the Muslim religious scholars, the ulama, as a quasi-priestly class."

[287] He estimates that conversion in Iraq, Syria, Egypt, and Tunisia reached the 80-percent conversion rate a century after Iran did. Bulliet 1979, 43–7, 81–3, 97, 102–3, 108–11, 124. "[E]arly conversion seems to have greatly enhanced the importance of Iran in the ninth, tenth, and eleventh centuries." Bulliet 1979, 130.

[288] Bulliet 1979, 47–9.   [289] Arjomand 2017, 69–79.   [290] Askari 2016, 159.

[291] Quoted in Askari 2016, 179; also 52.

(also known "mirrors for princes"). Several mirrors for princes were written (generally in Persian) by Muslim authors and promoted two Sasanian notions. One was the idea of religion–state brotherhood.[292] Many mirrors emphasized this idea with the maxim "religion and kingship are twins."[293] The other was the Sasanian hierarchical model of social stratification, which undermined the status of merchants. In the words of Marlow, merchants were despised in the "Sasanian model of socio-political hierarchy," given the "Iranian contempt for commercial activity."[294] Certain post-tenth-century Muslim mirrors promoted Sasanian models of four-fold social stratification,[295] in which the merchants had the lowest status, under priests, soldiers, cultivators, and artisans.[296]

Nizam al-Mulk's *Book of Government*[297] was a very influential mirror. It quotes several Sasanian maxims, including the famous one – "kingship and religion are like two brothers."[298] According to Marlow, Nizam al-Mulk's book was heavily influenced by Sasanian political thought, as reflected in "its strong attachment to hierarchy, the importance it ascribes to noble birth, its ideal of the king who keeps everyone in his proper place," and its detestation of "social mobility."[299]

The Sasanian influence on Muslim political thought shows once again that medieval Muslim ideas, even those of eminent Sunni ulema and officials, were influenced by pre-Islamic traditions. The Sasanian influence on notions of religion–state brotherhood and social hierarchy had existed for centuries, but

[292] Zoroastrianism "was the state religion of the Sasanian empire" and thus "the priestly hierarchy paralleled its administrative system." The chief priest, who was appointed by the king, shaped Zoroastrian doctrine, appointed the priests, acted as the supreme judge, and helped to regulate the succession of kings. Apostasy from Zoroastrianism was punishable by death. Morony 1984, 281–2. The punishment of apostasy was similar in Byzantium, where the "punishment for conversion to Islam was death." Mez 1937, 32.
[293] Tabatabai 2013, 117–18. In one of his mirrors, Mawardi (2015 [1032–40], 358) directly refers to Ardashir while quoting this maxim. See also Marlow 2016, 192.
[294] Marlow 1997, 8, 80. Lapidus (2002, 76) also argues that under Abbasid rule, a tension existed between the hierarchical mentality of Persian bureaucrats and the more egalitarian views of Arabs.
[295] According to Marlow (1997, 147), Mawardi's *The Laws of the Ministers and the Government of the Realm* promotes a Sasanian model of four-fold stratification (nobility, religious scholars, cultivators, and craftsmen), omitting the merchants. For her, "it is apparent here as elsewhere that al-Mawardi did not perceive any deep contradiction between Sasanian and Islamic notions of political organisation." See also al-Mawardi 2015 [1032–40], 375, 385, 401, 433, 475–6.
[296] Marlow 1997, 131; Morony 1984, 297.
[297] According to Javad Tabatabai (2013, 118), Nizam al-Mulk "follows precisely the Persian theory of kingship," especially in arguing that kings are chosen by God. See Nizam al-Mulk 1978 [1086–91], 9–11. See also Askari 2016, 185–96; Lingwood 2013, 45–60.
[298] Nizam al-Mulk 1978 [1086–91], 60.
[299] Marlow 1997, 130. Part II of Ghazali's *Book of Counsel for Kings* (1964 [c. 1107]) includes several Sasanian maxims. Crone and others have claimed that part II was likely written by another author. Crone (1987, 191) defines part II as "un-Islamic" and "yet another testimony to the survival of pre-Islamic values in Seljuq Iran." See also Said 2013, 20–4; Griffel 2009, 360.

they became influential in the eleventh century because they fitted transformations occurring at that time. These ideas particularly accorded with the changing class relations – the rise of the ulema and military elite, at the expense of the philosophers and merchants.

CONCLUSION

Between the eighth and eleventh centuries merchants and scholars produced major achievements in the Muslim world. This chapter has addressed two aspects of these intellectual and economic accomplishments. First, contemporary Islamists are wrong in envisioning this flourishing as a product of an orthodox notion of Islam. Instead, Muslim accomplishments, as many other examples from throughout human history, were products of diverse groups of people with different identities. Second, those who exaggerate the intercivilizational borrowings and diversity within Muslim populations, in order to undermine Muslims' original contributions, are wrong as well. Muslims created a progressive civilization by incorporating contributions of their predecessors and their non-Muslim contemporaries, as well as by achieving their own innovations. From a comparative perspective, Muslim lands experienced a virtuous circle of intellectual and economic progress, whereas Western Europeans suffered from something like a vicious circle at that time. Western Europe had neither a philosopher like Ibn Sina nor a city like Baghdad.

Religion-state relations have been a matter of degree in Muslim and other contexts, always including exceptions, complexities, and transformations. Yet in general, Islamic scholars enjoyed and insisted on more independence from state authorities from the eighth to the mid-eleventh century, in comparison to subsequent centuries. This chapter has tried to show that the contemporary perception of Islam and state as inseparable entities is a historical construction rather than an essential part of Islam.

Negative conditions began to develop in Muslim lands in the tenth and eleventh centuries in a multidimensional manner. Diminishing agricultural revenues weakened the old economic regime. The new economic regime, based on the revenue assignments to military personnel, *iqtas*, was associated with the militarization of the economy. Meanwhile, Sunni orthodoxy was already taking shape, though its full formation would require state power. In the increasingly militarized economic system, merchants began to lose their previously central role. This marginalization meant decreasing opportunities for private funding for Islamic scholars and an incentive for them to accept state patronage. Meantime, the political expansion of Shii forces provoked a Sunni reaction. These socioeconomic, religious, and political conditions made possible the emergence of the ulema–state alliance.

Seljuk ulema and rulers took advantage of these convenient conditions in the critical juncture of the eleventh century to establish an alliance. Nizamiyya madrasas constituted the institutional symbols of this alliance. These institutions started to train the ulema in a way that they would accept service to the state. The emerging ulema–state alliance used ideational hegemony and state violence to eliminate contenders, including Mutazilis, Shiis, and philosophers. Threatened by execution in this world and eternal hellfire in the hereafter, many Muslims were discouraged from intellectual exploration and creativity outside the boundaries drawn by the ulema–state alliance.

At this point, Ghazali played an important role by declaring certain Muslims with "heterodox" beliefs infidels punishable by death. Ghazali was not the founder of Sunni orthodoxy; he followed a path already created by such predecessors as Shafii, Ibn Hanbal, Ashari, Mawardi, and Caliph Qadir. Ghazali's ideas became influential because they suited the outlook and interests of the ulema–state alliance. Similarly, certain Sasanian political ideas, especially the four-fold social stratification, which prioritized the clergy and the rulers while undermining the merchants, became effective because they suited the changing class relations, particularly in Central Asia, Iran, and Iraq.

The transformations in the eleventh century negatively affected Muslim intellectual life in the subsequent centuries. Although Muslims continued to produce scientific and philosophical works, the quantity and quality of such production declined, and eventually reached a standstill. Some revisionist historians deny such negative transformations in Muslim intellectual history. I agree that knowledge expands in a dialectical manner; thus, debates between established notions and revisionist challenges are healthy. Yet revisionism should not promote an alternative reality. It is fine to challenge the image of the Early Middle Ages in Western Europe as "dark ages," but to define it as an age of rationality and progress would be an exaggeration. Similarly, to argue that Muslim intellectual production continued after the eleventh century is accurate; but to claim that Muslim intellectual decline never occurred simply contradicts historical reality. Progressive atmospheres have been very rare in human history. Muslims had such a precious experience, at least between the ninth and eleventh centuries. Later, however, Muslims gradually lost their progressive momentum and could not regain it until the present.

Almost a millennium has passed between the eleventh century and the present. What happened during the centuries immediately after the eleventh century? Didn't Muslim merchants and (independent, dissenting, or heterodox) scholars try to reclaim their previous influence? Weren't there any major challenges to the ulema–state alliance in the twelfth, thirteenth, and fourteenth centuries? How did Europe break its vicious circle of intellectual and economic backwardness? The next chapter will search for answers to these questions.

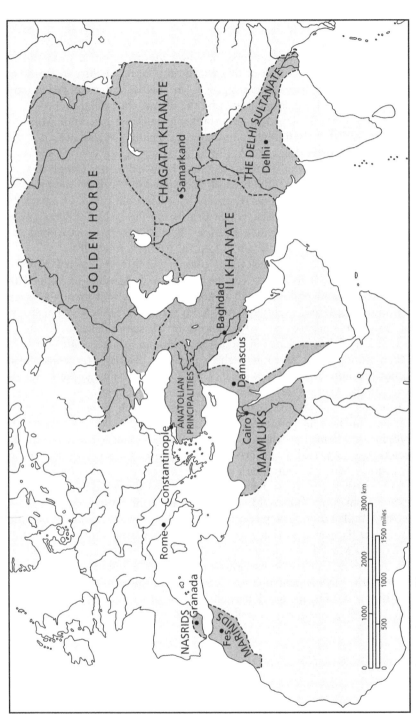

MAP 3 The Muslim World (c. 1300)

5

Crisis

The Invasions (Twelfth to Fourteenth Centuries)

From the twelfth to the fourteenth century Muslims experienced multiple and complex crises. Two military invasions, one coming from the west (Crusaders) and the other from the east (Mongols), destroyed the urban infrastructure and the public order across a vast geography. These security threats had contradictory impacts on the ulema–state alliance. On the one hand, the fall of most Muslim states, except the Ayyubids and then Mamluks in Egypt, and Berber dynasties in Morocco/Andalus, weakened this alliance. On the other hand, the perils of the Crusades and the Mongol invasions led many Muslims to seek safety from both the military state, as a possible protector against the invaders, and the ulema, as a provider of meaning to depressive conditions of invasions and massacres. Moreover, the Crusaders' emphasis on "religious war" resonated with similar sentiments on the Muslim side, further empowering the ulema–state alliance.

The invasions had also complex consequences for two other classes in Muslim lands: the merchants and philosophers. The Mongol invasion provided Muslim merchants with some opportunities by politically unifying Eurasia under the so-called Pax Mongolica. The Mongols also made some contributions to the natural sciences, for example, by patronizing the observatory in Maragha (Azerbaijan). Nonetheless, in general, both the Crusader and the Mongol invasions led to a deterioration of mercantile and scholarly activities in many Muslim cities. The Mongol invasions were particularly damaging in their destruction of irrigation systems and promotion of nomadic pastoralism. In this messy context, Sufism combined with Persian literature gained popularity in most Muslim lands.

Meanwhile Western Europe was protected from such destructive invasions after the end of the Hungarian and Viking raids and, later, the halt of the Mongol invasion in Eastern Europe. In addition to an expansion of agricultural production, Western Europe witnessed the emergence of a merchant class, particularly in the Italian city-states. Additionally, the separation between the Catholic Church and royal authorities became institutionalized, leading to deeper political decentralization, and universities began to be established, further challenging the intellectual hegemony of the Catholic clergy in Western Europe. This chapter will first analyze the Muslim world and then explore these Western European transformations.

THE INVADERS

The Crusaders

In the tenth and eleventh centuries, Muslim Turks established states and conquered lands beyond the borders of the Abbasid Empire. The Karakhanid state was extended from Transoxiana to the western Tarim Basin. The Ghaznavids took Afghanistan and parts of northern India under their rule. The Seljuk Empire defeated Byzantium at the Battle of Manzikert in 1071 and opened Anatolia for settlement. Meanwhile, Western Christians also expanded their zone of influence through the conversion of Hungarians, Poles, and Vikings to Christianity.[1]

The expansion of Western Europe's military capacity and its ability to fight collectively became apparent during the Crusades, from 1095 (the beginning of the First Crusade) to 1291 (the fall of Acre, the last Crusader stronghold).[2] The Crusades coincided with rising hostility between Sunni Seljuks and Shii Fatimids, as well as the internal divisions within both polities.[3] In Europe, multiple socioeconomic and political factors laid the foundations for the Crusades.[4] Yet they could also be defined as "from the beginning, papal enterprises."[5]

The Crusaders occupied such important cities as Antioch, Edessa, Tripoli, Acre, and Jerusalem, and almost entirely blocked Muslim access to the eastern Mediterranean Sea, except Egypt. Crusaders' anti-Muslim discourse intensified calls for jihad[6] and anti-Christian sentiments[7] among Muslims. Under these circumstances, Salah al-Din Yusuf ibn Ayyub (Saladin) (r. 1174–93), who recaptured Jerusalem from the Crusaders, emerged as a military hero. Saladin

---

[1] Logan 2013, 75–82, 90, 113; Bartlett 1993, ch. 1.

[2] If Christian campaigns against the Ottomans are counted as part of the Crusades, then the Crusades continued longer, arguably until the seventeenth century. Tyerman 2006, ch. 25, esp. 825.

[3] Runciman 1951; 64–82; Gabrieli 1969, xii.

[4] Madden 2013, 5–9; Elias 2000 [1939], 216–17; Logan 2013, 110–19; Watt 1972, 55.

[5] Küng 2007, 309. Pope Gregory VII was the first pope to "be preoccupied with a plan for a great campaign eastwards." He granted those who took part in certain wars against Muslims, "for example, to reconquer Spain – 'remission' of the punishments for their sins." Küng 2007, 308. See also Lewis 1988, 98.

[6] Berkey 2003, 199–201; Hodgson 1974b, 265–8; Armstrong 2014, 216–20.

[7] Runciman 1954, 474.

also replaced Shii Fatimid rule in Egypt with a new Sunni (Ayyubid) dynasty. A few decades later, Muslims faced an even more destructive invasion, this time coming from the east.

The Mongols

Having unified the Mongols and invaded northern China, Genghis Khan (r. 1206–27) marched in 1220 against the Khwarazm Shahs, who had replaced the Seljuks in Central Asia and Iran. The Mongols massacred virtually entire populations of some Muslim cities along their path. The reported numbers of murdered people in certain cities are exaggerations.[8] Nonetheless, I will still quote them to give an idea about the levels of destruction and terror: Herat (2,400,000), Nishapur (1,747,000), Merv (1,300,000),[9] and Rayy (500,000).[10] As another hyperbolic example, in the massacre of Gurganj, each of the 50,000 Mongol soldiers was reported to have executed twenty-four men, while children and young women were taken as prisoners.[11] According to a more conservative estimate, northwestern and northeastern parts of Iran (including Nishapur) had a total population of about 2.5 million before the invasion; the Mongols destroyed or dispersed about 90 percent of this population.[12]

The Mongols defeated both Chinese and Muslim forces and perpetrated these massacres, though their army comprised only around 129,000 fighters (all cavalry), and their total population was about only 1,000,000.[13] The Khwarazm Shahs had a larger army and population. The Jin dynasty in northern China had even a larger size in terms of both army and population.[14] Nonetheless, the Mongols defeated both the Chinese and Muslim states by exploiting their internal divisions, using defected Chinese and Muslims with various skills, and continuously expanding their army with soldiers from different ethnic groups.[15] Other reasons for Mongol military triumph included Genghis's draconian military discipline, effective intelligence network, and terrorizing by ethically unconstrained use of force.[16]

Barthold reports that Genghis sent a message to the Khwarazm Shahs' ruler Muhammad, informing him that he sought peace with him and "merchants

---

[8] Bulliet estimates Nishapur's population around the year 1000, at its peak, at about 150,000 and around the year 1160 at about 25,000. Bulliet 1995a, 136, 140–1. Hence, Mongols could not have killed 1.7 million people in that city.

[9] Lambton 1988, 19–20. Gibbon (2000 [1776–88], 376) reports similar numbers and calls them exaggerated.

[10] Daya 1982 [1223], 40.   [11] Barthold 1977 [1900], 436.   [12] Smith 1975, 291–2.

[13] Barthold 1977 [1900], 404; Saunders 1977, 56; Lambton 1988, 21.

[14] Alexseev 1997, 125; Lewis 1988, 191; Abu-Lughod 1989, 316.

[15] By the 1240s, the Mongol army included nomadic mounted archers (Turks, Tunguses, and Tibetians) and non-nomad soldiers (Chinese, Georgians, and Russians) from other ethnicities. Smith 1975, 273.

[16] Barthold 1977 [1900], 419; Kennedy 2002, 122, 130, 136–8; Alexseev 1997, 41, 139.

should be free to travel from one country to another." According to Barthold, the trade interests of Genghis "fully coincided with those of Muslim capitalists." Nevertheless, there was no such "harmony between Muhammad's political ambitions and the interests of the merchants of his kingdom."[17] Genghis also sent a caravan, including about 450 merchants, all Muslims, with merchandise. The frontier governor of Muhammad had all of them killed and the merchandise confiscated. In response, Genghis sent an envoy to protest and demand the surrender of the governor. Muhammad ordered the envoy to be killed as well.[18] When Genghis marched with a well-prepared army to take vengeance, Muhammad made another fatal mistake. Instead of meeting the Mongol army on the frontier with a unified force, he divided the army among the cities in Transoxiana. Muhammad was probably unable to assemble his troops in a single place because his generals were not "as docile an instrument in his hands as was the Mongol army" in those of Genghis.[19]

Barthold observes three main weaknesses of the Khwarazm Shahs that made possible their defeat against "the fresh forces of the nomads, united ... under one of the most talented organizers of all ages." First, the effective political structure created by the Abbasids and further developed by the Tahirids and Samanids in eastern Iran and Central Asia gradually broke down. The bureaucracy no longer functioned well under the Khwarazm Shahs. Second, the ulema and some other segments of society held deep grievances against Muhammad. Finally, there was a rivalry between Muhammad and his mother, Turkan Khatun, who shared the authority over commanders.[20] Against the Mongol invaders, neither Muhammad nor his mother showed effective leadership. It was Muhammad's son Jalal al-Din who led a vain but valiant resistance.[21]

After the death of Genghis, the Mongols continued their westward incursions into Muslim lands. In 1258, Hulagu, a grandson of Genghis, led the Mongol invasion of Baghdad, destroying its libraries, massacring its residents, and ending the Abbasid caliphate. Hulagu's army also sacked Aleppo and began to march toward Mamluk Egypt. Berke, another grandson of Genghis, disapproved of this military act. Berke was the first major Mongol prince to convert Islam.[22] He was the khan of the Golden Horde, which ruled territories to the north of the Black Sea, Caspian Sea, and Aral Sea. Berke was outraged by Hulagu's sacking of Baghdad and the killing of the Abbasid caliph. He was also angered by Hulagu's expansion toward the Caucasus. In this context, Berke provided some support to the Mamluks against Hulagu. Hulagu had to return eastward together with the larger part of his army due to not only the military challenge of Berke in Central Asia but also the death of the great khan. A small portion of Hulagu's army remained to fight the Mamluks. At the vital Battle of

---

[17] Barthold 1977 [1900], 394.   [18] Barthold 1977 [1900], 398–9.
[19] Barthold 1977 [1900], 405.   [20] Barthold 1977 [1900], 380.
[21] Barthold 1977 [1900], 404, 418–19, 430–1, 437–46.
[22] Barthold 1977 [1900], 484–5, 489–90.

Ain Jalut (1260) north of Jerusalem, the Mamluks won a decisive victory, halting the Mongol advance.[23]

Timur

Starting with Berke, the rulers and people of the Golden Horde underwent a process of Islamization. The Golden Horde eventually became a Muslim Turkic state. Meanwhile, Hulagu founded the Ilkhanate in the southwestern territories – Khurasan, the rest of Iran, Iraq, and parts of the Caucasus and Anatolia. The Ilkhanid elite gradually converted to Islam and adopted Persian culture.[24] Similarly, the Mongol state ruling Transoxiana and eastern Central Asia – the (western) Chagatai Khanate – gradually became Islamized and mostly Turkified (see Map 3).[25]

The Ilkhanate disintegrated by the mid-fourteenth century. Timur (r. 1370–1405), a Turko-Mongol warlord from Transoxiana, filled the power vacuum and established an empire over the former territories of the Ilkhanate and the (western) Chagatai Khanate. Notwithstanding his self-avowed Muslim identity, Timur sacked multiple Muslim cities and was responsible for the death of millions of Muslims in various regions including his own Central Asia. He weakened several powerful Muslim states, particularly the Golden Horde, the Delhi Sultanate, the Mamluks, and the Ottomans.[26] Marshall Hodgson depicts the aftermath of Timur's massacres as "towers of heads."[27] Timur failed to fulfill his goal of occupying all former Mongol territories,[28] but his conquests were as destructive as those of Genghis and Hulagu.[29] According to Janet Abu-Lughod, although the Arab Middle East survived the Crusader and the Mongol invasions, "it seems not to have survived the depredations" of Timur.[30]

The Invaders and the "Decline"

There has been a debate about the roles of Crusaders, Mongols, and Timur in Muslims' philosophical and scientific stagnation.[31] In his rebuttal against

[23] Al-Nuwayri 2016 [c. 1333], 250–2; Saunders 1977, 69–71.
[24] Dunn 1986, 83–8; Lambton 1991, 77.   [25] Soucek 2000, 117–18; Manz 1989, 7, 177n11.
[26] An exception was Timur's conquest of Smyrna (today's İzmir) from the Knights of St. John. Wittek 1936, 313.
[27] "Timur varied more routine methods of executing his enemies by throwing them over precipices or burning them alive." Hodgson 1974a, 433.
[28] Manz 1989, 14–15; Soucek 2000, 123–6.
[29] Timur "ruined Baghdad more thoroughly in 1401 than Hulagu had done in 1258." Saunders 1977, 127n21.
[30] Abu-Lughod 1989, 18. Timur's forces sacked Damascus and deported surviving Damascene artisans and craftsmen to Samarkand, the Timurid capital, striking a serious blow to the Mamluk economy. Lapidus 1984, 27; Lewis 1970, 113; Blair and Bloom 1995, 85.
[31] In his successful application to Ottoman authorities for receiving the permission to establish a printing press, İbrahim Muteferrika (1995 [1727], 288) argued that Genghis, Hulagu, and the

Renan's argument about the incompatibility between Islam and scientific progress, Ottoman intellectual Namık Kemal (1840–88) commented that the decline of Muslim scholarship was mostly due to the invasions of the Crusaders and the Mongols.[32] Syed Ameer Ali (1849–1928), an Indian Muslim reformist, also regarded the Mongol invasion as a turning point in Muslim history: "Rationalism, philosophy, the sciences and arts went down before that avalanche of savagery – never to rise again."[33] More recently, Amin Maalouf argued that the Crusades "led to long centuries of decadence" in the Middle East. "Assaulted from all quarters, the Muslim world turned in on itself. It became over-sensitive, defensive, intolerant, sterile – attitudes that grew steadily worse as world-wide evolution, a process from which the Muslim world felt excluded, continued."[34]

In addition to this intellectual argument, there is also an economic argument about the destruction wrought by the invaders. According to the latter, the Mongols destroyed Muslims' dams, canals, and kanats and turned Muslims' agricultural lands into pastures for their own herds. This destruction and appropriation led to long-term agricultural and thus economic decline in the Muslim world.

On the one hand, both arguments make sense in light of the damage the Crusader, Mongol, and Timurid invasions did to Muslim urban life. The Crusaders burned and plundered several libraries and schools,[35] while the Mongols destroyed many of them too.[36] The Mongol invasions resulted in the depopulation of cities and vacancy of previously cultivated lands, as a result of not only massacre but also the destruction of urban and agricultural infrastructure.[37] In the arid climate of Central Asia, Iran, and Iraq, rebuilding complex water supply and irrigation systems was very costly; the agricultural and urban damage in these areas was thus particularly hard to repair.

While the Mongols invaded the Muslim lands, Western Europe was ultimately spared a similar destruction. The Mongols reached Poland but then halted their westward expansion because their commanders had to return to their capital to elect a new great khan. According to John Saunders, this historical turning point facilitated progress in Western Europe while obstructing it in the Muslim world.[38] Bloch also notes that until roughly the year 1000, invasions from the south (Muslims), the east (Hungarians), and the north (Vikings) had

Spanish Catholics destroyed Muslims' books, and since that time there had been a scarcity of books in the Muslim world.

[32] Kemal 1962 [1910], 42, 44, 56. See also Kemal 1969 [1884].
[33] Ali 2012 [1902], 413; also 428–9.   [34] Maalouf 1984, 264.
[35] In their sacking of Tripoli (north of Beirut) in 1109, the Crusaders burned or pillaged all the books in the main library and schools. El-Abbadi 1990, 175; Mackensen 1935a, 84. See also Harris 1995, 84.
[36] Starr 2013, esp. 466.
[37] Barthold 1977 [1900], 436; Lambton 1991, 77; Shatzmiller 1993, 52.
[38] Saunders 1963, 712.

detrimental effects on Western Europe. But when the Hungarians and Vikings largely converted to Christianity, and the Muslim expansion in Spain and the Mediterranean islands ended, Western Europe was free from invasion. Hence, Western Europeans, unlike Muslims, enjoyed a unique opportunity for undisturbed (at least by outside forces) development.[39]

On the other hand, explaining Muslims' enduring problems as the result of solely foreign invasions has several weaknesses. After these invasions, Muslims achieved a geopolitical recovery. By the end of the thirteenth century, they took back all Levantine cities from the Crusaders. Crusaders intended to stop the Seljuk Turks' march in Anatolia, but after centuries of Christian campaigning, the Ottoman Turks still managed to cross the Danube.[40] A similar recovery followed the Mongol invasions. By the early fourteenth century, the ruling elite of three Mongol khanates – the Golden Horde, the Ilkhanate, and the (western) Chagatai – converted to Islam. In the sixteenth century, there were three powerful Muslim empires: Ottoman, Safavid, and Mughal. Muslims restored political order, military security, and wealth to rebuild their cities, including their libraries and schools. Until the European colonization, Muslims had centuries without foreign invasion. Hence, foreign invasions cannot solely account for the long-term intellectual stagnation in the Muslim world.

Moreover, during the post-Mongol era, Islam continued to spread into new territories. The conversion of Mongol khanates' elites cemented Islam's expansion into the Asian steppes. The Ottoman and Mughal Empires extended the political and religious borders of Islamic civilization to the Balkans in the west and to Bengal in the east.[41] In contrast to their early rule "from Nile to Oxus,"[42] Muslims began to rule the area "from the Balkans to Bengal."[43] Thus even if the Mongol invasions led to a severe decline in the agricultural fertility of Central Asia, Iran, and Iraq, this decline alone could not be the cause of a more general economic stagnation in Muslim lands, which had expanded well beyond these arid regions.

Even Archibald Lewis's book, which presents the Crusades and the Mongol invasions as a turning point in the geopolitical rivalry between Muslims and Western Europeans, recognizes Muslims' recovery after these attacks. Lewis argues that in the year 1000, Western Europe was "the most geographically remote and underdeveloped" among five great civilizations of Eurasia and Africa – the other four being Islamic, East Asian/Chinese, Indic, and Byzantine-Russian civilizations. Following the Crusades and the nomadic (mostly Mongol) invasions, he asserts, Western Europe "ended up the gainer,"

---

[39] Bloch 2014 [1940], 5–59. See also Jones 2003 [1981], 50–2.   [40] Runciman 1954, 469.

[41] Meanwhile, itinerant Muslim merchants and Sufis helped the conversion of populations in Sub-Saharan Africa, the Malay Peninsula, and the Indonesian archipelago. Hodgson 1993, 118–20, 175–6; Trimingham 1971, 102–4; Dunn 1986, 293–4.

[42] Hodgson 1974a, esp. 60–2.

[43] Ahmed 2015, esp. 18, 75. See also Hodgson 1974b, 271–9, 532–67; Eaton 1993, esp. part II.

while other civilizations weakened.[44] Nonetheless, contradicting himself, Lewis acknowledges that by the end of the fourteenth century, Muslims still challenged European maritime ascendancy in the Mediterranean Sea, restricted Europeans' access to the Indian Ocean and Central Asia, conquered lands in western Anatolia and the Balkans, and managed to convert the Mongol ruling class in western Eurasia. He also adds, "Perhaps more significant, Islam had proved capable of penetrating other cultures. It had done so in India and Indonesia ..., southern Russia and Byzantine Anatolia ... [and], the black world south of the Sahara and along the shores of East Africa." Thus, from a geopolitical perspective, "it was Islam and its civilization which ended up with the victory." For Lewis, this success is visible in Ibn Battuta's travel accounts.[45]

Ibn Battuta (1304–68/9) was a Moroccan traveler. He dictated his memoirs, *Travels*, to a writer. It is arguably "the biggest travel book ever written" and covers nearly 75,000 miles in Northwest Africa, Egypt, East Africa, Arabian Peninsula, Syria, Iraq, Iran, Anatolia, Crimea, Central Asia, India, Indonesia, and China.[46] Each of Ibn Battuta's three qualifications – as an Arabic-speaking Muslim, an expert on Islamic jurisprudence, and an advocate of Sufism – helped him during such an intercontinental travel.[47] Paradoxically, while Ibn Battuta's *Travels* documents Muslims' geopolitical expansion, it also reveals their intellectual stagnation. Ross Dunn makes this clear by comparing Muslim indifference toward Ibn Battuta with European interest in Marco Polo, and even Ibn Battuta himself:

> In contrast to Marco Polo's book, which was widely circulated and acclaimed in Europe in the later Middle Ages, the *Rihla* [*Travels*] appears to have had a very modest impact on the Muslim world until modern times ... Only in the mid-nineteenth century, half a millennium after it was written, did the narrative begin to receive the international attention it so profoundly deserved. The credit for that achievement, ironically enough, fell to scholars of Christian Europe, the one populous region of Eurasia Ibn Battuta had never bothered to visit in his travels.[48]

The overall Muslim indifference toward Ibn Battuta's book was not an isolated event but a reflection of a broader problem. I will mention later how the works of Ibn Rushd and Ibn Khaldun also received a similarly tepid, if not apathetic, Muslim reaction until the nineteenth century. The rise of the ulema, the military state elite, and the alliance between them – at the expense of philosophers and merchants – were the main factors for this intellectual

---

[44] Lewis 1988, 67, 195.   [45] Lewis 1988, 190.

[46] Mackintosh-Smith 2002, ix. See also Dunn 1986, 3.

[47] Himself a Maliki Sunni, Ibn Battuta (2002 [1355], 102) wrote approvingly that in Anatolia, Muslims were mostly Hanafi Sunni, and "there is not a Qadari, nor a Rafidi [i.e., Shii], nor a Mu'tazili, nor a Khariji, nor any innovators among them." Ibn Battuta (2002 [1355]). See also Dunn 1986, 11–12, 20–5.

[48] Dunn 1986, 317. The only Christian city he visited was Constantinople. Ibn Battuta 2002 [1355], 128–35.

stagnation. The foreign invasions contributed to this process; because of them, Muslims focused on security and survival and thus elevated the status of the military elites. In the case of the Mamluks, the military threat from the Crusaders and the Mongols "led to a defensive militarization of the region that eventually undermined civil society and its vital economic institutions."[49] Even the subsequent Ottoman, Safavid, and Mughal Empires were affected to various degrees by the Mongol legacy of the military state.[50] Moreover, the shocking massacres as well as religious discourse of the Crusaders motivated Muslims to further embrace their own religious discourses and support the leadership of the ulema.[51] Despite these negative conditions, Muslim philosophical and scientific tradition had such strong roots that it kept producing first-class scholars for a few more centuries, as indicated in the following section.

WANING OF PHILOSOPHERS: FROM GHAZALI TO IBN KHALDUN

Central Asia, Iran, and Iraq

Chapter 4 explained how in the eleventh century, several religious and political actors, particularly Ghazali, contributed to the establishment of an orthodox Sunni synthesis based on the integration of four Sunni schools of law[52] and the exclusion of Shiis, Mutazilis, and philosophers. This initiative continued in subsequent periods and successfully contained the political power of the Shiis, eliminated the Mutazilis, and marginalized the philosophers in the eastern territories (Central Asia, Iran, and Iraq). The campaign against philosophy entailed material as well as doctrinal measures. For example, in the mid-twelfth century, the Abbasid Caliph Mustanjid ordered the public burning of Ibn Sina's and Ikhwan al-Safa's books stored in libraries in Baghdad.[53]

---

[49] Abu-Lughod 1989, 243–4.

[50] This meant further militarization of Muslim states – a trend already started by the Ghaznavids and Seljuks, as noted in Chapter 4.

[51] Even the polymath Ibn al-Nafis (1968 [1268–77], 65–6) depicts the Mongol invasion as divine punishment for Muslims' sins, including drinking alcohol and homosexuality. Similarly, Bloch (2014 [1940], 58, 91) reports Western Christians' mystical explanations of Hungarian and Viking invasions. In the ninth century, there was an "atmosphere of legend and apocalypse" as well as a "belief that all these calamities were a divine chastisement." Many "believed that in the Hungarians they recognized the peoples of Gog and Magog, forerunner of Antichrist." Rulers too were seen as part of this apocalyptic scenario. In the eleventh and twelfth centuries, there was a "general conviction," which "was by no means confined to the clergy," that the end of the time was imminent. "In every wicked prince, pious souls believed that they recognized the mark of Antichrist, whose dreadful empire would precede the coming of the Kingdom of God."

[52] By the early thirteenth century, this integration effort had not yet succeeded fully, at least in some cities. In Ray, immediately before the Mongol invasion, there were ongoing clashes between the Hanafis and the Shafis. Algar 1982, 8, 10–11.

[53] Gutas 2014, II: 332; Ali 2012 [1902], 412. Fuat Sezgin (2011a, 158) claims, "Official opposition and condemnation like that of Averroes at the University of Paris or the Aristotle-prohibition by

Nonetheless, between the twelfth and fourteenth centuries, eastern Muslim territories were still producing philosophers and Islamic scholars engaging in philosophy. One example is Fakhr al-Din al-Razi (1150–1210). On the one hand, Razi attempted to reconcile reason and revelation.[54] He studied medicine, astronomy, and geometry in addition to Islamic studies, especially the exegesis of the Qur'an.[55] On the other hand, Razi made a contribution to the further consolidation of Sunni orthodoxy by promoting Ashari theology at the expense of Mutazili theology, and criticizing some of Ibn Sina's philosophical works.[56]

A more philosophically inclined polymath of the time was Abd al-Latif al-Baghdadi (1162–1231), who studied Islamic literature (including the work of Ghazali), philosophy (including works of Ibn Sina and Farabi), history, and medicine. Born and raised in Baghdad, he traveled through many cities, especially in Syria and Egypt, for about forty years, seeking knowledge and patronage. In Cairo, Baghdadi met such important figures as Saladin and Musa ibn Maymun (Maimonides).[57]

Despite their destructions, the Mongols still made an important contribution to scholarship by establishing the Maragha Observatory, where Nasr al-Din Tusi (1201–74) studied and taught.[58] Tusi gained this patronage through his services to the Mongols.[59] The research Tusi and his associates conducted in the observatory influenced Muslim and European astronomers until the sixteenth century.[60] In addition to astronomy, Tusi also wrote on such diverse issues as Shii theology, ethics, and politics.[61] He wrote a defense of Ibn Sina's philosophy against the critique of Razi.[62]

The most famous student of Tusi was Shirazi (1236–1311). Like his teacher, Shirazi was a polymath who studied a range of subjects such as astronomy, medicine, and philosophy.[63] In the early fourteenth century, the Maragha Observatory became inactive. Nevertheless, the Ilkhanid rulers' patronage of

---

Pope Innocence III in 1209 would have been inconceivable in the Islamic world." This is inaccurate given examples of official repression of philosophy by several Abbasid caliphs and various sultans, as explained in Chapter 4 and in this one.

[54] Jaffer 2014, esp. 11, 25. See also Anjum 2012, 163–8.

[55] Aminrazavi 2010a, 185–8; McAuliffe 1990.   [56] Jaffer 2014, esp. 56–7.

[57] Bonadeo 2015. According to Gutas (2014, VIII: 159), Abd al-Latif al-Baghdadi, "after personal inspection of over two thousand human skulls, observed against Galen that the lower jaw-bone is made of one suture-less bone, not of two bones joined at the chin." See also Gutas 2014, XIV: 91–3; XV: 9–26; Makdisi 1981, 84–91; Savage-Smith 1995, 104–5.

[58] Sayılı 1960, ch. 6.

[59] According to Hodgson (1974b, 291), Tusi was an advisor of the Mongols during their invasion of Baghdad. See also Darling 2013, 107. For an opposite view, see Dabashi 1996a, 529–37.

[60] Sezgin 2011a, 39. For Tusi's possible influence on Copernicus, see Saliba 2007, ch. 6; al-Khalili 2011, 204–22.

[61] Tusi 1964 [c. 1235].   [62] Adamson 2016, 333–5; Gutas 2014, XIV: 89.

[63] Ragep 2007b, 1054–5.

scientists continued. An eminent student of Shirazi was Nishapuri (1270–1328/9), who studied under this patronage. He wrote on astronomy, mathematics, and Qur'anic exegesis.[64]

Tusi, Shirazi, and Nishapuri were Shii Muslims. Their Sunni counterparts in eastern territories had an increasing tendency to focus on Islamic studies at the expense of philosophy and the natural sciences. Two prominent Sunni scholars of the thirteenth century, Taftazani (1322–c. 1390) and Jurjani (1340–1413), mostly concentrated on jurisprudence, Quranic exegesis, theology, Arabic linguistics, and logic.[65] Taftazani emphasized human free will more than Ashari theologians normally did.[66] Therefore, some scholars have considered his thought to be closer to Maturidi theology.[67] In later periods, the Muslim world produced so few ulema of the caliber of Taftazani and Jurjani that these two scholars' books continued to be taught in Ottoman, Mughal, and, to a lesser degree, Safavid madrasas for centuries.[68]

Eastern territories were the beacon of Muslim intellectual life from the ninth to the eleventh century. Between the twelfth and fourteenth centuries, however, they lost this status to two other Muslim regions: Egypt, Syria, and Anatolia, on one hand, and Andalus and Northwest Africa, on the other. Abd al-Latif al-Baghdadi's abovementioned westward travel was a sign of the westward shift of Muslim intellectual dynamism.

---

[64] "Nisaburi envisioned a cosmos under God's direct control ... to encourage humans' scientific investigation. If God wielded proximate control, then everything in the cosmos reflected ... [it] and the cosmos deserved humans' full understanding." Morrison 2007, 62.

[65] Jurjani's astronomical writings are only commentaries and constitute "a small part of his total corpus." Dhanani 2007, 603.

[66] Aminrazavi 2010b, 312. For Taftazani "there is a participation of man and God in the human actions." This participation is "not in a metaphorical, but in a real, sense" and implies a "very complex process." God creates human actions and provides man with "the power to accomplish the action he chooses." Corbin 1986, 376.

[67] Imam Maturidi's theology grants more space to human free will. He "attributes *ikhtiyar* [free choice] to God as well as humans. This is not supposed to imply that humans are similar to God, but rather that both possess complete freedom." Rudolph 2015, 305n346. Imam Maturidi followed Hanafi jurisprudence. Hence, his epistemology had "constant efforts to equally emphasize the three pathways of knowledge acquisition (the senses, transmission, and the intellect)." Rudolph 2015, 316; also 318–19; Rudolph 2016, 526n1071, 545–51. According to Fazlur Rahman (1982, 27), Maturidi theology eventually lost its emphasis on free will and reason by being "drowned by Ash'arism." For a late twelfth-century Maturidi text, which already showed signs of converging with Ashari views, see Es-Sabuni 1995 [c. 1184].

[68] Robinson 1997, 155, 174–84; Aminrazavi 2010b, 312–13; Moosa 2015, 110–14. These madrasas also kept teaching some medieval books on philosophy and logic, particularly Abhari's (c. 1200–64) *Guide on Philosophy* (a textbook on Ibn Sina's philosophy) and *Isagoge* (a summary of Aristotle's *Organon*). Çelebi 2007 [c. 1653], 208, 570; Özervarlı 2015a, 386; Gutas 2014, XIV: 94; Goldziher 1981 [1916], 208.

Egypt, Syria, and Anatolia

In Syria and Anatolia, several Muslim cities were occupied by the Crusaders. Some Syrian cities also experienced Mongol invasions. The ruler of Damascus, Nur al-Din Zengi (r. 1156–74), emerged as an effective military commander and defender of Islam against the Crusaders. Nur al-Din opened Sunni madrasas in Damascus. These and other Nizamiyya-type madrasas were funded by waqfs, which were private endowments. Nonetheless, they could not be simply defined as private or independent, because these madrasas fell under the doctrinal and political hegemony of the ulema–state alliance. Michael Chamberlain documents that in Damascus, from the beginning of the Nur al-Din's rule to 1350, the great majority of the madrasas were established by members of households of rulers and officials.[69]

Despite the foreign occupations and the solidification of Sunni orthodoxy, scholarly productions continued to a certain extent in Syria and Anatolia. In southern Anatolia, Jazari (1136–1206) wrote on mechanical engineering. His *Book of Knowledge of Ingenious Mechanical Devices* surpassed the ninth-century book by the Banu Musa brothers on the same subject. According to Hill, Jazari's book is "probably the most important engineering document from any cultural area before the Renaissance." It is "divided into six categories: (1) water-clocks and candle-clocks, (2) wine dispensers, (3) phlebotomy measuring devices and water dispensers, (4) alternating fountains and musical automota, (5) water-raising devices and (6) miscellaneous."[70]

Egypt was never occupied by Crusaders or Mongols, but it was still affected by the invaders' further militarization of the Muslim lands. In the 1170s, Saladin emerged as a military hero against the Crusaders. Initially he was a commander under Nur al-Din. He subsequently established the Ayyubid Sultanate (1171–1250) in Egypt and later extended it into Syria. Saladin followed Nur al-Din's model of promoting Sunni Islam by founding Nizamiyya-type madrasas in Cairo.[71]

In order to eradicate the legacy of the Shii Fatimids in Egypt, Saladin sold and disposed of books in that preceding dynasty's libraries and especially those housed in the library of Cairo, which was "presumably full of heretical Isma'ili books."[72] Ruth Mackensen notes that Saladin's dismantling of the library may surprise Western observers accustomed to looking upon Saladin as "one of the most enlightened gentlemen of the East." She explains the case "both as the regular accompaniment of conquest and as an attack of orthodoxy upon a

---

[69] Chamberlain 1994, 52; also 106. Similarly, in Aleppo, starting with the Nur al-Din era, madrasas undertook certain activities as "official institution[s]" and had "links with state authority." Tabbaa 1997, 128.

[70] Hill 1994, 27.   [71] Arjomand 1999, 271; Berkey 1992, 8.   [72] Lewis 2008, 217.

center of schism."[73] According to both Mostafa El-Abbadi and Bernard Lewis, the story about the Muslim destruction of the ancient library of Alexandria on Caliph Umar's order was fabricated in this context to provide precedent for Saladin's decision.[74]

Saladin's anti-philosophical measures also included his order for the execution of the philosopher-mystic Yahya Suhrawardi (1154–91) in Aleppo. Suhrawardi was influenced by Plato, Aristotle, Neo-Platonists, Ghazali, and especially Ibn Sina. Despite his execution at an early age after being accused of apostasy, Suhrawardi's writings continued to be influential and became foundational for the Illuminationist school.[75] Later Ayyubid rulers and ulema continued to take action against philosophy. Ashraf, the sultan of Damascus, made a statement at the beginning of his reign (1228–37) and prohibited the jurists "from studying anything but hadith, Koranic exegesis and law. He made clear that anyone studying logic and other 'foreign sciences' would be banned from the city."[76]

As in other parts of the Muslim world, in Syria and Egypt, the decline of the natural sciences and philosophy was relative, not absolute. Muslim scientists and philosophers continued writing and teaching in various institutional settings. Some grand mosques in major cities had *muwaqqit* (timekeeper) posts and thus provided research opportunities.[77] In Damascus, Ibn al-Shatir (c. 1304–75) worked as the head *muwaqqit* of the Umayyad Mosque, where he built a famous sundial. Ibn al-Shatir developed some non-Ptolemaic astronomical models as well.[78]

Another important Muslim institution was the hospital, which contributed not only to the social development of cities but also to advances in medical science. The pioneering Muslim hospital had been the Adudi Hospital in Baghdad, built by the Buyids in 981. Later, in 1154, the Zengis built another major institution, the Nur al-Din Hospital, in Damascus. The famous physician Ibn al-Nafis (1213–88) worked there. He then moved to Egypt, where he became a prominent physician. In 1285, the Mamluk sultan established the

---

[73] Mackensen 1935a, 100. According to El-Abbadi (1990, 176), Saladin's motive in selling or distributing these books could also have been to raise funds and to pay off his supporters.
[74] El-Abbadi 1990, 176–8. According to the mythical story, when the commander of the Arab conquerors of Egypt, Amr ibn al-As, asked Umar what to do with the library, the latter replied: "If these writings of the Greeks agree with the book of God, they are useless and need not be preserved; if they disagree, they are pernicious and ought to be destroyed." Books were used to heat the furnaces of four thousand bathhouses of the city. Lewis 2008, 213. Ibn Khaldun (2005 [1377], 373) narrates an almost identical story about books in conquered Persia and an order from Umar, which suggests the folkloric nature of both stories. Lewis 2008, 214–16; Mackensen 1935b, 117–22.
[75] Hodgson 1974b, 234–8; Fakhry 2004, 303–14; Ziai 1996a, 442–3; Corbin 1986, 286–9.
[76] Makdisi 1981, 137. Again in early thirteenth-century Damascus, the chief judge, Muhyi al-Din al-Qurashi, banned "the study of books on logic and dialectic." Makdisi 1981, 137.
[77] King 2004, 18. [78] Saliba 2007, 162–5; Ragep 2007a, 65.

Mansuri Hospital in Cairo, which surpassed earlier Muslim hospitals.[79] According to the encyclopedia of Nuwayri (1279–1333), in the Mansuri Hospital, "[p]hysicians, ophthalmologists, surgeons, and bonesetters were appointed to treat ... men and women," and "patients were placed in specialized wards with running water in most of them."[80] Ibn Nafis bequeathed his house and library to this hospital.[81]

Ibn al-Nafis is known as the first scholar to write about pulmonary circulation, long before its detailed explanation by Harvey in the seventeenth century.[82] Ibn al-Nafis wrote a theological novel *The Treatise of Kāmil on the Prophet's Biography*, as a response to Ibn Tufayl's philosophical novel, *Hayy bin Yaqzan (Alive, Son of Awake)*. In Ibn al-Nafis's novel, the hero (Kamil) learns things like language, cooking, and wearing clothes from the visitors to his island, rather than coming up with them himself. The novel stresses the necessity of revelation and prophecy, in contrast to *Hay bin Yaqzan*'s emphasis on humans' ability to reason truths on their own.[83]

In his analysis of Ibn al-Nafis, Nahyan Fancy tries to show that "there was not an all-out repression of the sciences by religious 'orthodoxy' during the thirteenth and fourteenth centuries."[84] He is correct at the individual level. The fact that Ibn Nafis was a Sunni expert on hadith, jurisprudence, and theology indicates the potential compatibility of Sunni Islam and scientific inquiry. Yet this individual example does not disprove the connection between the rise of religious orthodoxy and the stagnation of scientific development in Egypt. Ibn Nafis did not have students or successors of his caliber, and thus his writings on pulmonary circulation were forgotten until they were rediscovered in the twentieth century.[85]

Moreover, Fancy's own data indicate how religious intolerance hindered scientific development in the Mamluk Egypt. The endowment deed of the Mansuri Hospital "explicitly states that 'Christians and Jews were neither to be treated nor employed there.'"[86] This religious discrimination was probably

[79] Sezgin 2011a, 48; Dallal 2010, 21. See also Pormann and Savage-Smith 2007, 96–101; Endress 2006, 386–7.
[80] Al-Nuwayri 2016 [c. 1333], 257. Nuwayri was a retired Mamluk state servant and a litterateur. His encyclopedia had thirty-three volumes and covered five main topics: the heavens and the earth, the human being, animals, plants, and the history of Islam.
[81] Meyerhof and Schacht 1968, esp. 5.   [82] West 2008.
[83] Ibn al-Nafis 1968 [1268–77], 44–55. The novel ends with a science-fiction scenario which naturalistically explains Islamic ideas regarding the end of days and the resurrection. Ibn al-Nafis 1968 [1268–77], 71–5, 83. See also Fancy 2013, ch. 3.
[84] Fancy 2013, 34.   [85] Meyerhof 1935, esp. 118.
[86] On the same page, Fancy (2013, 24) provides two more points of evidence for the conflict between religious intolerance and philosophy/natural sciences. First, the anti-Christian attitude was not simply imposed by the Mamluk state; instead, it was encouraged by such Hanbali ulema as Ibn Taymiyya and his student Jawziyya, who were uncomfortable with the "disproportionate dominance of non-Muslim physicians." Second, these Hanbali ulema opposed not only philosophy but also medical science, because they "felt (justifiably) that medicine was too closely allied

motivated by the Crusaders' occupation of Muslim lands.[87] Whatever the motive, the discrimination was morally wrong and scientifically counterproductive. It shows the difference between Baghdad between the ninth and twelfth centuries – a cosmopolitan city, where Jewish and Christian physicians had career opportunities and science flowered[88] – and thirteenth-century Cairo – a city constricted by Sunni orthodoxy, where non-Muslim physicians and Muslim philosophers suffered discrimination, and scientific endeavors atrophied and faded.

Andalus and Northwest Africa

In contrast to eastern territories and Egypt-Syria, Andalus produced its most famous philosophers in the twelfth century. In the late tenth century, the vizier Mansur (r. 978–1002) became the de facto ruler of Andalus. Mansur was primarily a military leader and organized about fifty raids against Christian cities in northern Spain. In order to gain the support of the ulema and the masses, he targeted the famous library built by the previous ruler, Caliph Hakam II, in Cordoba. In this attack, Mansur destroyed books on philosophy and various sciences (with notable exceptions).[89]

After the rule of Mansur, internal power struggles in Andalus resulted in its partition into about two dozen small states, which facilitated the expansion of Catholic states in the region. In 1085, Toledo became the first major Andalusian city where Catholics fully regained control. A year later, armies of the Almoravids, a Muslim Berber dynasty, entered Andalus from Northwest Africa and halted the Catholic expansion. The Almoravids ruled Muslim cities in southern and eastern Spain until the mid-twelfth century.[90] The Almoravids allied with the Maliki ulema, constituting another example of an alliance between the ulema and the military state.

From the mid-twelfth to the mid-thirteenth century, another Berber dynasty, the Almohads, ruled Andalus and Morocco. The conditions of Christian and Jewish minorities in Andalus, which had already deteriorated as a result of constant warfare with Catholics and internal military struggles, severely worsened under the intolerant Almohads. In contrast to the Almoravids, the Almohads rejected the Maliki school of law. The Almohads had a puritanical

---

to a philosophical world-view." Thus, these ulema composed the *Tibb al-Nabi* (the Medicine of the Prophet) based on certain hadiths.

[87] Three Christian court physicians converted to Islam to be appointed to the hospital's teaching positions, the top of the Mamluk medical hierarchy. Ragab 2015, 130–1.

[88] In Baghdad, Ibn al-Tilmidh (1073–1165), a Christian, served as the chief physician of the Adudi Hospital. Sezgin 2011a, 158; Meyerhof and Schacht 1968, 8.

[89] The remaining books were mostly sold or stolen during subsequent military conflicts. Mackensen 1935a, 110–11.

[90] Lewis 2009, 322–3, 346–66.

understanding of Islam, which was paradoxically open to a "wide intellectual perspective" including elements of philosophy.[91]

Andalus produced eminent philosophers under both the Almoravids and the Almohads. Ibn Bajja (known in Latin as Avempace) (c. 1095–1138) was a polymath who wrote on philosophy, medicine, mathematics, astronomy, physics, and botany.[92] He influenced subsequent Andalusian philosophers. Ibn Bajja's argument that living an isolated life of contemplation was essential for attaining happiness and perfection represents an individualistic emphasis, which would be fully developed later in Ibn Tufayl's *Hayy bin Yaqzan*.[93]

Ibn Tufayl (c. 1110–85) was another Andalusian Muslim polymath. He served as a physician and advisor to the Almohad ruler Abu Yaqub. Ibn Tufayl's novel *Hayy bin Yaqzan* suggests that a human being living alone on an isolated island would be able to apprehend the meaning of life and the existence of a Creator solely through observation and contemplation, without the help of any religious text. Thus, the capacity for self-teaching and even metaphysical philosophy was inherent in human intellect. However, the book also stresses that the uneducated masses, unlike the elite, are unlikely to grasp philosophical truths on their own; therefore, they need revelation and to be disciplined with the promise of reward and punishment.[94] In the late seventeenth and early eighteenth centuries, this philosophical novel was translated into multiple European languages and read by several Enlightenment philosophers.[95]

Ibn Rushd

Among the Andalusian philosophers, the most influential was Ibn Rushd (1126–98). As Chapter 4 discussed, many scholars have judged Ghazali to be responsible for Muslims' intellectual stagnation. They have also interpreted Ibn Rushd in opposition to Ghazali, primarily because of the former's rebuttal to Ghazali's critique of philosophers, the *Incoherence*. A strong defender of this perspective was Jabri,[96] who called for a revival of Ibn Rushd's thought to revitalize the Muslim mind with its rationalism and critical approach.[97]

---

[91] Hodgson 1974b, 269.   [92] Fakhry 2004, 269–73; Corbin 1986, 319–26.

[93] Rosenthal 1958, 168; also 158–74.

[94] Ibn Tufayl 2005 [c. 1175]; Goodman 1996; Fakhry 2004, 273–80; Corbin 1986, 329–34.

[95] Israel 2006, 628–30.

[96] Al-Jabri 2011 [1984], 393–403; al-Jabri 1995, 119–48, 163–7. For similarly positive views on Ibn Rushd among some Egyptian intellectuals in the 1990s, see Najjar 1996, 14–16.

[97] Jabri (2011 [1984], 360–1) blames Ghazali for the marginalization of rationalism and the prevalence of mysticism in the Muslim world. For him, "al-Ghazali has left a deep wound inside Arab reason, which is still bleeding." Instead, Jabri (1995, 168) suggests making the ideas of Ibn Rushd central to Muslim and Arab thought, analogous to the status of Descartes' rationalism for French thought and Locke and Hume's empiricism for British thought.

It was Ibn Tufayl who presented Ibn Rushd to Abu Yaqub – a ruler deeply interested in philosophy – and commissioned Ibn Rushd to fulfill Abu Yaqub's vision of Arabic commentaries on Aristotle's works. Abu Yaqub appointed Ibn Rushd as a judge in Seville and then as the chief judge of Cordoba – where his father and grandfather had also served as judges. Ibn Rushd served the ruler as a physician as well. He wrote a large number of his treaties while serving in these public positions.[98]

Ibn Rushd promoted Aristotle's writings and was critical of the modifications of Aristotelian philosophy suggested by Farabi and Ibn Sina.[99] Yet Ibn Rushd was not a simple interpreter of Aristotle. His Islamic beliefs resulted in an understanding of God, God's creation of the world, and God's knowledge that diverged from Aristotle's ideas on several points.[100]

As an Islamic scholar, Ibn Rushd tried to bridge philosophy and Islam. In *Kitab Fasl al-Maqal wa Taqrir ma bayn al-Shari'a wa al-Hikma min al-Ittisal* (*Decisive Treatise: Determining the Connection between Islamic Law and Philosophy*), he shows that pursuing philosophy is obligatory for Muslims, because several Quranic verses order the faithful to contemplate animals, the earth, and the heavens. In order to better understand God and his creation, Ibn Rushd argues, one needs to learn demonstrative, dialectical, and rhetorical reasoning, which requires philosophical training.[101] There should be no contradiction between demonstrative reasoning and revelation; if a contradiction is perceived, then an interpretation is needed and must be achieved without destroying the linguistic framework of the text.[102]

The Quran, Ibn Rushd continues, explicitly states that some of its verses are "symbolic" and can be interpreted by "those firmly rooted in knowledge" (3:7).[103] It is normal, then, to see multiple interpretations, especially on

---

[98] Hourani 1961, 6–18; Leaman 1988, 3–5.

[99] Ibn Rushd 1954 [1180], 107–12. Ibn Rushd particularly criticized Ibn Sina and Farabi for defending the Neo-Platonic idea of emanationism, according to which all existence is a necessary outflow from God following a hierarchy, in which each category arises from the previous one and is degraded in comparison to it. Fakhry 2001, 5–11; Allard 1952–4, 25–7.

[100] Allard 1952–4, 36, 43, 49–55; Fakhry 2001, 84, 88–90.

[101] Ibn Rushd quotes a verse showing that these three methods of reasoning – demonstrative (wisdom), rhetorical (preaching), and dialectical (argument) – are reemphasized in the Quran: "Call to the path of your Lord by wisdom, fine preaching, and arguing with them by means of what is finest" (16:125). Ibn Rushd 2001a [c. 1179], 8; Ibn Rushd 2001b [c. 1179], 8 (the page numbers in the edition of *Fasl al-Maqal* and its translation [*Decisive Treatise*] by Charles Butterworth are identical).

[102] Ibn Rushd 2001a [c. 1179], 1–4. In the words of George Hourani (1961, 27), Ibn Rushd "was facing the dilemma of all religious modernists, who accept as true both a Scripture and the science of their day."

[103] Ibn Rushd puts the stop after "those firmly rooted in knowledge." Those who do the same, such as Seyyed Hossein Nasr et al. (2015, 129), read the verse (3:7) as "And none know its [i.e., a symbolic verse's] interpretation save God and those firmly rooted in knowledge. They say, 'We believe in it; all is from our Lord.'" In contrast, those who put the stop earlier, such as

theoretical issues, in different periods. Philosophers, such as Ibn Sina and Farabi, are among "those firmly rooted in knowledge," and they may have certain interpretations that seem wrong to others. Even their wrong judgments are to be rewarded in light of a well-known hadith: "If a judge makes a correct *ijtihad* (interpretation), he gets two (spiritual) rewards; if he makes a wrong *ijtihad* he gets one (spiritual) reward." In this regard, it is wrong to declare these philosophers as heretical innovators or apostates.[104]

Additionally, Ibn Rushd discusses Ghazali's and some other Ashari theologians' major criticisms of philosophers by mostly showing the complexity of philosophers' arguments. For him, on whether God knows the particulars or not, the philosophers' position is based on the categorical differentiation between God's knowledge and that of human beings.[105] Whether the world is eternal or not was another major debate between theologians and philosophers. Ibn Rushd defines it as a semantic discussion focused on "naming." He also defends the philosophers' position by stressing the difficulty in separating time from the universe: "Time does not precede ... the world.... Time is something that accompanies motion and bodies."[106]

Ibn Rushd takes an elitist position while accusing Ghazali of making a mistake against both religion and philosophy by discussing complex issues in dialectical and rhetorical works to be read by ordinary people. He similarly criticizes the Mutazilis and the Asharis for turning sophisticated religious interpretations into a matter of dialectical arguments and, furthermore, for teaching them to the masses. To Ibn Rushd, the popularization of these theological debates among the people produced hostile and clashing factions within the Muslim community.[107] Ibn Rushd also offers alternatives to the Ashari and Mutazili theology schools in certain issues, such as their ways of proving God's existence. For him, one alternative way of proving it is "invention": every invented thing reflects its inventor; all existing entities are invented; and thus existing entities reflect God. The other way is "providence": all existing beings

Marmaduke Pickthall (2017 [1930]), read it sharply differently: "None knows its [i.e., an allegorical verse's] explanation except God. And those who are of sound instruction say: 'We believe in it; the whole is from our Lord.'" Ibn Khaldun (2005 [1377], 354) also defends the second reading. Ibn Rushd finds the second reading self-contradictory because if "those deeply rooted in knowledge" had no knowledge on the matter, there would not be any reason to single them out; anyone can say, "We believe in it." The fact that God emphasizes their knowledge shows that they may know these verses' interpretations. Ibn Rushd 2001a [c. 1179], 12; also 20, 27.

[104] Ibn Rushd 2001a [c. 1179], 9–12, 17. Thus, Ibn Rushd makes an original argument that "philosophers are a group of Muslim *'ulama'* whose agreement is necessary to establish *ijma'*[consensus]." Hourani 1961, 31.

[105] Ibn Rushd 2001a [c. 1179], 13–14. See also Ibn Rushd 1954 [1180], 275–85, 325–6.

[106] Ibn Rushd 2001a [c. 1179], 14–15. "[T]he dependence of time on motion is much like the dependence of number on the thing numbered." Ibn Rushd 1954 [1180], 45.

[107] Ibn Rushd 2001a [c. 1179], 21, 26–30.

are suited to man's existence, and this suitability cannot be due to chance, but indicates a willing agent – God.[108]

Ibn Rushd elaborates his criticism of Ghazali at length in *The Incoherence of the Incoherence*. He particularly criticizes Ghazali's notion of causality. Ibn Rushd notes that as a result of Ghazali's and other Asharis' rejection of causality and their definition of God's creation as unpredictable, "there would no longer ... be any permanent knowledge of anything," because Asharis suppose God "to rule existents *like a tyrannical prince* ... of whom no standard or custom is known to which reference might be made."[109] Ibn Rushd also cites the Quranic verse "You will never find in God's course any alteration" (33:62, 35:43, 48:23) to emphasize the established order and causality in the world.[110]

On the relationship between the divine will and human free will, Ibn Rushd's explanations would be relevant to modern discussions on agent–structure relations. For him, what is referred to as God's decree is the external and internal conditions that constrain human free will. God gives humans faculties to choose between opposite options. Nevertheless, the causes outside and inside of individuals' bodies also affect their will.[111]

After the death of Ibn Rushd's patron, Abu Yaqub, his son, Yaqub al-Mansur (r. 1184–99), became ruler. Initially, he followed his father in supporting Ibn Rushd. Nonetheless, in 1195, Yaqub al-Mansur, motivated by the reactionary ulema and their public allies, ordered the burning of Ibn Rushd's books, put him in exile in a small town, and similarly punished other scholars for their engagement in philosophy. Ibn Rushd went into exile for around two years, and he died shortly after being exonerated.[112]

Ibn Rushd was mostly disregarded or forgotten in Muslim lands,[113] but he profoundly influenced European thought. Jewish philosophers and translators played a pivotal role in the diffusion of his ideas.[114] Besides his treaties on Islamic theology, Islamic jurisprudence, and medicine, we know today thirty-eight commentaries by Ibn Rushd on Aristotle's work. Only nineteen of his commentaries have survived as Arabic manuscripts in Arabic characters; nine have survived as Arabic manuscripts in Hebrew characters; and the rest have survived only as Latin and/or Hebrew translations.[115] That the Muslim world and Europe treated Ibn Rushd's ideas in such divergent ways indicates the

---

[108] Ibn Rushd 2001c [1179–80], 33–4.
[109] Ibn Rushd 1954 [1180], 325 (emphasis added). Ibn Rushd (2001c [1179–80], 87) claims that Asharis' rejection of natural causes is counterproductive: "[T]he thesis of contingency is more likely to lead to denying the existence of the Maker, rather than affirming it ... [If] there are no intermediaries ..., there will be no order or organization ... [and thus] no indication that these existing entities have a willing and knowing agent."
[110] Ibn Rushd 1954 [1180], 333. See also Van den Bergh 1954.
[111] Ibn Rushd 2001c [1179–80], 109.   [112] Fakhry 2001, 1–4; Butterworth 2001, xiv–xv.
[113] "Ibn Rushd had scarcely had any disciples or successors in the Muslim" world. Fakhry 2004, 285.
[114] Leaman 1988, 175; Renan 1882 [1852], 173–99.   [115] Wolfson 1963, 90–4.

beginning of an intellectual reversal between the two realms – the former began to undermine philosophy, while the latter started to appreciate it.

After Ibn Rushd, Andalus and Northwest Africa continued to produce great scholars for two more centuries. These scholars included Maimonides (c. 1135–1204), one of the most important medieval Jewish philosophers. Born in Cordoba, Maimonides lived for a few years in Morocco and eventually settled in Egypt. He tried to bridge Judaism and Aristotelian philosophy. He also wrote treatises on medicine and worked as a physician for Ayyubid rulers, including Saladin. Maimonides was influenced by Farabi, Ibn Sina, and Ibn Rushd and influenced both Jewish and Muslim scholars.[116] Ibn Arabi (1165–1240) was also born in Andalus. He traveled all around Muslim lands, including Morocco, the Arabian Peninsula, Syria, Iraq, and Anatolia. Ibn Arabi's work combines philosophy and Sufism. He defines God as the only reality and human beings as mirrors of God's beautiful names.[117]

By the mid-thirteenth century, Cordoba and Seville had fallen to the Reconquista, and Muslim rule in the Iberian Peninsula was limited to Granada under the Nasrid dynasty. Despite its challenging political conditions, Granada remained an impressive example of Islamic civilization in terms of arts and architecture[118] and produced a prominent Sunni jurist, Shatibi (c. 1320–88). Shatibi elaborated the concept of the five "higher objectives of Islamic law" (*maqasid al-sharia*). The five higher objectives, as previously formulated by Ghazali, are the protection of religion, of life, of intellect, of progeny, and of property.[119] This formulation is based on the jurisprudential interpretation that "people's well-being" (*maslaha*) should be taken as an essential criterion in Islamic law. Ghazali was very cautious not to permit the principle of *maslaha* to supersede Quranic verses and hadiths. Shatibi, however, attached great importance to *maslaha* and legitimized many legal exceptions based on that principle. His methodology would reach "the point that any ruling potentially could be considered" an exception and "adapted according to circumstances," even by disregarding a ruling based on a Quranic verse or hadith.[120] In this regard, Shatibi's methodology provides the most flexible understanding of Islamic law, which has increasingly appealed to Muslim modernists since the late nineteenth century.[121] Another fourteenth-century Muslim scholar, Ibn Khaldun, has received much more modern academic and political attention than Shatibi or any other Muslim scholar.

---

[116] Broadie 1996, esp. 725–6. For Maimonides and other Andalusian Jewish philosophers, see Adamson 2016, 208–91.
[117] Chittick 1989; Knysh 1999; Schimmel 1975, 263–74; Corbin 1986, 402–8.
[118] Blair and Bloom 1995, 124.   [119] Masud 1995; al-Raysuni 2005, esp. 16–20.
[120] Opwis 2010, 348; also 350, 352.
[121] Ramadan 2003, 38–43; Ramadan 2009, 65–76, 122–39.

Ibn Khaldun

Ibn Khaldun (1332–1406) has been regarded as a founder of social science as a discipline distinct from religious sciences, philosophy, and natural sciences.[122] In fact, Ibn Khaldun himself also acknowledges that he initiated "an independent science with its own peculiar object – that is, human civilization and social organization."[123]

Ibn Khaldun was born in Tunisia into a family of Andalusian descent. Having lost his parents and some teachers during the Black Death, he moved to Morocco and then Granada. Ibn Khaldun became advisor of various rulers; his political engagements ended with these rulers' failures. Politically disappointed, he focused on writing a history of the world. Like Shatibi, Ibn Khaldun was a Maliki jurist. In Cairo, where he settled in the last third of his life, the Mamluk authorities appointed him to various posts, such as the chief judge of the Maliki school, professor of law, and head of a prominent Sufi lodge.[124] As a Mamluk representative, he went to Damascus, which at the time was under siege by Timur's army. Ibn Khaldun had a month-long series of conversations with Timur before the latter sacked the city in 1401.[125]

The most famous book of Ibn Khaldun is the *Muqaddimah*, the introduction to his multivolume world history. The *Muqaddimah* analyzes complex socioeconomic and political causes behind historical events. In this book, Ibn Khaldun develops two concepts of social life: *umran badawi* (rural, simple culture) and *umran hadari* (urban, complex culture). In a nutshell, these concepts capture the dichotomy between nomadic tribes and sedentary people. In a detailed analysis, however, they mark a continuum – *umran badawi* refers to lifestyles of desert nomads (Bedouins), semi-nomads, and the inhabitants of

---

[122] According to Antony Black (2011, 181), Ibn Khaldun was "the first to distinguish the study of human cultures from both metaphysics and natural sciences. He identified for the first time the field of knowledge which we call sociology." Ernest Gellner (1983, 30; also 16–35, 73–7) writes, "It is remarkable how very much Ibn Khaldun is a positive sociologist rather than a normative political philosopher." Abdesselam Cheddadi (2006, 184, 200, 459–80) depicts Ibn Khaldun's approach as similar to that of modern anthropology. In the words of Yves Lacoste (1998 [1966], 187), "Before the nineteenth century, Thucydides was surpassed by only Ibn Khaldun. The former was the inventor of history and the latter marked the emergence of history as a science."

[123] Ibn Khaldun 2005 [1377], 38–9; also 40–3, 459. Cheddadi (2006, 197) translates Ibn Khaldun's phrase *"ilm al-ijtima' al-insani wa-al-'umran al-bashari"* as "science of human society and civilization."

[124] Ibn Khaldun 1980 [1405]; Cheddadi 2006, 18–168; Dale 2015, chs. 1–3; Fromherz 2010, chs. 1–4; Alatas 2013, ch. 1; Talbi 1971, 825–30.

[125] Ibn Khaldun (1952 [1405], 36; 1980 [1405], 234) told Timur that his power was an effect of the strong *asabiyya* of the Turks under his leadership. He probably saw in Tamerlane "further confirmation of his theories." Goodman 2003, 207. See also Fischel 1967, 42–65, 93–108.

mountains and outlying villages, while *umran hadari* refers to lifestyles of those living in suburban villages, towns, and cities.[126]

Sedentary people develop sciences and arts, but they have two main weaknesses. The first is their political and military docility, which grows as the state disarms and subjugates them. The second weakness comes with the luxurious urban lifestyle: "[S]edentary people have become used to laziness and ease. They are sunk in well-being and luxury." These two characteristics are interrelated; sedentary people become more militarily dependent on the state as they eat more and become lazier, and vice versa.[127]

People of nomadic tribes, in contrast, are used to hard conditions, ready to fight, and likely to be courageous. "They have no walls or gates. Therefore, they provide their own defence ... They always carry weapons." More importantly, they have strong *asabiyya* (group feeling). *Asabiyya* is the vital factor that "restrains people from splitting up and abandoning each other. It is the source of unity and agreement."[128] It accounts for nomads' ability to invade and conquer cities. Nomads have negative characteristics as well. "Places that succumb to the Bedouins are quickly ruined," stresses Ibn Khaldun. He defines their "natural disposition" as "the negation and antithesis of civilization," characterized by the tendency to plunder other people's possessions.[129]

According to Ibn Khaldun, there is a complex relationship between *asabiyya* and royal authority. On the one hand, the goal of *asabiyya* is to establish royal authority. On the other hand, royal authority eventually weakens the people's *asabiyya* by removing their weapons and subduing them. In his definition, "[r]oyal authority means ... to rule by force."[130] In some cases, when their people no longer have *asabiyya*, rulers seem to govern easily. Nonetheless, in general, the weakening of the people's *asabiyya* implies the weakening of the state too. In the short run, despotic dynasties can maintain authority and military might by employing foreign mercenaries and slave soldiers. In the long run, however, their rule deteriorates.[131]

---

[126] Ibn Khaldun 2005 [1377], 43. See also Lacoste 1998 [1966], 127; Mahdi 1964, 193n7; Cheddadi 2006, 294.

[127] Ibn Khaldun 2005 [1377], 94.

[128] Ibn Khaldun 2005 [1377], 95, 170. *Asabiyya* implies "willingness to fight and die for each other." Ibn Khaldun 2005 [1377], 123. *Asabiyya* is also translated as "group solidarity," "group loyalty," and "esprit de corps." Lacoste 1998 [1966], 134–45; Cheddadi 2006, 289–90, 470; Baali 1988, 43–9.

[129] Ibn Khaldun 2005 [1377], 118; also 119–22.

[130] Ibn Khaldun 2005 [1377], 108; also 107–11, 285. This is to some extent similar to Weber's (1946 [1919], 78) definition of the state as "a human community that (successfully) claims the *monopoly of the legitimate use of physical force* within a given territory" (emphasis in original).

[131] Ibn Khaldun 2005 [1377], 124, 131, 136, 246–8. According to Ibn Khaldun, at the time of state formation, both royal authority and *asabiyya* are strong; at the time of collapse, both are weak. His analysis resembles Joel Migdal's (2001) examination of state–society relations.

In addition to despotism, another major characteristic of a declining dynasty is corruption. Due to its addiction to luxury and spending, the dynasty over-taxes the people. Moreover, it plunders: "Its hand reaches out to seize some of the property of the subjects, either through customs duties, or through commercial transactions, or, in some cases, merely by hostile acts directed against (property holdings), on some pretext or even with none." The people do not rebel because the dynasty "has coloured the souls of its subject people with the habit of subservience and submission for so many long years." Finally, the dynasty falls, usually leading to both political and social collapse. The declining sedentary group is replaced by a new nomadic group with strong *asabiyya*. The cycle continues.[132]

Ibn Khaldun uses this theory to explain political transformations in Muslim history. Religions, including Islam, may play a unifying role, but they cannot single-handedly shape sociopolitical events; they need the support of a powerful group with strong *asabiyya*.[133] When the Abbasids lost their *asabiyya*, they tried to keep the power by employing Turks and other ethnic groups as soldiers. Later, non-Arab groups with strong *asabiyya*, such as the Buyids and then the Seljuks, gained control of Baghdad. Finally, nomadic Mongols invaded eastern territories and destroyed the Abbasid caliphate. The case of the Iberian Peninsula was similar. Once the Umayyads' *asabiyya* became weak, small principalities divided their territory. Subsequently, a nomadic Berber force with strong *asabiyya* (and religious dynamism), the Almoravids, came and took Andalus under its control.[134]

In certain parts of the *Muqaddimah*, especially the section entitled "A Refutation of Philosophy. The Corruption of the Students of Philosophy," Ibn Khaldun criticizes such Muslim philosophers as Farabi and Ibn Sina, particularly for their metaphysical views.[135] Religiously, Ibn Khaldun was more an orthodox Sunni than these philosophers. Methodologically, Ibn Khaldun preferred to make inferences from historical data, unlike these philosophers, who largely relied on syllogism and drew normative conclusions.[136] Yves Lacoste defines Ibn Khaldun as a unique personality who was both an orthodox Muslim and an empirical scientist. Lacoste points out that these two characteristics were complementary and even necessary for Ibn Khaldun to develop a scientific approach independent of (Aristotelian) logic and (metaphysical) philosophy, which dominated sciences at that time.[137]

---

[132] Ibn Khaldun 2005 [1377], 248–9; also 107–11, 246–7, 285–9. See also Gibb 1933, 31.

[133] "[N]o religious or political propaganda can be successful, unless power and group feeling exist to support" them. Ibn Khaldun 2005 [1377], 258. Ibn Khaldun (2005 [1377], 259) warns about utopic and dangerous expectations of a religious savior, a Mahdi. For him (2005 [1377], 126, 255; 1967 [1377], I: 320–2), early Muslims' rapid military achievement had some unique aspects, though it can also be explained as a successful combination of religious dynamism and strong *asabiyya*.

[134] Ibn Khaldun 2005 [1377], 124–5.   [135] Ibn Khaldun 2005 [1377], 353, 357, 398–405.

[136] Fakhry 2004, 335–8.   [137] Lacoste 1998 [1966], 214–15, 247, 261.

Although Ibn Khaldun criticizes philosophers, his approach also diverges from orthodox Sunni perspectives in some respects. One divergence pertains to the authentication of hadiths. Orthodox scholars generally check two things: (1) whether a hadith contradicts apparent meanings of Quranic verses and (2) whether the person who transmits the hadith is reliable. Ibn Khaldun argues that rational criticism should have priority over criticism of transmitters regarding hadiths and other historical reports: "[I]t is necessary to investigate whether it is possible that the (reported facts) could have happened. This is more important than, and has priority over, personality criticism."[138]

Ibn Khaldun's general theory is structuralist, in a sense that it explains events through broad geographical, socioeconomic, and political factors, rather than the roles of particular actors or ideas. He does not depict history as a struggle between belief and unbelief, or between good and evil. For him, sedentary and nomadic groups are interdependent entities, which jointly constitute dynamics of social history in a dialectical manner.[139]

To explain the state of Muslims' intellectual life, Ibn Khaldun again uses a structuralist perspective. He regards scholarship as a consequence of certain sociopolitical conditions, particularly the existence or absence of sedentary culture. There had been a flourishing of sciences in eastern territories, while "Iraq, Khurasan, and Transoxiana retained their sedentary culture." Yet "when those cities fell into ruins, sedentary culture, which God has devised for the attainment of sciences and crafts, disappeared from them." Consequently, scholarship "disappeared from among the Persians, who were now engulfed by the desert attitude." He refers to Tusi as the last great Persian scholar. He also mentions Taftazani as a great scholar who indicates that in his region, Transoxiana, sedentary culture still survived in some cities. In the same vein, in Andalus and Northwest Africa, "sciences decreased with the decrease of civilization." Ibn Khaldun appreciates the Cairo of his times as "the great center of Islam," the paramount example of sedentary culture, and a fount of scholarship.[140]

Nonetheless, after his death, Ibn Khaldun's work did not have much influence even in Cairo, let alone other parts of the Muslim world.[141] Beginning in the seventeenth century, Ottoman analysts of imperial decline became interested in the *Muqaddimah*, but they focused almost exclusively on its explanation of the dynastic life cycle.[142] "No famous thinker has suffered such long

---

[138] Ibn Khaldun 2005 [1377], 38; also 11–26, 35–7. Ibn Khaldun's approach inspired some modern critics of certain hadiths. Using Ibn Khaldun's approach, Barakat Ahmad (1979, esp. 2, 67–94) refutes historical reports about Muslims' killing of 600–900 Jews of the Banu Qurayda tribe in Madina in 627. See also Alatas 2013, 41–6, 130–4.

[139] Lacoste 1998 [1966], 209–11; Cheddadi 2006, 283–96, 474–8; Fromherz 2010, 127–43.

[140] Ibn Khaldun 2005 [1377], 375, 430–1; Ibn Khaldun 1967 [1377], III: 315. In 1350, Cairo had an estimated population of 350,000 and was the third largest city in the world, after two Chinese cities. Chandler 1987, 475.

[141] Cheddadi 2006, ch. 11.   [142] Fleischer 1983, 198–203. See also Okumuş 2008.

and strange neglect as Ibn Khaldun," writes Saunders. "It was his misfortune to live when Arabic culture, of which he was so bright an ornament, was in full decline, and Western Europe had ceased to borrow from it."[143] Ibn Khaldun was a lost opportunity for Muslims to revive their waning intellectual dynamism.

SUFISM

Sufism Replacing Philosophy

The process of discrediting philosophers in the Muslim world that began in the eleventh century continued in subsequent centuries. Even Ibn Khaldun strongly criticized philosophers, as previously noted.[144] The ulema and the Sufis filled the vacuum left by the gradual disappearance of philosophers. With its syncretic and flexible discourses, Sufism became popular among certain segments of Muslim elites and masses, who saw madrasa-centered orthodox scholarship as rigid and tedious.[145] Sufism's mixture with poetry was also a major reason for its popularity.[146] Another appealing aspect of Sufism has been its esotericism. According Hodgson, the Sufi claim of mystical knowledge was a way of bypassing the censorship of the ulema. The concealment of knowledge gradually became "a pattern for all thinkers who did not conform to the narrow range approved by the official 'ulama.'" As a result, "the more imaginative sides of intellectual culture in Islam … tended to become esoteric."[147]

In this context, some eminent Sufis such as Ibn Arabi (d. 1240) developed philosophical thought under the name of Sufism. Nonetheless, Fazlur Rahman, Jabri, and several other modern critics have seen the enduring influence of Sufism on Muslim intellectual life as predominantly negative for two main reasons. First, to Sufism's critics, while the philosophy of the philosophers had been rational, the philosophy of the Sufis was mystical. Sufism has

---

[143] Saunders 1966, 342. This statement makes sense when we compare pre-modern Europeans' interest in Ibn Rushd and their ignorance of Ibn Khaldun.

[144] Regarding Ibn Khaldun's relationship with philosophy, I disagree with Muhsin Mahdi (1964, 108–12, 225, 285–95), who categorizes the *Muqaddimah* as a work of (and a minor contribution to) Muslim Aristotelian/Platonic philosophy. I agree with Cheddadi (2006, 195–218), who notes that Ibn Khaldun makes an original contribution and takes every opportunity to distance himself from philosophers, though his new science has some philosophical roots. See also Dale 2015, 2–6, 23–31, 77–117.

[145] For the importance of memorizing texts in Mamluk madrasas, see Berkey 1992, 28–30; Hodgson 1974b, 438–45.

[146] In Anatolia, Rumi's (1207–73) Persian Sufi poetry and Yunus Emre's (1238–1321) Turkish Sufi poetry became very popular. Rumi 2004 [1258–73]; Emre 2102 [c. 1321]; Schimmel 1975, 309–28, 329–37; Hodgson 1974b, 244–54.

[147] Hodgson 1974b, 194–5.

emphasized mystical knowledge (*irfan*), which is unveiled to illuminated hearts, at the expense of reason, declaring the latter to be fallible and misleading.[148]

Second, the Sufi understanding of spiritual hierarchy is seen as contradicting Sunni Islam's original message of egalitarianism. The Sufi shaykhs have claimed a monopoly over the Quranic terms *wali* (singular) and *awliya* (plural), meaning friend(s) (of God). This dynamic is similar to the ulema's monopolization of broad Quranic terms *ilm* (science) and *ulema* (those who are knowledgeable), by reducing the former to Islamic studies and the latter to themselves. The Sufi shaykhs did not stop there. They have even argued for the existence of a perfect man – the *qutb* ([spiritual] pole) – at the top of the spiritual hierarchy. Hence, the duty of ordinary Muslims was to follow this perfect man.[149] Sufism's hierarchical outlook was not confined to spiritual matters and contributed to the authoritarian tendencies in Muslim sociopolitical life, as explored in the following section.

Sufism and the State

In addition to allying with the ulema, Sunni rulers and officials, such as Nizam al-Mulk, Nur al-Din, and Saladin, patronized Sufis. Their patronage helped these rulers both keep Sufis under control and benefit from their popular legitimacy.[150] In the late twelfth and early thirteenth centuries, Caliph Nasir (r. 1180–1225) tried to reassert Abbasid religiopolitical authority by building close alliances with the ulema and Sufi shaykhs. He also restructured *futuwwa* orders (men's clubs organized around codes of honor) under his leadership. As one component of this broader support for Sufism, Nasir provided a prominent Sufi shaykh, Umar Suhrawardi, with an official position.[151]

In order to strengthen Nasir's network, especially following the Mongol invasions, Suhrawardi visited Anatolia. He arranged a meeting between the sultan of the Anatolian Seljuks, Alaeddin Keykubad (r. 1220–37), and the eminent Sufi shaykh Najm al-Din Razi (known as Daya) (1177–1256). Daya had fled the Mongols from Khurasan to Anatolia. He submitted his Sufi compendium, *The Path of God's Bondsmen from Origin to Return*, to the sultan.[152]

---

[148] Rahman 1965, 115; al-Jabri 2011 [1984], 312, 340, 360, 396; al-Jabri 1995, 119–48; Ali 2012 [1902], 418.

[149] Ibn Khaldun was sympathetic to Sufism but also critical of these Sufi concepts. He sees the notion of the perfect man as illogical and incompatible with Sunni Islam. For him, the Sufis adapted this idea from the Shii notion of infallible imam. Ibn Khaldun 2005 [1377], 367; Ibn Khaldun 1967 [1377], II: 186–7, III: 92–3. See also Trimingham 1971, 102–4; Hodgson 1974b, 227–9, 241–3; Karamustafa 2007, 42.

[150] Ohlander 2008, 19; Trimingham 1971, 9; Lapidus 1984, xiii.

[151] Ohlander 2008, 19–27, 89–112; Hodgson 1974b, 279–85; Hanne 2007, 204.

[152] Daya 1982 [1223], 45–50.

The *Path* provides a Sufi framework for the orthodox Sunni synthesis. It condemns the philosophers for their metaphysical views. It particularly criticizes Omar Khayyam for his poems questioning the meaning of life in an unorthodox manner.[153] The *Path* reflects the influence of the Sasanian notion of social stratification in which the rulers and the clergy constitute the dominant classes, while the merchants are subordinated and the independent scholars eliminated. The *Path* follows this stratification and establishes the following social hierarchy: kings, kings' viziers and deputies, ulema (jurists, judges, and preachers), holders of wealth, farmers, merchants, and craftsmen.[154]

The *Path* quotes several fabricated hadiths to justify such a hierarchy. It depicts kings as sacred people: "The Prophet, upon whom be God's peace and blessings, said: 'The king is the shadow of God upon earth.'"[155] The ulema have lower but still sacred status: "The Prophet may be thought of as saying '... What need henceforth for prophets, for each of the scholars of my religion shall be equal to a prophet?'"[156] Shaykhs are also presented as sacred: "The Prophet said: 'The shaikh among his following is like the prophet among his people.'"[157] Last but not least, it repeats a version of the famous fabrication: "[T]he Prophet said: 'Justice and kingship are twins.'"[158]

The *Path* was widely read in Muslim lands and promoted hierarchical political and religious views. Modern investigations discovered a large number of copies of its original and translations in Turkey, Iran, Central Asia, the Indian subcontinent, and China. It exerted "great influence in Turkish Anatolia, the land of its composition, in both the Persian original and a much-read Turkish translation made in the fifteenth century." Versions of it were dedicated to two Ottoman sultans, Murad II and Bayezid II – the father and son of Fatih, respectively.[159]

Another important work that promoted similar themes was the mirror for princes written in Persian by the famous poet Saadi (1209–91). Saadi emphasizes the need for a strong connection between the ruler, the ulema, and the Sufi orders. He writes, "The ruler must treat religious leaders and clergymen with reverence, offer them a prominent seat, and rule as they deem it advisable so that kingship is in compliance with the shari'a and not vice versa." While listing "the most important tasks of the state," he first mentions "the construction of mosques [and] houses of dervishes" followed by "bridges, water reservoirs, and roadside wells."[160]

---

[153] Daya 1982 [1223], 54, 482.   [154] Daya 1982 [1223], 395–493.

[155] Daya 1982 [1223], 395; also 49, 156. In the following quotations, I removed the phrase "upon whom be God's peace and blessings."

[156] Daya 1982 [1223], 178; also 445. This statement is an exaggerated adaptation of an authenticated hadith.

[157] Daya 1982 [1223], 235; also 178.   [158] Daya 1982 [1223], 414.   [159] Algar 1982, 15, 20.

[160] Saadi 2013 [c. 1258], 62.

The hierarchical understandings of state–society and state–religion relations were not merely reflected in certain Sufi writings. As the next section will show, they characterized Muslim political thought between the twelfth and fourteenth centuries.

MUSLIM POLITICAL THOUGHT

If one thinks about some medieval ulema whose political views have influenced Muslims into the twenty-first century, the three most prominent examples would be Mawardi, Ghazali, and Ibn Taymiyya. I already covered Mawardi and Ghazali, whose ideas were shaped by the political conditions in Iraq-Iran mostly in the eleventh century. Ibn Taymiyya (1263–1328) lived about two centuries later, in Egypt-Syria.[161] His radical views about declaring some heterodox groups (Alawites and Druzes) and Muslims who did not observe Islamic law (Mongol rulers who converted to Islam) as unbelievers and thus people who could be killed[162] were informed by the experience of war between his country, the Mamluk Sultanate, and its enemies – the Mongols, the Crusaders, and disobedient heterodox Muslims.[163]

Beyond the issue of violence, Ibn Taymiyya's ideas have been influential in the formation of contemporary Salafism. As a (neo-)Hanbali, Ibn Taymiyya attached importance to literal understandings of the Qur'an and hadiths; thus he emphasized the text at the expense of reason while interpreting Islamic law. Ibn Taymiyya attacked those who advocated the use of logic, including not only philosophers such as Ibn Sina, but also theologians such as Ghazali and Razi. His criticisms unsurprisingly targeted Sufis and Shiis too.[164]

In his influential *Al-Siyasah al-Shar'iyah fi Islah al-Ra'i wa al-Ra'iyah* (*Sharia-Based Governance in Reforming Both the Ruler and His Flock*), Ibn Taymiyya emphasizes the importance of the ulema–state alliance. He depicts political authority as an absolute necessity: "Sixty years with a despotic ruler are better than one night without a ruler."[165] He also notes that political authority and religious authority are dependent on each other: "If political authority is isolated from religion, or religion from political authority, then the people's order would be destroyed." In this regard, Ibn Taymiyya interprets the phrase *"uli'l-amr"* in the Quran (4:59) ("O you who believe! Obey God and obey the Messenger and *those in authority [uli'l-amr]* among you") as referring

[161] For analyses of the complex dimensions of Ibn Taymiyya's thought, see Anjum 2012; Vasalou 2016; Hallaq 1993.
[162] Griffel 2007, 133; Ibn Taymiyya 1994a [1309–14], 152–6; Ibn Taymiyya 1994b [1309–14], 185–90; Ibn Taymiyya 1966 [1309–14], 142–8.
[163] Laoust 1939, 45, 59–65, 117–25. See also Chapter 1.
[164] Hallaq 1993, esp. xiv; Jaffer 2014, 122–30.
[165] Ibn Taymiyya 1994a [1309–14], 187. French translation: Ibn Taymiyya 1994b [1309–14], 232; English translation: Ibn Taymiyya 1966 [1309–14], 188. Ibn Jamaah also quotes this saying. Lambton 1981, 139, 140; Rosenthal 1958, 44. See also al-Ghazali 1964 [c. 1107], 77.

to two leading classes: the *"umara"* (rulers and officials) and the ulema.[166] This view marked a departure from Mawardi's theory of the ideal caliphate, in which a single imam represents both political and religious authority.[167]

Ibn Taymiyya's shift from the ideal of caliphate to a more realistic notion of ulema–state alliance seems to have resulted from the abolishment of the Abbasid Caliphate and the Mamluk sultans' military-based political authority. It is not a coincidence that another famous Mamluk jurist of that time, Ibn Jamaah (1241–1333), held similar views on the political importance of the ulema.[168] Ibn Taymiyya's harsh and wide-ranging criticisms earned him many enemies. As a result, he was imprisoned several times and eventually died in prison. Some of his ideas, such as his criticism of Sufism and his literalism, mostly remained peripheral until the twentieth century, while his stress on the ulema–state alliance has continually attracted attention.

Ibn Rushd and other philosophers offered alternative political views, but they gained neither the support of the masses nor the approval of those in power. In his commentary on Plato's *Republic*, Ibn Rushd endorses and even expands the Platonic view on women's sociopolitical participation. He notes that women can hold any sociopolitical status, including those of "philosophers and rulers."[169] Ibn Rushd even argues that keeping women out of sociopolitical life hindered prosperity in the Muslim cities of Andalus. In these writings, Ibn Rushd challenges both the established notion of gender relations in his own Muslim society and certain views of Aristotle on this issue:[170]

The competence of women is unknown, however, in these cities since they are only taken for procreation and hence are placed at the service of their husbands and confined to procreation, upbringing, and suckling. This nullifies their [other] activities. Since women in these cities are not prepared with respect to any of the human virtues, they frequently resemble plants . . . Their being a burden upon the men is one of the causes of the poverty of these cities . . . [Women] should be trained in the same way through music and gymnastic.[171]

---

[166] Ibn Taymiyya 1994a [1309–14], 190, 184, respectively; Ibn Taymiyya 1994b [c. 1309–14], 237, 228; Ibn Taymiyya 1966 [1309–14], 192, 183. See also Anjum 2012, ch. 6.

[167] Mawardi (1996 [1045–58], 3) quotes this verse (4:59) at the beginning of his case for a caliph. He argues that God "made it obligatory for us to obey those in authority; namely, the sovereigns with power over us." See also Afsaruddin 2015, 33.

[168] Lambton 1981, 139.

[169] Ibn Rushd 1974 [c. 1194], 58. On women's ability to share sociopolitical functions with men, Ibn Rushd "is clearly in agreement with Plato," whereas on some other issues "such as the community of women and property, he resorts to the purely narrative style, simply reporting what Plato has said." Fakhry 2001, 111.

[170] "[T]he male is by nature superior, and the female inferior; and the one rules, and the other is ruled." Aristotle 1996b [c. 350 BCE], 17. "[W]oman should just obey and be silent." Aristotle 1996b [c. 350 BCE], 29.

[171] Ibn Rushd 1974 [c. 1194], 59.

Nonetheless, such egalitarian views on gender relations never became popular in Muslim societies until the twentieth century. Instead, patriarchal, if not misogynistic, views, including those of Ghazali[172] and Ibn Taymiyya,[173] as well as those of some philosophers such as Tusi,[174] represented the mainstream.[175]

Ibn Rushd's views on education and political regimes in his commentary on Plato's *Republic* were also completely ignored by Muslims.[176] On education, Ibn Rushd approvingly paraphrases Plato's emphasis on teaching philosophy, gymnastics, and music to students.[177] On political regimes, Ibn Rushd briefly analyzes early Islamic history through the lens of the Platonic framework. While explaining Plato's notion of the transformation from the virtuous regime (based on reason and wisdom) to timocracy (based on spiritedness and honor), and then to three other regimes (based on appetite and desires) – oligarchy (the rule of the wealthy few), democracy (the rule of the poor majority), and tyranny – Ibn Rushd refers to cases from early Islamic history. For him, "the case of the governance of the Arabs in early times" – i.e., the rule of the Prophet and the Four Caliphs – "used to imitate the virtuous governance." Afterward, the Arabs "were transformed into timocrats in the days of Mu'awiya."[178] Likewise, he briefly explains the political achievements and failures of the Almoravids and the Almohads as a transformation from regimes based on wisdom to regimes based on honor and desire.[179]

Ibn Rushd explains that he commented on Plato's *Republic* because "Aristotle's book on governance has not yet fallen into our hands."[180] Interestingly, Aristotle's *Politics* was not translated into Arabic until 1957.[181] Scholars have debated the reasons for this delay.[182] *Politics'* translation into Latin and then vernacular languages, beginning in the mid-thirteenth century, had a substantial impact on the transformation of Western European thought,[183]

---

[172] See Chapter 2.

[173] Ibn Taymiyya 1994a [1309–14], 179; Ibn Taymiyya 1994b [1309–14], 222–3; Ibn Taymiyya 1966 [1309–14], 177–8.

[174] Tusi 1964 [c. 1235], 161–6, 173. See also Dawani 1839 [c. 1477], 268–74.

[175] For a comparison of Ibn Rushd's, Ghazali's, and Ibn Taymiyya's views on gender relations, see Harhash 2016, esp. 18–41.

[176] This commentary's Arabic original has been lost; it was translated into English from a fourteenth-century Hebrew translation written in southern France.

[177] Ibn Rushd 1974 [c. 1194], esp. 27–31, 50.

[178] Ibn Rushd 1974 [c. 1194], 121; also 75. Erwin Rosenthal (1966, 15, 297–9; also 1958, 176–7, 190–209) argues that Ibn Rushd identifies Plato's ideal state with the sharia-based state. Critics, however, refute this argument by noting that Ibn Rushd's perspective is universal political philosophy. Pines 1957, 126–8; Teicher 1960, 192–3; Berman 1968–9, 436–7; Lerner 1974, ix, xvii–xxi.

[179] Ibn Rushd 1974 [c. 1194], 121, 125, 133–4, 144–5.   [180] Ibn Rushd 1974 [c. 1194], 4.

[181] Fakhry 1988, 90.

[182] Pines 1975; Brague 1993, esp. 433; Parens 1995, 149–50, 153n39; Fakhry 2001, 97.

[183] Tierney 1988, 2, 98; Starr 2013, 138, 190–1.

particularly on its conceptualization of citizenship, political community, and the common good.[184]

In short, the jurisprudential approach (represented by Ibn Taymiyya) was dominant, while the philosophical approach (represented by Ibn Rushd) was mostly marginal in Muslim political thought between the twelfth and fourteenth centuries. The ulema class had dozens, if not hundreds, of madrasas and thousands of members to disseminate its ideas,[185] whereas the philosophers lacked institutional and financial bases except for arbitrary political patronage, particularly after the weakening of the merchant class, which had previously supported both philosophers and independent Islamic scholars.

A third approach was the advice (or mirrors for princes) literature. It was much more eclectic and pragmatic than the jurisprudential and philosophical alternatives. Works of this category combined Sasanian realpolitik, Greek philosophy, and Islamic political thought in various degrees. Tusi's philosophical book, *Nasirean Ethics*, could be categorized as a book of advice literature. Originally it was intended to be a Persian adaptation of Miskawayh's book on ethics,[186] but it subsequently became an important book in its own right. The main sources Tusi used were Miskawayh and Aristotle (on ethics), Ibn Sina and Bryson (on household management), and Farabi and Plato (on politics). Tusi's synthesis of Platonic, Sasanian, and Islamic ideas is visible in the following paragraph about the ideal polity and the religion–state brotherhood:

The people of the Virtuous City, however, albeit diversified throughout the world, are in reality agreed . . . In their close-knit affection they are like one individual; as the Religious Legislator says (peace be upon him!): "Muslims are (like) a single hand against all others, and the Believers are as one soul." Their rulers, who are the regulators of the world, have control of the enactments of laws and of the most expedient measures in daily life . . . This is the reason for the interdependence of faith and kingship, as expressed by the Emperor of the Iranians, the Philosopher of the Persians, Ardashir Babak: "Religion and kingship are twins, neither being complete without the other." Religion is the base and kingship the support: just as a foundation without support avails nothing, while a support without foundation falls into ruin, so religion without kingship is profitless, and kingship without faith is easily broken.[187]

Tusi's *Nasirean Ethics* influenced the elite in the Middle East and India for centuries.[188] Ziauddin Barani (1285–1357), a Muslim political thinker in the Delhi Sultanate, produced another important book of advice literature. He was an unapologetic defender of the Sasanian notion of realpolitik. For Barani,

[184] Aristotle 1996b [c. 350 BCE], esp. 11–14, 31–3, 61–9.
[185] Nur al-Din, Saladin, and following Ayyubid rulers established about ninety madrasas in Damascus. The Ayyubids (1171–1250) also established thirty-two madrasas in and around Cairo. Berkey 1992, 8.
[186] Miskawayh 1968 [c. 1030]; Tusi 1964 [c. 1235], 25.
[187] Tusi 1964 [c. 1235], 215. See al-Farabi 1985 [c. 940], 260–1.
[188] Fakhry 1991, 131–42; Arjomand 2010, 248; Alam 2013, 168–75.

governance was inherently immoral. Thus, it should be designed by Sasanian traditions, instead of Islamic ethical principles:

But just as the eating of carrion, though prohibited, is yet permitted in time of dire need, similarly the customs and traditions of the pagan Emperors of Iran – the crown and the throne, ... high palaces, court ceremonials, asking people to prostrate themselves before the king, collecting treasures, misappropriating properties, ... putting people to death on grounds of state-policy, ... spending recklessly without any right ... – should from the viewpoint of truth and the correct Faith, be considered like the eating of a carrion in time of dire need ... Know well that kingship is not possible without following the traditions of the Emperors of Iran, and it is known to all religious scholars that these traditions are opposed to the traditions of the Prophet and to his mode of life and living.[189]

In the same vein, even Ibn Khaldun justifies certain Sasanian political customs in Muslim states. "The decisions of the ruler," he notes, "as a rule, deviate from what is right."[190] Thus, he explains how various Sasanian political attitudes replaced Islamic ones. The Prophet Muhammad and the Four Caliphs received the *bay'a*, a handshake between the leader and the person who renders his or her oath of allegiance (the Prophet received *bay'a* from both men and women). *Bay'a* implied a contractual relationship, resembling a handshaking for a trade deal – in the words of Ibn Khaldun, "something like the action of buyer and seller." Later, Muslims adopted "the Persian custom of greeting kings by kissing the earth, or their hand, their foot, or the lower hem of their garment." This behavior "replaced the handshake which was originally used, because shaking hands with everybody meant that the ruler lowered himself and made himself cheap, things that are detrimental to leadership and the dignity of the royal position."[191]

In general, the methodological and theoretical approaches of Ibn Khaldun could have lifted Muslim political thought to a much higher level had they not been ignored for centuries. His empirical methodology could have fixed the main problem with the ulema's literalist epistemology – the exclusive focus on the text without consideration of the context. Moreover, Ibn Khaldun's social-scientific theoretical approach, which explains cause and effect relations, could have offered novel perspectives on sociopolitical analysis beyond those provided by philosophy or advice literature.

In a narrow sense, Ibn Khaldun's theoretical framework based on *asabiyya* became irrelevant by the sixteenth century as a result of the Ottomans' and other states' effective use of gunpowder against various nomadic horsemen.[192]

---

[189] Barani 1961 [c. 1358–9], 40; also 39. For Barani's thought, see Aquil 2008, esp. 185; Alam 2004, 31–43.

[190] Ibn Khaldun 2005 [1377], 154.   [191] Ibn Khaldun 2005 [1377], 166–7.

[192] Black (2011, 183–4) argues that Ibn Khaldun's framework may be "to some extent peculiar to the Islamic world" but does not explain non-Muslim cases such as China and medieval Europe, which had stronger state traditions. Francis Fukuyama (2011, 294), however, claims the opposite: in certain periods of Chinese history, "the source of military pressure was pastoral

Later, Western European states developed even more disciplined military forces armed with more sophisticated weapons.[193] Furthermore, nationalism and national armies made urban people militarily much stronger than Ibn Khaldun could have imagined.[194] In a broader sense, however, Ibn Khaldun's framework may still be seen as relevant for understanding such modern phenomena as peasant revolts, center–periphery relations, and migration.

While discussing political issues, Muslim scholars generally did not systematically explore economic affairs. An exception was, again, Ibn Khaldun. He stresses the interconnection between political sociology and economics while also elaborating certain rules of economics. Although Ibn Khaldun might have had a few forerunners who studied the economy as a subject in and of itself,[195] he still was the first and, until the nineteenth century, the only Muslim thinker to develop systematic ideas on economics.[196] He argues that extravagant spending weakens dynasties and that despotic dynasties overtax to fund extravagancy. Nevertheless, in a declining dynasty, higher tax rates do not mean higher revenues; instead, they lead to lower revenues.[197]

nomads ... In the particular geography of China, the Middle East, and Europe, bordering as they did on the vast steppes of Central Asia, this led to the repeated cycle of decadence, barbarian conquest, and civilized renewal noted by the Arab philosopher Ibn Khaldun." For the nomadic invasions in China and India, see Braudel 1993, 164–7. According to Bloch (2014 [1940], 57), Ibn Khaldun's approach not only explained invasions in early medieval Europe but also "had an almost universal validity – at least till such time as the sedentary people could call to their aid the resources of an improved political organization and of a really scientific military machine."

[193] These dynamics are articulated by Smith (1993 [1776], 174): "The frequent conquests of all the civilized countries in Asia by the Tartars [i.e., Mongols], sufficiently demonstrates the natural superiority, which the militia of a barbarous, has over that of a civilized nation. A well-regulated standing army ... can best be maintained by an opulent and civilized nation, so it can alone defend such a nation against the invasion of a poor and barbarous neighbor."

[194] "[F]rom Ibn Khaldun's viewpoint, nationalism is wildly paradoxical. It operates in a milieu and on individuals who, from Ibn Khaldun's viewpoint, should exemplify the very opposite of any social cohesion ... deeply sunk in an urban-style life of specialism and individualism. And yet, nationalism ... proved a powerful social bond." Gellner 1983, 92; also 90–8. See also Smith 1993, 160–2.

[195] For Dimashqi (1995a [c. 11th century]), see Chapter 4. See also Ghazanfar and Islahi 2003, 58–69.

[196] Issawi 1980, 493–5.

[197] Ibn Khaldun 2005 [1377], 230–1, 289. See Rosenthal 1958, 246–50. Arthur Laffer (2004, 1) refers to Ibn Khaldun's thinking as an antecedent of the "Laffer curve," which represents the relationship between tax rates and government revenues. In 1993, former president Ronald Reagan ended his open letter to President Bill Clinton by referring to him: "[M]ay I offer you the advice of ... Ibn Khaldun, who said: 'At the beginning of the empire, the tax rates were low and the revenues were high. At the end of the empire, the tax rates were high and the revenues were low.'" "There They Go Again," *New York Times*, February 18, 1993. Previously, Manfred Halpern had criticized Reagan for misrepresenting Ibn Khaldun. For him, Ibn Khaldun observed the ineffective overtaxation as a consequence of despotism and corruption, rather

Jean Boulakia defines Ibn Khaldun as a pioneer theorist of production, value, money, prices (determined by demand and supply), distribution, the population cycle, and the public finance cycle.[198] Joseph Spengler notes that Ibn Khaldun's economic views embrace "market, price, monetary, supply, and demand phenomena, and hinting at some of the macro-economic relations stressed by Lord Keynes" six centuries later. For Spengler, Ibn Khaldun's economic views did not lead to the creation of economics as an independent discipline because they were too deeply embedded into his general sociological analysis, which "intended to explain the behavior over time of interrelated economic and non-economic phenomena." Otherwise, he could have led "economic inquiry ... [to be] carried forward effectively in the Muslim world, at least in the absence of oppressive governmental or ecclesiastical action."[199] Indeed, governmental and clerical suppression of critical inquiry into politics and the economy became increasingly dominant in the Muslim world. This problem was directly linked to the trivialization of not only economic thought but also the merchant class at the hands of the state–ulema alliance.

MARGINALIZATION OF MERCHANTS

I have explained how the Seljuk model of ulema–state alliance gradually spread from the eastern territories toward Egypt and Syria under the Ayyubids and then the Mamluks. This alliance weakened social roles of merchants, who had previously funded certain philosophers and independent (i.e., not state-servant) Islamic scholars. Another dimension of the Seljuk model was the *iqta* system of land revenue assignments. In Egypt, the *iqta* system was developed under the Ayyubids and further institutionalized under the Mamluks. It became a foundation for the Mamluk centralization and militarization of the economy.[200] Particularly during the second period of Mamluk rule, central state policies marginalized merchants.[201]

Following the Mongol invasion of the eastern territories, including the destruction of the Abbasid caliphate in Baghdad, the Mamluk Sultanate, which ruled Egypt and Syria from the mid-thirteenth to the early sixteenth century, gained central importance in the Muslim world. In this regard, the Mamluk

---

than prescribing supply-side economics. "Khaldun Was Nowhere Near the Supply Side," *New York Times*, October 11, 1981.

[198] Boulakia 1971, 1106–17.   [199] Spengler 1964, 304.

[200] Under the Mamluk *iqta* system, land grants were assigned to officials as payment and "on condition of maintaining a certain number of Mamluk soldiers, varying between five and a hundred ... The system was based on the permanent eviction of the Arabized descendants of the Mamluk officers by newly imported Mamluks, thus preventing ... the formation of a hereditary landing aristocracy." Lewis 1970, 112.

[201] During the first period (1250–1382), ethnically Turkish Mamluks were ruling, while in the second period (1382–1517), the Circassians ruled. Al-Nuwayri 2016 [c. 1333], 295. The Circassian period had more negative state policies toward merchants. Ashtor 1983, 271–4.

case is crucial to understanding the ulema–state alliance and state–merchant relations in this period. The Mamluks officially sanctioned the idea of the "equality and full orthodoxy" of the four Sunni jurisprudential schools "as never before."[202] Under the Mamluks, Lapidus stresses, the ulema were not only "the undisputed interpreters of the divine law" but also "the administrators of the community's familial, commercial, educational, and legal affairs." The weakening of private economic enterprises coincided with the strengthening of Mamluk control over religion: "Muslim religious life was rebuilt around formal schools and endowed properties, and was increasingly subordinated to state control."[203]

The Black Death in 1348–9 killed about one-third of the population of Egypt and Syria.[204] The Black Death affected almost the entire Old World, and its death rate was even higher (around two-fifths of the population) in Europe.[205] Plague continually struck the Mamluk territories until the early fifteenth century and, according to Michael Dols, had "a cumulative effect far greater than that of the Black Death itself."[206] Dols narrates an anecdote about the plague of 1429–30. The Mamluk sultan of the time gathered the ulema in Cairo for consultation. A judge complained that the sultan himself had a production and trade monopoly on certain goods, including sugarcane and spices, which led to substantial hardship for merchants. "In response, the sultan merely ordered the judges and amirs [officials] to instruct the people to be penitent and to increase their pious deeds."[207] This anecdote shows how the Mamluk sultan disregarded the worsening conditions of merchants even when the issue was raised by a member of the ulema.[208]

The Mamluks subordinated Karimi merchants, who had conducted Egypt-based intercontinental trade for centuries.[209] In certain cases of fiscal need, the Mamluk state seized money from Karimi merchants through forced loans or forced purchases. "Fiscal abuses were so common as to be natural," writes

[202] Madelung 1985, 166.
[203] Lapidus 1984, 130, xiii, respectively. Under the Mamluks, the appointment of judges, preachers, and prayer leaders needed official confirmation. Lapidus 1984, 135. See also Zubaida 1972, esp. 325–8.
[204] Dols 1977, 215. [205] Logan 2013, 264; North and Thomas 1973, 72–4.
[206] Dols 1977, 4. From the mid-fourteenth to the early fifteenth century, the Mamluk Sultanate faced other crises, including droughts, internal military struggles, and Timur's invasion of Syrian cities. Abu-Lughod 1989, 181, 235–8; Ayalon 1956, 104.
[207] Dols 1977, 276. See also Borsch 2005, 48–9, 113.
[208] "The Mamluk system was essentially a mechanism for mobilizing the natural resources and labor of the country to support an elaborate military machine and the luxurious style of life of its alien elite." Abu-Lughod 1989, 239.
[209] Karimi merchants included Muslims and Jews. They flourished under Fatimid rule and remained effective even during the first Mamluk period. Ashtor 1983, 271–4.

Lapidus. Beyond state needs, personal corruption of Mamluk officials caused problems for merchants too. In this regard, "what protection merchants could obtain depended on patronage, appeals to higher officials against the abuses of lesser ones, the intercession of the religious notables, and above all on bribery and compromise."[210]

In the fifteenth century, the Mamluk state's control of the economy tightened even further. The Karimi merchants were largely marginalized. In general, an increasing number of merchants began to serve as the sultan's agents, and numerous officials started to function in commerce. In other words, "giant steps were taken toward the fuller assimilation of the merchants into the state and the reduction of the independent merchant class,"[211] leading to "the decline of the upper bourgeoisie."[212]

The restrictions on private property led to an enormous expansion of waqf properties.[213] In particular, officials tended to endow their properties as waqfs in order to protect them from state seizure. Ibn Khaldun observes that in Egypt, "the Turkish amirs [officials] under the Turkish dynasty [Ayyubids and early Mamluks] were afraid that their ruler might proceed against ... [their] descendants ... because chicanery and confiscation are always to be feared from royal authority." Thus, "they built a great many colleges, hermitages, and monasteries, and endowed them with mortmain endowments that yielded income." Some intended that "their children would participate in these endowments, either as administrators or by having some other share in them," while others were "inclined to do good deeds and hoped for (a heavenly) reward for their aspirations and actions."[214] While increased waqf funding supported more students and teachers, as Timur Kuran emphasizes, these measures also led to economic inefficiency and stagnation.[215]

This economic stagnancy can be deduced from Shatzmiller's data. Analyzing historical documents, including urban market administrator guidelines (e.g., *hisba* manuals), written in Iraq, Syria, Egypt, North Africa, and Andalus, she compares the period between the eighth and eleventh centuries with that between the twelfth and fifteenth centuries. From the first period to the second, the number of occupational terms pertaining to "commerce" almost remained stable (from 233 to 220), whereas the number pertaining to "bureaucracy and military" increased from 97 to 303, and the number pertaining to "education, law, and religion" increased from 33 to 180 (see Table 5.1). The changing numbers indicate the higher degree of specialization and division of labor in the

[210] Lapidus 1984, 124–5.   [211] Lapidus 1984, 126–8.   [212] Ashtor 1976, 320.
[213] Most Mamluk monuments were built in Cairo. Blair and Bloom 1995, chs. 6–7. Mamluk officials, who were granted revenues of lands all over Egypt, mostly stayed in Cairo. Thus, revenue generally poured into Cairo while neglecting other parts of Egypt. Dunn 1986, 49.
[214] Ibn Khaldun 1967 [1377], II: 435. See also Berkey 1992, 130–46; Arjomand 1999, 286.
[215] Kuran 2011, esp. 128–31. For Kuran's analysis, see the next chapter.

TABLE 5.1 *Occupational Terms in Industrial and Public Services*

		Eighth to eleventh centuries	Twelfth to fifteenth centuries
	Commerce	233	220
	Transportation	30	25
Industrial services total		263	245
	Bureaucracy/ military	97	303
	Educational/ legal/religious	33	180
Public services total		130	483

Source: Shatzmiller 1993, 288–323.

sectors related to the officials and ulema in comparison to the sectors related to the merchants.[216]

The hardship of Muslim merchants within the Mamluk Sultanate coincided with their increasing competition with European merchants. In the twelfth century, both the growing European markets and Crusaders' invasion of Levantine port cities helped Italian merchants become active in the Eastern Mediterranean trade. In the thirteenth and fourteenth centuries, Italian merchants expanded their influence in Eastern Mediterranean ports.[217] Relatedly, in Western Mediterranean trade, Italian, French, Catalan, and Portuguese merchants became effective in the twelfth century and dominant in the thirteenth and fourteenth centuries.[218]

Why were European merchants able to eventually surpass their Muslim competitors in Mediterranean trade? One way of answering this question is to follow Avner Greif's well-known comparison between Maghribi (North African) and Genoese traders in the eleventh and twelfth centuries. Greif claims while the Maghribi Jewish traders belonged to a collectivist culture of Muslim North Africa, the Genoese traders were products of a more individualist Western European culture. Collectivist culture promoted reputation-based community enforcement mechanisms at the expense of formal institutions, whereas individualist culture generated and strengthened formal institutions. For Greif, this cultural difference explains how European traders became more successful than their Muslim competitors in the long run.[219]

---

[216] Shatzmiller 1993, esp. 70, 169–287, 288–323. See also Kuran 2011, 68–71.
[217] İnalcık 1994, 315; Shatzmiller 2000, 473; Findlay and O'Rourke 2007, 92–5; Paine 2013, 316.
[218] Shatzmiller 2000, 473.   [219] Greif 1994, esp. 943; Greif 2006, 272–3, 300–1.

I have two main reservations with respect to Greif's argument. First, Greif provides sufficient evidence for neither his characterization of North African Jewish/Muslim culture as "collectivist" nor the weakness of formal institutions in North Africa at the time. Shatzmiller stresses Greif's lack of evidence on collectivist characterization and shows fairly strong formal institutions in a North African case. Shatzmiller refers to eleventh-century legal documents on commercial and maritime issues in Tunisia, which indicate that "[l]egal principles and court decisions were enforced, and rules on partnerships and contracts were codified and enforced throughout."[220]

Jeremy Edwards and Sheilagh Ogilvie have also reevaluated the ways Greif interpreted his main source for the Maghribi traders – the Geniza documents discovered in an Old Cairo synagogue. They reached an opposite conclusion: "The Maghribi traders combined reputation-based sanctions with legal mechanisms, in ways that resemble the practices of medieval European merchants. We find no evidence that the Maghribi traders had more 'collectivist' cultural beliefs than their European counterparts."[221]

Second, Greif's references to religious differences, intended to explain the alleged individualist/communitarian dichotomy, are not convincing. He argues that "Christianity during that period placed the individual rather than his social group at the center of its theology," and that it stressed the individual's salvation as "personal and private" affair.[222] Nonetheless, salvation in Islam has been a personal and private affair too. Unlike Catholicism, Islam never accepted confessing one's sin to a priest. There is no reason to think that Islam was any less individualistic than Catholicism.

Thus, the increasing success of Italian Catholic merchants vis-à-vis their North African Jewish/Muslim competitors requires some other explanation. My analysis has shown that the answer lies in the marginalization of Muslim/Jewish merchants by the ulema–state alliance. In contrast, the Catholic merchants began to gain better positions in the republics of Genoa and Venice,[223] as well as several other parts of Western Europe, due to changing class relations, as I will elaborate later.

Given these circumstances, Muslim merchants could not respond to their European competitors in a reciprocal way. Muslim merchants "failed to notice the evolving markets in Northern Europe."[224] In fact, even intellectually, Muslims were never sufficiently interested in Western Europe.[225] There is no

---

[220] Shatzmiller 2011, 136–7; also 134–5.

[221] Edwards and Ogilvie 2012, 421. For his reply, see Greif 2012.

[222] Greif 1994, 923. See also Greif 2006, 279–80, 301.

[223] In such Italian republics as Genoa and Venice, the merchant class ascended "to a place of privilege and authority." Paine 2013, 317.

[224] Shatzmiller 2000, 473.

[225] Lewis's *The Muslim Discovery of Europe* effectively documents this indifference. Yet it includes essentialist generalizations and Eurocentric biases. For example, Lewis (2001 [1982], 218–19) depicts the French trial of Suleiman al-Halabi, an Al-Azhar student who assassinated the

noteworthy reference to even the Crusaders in the writings of Ghazali (who traveled to Jerusalem right before the Crusades and lived long enough to write after its invasion)[226] or the *Muqaddimah* of Ibn Khaldun (who was, after all, a historian analyzing invasions). There is one famous paragraph in the *Muqaddimah* about the development of philosophical education in Western Europe, which seems to be an exception that proves the rule.[227] While Muslims were mostly indifferent to Western Europeans, the latter were experiencing substantial transformations.

TRANSFORMATION OF WESTERN EUROPE

March Bloch analyzes two periods of medieval Western Europe. The first period begins with the collapse of the Carolingian Empire (800–88) and was characterized by the weakening of central political authority. During this period, which lasted to the mid-eleventh century, population density was low, communication and transportation opportunities were restricted, and commerce was limited. Circulation of gold depended on Arab and Byzantine coins and imitations of them.[228]

The second period lasted from the mid-eleventh to the late thirteenth century. During this period, Western Europe experienced agricultural development, population growth, strengthening of monarchical powers, improvement in transportation, circulation of money, and expansion of commerce. Merchants, who previously had only an inferior status, became more numerous and indispensable for the developing urban life. In 1252 an indigenous Western European gold coin began to be minted.[229] Fernand Braudel regarded this monetary development as a landmark event: "if one had to choose a date to mark the end of Europe's apprenticeship in trade to the cities of Islam and Byzantium, that of 1252 ... seems as good a date as any, if indeed what was essentially a slow evolution can be dated."[230]

In addition to urbanization and economic growth, another transformation in Western Europe was the beginning of institutional balance of power, diversity,

---

commander of the French occupation forces in Egypt in 1800, as an example of European justice and due process. Lewis hides the facts that the French authorities executed Halabi by impalement, which caused four hours of suffering, and sent his remains to France for display, ultimately in a museum. Laurens 1989, 274–5, figure 55.

[226] Laoust 1970, 112, 135–6; Lambton 1981, 109; Hourani 1984, 291.

[227] "We further hear now that the philosophical sciences are greatly cultivated in the land of Rome and along the adjacent northern shore of the country of the European Christians. They are said to be studied there again and to be taught in numerous classes. Existing systematic expositions of them are said to be comprehensive, the people who know them numerous, and the students of them very many." Ibn Khaldun 2005 [1377], 375.

[228] Bloch 2014 [1940], 65–74. For Bloch's and others' views on this period, see also Chapter 4.

[229] Bloch 2014 [1940], 75–8, 401, 443.   [230] Braudel 1982, 559.

and differentiation. The eleventh-century reform of the Catholic Church was an important part of this broader institutional development.

A well-established perception about the differences between Catholicism and Islam is that the former essentially embraces religion–state separation whereas the latter essentially rejects it. Defenders of this perception provide some textual evidence for their position. To show religion–state separation in Christianity, they quote a biblical phrase, "render unto Caesar the things that are Caesar's, and unto God the things that are God's" (Luke 20:25). To argue that such a separation is not possible in Islam, they refer to the abovementioned fabricated hadith about "religion–state brotherhood." I have shown that a certain level of separation between religious and political authorities was maintained in early Islamic history. Hence, the ulema–state alliance is not an essential aspect of Islam, but a historical construct of the eleventh century and its aftermath. Similarly, religion–state relations in the history of Western Christianity were too complex to be explained by a single biblical phrase. As the history of France exemplifies, the Catholic Church's struggles with political authorities continued even in the twentieth century.[231] Interestingly, developments in the eleventh century also shaped the historical construction of church–state separation in Western Christianity.

In the eleventh century, several members of the Catholic hierarchy claimed superiority over kings, while certain kings tried to dominate the Church; neither side had a clearly defined notion of church–state separation. The struggles between the clergy and royal power at that time included both doctrinal debate and military conflict. Cardinal Humbert – who also played a leading role in the Great Schism between the Catholic and Orthodox Churches – was a principal defender of the Catholic Church's supremacy over royal authority. He argued, "Just as the soul excels the body and commands it, so the priestly dignity excels the royal."[232] Beyond such statements, the Church took initiatives to restrict lay rulers' interventions in ecclesiastical appointments. In 1059, the pope's election by cardinals was institutionalized. Henry IV, king of Germany (and later Holy Roman emperor), however, sought the authority to appoint bishops. The Church responded with additional reforms – called either the "Eleventh-Century Reform" or Gregorian Reform (named after Pope Gregory VII) – to maintain the Church's institutional independence from political authorities.[233] In 1075, Gregory issued "The Dictates of the Pope," which asserted the pope's supreme status. Its twenty-seven articles include these two: "That the Pope is the only one whose feet are to be kissed by all princes" and "That he may depose Emperors."[234]

---

[231] Kuru 2009, ch. 3.   [232] Quoted in Tierney 1988, 35.   [233] Logan 2013, 98–9; also 101–7.
[234] Quoted in Tierney 1988, 49; also in Southern 1970, 102. During these struggles, the clergy wanted to "humble the rulers of men's bodies before the rulers of their souls." Bloch 2014 [1940], 401; also 114, 371.

Henry did not accept the Reform and deposed Gregory, while Gregory excommunicated Henry, more than once.

Other struggles pitted popes and monarchs against each other in the early twelfth century, resulting, for example, in a pope's imprisonment by a German monarch. According to Brian Tierney, during all these struggles, kings tried to found a "royal theocracy," while popes tried to establish a "papal theocracy." Yet both endeavors largely failed; neither side was able to fully subdue the other. This mutual failure institutionalized the coexistence of the Church and royal authority as two separate entities.[235]

Another transformation that led to institutional diversity and differentiation in Western Europe was the establishment of universities. Latin translations of Arabic sources became a component of these universities' curricula.

MUSLIM INFLUENCE ON WESTERN EUROPE

Western Europeans interacted with Muslims in various ways, including conquest and commerce. Muslim influence on Western Europeans may be traced by words in European languages with Arabic origins, e.g., admiral, alchemy, alcohol, algebra, checkmate, giraffe, guitar, mattress, saffron, sugar, and syrup.[236] Between 700 and 1100, Muslims developed the cultivation of various new crops, many of which spread to Europe and whose English names (artichoke, cotton, lemon, orange, and spinach) originally come from Arabic.[237]

In terms of commerce, according to Braudel, "anything in western capitalism of imported origin undoubtedly came from Islam." He writes, "The long-distance trade of early European capitalism, carried on by the Italian city-states, was not an inheritance from the Roman Empire." Instead, it inherited the model created by Muslims.[238] In terms of technology, paper production was imported from Muslim lands to Christian Europe through Andalus.[239] Some Muslim paper mills fell to the Catholic states during the Reconquista. The first European paper mill outside the Iberian Peninsula was established near Rome in the late thirteenth century – about five centuries after the first paper mill opened in Baghdad. Paper mills were established in other parts of Western Europe even later: in the fourteenth century in France and Germany, and the late fifteenth century in England.[240]

Muslim scholarly influence on Europe flowed through the translation of Arabic books into Latin and Hebrew. The Iberian Peninsula, including Toledo, which was reconquered by Catholics in 1085, was a center for such

---

[235] Tierney 1988, 86. See also Black 2008, 133–8; Philpott 2019, ch. 7.
[236] Hodgson 1993, 167; Runciman 1959, 14–15; Hunke 1984 [1960], esp. 1–9.
[237] Watson 1983, 31–50, 62–5. See also Beckert 2014, 22–3.   [238] Braudel 1982, 559.
[239] Glick 2005, 279–80.   [240] Kilgour 1998, 79.

translations.[241] Translation of Arabic works continued in some other parts of Europe, such as southern France, in the twelfth and thirteenth centuries.[242] Translated Arabic books included both original Muslim contributions and Arabic translations of Greek books.[243] Despite the increasing number of translations, Western European libraries still had limited numbers of books at that time.[244]

In the thirteenth century, Latin and Hebrew translations of Ibn Rushd's commentaries on Aristotle exerted a strong influence on various European thinkers,[245] such as Thomas Aquinas (d. 1274).[246] Ibn Rushd's influence was so deep that Catholic clergy took action against it, by condemning Ibn Rushd and his followers – Averroists – in several cases from the thirteenth[247] to the sixteenth century.[248] Ibn Rushd's appearances in both Dante's *The Divine Comedy*,[249] written in the fourteenth century, and Raphael's "The School of Athens," painted in the sixteenth century, indicate his fame among the European elite.[250]

[241] Burnett 2009, VII: 249–73; al-Hassan 2001, esp. 133–42. Norman King Roger II's (1130–54) court in Sicily was a meeting place for Muslim and Catholic cultures. He commissioned al-Idrisi's world map. Turner 1995, 127; Watt 1972, 5, 29.

[242] Sarton 1931, 167–79, 338–46; Grant 1996, ch. 2; Watt 1972, 58–71; Guillaume 2005 [1931]; Ülken 2016 [1935], 161–212. Adelard of Bath (c. 1080–1150) was a pioneering translator from Arabic into Latin. Burnett 2009, III: 89–107; Lyons 2010.

[243] Some scholars argue that there was no substantial Muslim intellectual influence on Western Europe. Huff 2011, 178–9, 259–63, 291; Duchesne 2011, 66–7; Gouguenheim 2008. For a rebuttal to the last work, see Büttgen et al. 2009.

[244] "Durham's cathedral library had only about 600 volumes in 1200 ... Canterbury, one of the largest cathedral libraries, possessed about 5,000 books in 1300, but this was exceptional." Harris 1995, 98. In 1338, the library of the Sorbonne in Paris, which possessed the largest university collection in Western Europe, had only 2,066 books. Martin 1994, 187–8.

[245] Ibn Rushd's works were "translated into Latin 30 years after his death and produce[d] a shock wave in Christendom a generation after that." Collins 2000, 445. Today, thirty-six Hebrew and fifteen Latin translations of Ibn Rushd's books from that period are extant. Wolfson 1963, 90–4.

[246] Fakhry 2004, 285.

[247] "[T]here came into existence a group of (mostly young) 'extremists' whose laudation of Averroistic Aristotle gave the official spokesman of the Church much to think of and worry about. A long list of *errores condemnati* [issued in Paris in 1270 and 1277] followed the Church's effort to stem the Averroistic turbulence in philosophical and theological circles." Nisbet 1980, 89–90. See also Grant 1996, ch. 5.

[248] Fakhry 2001, 134–64; Leaman 1988, 165–9; Renan 1882 [1852], 200–320.

[249] For Islamic influences on Dante's *The Divine Comedy*, see Palacios 2008 [1919]. See also Ziolkowski 2007; Cantarino 2007.

[250] Another example of a Muslim philosopher's portrayal by a Renaissance artist is Giorgione's "The Three Philosophers" (c. 1509), which is on the cover of the present book. This painting arguably depicts a Muslim philosopher between an ancient philosopher and a Renaissance philosopher. For cultural interactions between Muslims and Catholics during the Renaissance, see Brotton 2002. For the impact of Ibn al-Haytham's optical theory on fifteenth-century Italian Renaissance art, see Belting 2011.

Newly established universities were essential in circulating the thought of Ibn Rushd, Aristotle, and others in Western Europe. The introduction of Aristotle's ideas by scholars such as Aquinas (teaching at the University of Paris) transformed European scholarship.[251] The number of European universities kept increasing – in 1300, it was twenty; in 1400, it was forty-four; and in 1500, it reached sixty-six.[252] European universities differed from Muslim madrasas in several respects. While European universities increasingly taught more secular subjects and became open to new ideas, madrasas were focused more on religious education and defending the tradition. Universities had strong institutional bases and issued institutional licenses. Madrasas, by contrast, were based on personal relationships; each professor was granting personal licenses (*ijaza*s) to certify his students' expertise to teach particular books and/or issue legal opinions.[253] Institutionalization helped universities become stronger against the pressures of the political and religious authorities, whereas relatively uninstitutionalized madrasas remained weak against such pressures.

In sum, many facets of Western European development – from the cultivation of new crops to intercontinental trade, and from paper production to the engagement with Aristotelian philosophy – bear the deep imprint of Muslim influence.

CONCLUSION

From the twelfth to the fourteenth century, Muslims suffered devastating invasions: by the Crusaders, Mongols, and Timurids. Nonetheless, Muslims recovered geopolitically after these invasions by defeating Crusaders, converting Mongols, and establishing powerful empires. The truly enduring negative effects of these invasions were their contributions to the cementing of the ulema–state alliance. These invasions highlighted the need for survival and order, strengthening the military elites and their alliance with the ulema at the expense of philosophers and merchants throughout the Muslim world, particularly in Syria and Egypt.

The marginalization of philosophers did not lead to a complete lack of major Muslim scholars throughout these three centuries. This period witnesses several important Muslim thinkers, from Ibn Rushd to Ibn Khaldun. However, these scholars were either persecuted or ignored. Ibn Taymiyya

---

[251] See Aquinas 1988 [1265–72].

[252] Buringh and Van Zanden 2009, 431. Collins's (2000, 516) numbers are close: 1300 (18), 1400 (34), and 1500 (56). See also Grant 1996, ch. 3; Lindberg 2007, 218–24; Cubberley 1948 [1920], 215–35.

[253] Makdisi 1970, 260; Burak 2015, 27. For Mamluk madrasas, see Berkey 1992, ch. 2. For madrasas in Timurid Iran, see Subtelny and Khalidov 1995, 214. For the possible influence of the Muslim waqf model on European educational endowments, see Gaudiosi 1988, 1231–2; Makdisi 1981, 287.

too experienced persecution; nonetheless, his concept of the rulers and the ulema jointly holding public authority was the established norm under the Mamluks. Some prominent Sufi thinkers, such as Ibn Arabi, partially filled the vacuum created by the elimination of philosophers. These Sufi thinkers influenced both the elites and the masses in the Muslim world, with their emphasis on mystical knowledge, as well as their justification of spiritual and sociopolitical hierarchy.

Between the twelfth and fourteenth centuries, hierarchy and stratification replaced the more egalitarian sociopolitical structure in early Islamic history. Sociopolitical hierarchy became a major problem in the most important Muslim state of that time, the Mamluk Sultanate. To use Ibn Khaldun's theoretical framework, the ulema–state alliance under Mamluk rule imposed obedience on the people by using both state power and religion, and thus turned the people into docile bodies without *asabiyya* – the group feeling to determine their own political destiny. The ulema monopolized the authority to interpret Islam, used waqf funds, and held judicial and other official positions. In exchange for these privileges, the ulema legitimized the Mamluk rulers' acts, even the seizure of private properties and the levying of extraordinary taxes. The ulema were supposed to function as social leaders. Instead, by cooperating with the Mamluk military elite, the ulema delegitimized resistance against corrupt and oppressive rulers.[254]

This religiopolitical structure was undoubtedly elitist. Nikki Keddie argues that, from the twelfth century on, the elite's domination of the masses in the Middle East was visible even in the nature of its manufactures. For her, the region became "increasingly known for the complex production of luxury goods," which indicates that it "moved away from its earlier, more egalitarian phase" and that "manufacture was increasingly controlled by rulers and the wealthy."[255]

During this period, Western Europe underwent profound transformations. Increasing agricultural production and population growth led to the development of commerce. These processes contributed to the emergence of merchants and artisans/craftsmen as important urban classes, alongside the already-influential classes – the (military) aristocracy and the clergy. Institutionally, this era witnessed diversification. The balance of power between the Catholic Church and monarchs became institutionalized. Universities were established and supported the flourishing of Aristotelian philosophy, which was initially transmitted to Europe through Arabic translations.

This chapter has emphasized that the essentialist argument about the inherent difference between Islam's and Christianity's relations with state

---

[254] Lapidus 1984, 135, 141.

[255] Keddie 1984, 719; also 723. For the luxury products Muslim countries exported to Italy, and their influence on Renaissance art, see Mack 2002. For egalitarianism in early Islamic history, see Chapter 4.

authority is inaccurate. The eleventh century was a critical juncture in the historical construction of both the ulema–state alliance in the Muslim world and church–state separation in Western Christianity. These historical constructions – together with the marginalization of merchants and philosophers in the Muslim world, in contrast to the emergence of an influential merchant class and the establishment of universities in Western Europe – would have long-lasting effects on these two cultural zones, as will be explored in subsequent chapters.

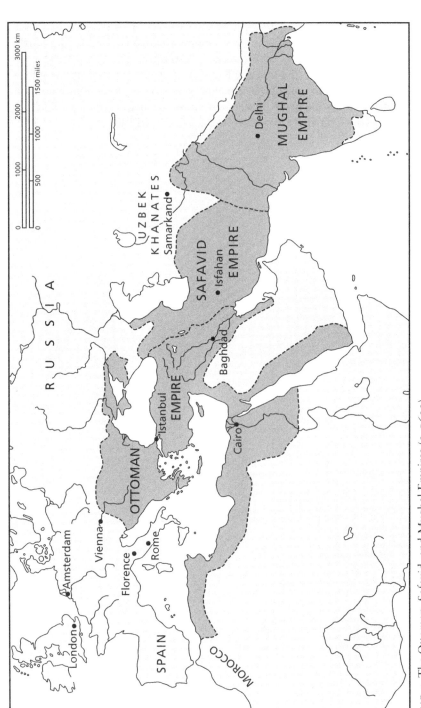

MAP 4 The Ottoman, Safavid, and Mughal Empires (c. 1600)

6

Power

Three Muslim Empires (Fifteenth to Seventeenth Centuries)

The Ottomans experienced a decade of chaos after their defeat by Timur at the Battle of Ankara in 1402. Three years later, Timur died, and his empire was divided amid the power struggles among his sons and grandsons.[1] Meanwhile, the Ottomans recovered in an impressive way. In 1453, Mehmed the Conqueror (Fatih), succeeded in conquering Constantinople, in part thanks to the use of cannons, ending the millennium-old Byzantine Empire and transforming the Ottoman state into an empire. In the early 1500s, the main challenge to the Ottomans came, once again, from the east and from a nomadic force.

Shah Ismail (r. 1501–24) founded a Shii state – the Safavids – in Iran and eventually converted the Iranian population into (Twelver) Shiism by force. Supported by nomadic Turkmen tribespeople from Anatolia and Azerbaijan (called the Kizilbashs), Ismail had ambitions to invade Sunni Ottoman lands. Over a century after their defeat against Timur, the Ottomans won a victory against Ismail at the Battle of Chaldiran in 1514. Sultan Selim's (r. 1512–20) artilleries and musket-armed Janissaries defeated the strong cavalry of the nomadic enemy,[2] breaking the "Ibn Khaldunian circle" of nomadic conquest, urbanization, and subsequent conquest by new nomads. Although Ismail was defeated and his image of being an untouchable holy person was damaged, the state he founded survived. In fact, the Safavids gradually minimized their nomadic features by embracing slave soldiers and gunpowder as military

---

1 Manz 1989, 128–47.

2 Uzunçarşılı 1983, 268; Lindner 1983, 105–11. The Janissaries were an Ottoman elite infantry unit, constituted mostly by Christian boys converted to Islam. It was an adaption of earlier Muslim models of slave soldiers. Previously, in the Fatih era, the Janissaries equipped with firearms defeated another strong nomadic cavalry force (the Akkoyunlus led by Sultan Uzun Hasan). Akdağ 1971, 119; Imber 2009, 285.

instruments.[3] The rivalry between the Ottomans and the Safavids continued
for two more centuries, until the end of the Safavid dynasty.[4]

Three years after Chaldiran, the Ottomans defeated the Mamluks in Egypt.
The Ottomans eventually ruled all of Middle East and North Africa, except
Iran and Morocco. The Mamluks had already been suffering economic collapse
and social/demographic crisis.[5] Beyond Syria and Egypt, other Arab cities were
dealing with various problems at the time of the Ottoman conquest. Baghdad
was still suffering the consequences of Timur's sacking. In short, "it was an
impoverished Arab world with fallen capitals that the Ottomans conquered
between 1516 (occupation of Syria) and 1574 (definitive conquest of
Tunisia)."[6] Demographic data support this observation: the estimated total
populations of Iraq, Syria, Egypt, and North Africa was only 11 million in
1500, showing a decline from 13.5 million in 1300.[7]

During the sixteenth and seventeenth centuries, the Ottoman and Safavid
Empires were the two most powerful Muslim-majority states. There was an
equally powerful empire in India ruled by the Muslim Mughal dynasty, which
was founded by Babur (r. 1526–30), a descendant of Timur. Like the Ottoman
and Safavid Empires, the Mughal Empire had a Turkic dynasty, an Islamic
madrasa system based on Arabic, and a heavily Persian literature.[8] But demo-
graphically, the Mughal Empire was Hindu-majority.[9] Other Muslim-majority
countries of the sixteenth and seventeenth centuries included Morocco in North
Africa and the Uzbek khanates in Central Asia; but these were relatively smaller
polities (see Map 4).[10]

This chapter primarily focuses on the Ottoman Empire for three reasons.
First, the Ottoman Empire (1299–1922) lasted much longer than the Safavid
(1501–1722) and Mughal (c. 1526–1707) Empires, almost from the Mongols'
destruction of the Abbasid caliphate to World War I. Second, unlike the Shii
Safavid Empire and the Hindu-majority Mughal Empire, the Ottoman Empire
was more likely to represent Sunnis, who have constituted the vast majority of

---

[3] In 1528, the Safavids used wagons mounted with guns to defeat nomadic Uzbeks in eastern Iran. Bulliet 1990, 260.

[4] Besides their military conflicts, the Ottomans and the Safavids had religious animosity against each other. The Ottoman ulema deemed the Safavids "heretics" and approved the war against them. İnalcık 1994, 21.

[5] Lapidus 1984, 11, 38–43; Dols 1977, 282; Abu Lughod 1989, 358; Erünsal 2014, 38–76.

[6] Raymond 1979–80, 85.

[7] Under the Ottoman rule, the population of these Arab lands increased, but only to 12.5 million by 1800. Bosker et al. 2008, 39.

[8] Alam 2004, ch. 4. As another common characteristic of these three empires, Sufi orders were important social actors in them. Green 2012, ch. 3.

[9] "The population of Mughal India in 1600 has been estimated at about 100 million." Chaudhuri 1990, 382. This figure is more than double the combined populations of the Ottoman and Safavid Empires.

[10] Hodgson 1974c, esp. 47. There also existed small Muslim-majority or Muslim-run states in Southeast Asia. Lombard 2000; Reid 1993a; Reid 1993b.

the Muslim population. The Ottomans ruled all four previous centers of the Muslim caliphate – Medina, Damascus, Baghdad, and Cairo – in addition to claiming Istanbul as the new center. Finally, the Ottomans collaborated militarily and religiously with various Muslim groups across a vast geography from Morocco to the Horn of Africa, from the Balkans to Crimea, and from India to Aceh. Neither the Safavids nor the Mughals ever held such a central position in the Muslim world.

The ulema–state alliance was effective in the Ottoman, Safavid, and Mughal Empires to varying degrees and with different characteristics. The natural sciences and philosophy had some favored moments in the history of these empires, but they lacked a permanent institutional basis comparable to European universities. Trade was crucial for all three empires, but none accorded merchants an influential political position. In short, the Ottomans, Safavids, and Mughals had world-scale military powers, but their attitudes toward the intellectual and economic spheres were far from impressive. This underestimation of scholarship and commerce might have been less crippling in the long term had the Muslim empires had no competitors in those fields. Yet the reality was the opposite. Western Europe was progressing intellectually and economically, while these Muslim empires focused almost entirely on their military capabilities.

Even militarily, European states became increasingly more powerful and occupied various Muslim-populated territories. The Spaniards invaded the last Muslim state (Granada) in the Iberian Peninsula in the late fifteenth century; the Portuguese occupied several Muslim ports across the Indian Ocean in the early sixteenth century; and the Russians conquered the Volga Tatar khanates in the mid-sixteenth century. Neither the Safavids nor the Mughals attempted a serious response to these European challenges.[11] The Ottoman Empire was the only Muslim power that tried to strategically address them in the sixteenth century.

The Ottomans provided some support to Andalusian Muslims in their resistance against Spanish monarchs.[12] Against the Portuguese, the Ottoman navy organized expeditions in the Indian Ocean with ships built in the Red Sea using wood brought from Anatolia. In order to give their main fleet access to the Indian Ocean, the Ottomans planned to dig a canal in Suez.[13] Similarly, against the Russians, the Ottomans started to dig a canal between the Don and Volga Rivers in order to use their fleet to save the Volga Tatars, while also descending on the Caspian Sea to contain Iran from the north.[14] Nonetheless, due to various reasons, including technological difficulties as well as exhausting wars with the Habsburgs and the Safavids, these two canal projects never materialized.

---

[11] Hodgson 1993, 197.   [12] Hess 1968, 13–21.
[13] Barkan 1940, 452–4; Casale 2010, 162, 202.   [14] İnalcık 1994, 330.

Meanwhile, the Ottomans faced European challenges even in the Mediterranean Sea. In 1538, the Ottoman fleet won a victory against a European armada assembled by the pope in Preveza. However, in 1571, another united European armada defeated the Ottomans in Lepanto.[15] The Ottoman army was by and large superior to any single European army until the early seventeenth century.[16] At the end of the century, the failure of its second siege of Vienna (1683) halted Ottoman expansion into Central and Eastern Europe. The major failure of the Ottomans, however, was not their geopolitical strategies; instead, it was their inability to catch up with Western Europeans' progress in the intellectual and socioeconomic realms. The ulema–state alliance was primarily responsible for this failure.

THE ULEMA–STATE ALLIANCE

According to Halil İnalcık, there were two main classes in Ottoman society. "The first one, called *askeri*, literally the 'military,' included those to whom the sultan had delegated religious or executive power." This class included the ulema, the army, and officers of the court. All other segments of Ottoman society, regardless of their religious identities, constituted the second class, the *reaya* (subjects). In contrast to the ruling elite, the subjects worked for production, paid taxes, and did not participate in government.[17]

On the one hand, the ulema had a pivotal position in the Ottoman state. They monopolized the interpretation of Islam, which was the basis of the legal system and public discourse. The Ottoman ulema made laws (as jurists), ruled the courts (as judges), and ran the main educational institutions, the madrasas (as professors). The ulema exercised power from the Imperial Council down to the smallest unit of government. In the former, the leading ulema – the shaykh al-Islam (*şeyhülislam*) and chief judges – worked with the viziers. In the latter, the ulema acted as local judges, who gave order to *subaşı*s, the local "chiefs of police." On the other hand, their bureaucratic status made the ulema state servants who were dependent on public salaries and government appointments.[18]

Given the significant governmental roles of the Ottoman ulema, one might misconstrue the Ottoman Empire as an exclusionary Islamic theocracy. This characterization would be inaccurate for two main reasons. First, the

[15] According to Braudel (1976, 1088), by Lepanto "[t]he spell of Turkish supremacy had been broken." Nonetheless, seven years later, in the Battle of Alcazar, the Ottomans and their Moroccan allies won a decisive victory against the Portuguese and their Moroccan allies. Hence, the Ottomans were still militarily powerful in North Africa. Hess 1972, esp. 72–3. See also Grant 1999, 185–6; Parker 1996, 87–9.
[16] Agoston 2005, 194–202; Imber 2009, 331.   [17] İnalcık 1964, 44. See also İnalcık 1970, 217.
[18] Schacht 1964, 89–90; Lapidus 1996, 17; Atçıl 2016, parts I and II.

legislative authority of the Ottoman jurists was shared by the sultans, who issued non-religious laws (*kanun*s).[19] Because of his extensive legislation, Suleyman the Magnificent (r. 1520–66) was called the lawgiver – Kanuni. Second, the Ottoman Empire accommodated a certain level of religious diversity and was at least more tolerant of diversity than its Western European counterparts. The Ottoman sultan recognized and superseded the religious authorities of his subjects, including the shaykh al-Islam and the Greek Orthodox patriarch. In a nutshell, the Ottomans ruled a diverse empire, where "Muslims, Christians, and Jews worshipped and studied side by side."[20]

The Ottoman ulema–state alliance entailed a reciprocal relationship. The ulema had certain religious, legislative, judicial, and educational prerogatives. In some cases, the ulema also cooperated with the Janissaries in deposing certain sultans.[21] Nonetheless, the sultans used executive powers, including coercion and finance, to dominate the ulema. Sultanic power could pressure the ulema to legitimize such problematic deeds as the killing of several male dynasty members and top bureaucrats, as well as the confiscation of private properties of various individuals.[22] In sum, the relationship between the Ottoman ulema and the sultan meant a mutual alliance, rather than one-way royal dominance over the clergy, or vice-versa.[23]

The Ottoman ulema–state alliance followed earlier Sunni models explored in previous chapters. The Safavids, however, were innovative in establishing a Shii ulema–state alliance,[24] although their system could also be seen as an adaption of Sunni models.[25] Appointed by the shahs to judgeships as well as consultative and teaching positions, the Shii ulema became a major component of the Safavid state structure.[26] The Safavid shahs had two main motives for importing Twelver Shii ulema from various parts of the Middle East and establishing a strong alliance with them. The first one was the shahs' policy of forcing the majority of the Iranian population to convert to Shii Islam. The ulema helped the shahs implement this policy and eliminate Sunnis and various Sufi groups.[27] The second motive was to undermine the Kizilbashs ("red-headed ones"). The Kizilbashs were religious zealots who believed in Shah Ismail's messianic claims and regarded him as a divine figure.[28] In contrast, the Ottoman sultans never made messianic

---

[19] İnalcık 2000 [1973], 70–5. Sharia was "the law of a religious community," while *kanun* was "the law of an [e]mpire." Ottoman rulers and ulema bridged these two "distinct bodies of law." Imber 1997, 24.
[20] Braude and Lewis 1982, 1. See also Barkey 2008, esp. 105; Barkey 2012.
[21] İnalcık 2000 [1973], 63–4.   [22] Timur 1979, 108, 117; Platteau 2017, 5.
[23] İnalcık 2000 [1973], 169–72; Burak 2015, 46–7.   [24] Halm 1997, esp. 108.
[25] According to Lapidus (1999, 367), the Safavids adopted the Seljuk model of state patronage of religion, "but went much further in centralizing control of the ulama in the hands of the shahs."
[26] Lapidus 1996, 18.   [27] Arjomand 1984, 105–87; Matthee 2012, 173–5; Alatas 2014, 123–9.
[28] Moin 2012, 74–84, 88–91; Yıldırım 2008; Barkey 2008, 175–8.

claims.[29] Even in the Safavid case, the Kizilbash messianism clashed with the state-building efforts. In order to subdue the Kizilbashs, the shahs used Twelver Shii ulema as allies. This suppression of messianism did not mean the total abolishment of shahs' holy status; the Safavid shahs continued to enjoy "religious legitimacy as the descendant[s] of the holy Imams."[30]

The Safavid shahs succeeded in converting the population but generally failed to subdue the Kizilbashs. In order to balance Kizilbash military power and centralize state authority, Shah Abbas (r. 1588–1629) recruited slave soldiers, particularly Georgian converts.[31] Abbas's policies did not work effectively, because the Safavid Empire had a large tribal nomadic population, in contrast to "the Ottoman and the Mughal empires, the great majority of whose subjects were sedentary cultivators."[32]

The ulema–state relationship in the Mughal Empire were much more complex. The Mughal dynasty was Sunni but did not follow a sectarian policy. Furthermore, the majority of the Mughal Empire's population was Hindu. Unlike the Ottoman policy, the Mughals recruited non-Muslims (i.e., Hindus) to the military without requiring conversion to Islam. Like the Ottoman rulers, the Mughal rulers produced a set of laws (*zawabit*) independent of and coexistent with sharia. Akbar (r. 1556–1605) – the least religiously conservative Mughal ruler – abolished the poll tax imposed on non-Muslims in the two other Muslim empires, as a significant example of *zawabit*.[33] Akbar also appointed numerous Hindu officials and had a wife following Hindu rituals in the royal palace.[34]

During the rule of Aurangzeb – the most religiously conservative Mughal ruler – the public influence of the ulema became more salient. Aurangzeb tried to implement aspects of Islamic law, some of which discriminated against Hindus.[35] In various periods of Mughal history, "there were always conservative *'ulama* who insisted on the emperors' 'duty' to convert the Hindu 'infidels' to Islam," but the rulers, including even Aurangzeb, did not pursue such a policy.[36]

The Ottoman, Safavid, and Mughal ulema had many similarities in terms of the curricula they followed in madrasas.[37] Moreover, the ulema in these three empires shared a generally negative attitude, or at least indifference, toward the

---

[29] The only scholarly debate on this issue was about whether the Ottoman state's initial raison d'être was the expansion of Islam (e.g., Paul Wittek's "gazi thesis") or not. Wittek 1936; Wittek 1938; Lindner 1983, ch. 1; Kafadar 1995, c. 1.

[30] Arjomand 1988, 12. See also Newman 2001, 34–46.

[31] Matthee 2012, 178; Alatas 2014, 123–7.   [32] Arjomand 2010, 473.

[33] Ahmad 2009, 148–9. See also Alam 2013, 169.

[34] Dale 2010, 98–100. Other pro-Hindu policies of Akbar included banning cow-slaughter. "He also abolished discriminatory taxes such as those levied on Hindu pilgrims, admitted Hindu sages into his private audience and Rajput chieftains into his ruling class, ordered the translation of Hindu sacred texts into Persian, and celebrated Hindu festivals." Eaton 1993, 159n2.

[35] Zaman 2002, 19–20.   [36] Eaton 1993, 134; also 192–3.   [37] Robinson 1997, esp. 181–4.

natural sciences and philosophy. The next section examines some exceptional Muslim scholars' scientific and philosophical works. It also analyzes the roles of the ulema and rulers in the ultimate waning of the natural sciences and philosophy in these empires.

THE NATURAL SCIENCES AND PHILOSOPHY

A major Muslim center of sciences in the first half of the fifteenth century was the observatory of Ulugh Beg in Samarkand. Ulugh Beg was not only an eminent astronomer, but also a Timurid ruler. Ulugh Beg's observatory followed major observatories Muslims built and/or ran, including the Abbasid caliph Mamun's observatory in Baghdad (ninth century), the Buyid Sharaf al-Dawla's observatory in Baghdad (tenth century), the Seljuk Malikshah's observatory in Isfahan (eleventh century), the observatory patronized by the Mongol Hulagu and run by Tusi in Maragha (thirteenth century), and the Ilkhanid Ghazan Khan's observatory in Tabriz (fourteenth century).[38]

Ulugh Beg and the Ottomans were connected through certain scientists. Kadizade al-Rumi (1364–1436) was an eminent astronomer who was born and raised in Bursa, then the Ottoman capital. He later moved to Samarkand and joined Ulugh Beg's team of scholars, who produced the most accurate star catalogue of the time. Ali Kushji (1403–74), a student and co-worker of Kadizade and Ulugh Beg, followed the opposite geographical trajectory. After the death of Ulugh Beg, the observatory was destroyed and Kushji left Samarkand and ended up in Istanbul, the new Ottoman capital, where he accepted Sultan Fatih's offer to continue his teaching and research career.[39]

In addition to patronizing scientists, Fatih (r. 1451–81) was also interested in European arts. He invited the Italian Renaissance painter Bellini to paint his portrait.[40] This was an exceptional attitude given that the Sunni ulema forbade the depiction of human beings and animals on religious grounds. Hence, Islamic arts were mostly aniconic and focused on calligraphy and geometric and vegetable patterns.[41]

Fatih took some steps forward in encouraging philosophy too.[42] He commissioned two ulema of the time to write separate books that would rethink Ghazali's *Incoherence* and his arguments on philosophy and Islam. Hocazade's

---

[38] Sayılı 1960, esp. 260, 393. See also Çelebi 2007 [c. 1653], 777–83; Sezgin 2011b, 28–52; Nusseibeh 2016, 185–98. According to Sayılı (1960, 400), the observatory as a research institution was a Muslim innovation.

[39] King 1999, 44–5, 128–9; Fazlıoğlu 2003, 8–34; Adıvar 1982 [1939], 18–20, 47–9; Kazancıgil 1999, 92–3. For the possible influence of Kushji on Copernicus, see Ragep 2007a, 72–5.

[40] Wittek 1936, 317; Adıvar 1982 [1939], 39–40.   [41] See Blair and Bloom 1995.

[42] Çelebi 2008 [1656b], 21.

book appeared to be the more acclaimed than the contender.[43] Muhabat Türker revealed that various scholars had misrepresented Hocazade's book as a comparison of Ghazali's *Incoherence* and Ibn Rushd's *Incoherence of the Incoherence*. In reality, Hocazade did not even refer to Ibn Rushd or his book.[44]

Later sultans did not match Fatih's positive attitude toward the arts, the natural sciences, and philosophy. The last noteworthy semi-philosophical Ottoman book was written in the mid-sixteenth century. Kinalizade, who wrote *High Ethics* (*Ahlak-ı Alai*) in 1565, was a judge in Damascus. He was later appointed as the chief judge of Anatolia, and his book became the most influential book on ethics ever written in Ottoman Turkish. In terms of the structure, Kinalizade followed Tusi's and Dawani's ethics books. In terms of the contents, Kinalizade's main sources also included Ghazali's work, particularly the *Revival*, and several poets, especially Hafiz and Saadi.

One influential concept Kinalizade popularized among the Ottoman elite was the Circle of Justice:

> Justice is the cause of the well-being of the world
> The world is a garden whose wall is the state
> The state is based on Islamic law
> Islamic law cannot stand without royal authority
> Royal authority relies on the army
> The army cannot be maintained without money
> Money is provided by the subjects
> The subjects obey the sultan because of justice.[45]

Kinalizade quoted the Circle of Justice from Dawani[46] with some modifications.[47] Previously, Ibn Khaldun had already quoted three versions of this Circle,[48] from a Sasanian priest, a Sasanian ruler,[49] and *The Secrets of Secrets*.[50] As presented by Kinalizade, the Circle of Justice suited the Ottoman

---

[43] Çelebi 2007 [c. 1653], 444. Although Hocazade generally agrees with Ghazali, on some issues, he criticizes Ghazali, especially for misrepresenting Ibn Sina and unfairly declaring him as an apostate. Türker 1956, 383–6. See also Arslan 1999, 265–7; Özervarlı 2015a, 390–6.

[44] Türker 1956, 56–60, 385–8. The scholars criticized by Türker include Adnan Adıvar (1982 [1939], 54) and Şemsettin Günaltay (1987 [1938], 444).

[45] Kınalızade 2012 [1565], 532.   [46] Kınalızade 2012 [1565], 529; Dawani 1939 [c. 1477], 249.

[47] For the background of the Circle of Justice, see Tusi 1964 [c. 1235], 230; Dawani 1839 [c. 1477], 372–4, 388–90; Kınalızade 2012 [1565], 451, 479–80.

[48] Ibn Khaldun 2005 [1377], 40–1, 239. For Sasanian versions, Ibn Khaldun cited Masudi. According to Masudi (Maçoudi 1863 [947], 210), the Sasanian King Anushiruwan (r. 531–79) said: "Royal authority relies on the army, the army on money, money on taxes, taxes on agriculture, agriculture on justice, justice on the loyalty of officials, and that on the forthrightness of ministers." See also Hacib 1974 [1070], 155.

[49] Linda Darling (2013) explains that the historical background of the Circle of Justice goes back even earlier than the Sasanians in the Middle East and Central Asia.

[50] As his source, Dawani (1939 [c. 1477], 244) also referred to *The Secrets of Secrets* – an advice work falsely attributed to Aristotle. Modern scholars revealed that it was anonymously compiled in the tenth and eleventh centuries. Darling 2013, 6, 75.

ulema–state alliance with its emphasis on the interdependence of Islamic law, the state, the army, and royal authority.

The transformation of Muslim ethics books from Tusi to Dawani and Kinalizade shows the declining role of philosophy and increasing status of religious preaching in Muslim intellectual life. As mentioned in Chapter 5, Tusi's *Nasirean Ethics* was a deep philosophical work with universal questions. Dawani largely paraphrased Tusi's book in his *Jalalean Ethics* and added more Islamic tone. Kinalizade's *High Ethics* was much less philosophical and more focused on Islamic preaching than even Dawani's book.

The Ottoman disinterest in non-religious sciences was not confined to philosophy but extended to such newly advancing fields as cartography and navigation. An exceptional figure was Piri Reis, an admiral, geographer, and cartographer. Piri Reis drew his (now famous) world map in 1513 and submitted it to Sultan Selim. Today only one part of the map is extant – that on the Atlantic showing coasts of Western Europe, Africa, and the Americas (as known at the time). Piri Reis acknowledged that he used many sources, including a map of Columbus, which did not survive. Later, Piri Reis wrote his *Book of Navigation*, a detailed book in Ottoman Turkish on sailing along coasts of the Mediterranean Sea that also reported the Iberian explorations in the New World and the Indian Ocean.[51] He presented this book to Suleyman the Magnificent. In 1554, in his late eighties, Piri Reis was executed due to some political intrigues related to his job as an admiral.[52]

Piri Reis's execution was a tragic end to a productive life; but it was also tragic that his work did not earn him an intellectual legacy. As Stevan Soucek notes, the Ottoman ruling elite "failed to use Piri Reis in the fields where he excelled, cartography and navigation at a time when cartographers and navigators of his stature were the pampered consultants of Europe's monarchs." After Piri Reis, "[t]here is no evidence of any attempt, on the part of the Ottoman government or anyone else, to establish a school of navigation and cartography, or an office of overseas exploration and trade, features so characteristic of southern and western Europe."[53]

After Piri Reis, two Ottoman authors briefly mentioned the New World in their writings.[54] Finally, in around 1580, a major work on the subject was written. An anonymous author compiled *The History of West Indies* (*Tarih-i Hind-i Garbi*). Based on Italian translations of Spanish sources, the book presented Spanish explorations and conquests in the New World to Ottoman Turkish readers. It included world maps and various illustrations on American zoology and botany.[55] This book was so important for the Ottoman elite that Ibrahim Muteferrika included it in 1730 in the select group of books he printed

[51] Reis 2013 [1521].   [52] McIntosh 2000; Hess 1974; Tekeli 1985.   [53] Soucek 1994, 134–5.
[54] Goodrich 1990, 11–14.
[55] *Tarih-i Hind-i Garbi* 1990 [1580]. See also Goodrich 1990, esp. 32–5; Çelebi 2007 [c. 1653], 287–8; Togan 1942–7, 127.

in the first Ottoman press. Although Muteferrika updated the maps in the book, he printed the text in its original form. Its modern translator into English, Thomas Goodrich, reacted to this choice: "How unusual to print a book in 1730 already a century and half old! Even more extraordinary that it was reprinted in 1875!" The uniqueness of the book was not about its quality, but the fact that there was no other major book written by an Ottoman on the New World until that time.[56] Goodrich speculates on the possibility that the author of *The History of West Indies* concealed his name because of his association with the destroyed observatory in Istanbul.[57] Why would anyone associated with the observatory be so scared around 1580? To answer this question, we should examine the observatory.

A century after the reign of Sultan Fatih, Sokollu Mehmed Pasha appeared as a powerful Ottoman official who supported the arts and natural sciences. Born to a Balkan Christian family and then converted to Islam and educated by the state, Sokollu served in various top bureaucratic positions, finally as the grand vizier (1565–79). He patronized an important astronomer, Takiyuddin, in founding an observatory in Istanbul in 1577.[58] Takiyuddin was also a prominent scholar of mathematics and clocks.[59] Sultan Murad III permitted him to establish the observatory with astrological expectations. In the following years, however, conditions worsened for the observatory: Sokollu died; Murad was disappointed because the observatory did not satisfy his astrological expectations; and Shaykh al-Islam Ahmed Şemseddin demanded the destruction of the observatory, arguing that it brought misfortune. The observatory was destroyed by Ottoman navy artillery in 1580.[60]

The Istanbul observatory was the last chance for reenergizing scientific research in the Ottoman Empire. Its destruction by the navy following the shaykh al-Islam's opposition symbolized the decline of the natural sciences under the domination of the ulema–state alliance. Meanwhile, Western Europeans were surpassing Muslims in terms of astronomical knowledge. At around 1580, when Takiyuddin's observatory was destroyed, Tycho Brahe established the first observatory in Western Europe with the patronage of the king of Denmark.[61]

By 1543, Copernicus had already published his heliocentric model, which placed the sun at the center of the universe, contra the dominant Ptolemaic geocentric model. Brahe's observations provided necessary data to (his assistant) Kepler. Inspired by Copernicus's ideas, Kepler (1571–1630) explained the laws of planetary motion. Galileo (1564–1642) was another European scientist

[56] Goodrich 1990, 2, 15.   [57] Goodrich 1990, 20.   [58] Casale 2010, 119–20, 162, 195–6.
[59] Takiyüddin 1966 [1556]; Tekeli 1966. For Takiyuddin's clock designs, see Sezgin 2011c, 118–22.
[60] Sayılı 1960, 289–92; Adıvar 1982 [1939], 99–109; Ünver 1969, 51–4. For instruments of the Istanbul Observatory, see Sezgin 2011b, 53–61.
[61] Sayılı 1960, 374; al-Hassan and Hill 1986, 282.

who played a leading role in the development of laws of motion and recognition of Copernicus's heliocentric model. His experiments were significant for the development of modern scientific methods.[62]

At that time, the intellectual apathy among Muslims was so pervasive that they remained indifferent to these scientific developments. The telescope was invented in the Netherlands in 1608; Galileo improved it in the following year and so did Kepler two years later. Within few decades, several telescopes were brought to the Ottoman and Safavid Empires. Yet Muslims in these places did not use this innovation to advance astronomical knowledge.[63] If Muslims had had access to telescopes in previous centuries, when they had prominent astronomers and observatories, their response would have been sharply different.[64]

Western Europe also achieved major progress in medical science in the sixteenth and seventeenth centuries.[65] In 1543, Vesalius published his collection on human anatomy, refuting many of Galen's inaccurate anatomical views, which had influenced physicians over a millennium.[66] Vesalius and some other European physicians dissected human cadavers in conducting their research. The Catholic Church tried to limit human dissection but was unsuccessful due to political decentralization and the existence of universities in Western Europe. In the Muslim world, however, the ulema were relatively more successful in discouraging human dissection thanks to their support from the centralized state authorities and complete control over the madrasas.[67] A complementary factor was the ulema's prohibition of painting or sculpting the human body. In Western Europe, by contrast, dissection and anatomic depictions followed the rising artistic interest in understanding and portraying the human body. As Seyyed Hossein Nasr stresses, during centuries without

---

[62] Daly 2014, 202–6.

[63] Huff 2011, 133. In 1720s and 1730s, Jai Singh, a Mughal general and Hindu ruler and scholar, established five observatories in India, which became the last examples of the observatory tradition previously represented by that of Ulugh Beg. Sezgin 2011b, 72–7. "The good start made by Jai Singh," however, "came to an abrupt end at his untimely death in 1743." Sen 1971b, 103.

[64] Other European inventions between 1590 and 1660 included microscope, thermometer, barometer, and pendulum clock. McNeill 1991 [1963], 594–5.

[65] According to Brentjes and Morrison (2010, 634), in the Ottoman Empire "since the sixteenth century if not earlier ... [s]everal head physicians were Jewish refugees ... Christian physicians from Ottoman Greek and Armenian communities as well as from France, Italy and other Catholic or Protestant countries in Europe also served at the Ottoman court. Most of the Jewish and Ottoman Christian physicians had studied medicine at Italian or Spanish and Portuguese universities." Hence, the Ottomans did not have sufficient institutions to train physicians to serve in their own court.

[66] Daly 2014, 199–200.

[67] Some exceptional Muslim physicians could have performed dissection. It is unknown whether Ibn Nafis did so for his study on pulmonary circulation, which refuted Galen's theory. Savage-Smith 1995, 99–104; Fancy 2013, 111; Meyerhof 1935, 115–18.

dissection, "Muslims relied heavily upon Galenic anatomy and physiology."[68]
The prohibition of and disinterest in dissection in Muslim countries largely
continued until the Westernizing reforms of the mid-nineteenth century.[69]

Instead of paying attention to scientific developments in Western Europe, the
Ottoman ulema focused more on religious studies in madrasas, further marginalizing the natural sciences and philosophy in curricula in the late sixteenth
century and afterward.[70] Even this level of conservatism was not sufficient for
the Kadizadeli movement, which became influential in seventeenth-century
Istanbul. This movement was critical of the mainstream ulema, although it also
included some members of the ulema, particularly certain preachers.[71] The
Kadizadelis resembled modern Salafis in promoting a literalist and puritanical
understanding of Islam and condemning particular rituals and notions of Sufis.

The most prolific Ottoman scholar of the time, Katip Çelebi (Haji Khalifa)
(1609–57), engaged in the debate between the Kadizadelis and the Sufis. In *The
Balance of Truth*, he searched for a middle way between these two groups by
treating their arguments as two opposite extremes.[72] Katip Çelebi wrote on
various topics, including the history of Ottoman naval wars and the problems
of the Ottoman state structure.[73] His most comprehensive book was *The
Removal of Doubt from the Names of Books and the Sciences* – a multivolume
annotated bibliography, which included about 9,000 authors and 15,000
books in Arabic, Persian, and Turkish. This work included the earliest known
explicit Ottoman references to Ibn Rushd's *Incoherence of the Incoherence* and
Ibn Khaldun's *Muqaddimah*.[74] In his geographical writings, Katip Çelebi used
Latin sources.[75] He also played a leading role in translation; with the help of an
associate, he translated a history book and a geography book from Latin into
Ottoman Turkish.[76]

Katip Çelebi was the exception that proved the rule in the seventeenth-
century Ottoman intellectual life. Thanks to the family fortune he inherited,
he was able to spend time studying broad range of issues, including Islamic
studies. Like Piri Reis, Katip Çelebi was originally a bureaucrat, rather than a

[68] Nasr 1976, 163.
[69] As late as the early nineteenth century, human dissection was still not a common method of
medical research in Istanbul or Cairo. At that time, Hasan al-Attar, a reformist Islamic scholar
and the shaykh of Al-Azhar, defended the necessity of conducting dissection. See Gran 1979,
104–5, 170–2.
[70] Çelebi 2008 [1656b], 21; Adıvar 1982 [1939], 126–7; Unat 1964, 3–6. Starting with the late
sixteenth century, the Ottoman ulema "tended to interfere more and more in the administration
and in the laws promulgated by the crown." This "clerical influence reinforced Sunnite conservatism and severely curtailed the government's freedom of action in response to changing conditions." İnalcık 1994, 23.
[71] Zilfi 1988, 39; İnalcık 2000 [1973], 179–85; Baer 2007, 65–76.
[72] Çelebi 2008 [1656b], esp. 39–40, 65–70.   [73] Çelebi 2007 [1656a]; Çelebi 1982 [c. 1652].
[74] Çelebi 2007 [c. 1653], 443–4, 1007, 262, 566–7, 598, 684, 899; Özervarlı 2015a, 388; Fleischer
1983, 199; Okumuş 2008, 83–6.
[75] Çelebi 2008 [1654].   [76] Ülken 2016 [1935], 233–9.

member of the ulema. His lack of a formal madrasa education helped make him the creative and prolific scholar he was. The conservative nature of madrasas was not confined to the Ottoman Empire. Madrasas in the (Sunni) Mughal and (Shii) Safavid Empires were also conservative and taught similar curricula, notwithstanding their sectarian differences.[77]

Despite these handicaps, the Savafid Empire produced eminent philosophers. Mir Damad (1543–1631) emerged as a leading philosopher and Shii theologian. His work "was the impetus for the revival of philosophy known as the 'School of Isfahan.'"[78] The most prominent student of Mir Damad was Mulla Sadra (1572–1640), who became even more famous than his tutor.[79] The existence of such eminent philosophers, however, did not negate the restrictions the established ulema put on philosophy. According to Hamid Dabashi, the Safavid madrasa system and "its total reliance on religious endowments prohibited any financial support for students who were attracted primarily to philosophy." He explains that the works of Mir Damad and Mulla Sadra were exceptions:

Having a wealthy and influential father, as in the case of Mir Damad and his student Mulla Sadra, was a crucial factor in facilitating a philosophical career. But even these two independently wealthy Shi'i philosophers were not totally immune to financial difficulties. In one of his extant letters to Mir Damad, Mulla Sadra complains in almost the same breath of his financial burdens in supporting his family and of harassments to which he has been systematically subjected.[80]

In short, in the Safavid Empire, "the practice of philosophy was a precarious act that Persian philosophers pursued at their own peril." There was not "the slightest recognition of the legitimacy of the philosophical discourse on the part of Shi'i legal orthodoxy." Therefore, Dabashi continues, philosophers "in or out of the 'School of Isfahan,' remained the constant targets of suspicion." Mir Damad "sought refuge from anti-philosophical doctors of law in his convoluted discourse," whereas Mulla Sadra "practically fled persecution and lived a life of exile for some years in a small village." Some other philosophers "sought a poetic or satirical discourse as haven."[81] Dabashi's depiction of unfavorable conditions is supported by the fact that Iran did not produce a philosopher of the same caliber after Mulla Sadra.

The public functions of the ulema and the problems caused by conservatism were more complex in the Hindu-majority Mughal Empire. Moreover, Mughal state policies toward these issues varied widely under different rulers. Aurangzeb (r. 1658–1707) has been regarded as not only the last great Mughal emperor, but also the most religiously conservative one. Under his authority, the *Fatawa al-Hindiyya*, the famous compendium of Islamic law,

---

[77] Robinson 1997, 174–84; Ahmed 2015, 18–19, 76–8.   [78] Ziai 1996b, 636.
[79] Corbin 1986, 462–72; Adamson 2016, 379–99.   [80] Dabashi 1996b, 600.
[81] Dabashi 1996b, 600, 632. See also Ziai 1996b, 637; Fakhry 2004, 314–22.

was written.[82] Even this conservative emperor was unhappy with the madrasa-style classical education he received, as seen in his reported statement to his quondam teacher:

But what was the knowledge I derived under your tuition? You taught me that the whole of Franguistan [Western Europe] was no more than some inconsiderable island, of which the most powerful Monarch was formerly the King of Portugal, then he of Holland, and afterward the King of England. In regard to the other sovereigns of Franguistan, such as the King of France and him of Andalusia, you told me they resembled our petty Rajas, and that the potentates of Hindoustan [India] eclipsed the glory of all other kings ...

A familiarity with the languages of surrounding nations may be indispensable in a King; but you would teach me to read and write Arabic; doubtless conceiving that you placed me under an everlasting obligation for sacrificing so large a portion of time to the study of a language wherein no one can hope to become proficient without ten or twelve years of close application. Forgetting how many important subjects ought to be embraced in the education of a Prince, you acted as if it were chiefly necessary that he should possess great skill in grammar, and such knowledge as belongs to a Doctor of law; and thus did you waste the precious hours of my youth in the dry, unprofitable, and never-ending task of learning words![83]

According to Fazlur Rahman, Aurangzeb's statement was exemplary: "There is hardly a more eloquent and pungent criticism of the narrowness of the curriculum" of madrasa-style Islamic teaching.[84]

In fact, unimaginativeness was visible even in famous advice reports submitted to Ottoman sultans in the seventeenth century. Kochi Bey, a high-level state servant, submitted two treatises to two subsequent sultans (in 1631 and 1640). For him, the Ottoman system was deteriorating, and the main problem was corruption – specifically favoritism and bribery in judicial and governmental appointments, and the dwindling *timar* (military land tenure and tax farming) system. Kochi Bey recommended that the sultans use their central authority to reestablish a fair system of appointments and fix the *timar* system.[85] A decade later, Katip Çelebi submitted a treatise to a third sultan. Inspired by Ibn Khaldun's idea of cyclical history, Katip Çelebi regarded the Ottoman problems as natural consequences of the empire's aging. He also stressed corruption, particularly the fact that offices were sold to unqualified individuals who then overtaxed the people to compensate for the losses they had incurred to bribe officials. Additionally, Katip Çelebi pointed to the increasing imbalances in government's revenues and military expenses. He recommended reestablishing a just rule and balancing the government budget. Like Kochi Bey, Katip Çelebi emphasized the need for a decisive sultan as the ultimate solution.[86]

---

[82] *Fatawa al-Hindiyya* was known among Ottoman jurists. Another Mughal/Indian text read by Ottoman Muslims was *The Letters* (*Mektubat*) of Naqshbandi Sufi shaykh Ahmad Sirhindi (1564–1624).
[83] Quoted in Bernier 1891 [c. 1668], 155–7.   [84] Rahman 1968, 230.
[85] Bey 1972 [1631–40], 48, 68–70, 84.   [86] Çelebi 1982 [c. 1652], 24–5, 32.

Kochi Bey's and Katip Çelebi's reports were pragmatic and based on observations and financial data. They were realistic enough to acknowledge that the Ottoman system was in a worse condition compared with earlier periods. But they focused exclusively on the Ottoman state structure, while ignoring broader educational and economic problems, e.g., deteriorating conditions of scholars and merchants. They also lacked insights about developments in Europe. Modern scholars who have written on Muslim political thought in the seventeenth century generally referred to Kochi Bey and Katip Çelebi as two of the most prominent thinkers of the time.[87] In terms of political thought, however, these two scholars did not have the depth of Tusi and Ibn Khaldun, or Machiavelli and Hobbes.[88]

THE DECLINE THESIS, AGAIN

Some prominent scholars have presented the Ottoman case as evidence against the idea of Muslim intellectual decline. As mentioned in the earlier analysis of the decline thesis (in Chapter 4), such a revisionist history may provoke interesting questions, contribute to the expansion of knowledge via alternative arguments, and question the superiority of the West. However, these positive aspects notwithstanding, revisionist readings of the Ottoman history as a period of intellectual dynamism are still inaccurate.

I will examine two leading examples of these revisionist scholars. One of them is Dimitri Gutas. He criticizes those who argue that a philosophical and scientific decline took place in Muslim lands because of the "orthodox" Sunni ulema. He refers to the Maragha Observatory, run by Tusi, to prove his point: "During the high time of the period when Muslim 'orthodoxy' was supposed to be at its most inimical to the ancient sciences, a very significant ancient science was not only cultivated in Islam but also institutionalized through the foundation of an observatory."[89] This is an erroneous example. As Gutas acknowledges, the Maragha Observatory was built by the Mongols a year after Hulagu's invasion of Baghdad and destruction of the Abbasid Caliphate. It was not a "high time of Muslim orthodoxy"; it was one of its lowest times. Even before the Mongol invasion, Tusi had spent about twenty years in the Alamut Castle under the patronage of the Ismailis (who had been defined as apostates by Ghazali). Tusi was a Shii theologian, and the observatory he directed, regardless of whether some Sunnis also worked there,

---

[87] Rosenthal 1958, 224–33; Black 2011, 264–7; Adamson 2016, 407–8.
[88] Machiavelli 1996 [c. 1513]; Hobbes 1994 [1651].
[89] Gutas 1998, 172. George Saliba (2007, 243) also points to Tusi while criticizing the decline thesis. He claims that Tusi "save[d] about 400,000 manuscript before the sack of Baghdad." Saliba does not cite any particular source for this dubious claim.

cannot be presented as an example of the compatibility between the Sunni "orthodoxy" and scientific development.

Gutas extends his claim to as recent as the eighteenth century: "Avicennan philosophy and its subsequent development found eager cultivators among Ottoman scholars of the sixteenth through the eighteenth centuries."[90] I have three main reservations regarding this claim. First, instead of giving them credit for commenting on Ibn Sina – centuries after him – one can criticize Ottoman scholars for not producing their own original works. Second, Gutas does not explain who these eager cultivators were. He merely quotes Katip Çelebi referring to the names of some early Ottoman scholars, including Hocazade. Elsewhere, Gutas defines Hocazade's abovementioned book on philosophy and Islam as a "refutation of Averroes."[91] Yet Türker and subsequent experts on this subject have emphasized that Hocazade did not even cite Averroes (Ibn Rushd).[92] Finally, Gutas quotes only the initial part of Katip Çelebi's passage,[93] where the latter mentions Hocazade, Kadizade al-Rumi, Ali Kushji, and Kinalizade as exemplary scholars of both philosophy and Islamic studies in the early and middle periods of the Ottoman history. In the following part, however, Katip Çelebi also stresses that, after Kinalizade (d. 1572), a period of decline began in Ottoman intellectual life. He blames certain Islamic jurists for prohibiting philosophy. Consequently, Katip Çelebi adds, philosophy and the natural sciences waned with a few exceptions, indicating the Ottoman state's general decline.[94]

The second scholar who provides examples from Ottoman history to reject the thesis of Muslim intellectual decline is Khaled El-Rouayheb. In *Islamic Intellectual History in the Seventeenth Century*, El-Rouayheb primarily focuses on the Ottoman case to show the continuing vibrancy of Muslim scholarship.[95] For him, Dawani (1426–1502) was a prominent Muslim philosopher who had a long-term impact on Ottoman scholars. In the words of El-Rouayheb, "Dawani, active in western Iran (especially in Shiraz and Tabriz), is arguably the most significant Islamic philosopher active after the thirteenth century and before the seventeenth century."[96]

Indeed, Dawani's *Jalalean Ethics*,[97] which was written in Persian for Akkoyunlu Sultan Uzun Hasan, did influence Ottoman scholars, as previously seen in the case of Kinalizade. Nonetheless, it would be an exaggeration to define this influence as a continuation of philosophical creativity and productivity. Many other scholars have questioned the originality and philosophical depth of Dawani's works, particularly given that his well-known *Jalalean Ethics* was an adaptation of Tusi's *Nasirean Ethics*[98] with a more religious

[90] Gutas 1998, 173.   [91] Gutas 2014, XIV: 88.
[92] Türker 1956, 53–60, 385–7; Arslan 1972, 21; Özervarlı 2015a, 385–9.   [93] Gutas 1998, 173.
[94] Çelebi 2007 [c. 1653], 567–8.   [95] El-Rouayheb 2015, 1–2, 356–61.
[96] El-Rouayheb 2015, 30. See also El-Rouayheb 2010, esp. 254–9.   [97] Dawani 1839 [c. 1477].
[98] Tusi 1964 [c. 1235].

tone.[99] For Erwin Rosenthal, Dawani was not "a philosopher like the *Falasifa* from Kindi to Ibn Rushd, nor even like his source and model Tusi ... We no longer sense in his pages their passionate zeal for Truth, their inquiring mind, or their intellectual curiosity and striving."[100] Even if we accept Dawani as a first-rate philosopher, his case cannot refute the decline thesis. Of course, there were some philosophical and scientific advances during the six-century-long history of the Ottoman Empire. But when these works are contrasted with those in Western Europe during the same period or even those in Muslim lands in the previous six (eighth to thirteenth) centuries, the Ottoman period appears to be one of intellectual stagnation. This stagnation was associated with the marginalization of merchants, as explored in the next section.

TRIVIALIZATION OF MERCHANTS

All three Muslim empires – the Ottoman, the Safavid, and the Mughal – were military states in which the bureaucracy and land revenue system were designed with military focus. Trade was an important source of revenue, but merchants were not an influential class.[101] While explaining the military nature of these three states, Hodgson pointed to both their new weaponry – by calling them "gunpowder empires" – and the influence of the Mongol administrative model, in which "the whole state apparatus was organized as a single massive army."[102]

Under the Ottomans, the *timar* system, which was a continuation of old *iqta* system in previous Muslim dynasties, became an important institution of land regime. Through the *timar*, the Ottoman state authorized military personnel, particularly the *sipahi*s (free Turkish cavalrymen), to manage lands and to collect agricultural taxes/revenues. Like earlier Muslim *iqta* systems and unlike European feudalism, in the Ottoman *timar* regime, land revenue assignments were not hereditary, and peasants were free to organize their activities. A *timar*-holder could not impose forced labor or arbitrary taxes on the peasants under him.[103]

According to Şevket Pamuk, state ownership of land and restrictions on private capital were main characteristics of the Ottoman economic system until

---

[99] Darling 2013, 117; Fakhry 1991, 143; Fleischer 1983, 201.
[100] Rosenthal 1958, 223; also 211–12.
[101] The Ottomans and the Safavids occasionally imposed blockades against each other, which hindered the exports of such items as Iranian silk. İnalcık 1994, 246. Sectarian wars prevented merchants from safely traveling between the Sunni Ottoman, the Shii Safavid, and the Sunni Uzbek realms. Rossabi 1990, 351, 361; Soucek 2000, 151. The decision-makers of this commercially harmful conflict, however, included the ruling elites and ulema and excluded the merchants.
[102] Hodgson 1974c, 16; Hodgson 1974b, 408.
[103] İnalcık 2000, 503. See also İnalcık 1994, 114–73.

the nineteenth-century reforms.[104] Murat Çizakça describes the general Ottoman economic system as extremely state-centric, in which the state "firmly
controlled all the basic factors of production and physical capital, possessed
nearly all mines and metallurgical establishments, and exerted a firm control
over factor prices and mercantile profits – in short, it effectively controlled and
dominated the economy." For Çizakça, this economically inefficient Ottoman
system was "a major divergence" from the capitalist-friendly economic model
of early Islamic history.[105]

In this context, the Ottoman military elite received either salaries (for Janissaries and the sultan's other soldiers) or land revenue assignments (for *sipahi*s).
Similarly, certain ulema received salaries, while madrasas depended on waqf
revenues. The bureaucrats were another group that received salaries from the
state. As noted above, the military elite, ulema, and bureaucrats constituted the
politically dominant class, called *askeri* – the "military." Certain military titles
given to high-ranking ulema and bureaucrats indicated the military character of
the Ottoman state structure. The chief judge of Anatolia (as well as that of the
Balkans) was called *kadıasker* (military qadi), though he was a civilian and a
member of the ulema. Similarly, governors and some other top bureaucrats
could receive the title pasha (general) even if they were actually civilians.[106]

The other (and lower) social class comprised all subjects. Peasants, artisans
and craftsmen, and merchants were all in this category. They were producers
and taxpayers, but they could not participate in government or carry
weapons.[107] In Ibn Khaldun's terminology, they were supposed to lose *asabiyya*. The "military" class monopolized both the use of force and law-making,
two components of politics; thus, the subjects were pacified, unless they
revolted. Unlike various Western European countries with city councils and
parliaments, the Ottoman Empire, until the late nineteenth century, had no
institutions in which merchants could participate in law- and policy-making,
including the setting of tax rates.[108]

The primacy of military concerns in the Ottoman, Safavid, and Mughal
Empires was reflected in their selective adoption of Western European technologies. Among the three technologies Western Europeans used very

---

[104] Pamuk 2004, 246. According to İnalcık (2000 [1973], 110), in 1528, about 87 percent of the
Ottoman land was state-owned (*miri*).

[105] Çizakça 2011, xxii–xxiii.

[106] "The Ottoman Empire was, above all, a military organization ... There was no clear distinction
between civil government and military command ... [V]iziers and provincial governors [were]
acting also as commanders in war." Imber 2009, 330.

[107] Akdağ 2009 [1963], 178.

[108] This was the opposite of "the Italian, German, Flemish and Dutch city-states," where "traders
and craftsmen were in fact the predominant power, and shaped economic policy to suit their
interests." Issawi 1980, 500–1. Encompassing members of the aristocracy, the clergy, and the
bourgeoisie, parliaments spread to many parts of Europe (except the Byzantium) after the
opening of the first one in 1188 in Spain. Van Zanden et al. 2012, esp. 846–7.

effectively – gunpowder, printing, and the nautical compass[109] – these Muslim empires effectively adopted only gunpowder, which suited the interests of their influential military elites.[110] These empires did not establish printing presses (until the Ottoman press in 1727) in part because they lacked influential merchant classes who would support this technology for their commercial interests. Instead, these empires had influential ulema who regarded printing technology as unnecessary, if not dangerous.

The story of these Muslim empires' disinterest in the nautical compass and long-distance maritime trade was similar. The Safavids and Mughals had influential military elites who focused on maintaining and improving their armies. Neither of them had a first-rate navy or merchant fleet.[111] Only the Ottomans had an effective navy; it fought against the Portuguese in the Indian Ocean by using its ports in the Red Sea and the "Basra" (Persian) Gulf.[112] Yet even the Ottoman expeditions, which included such distant places as Mombasa (East Africa), Diu (India), and Aceh (the Indonesian archipelago), were mostly limited to military purposes and took place only between the 1530s and the 1580s.[113] Even in the Mediterranean, Ottoman sailing was primarily military.

Some scholars have explained the Ottomans' indifference toward long-distance maritime trade with reference to cultural factors and ideas. Sabri Ülgener argued that, beginning in the thirteenth century, the Sufi actors and ideas promoted asceticism at the expense of economic competition in

---

[109] "[P]rinting, gunpowder and the nautical compass ... have changed the face and condition of things all over the globe: the first in literature; the second in the art of war; the third in navigation." Bacon 2000 [1620], 100. "Gunpowder, the compass, and the printing press were the 3 great inventions which ushered in bourgeois society. Gunpowder blew up the knightly class, the compass discovered the world market and founded the colonies, and the printing press was the instrument of Protestantism and the regeneration of science in general." Marx 1991 [1861–3], 403. See also Braudel 1981, 385–408. These technologies were invented in China. Needham 2004, 214; Andrade 2016, chs. 2–4.

[110] See Agoston 2005, 19, 59–60, 194. The Ottomans used cannons, harquebus, and handguns against the Mamluks while conquering Egypt in 1517. When Sultan Selim discussed his victory with a Mamluk general, the latter famously accused the Ottomans of deviating from the Islamic way of fighting "with sword and lance." In reality, the Mamluks had used artillery in sieges as early as 1389. Yet they did not use gunpowder in the battlefield, because, unlike the Ottoman Janissaries, the Mamluks were mostly cavalry, who could not easily use guns on horseback. Moreover, while Ottoman territories had deposits of required ores for producing firearms, the Mamluks had to import most of their metals. Ayalon 1956, 27, 89, 94–6, 102–3.

[111] For "the failure of the Mughals ... to create a permanent navy," see Parker 1996, 108, 219n76.

[112] Giancarlo Casale (2010) refers to certain successes of Ottoman naval expeditions against the Portuguese to argue that there was an "Ottoman Age of Exploration" comparable to European explorations. In my view, these successes should not be exaggerated, because the Ottoman Empire had inherent advantages. It had access to the Indian Ocean via the Red Sea, whereas the Portuguese ships had to sail around Africa; it had a much larger population than Portugal; and it had easier ways of communicating with many rulers and merchants in the Indian Ocean through shared Islamic culture.

[113] İnalcık 1994, 320–40.

184 History

Anatolia.[114] One could support this argument with some passages from Ghazali's *Revival*, which was a very influential Sufi-based text in Anatolia. It was translated into Turkish as early as the fourteenth century in an Anatolian principality. In the mid-sixteenth-century Ottoman Empire, it was (partially) translated again into Turkish.[115] A century later, Katip Çelebi recorded a common saying: "If all other Islamic books disappeared, the *Revival* would be alone sufficient."[116] The *Revival* discourages merchants from concentrating on maximizing profit. It asks them to avoid coming to the bazaar early and leaving it late. It urges those who earn enough to leave the bazaar early and focus on worship. The *Revival* also claims that merchants should not participate in maritime trade. It even cites a fabricated hadith to support this judgment: "Do not travel in the sea except for pilgrimage or jihad."[117]

Although these passages can give an idea about the cultural milieu of Anatolia and possibly other Muslim-populated parts of the Ottoman Empire, one still should not exaggerate their impact on merchants' attitudes. Unlike Muslims in the Ottoman Empire, Arab Muslim merchants in the Indian Ocean were very successful in seafaring trade until the Portuguese destroyed their ships and occupied their ports.[118] In sum, Ottoman merchants could not compete with their European counterparts in long-distance maritime trade primarily because the former were marginalized by the ulema–state alliance at home.

Ottoman rulers were not preoccupied with the poor conditions of merchants because their main economic concern was "to ensure an uninterrupted flow of the principal food-stuffs" for cities, particularly Istanbul.[119] As long as cities did not have a shortage or high prices, Ottoman rulers did not care much whether foreign or local merchants supplied goods. Due to this provisionist policy, the Ottoman state sometimes banned exports to other countries.[120] Moreover, Ottoman sultans willingly signed capitulations – contracts providing privileges to foreign merchants – with certain European states. Although capitulations were bilateral agreements based on mutual benefits, they gradually served European merchants' domination of the Ottoman markets. Geopolitical considerations also informed the sultans' consent to these agreements, which harmed Ottoman merchants' and manufacturers' interests. By consenting to such capitulations, the sultans hoped to give France (1569),

[114] Ülgener 1981, 58–94. See also Sayar 1986, 125, 134–6.
[115] Ülken 2016 [1935], 138; Özervarlı 2015b, 254.   [116] Çelebi 2007 [c. 1653], 71.
[117] Gazali 1974b [1097], 223–4; al-Ghazali 1963 [1097], 73.
[118] "Arabs remained the leading traders and mariners of the Indian Ocean" for centuries until "the entry of the Portuguese." Hourani 1995 [1951], 83. The Portuguese arrived in 1498 – about three decades before the foundation of the Mughal dynasty – and "engaged in exemplary violence because they knew that their opening of a new spice route round the Cape would meet resistance." Ferguson 2011, 34.
[119] İnalcık 1994, 179. See also Genç 2000, 41–4, 80–5, 92–4, 199. Istanbul's estimated population was 700,000 in 1600 and 1700 – the largest in the world in 1700. Chandler 1987, 20–1, 481–3.
[120] Pamuk 2004, 235; İnalcık 1970, 217.

England (1580), and the Dutch Republic (the Netherlands; 1612) advantages against the Habsburgs.[121] European governments of the time, by contrast, were largely mercantilist: they supported their own merchants and manufacturers by opening (at times by force) markets for exports[122] while restricting imports.[123]

According to İnalcık, by the end of the seventeenth century, the Dutch and English economies threatened Ottoman economic interests thanks to the mass production of crops like cotton and sugar in their colonies and the superior quality of many of their manufactures. Yet in response to these challenges, the Ottomans had "no systematic policy ... to protect and improve native industries." Nor were the Safavids in a better position against these European competitors.[124]

THE RISE OF WESTERN EUROPE

Between the fifteenth and seventeenth centuries, Western Europe achieved intellectual, economic, and military advances often referred to collectively as "the rise of the West." Many scholars have pointed to the political decentralization in Europe as the cause of these developments and have contrasted them against political centralization in the Muslim world and China. On the one hand, one should not exaggerate the role of political decentralization in the rise of Western Europe. Political decentralization is not always a positive factor; under certain circumstances, it may imply disorder. After the fall of Rome, Western Europe had centuries of general political decentralization without anything resembling the economic and intellectual progress that it would enjoy in later centuries. The Carolingian Empire's relatively centralized rule in the ninth century is generally regarded as a positive exception. Five centuries after Rome's fall, around 990, there were "hundreds of principalities, bishoprics, city-states, and other authorities" in Western Europe,[125] which was still a backward corner of the Old World.

On the other hand, the combination of political decentralization with other factors, such as a creative scholarly class and dynamic merchant class, would become a cause of intellectual and economic progress, as seen in some periods of early Islamic history. Chapter 5 explored multiple transformations in Western Europe between the eleventh and fourteenth centuries, including economic growth and institutional diversification. Economic growth led to the emergence

---

[121] İnalcık 1994, 21, 189–95.
[122] Issawi 1982, 17–19. The Ottoman statesmen did not provide "encouragement of search for new markets as trade shrank. There was no Ottoman counterpart to King Henry the Navigator of Portugal's activity in this respect, nor to such policies as are exemplified in Queen Elizabeth's patronage of the Levant Company." Mardin 1969, 261.
[123] Western European states were pursuing protectionist policies. The British state imposed a high customs duty against Indian textiles starting in 1685. Parthasarathi 2011, ch. 5, esp. 126.
[124] İnalcık 1994, 353–4, 359. See also İnalcık 1970, 212.   [125] Tilly 1992, 40.

of merchants and artisans/craftsmen as challengers to the two dominant classes, the military elite and the clergy. The main causes of institutional diversification were the opening of universities and the emerging balance of power between the Catholic Church and monarchs. Combined with these transformations, political decentralization turned into a positive factor for the multidimensional rise of Western Europe.

Similarly, political centralization is not inherently a regressive factor, as long as it coexists with a certain level of doctrinal and institutional diversity. The main problematic aspect of political centralization in the Ottoman, Safavid, and Mughal Empires was its maintenance of doctrinal and institutional hegemony – what I call the ulema–state alliance. Some scholars have presented Ming China (1368–1644) as a case where a centralized state established the doctrinal hegemony of Confucianism.[126] Possibly as a reaction to alien rule under the preceding Mongol Yuan dynasty, the Ming promoted cultural conservatism, particularly through its educational system, which required years-long memorization of Confucian texts to succeed in the civil service examinations, thus hindering creativity and innovation.[127]

According to Charles Tilly, by around 1200, Western Europe had hundreds of political authorities, particularly in the territories of Holy Roman Empire, which encompassed present-day Germany and northern Italy. In fact, "the Italian peninsula alone hosted two or three hundred distinct city-states."[128] This decentralization led to economic, intellectual, and artistic competition and creativity.[129] Among the Italian city-states, Venice and Genoa led in intercontinental trade, while Florence gained wealth from trade and banking and promoted literature and arts. From the mid-fifteenth to the mid-sixteenth

---

[126] According to Paul Kennedy (1987, xvi–xvii), in the early sixteenth century, all power centers in the East, including the Ottomans, the Mughals, and Ming China, had "a centralized authority which insisted upon a uniformity of belief and practice, not only in official state religion but also in such areas as commercial activities and weapons development." In Western Europe, by contrast, the "lack of any such supreme authority" and constant rivalries led to a "competitive, entrepreneurial environment," which eventually resulted in Western economic and military supremacy.

[127] Another characteristic of the Ming dynasty was the declining role of the merchants – who were an influential class during the Song dynasty (960–1279). Lin 1995, 285–6; Kennedy 1987, 6–9; McNeill 1991 [1963], 525–34; Mokyr 2016, ch. 16.

[128] Tilly 1992, 40. See also Spruyt 1994, part II.

[129] Van Zanden 2009, ch. 2; Cosandey 1997, 101, 255–61; De Long and Shleifer 1993. Daniel Chirot (1994, 63) regards decentralization and powerful towns as a necessary condition for European intellectual dynamism: "Only where it was possible for a thinker to flee to a safe haven could the continuing development of rational thought take place." At this point Collins (2000, 418) finds a similarity between Ibn Sina, who had fled from Mahmud of Ghazni, and Descartes: "Ibn Sina … moved into western Persia, becoming court physician, sometimes vizier, and sometimes living under private patronage at Rayy, Hamadan, and Isfahan … [H]is travels are reminiscent of those of Descartes, who moved between Catholic and Protestant battle lines."

century, Florence was the center of the Italian Renaissance under the leadership of the Medicis, a bourgeois family who patronized artists, including Botticelli, Leonardo da Vinci, and Michelangelo, and scholars, including Galileo. The Medicis represented the political influence of the bourgeoisie (including merchants, bankers, and manufacturers) in European politics: in the sixteenth and early seventeenth centuries, the Medicis produced three popes and two regent queens of France.[130]

While Italian cities led Western Europe in an artistic revival, a German city took the lead in printing. In Mainz, Gutenberg, who used private loans, printed the first mass-produced book, the Gutenberg Bible, with metal movable type in 1455. Gutenberg's efforts initiated a "printing revolution" across Western Europe.[131] By 1480, printing presses were operating in 110 Western European towns, mostly in Italy and Germany. By 1500, Western European presses produced 10,000–15,000 different books and an estimated 15–20 million copies of books.[132]

It was unthinkable in the Ottoman Empire for a private entrepreneur to take such a groundbreaking initiative. As Chapter 7 will explain, about three centuries after Gutenberg, an Ottoman state servant established the first Muslim printing press only with the direct support of some high-ranking officials and the permission of the sultan and shaykh al-Islam.

In *The Long Road to the Industrial Revolution*, Van Zanden explains that the establishment of printing presses was both an effect of the growing demand for books and a cause of the subsequent flourishing of book publishing. For Van Zanden, the highly tentative estimates of the average literacy rates in Western Europe – calculated based on percentages of those signing their names in documents such as marriage contracts – showed an increase from 1.3 percent in the eleventh century to 3.4 percent in the twelfth century, 5.7 percent in the thirteenth century, 6.8 percent in the fourteenth century, and 8.6 percent in the first half of the fifteenth century. Estimates of Western European manuscript production also indicate a similar growth, from around 11,000 in the seventh century to 44,000 in the eighth century, 202,000 in the ninth century, 136,000 in the tenth century, 212,000 in the eleventh century, 769,000 in the twelfth century, 1.7 million in the thirteenth century, 2.7 million in the fourteenth century, and about 5 million in the fifteenth century.[133] The increase in manuscript production from the twelfth century on was associated with the rising number of universities.[134]

[130] Niccolo Machiavelli (1996 [c. 1513], 502) dedicated the *Prince* to a member of the House of Medici. Dupouey 1998, 11, 21.
[131] Eisenstein 2005 [1983], esp. part I; Febvre and Martin 1997 [1958], esp. 55–6.
[132] Febvre and Martin 1997 [1958], 182, 186, 248.
[133] Van Zanden 2009, 77, 86, 89. See also Buringh and Van Zanden 2009, 416.
[134] Buringh and Van Zanden 2009, 431–2, 440.

Printing presses sharply reduced the cost of book production.[135] The estimated number of books printed in Europe (including Russia) per century kept increasing, from 12.5 million in the second half of the fifteenth century to 218 million in the sixteenth century, half a billion in the seventeenth century, and nearly one billion in the eighteenth century. In Europe, just in the year 1550, the number of printed books was 3 million, more than the total number of manuscripts produced during the entire fourteenth century.[136] This increased printing admittedly coincided with substantial population growth in Europe.[137] Nevertheless, the increase in book production was still revolutionary – a "30-fold increase European per capita production from 1450/1500 to 1700/1800."[138] Although China had a larger population and was the origin of printing technology, it fell behind Western Europe; between 1522 and 1644, the estimated average annual book production in Western Europe was forty times higher than that in China.[139]

Benedict Anderson points to print-capitalism, which combined printing technology and capitalist entrepreneurs, as an engine for epochal transformations in Western Europe, particularly the rise of popular nationalism.[140] According to Anderson, print-capitalism led to both secularization and vernacularization. Secularization – that is, the declining public importance of religion – included the replacement of a messianic conception of time with a more secular conception.[141] Vernacularization implied the rise of vernacular languages at the expense of Latin. A parallel process was the Protestant Reformation, which challenged the continental hegemony of the Catholic Church.[142]

The Protestant Reformation received substantial support from printing presses, particularly in German cities.[143] Luther (1483–1546) published his "Ninety-Five Theses" in 1517 and his German translation of the New Testament five years later.[144] The role of the Protestant Reformation in the rise of Western Europe has been a controversial topic.[145] It would be reasonable to see the rising bourgeoisie, printing presses, the increasing literacy rate, and the

---

[135] With the printing press, the book production cost declined "perhaps as much as 85 to 90 percent." Van Zanden 2009, 186.

[136] Buringh and Van Zanden 2009, 417, 419. See also Febvre and Martin 1997 [1958], 262.

[137] The estimated total population of Western Europe increased from roughly 48 million in 1400 to around 65 million in 1500, 83 million in 1600, 94 million in 1700, and 137 million in 1800. Bosker et al. 2008, 39.

[138] Van Zanden 2009, 194.

[139] The large gap between Chinese and European book production continued to exist between 1644 and 1911. Buringh and Van Zanden 2009, 437.

[140] The book became "the first modern-style mass-produced industrial commodity." Anderson 1983, 34.

[141] Anderson 1983, 22–36. See also Bloch 2014 [1940], 91–3.   [142] Anderson 1983, 12–19.

[143] Eisenstein 2005 [1983], ch. 6.

[144] Edwards 1994, chs. 1 and 5; Febvre and Martin 1997 [1958], 288–95.

[145] See Weber 1998 [1905]; Becker and Woessmann 2009; Ekelund et al. 1996, ch. 9.

Reformation as interconnected processes.[146] This interconnection was visible in England, which established its Church of England, and the Netherlands, which mostly embraced Calvinism – both of which had influential bourgeois classes shaping parliamentary politics[147] and attained high literacy rates. In England the estimated literacy rate increased from 15 percent in 1600 to over 50 percent in 1800. In the Netherlands, the estimated rates were even more impressive: over 45 percent in 1600 and 75 percent in 1800.[148]

Two Catholic countries, Spain and Portugal, did not make significant contributions to either the Renaissance or the printing revolution, but both were pioneers in geographical explorations, which owed much to royal funds and efforts.[149] With the support of the Spanish monarchs, Columbus reached the New World in 1492. The Spanish crown sponsored other explorations, including Magellan and Elcano's circumnavigation of the globe in 1519–22. Following these initial ventures, Spain colonized the Americas. Given their technological and military superiority, the Spaniards dominated the natives, who did not have horses, wheels, steel, or gunpowder.[150] Moreover, the Spaniards carried foreign germs and infectious diseases into the Americas,[151] killing much of the indigenous population, which lacked immunity to them.[152]

Almost simultaneously, the Portuguese crown organized its own expeditions. In 1498 Vasco da Gama reached India by sailing around the Cape of Good Hope, and Cabral reached (what would be called) Brazil in 1500.[153] Like the Spaniards in other parts of the Americas, the Portuguese dominated the

---

[146] Rubin 2017, 119–40; De Vries and Van der Woude 1997, 165–72; Van Zanden 2009, 90–1, 195.

[147] Van Zanden et al. 2012, 851n55, 856–60; Zaret 2000, ch. 2.

[148] In the Catholic France, the estimated literacy had more modest rates: over 20 percent in 1700 and 35 percent in 1800. Van Zanden 2009, 191.

[149] Paine 2013, 385–405.   [150] Diamond 1997, ch. 3.

[151] "[I]n many specific cases, the Europeans specifically and intentionally introduced smallpox or other microbes as an early form of bacteriological warfare … [T]he repeated abuse, rape and massacre, the scorched-earth destruction of agricultural crops and animals, the starvation, induced trauma and psychic numbing, which [came] interdependently with microbes, sapped the indigenes' will to live." Levene 2005, 11.

[152] The "central Mexican population of about eleven million in 1519 had shrunk to a mere 2.5 million by 1600." McNeill 1991 [1963], 601. It is estimated that the total native population in the Americas declined by 80 percent after the arrival of Europeans. The precise decrease is difficult to ascertain, in part because estimates of the native population range from 13 to 112 million. Engerman and Sokoloff 2012, 216, 216n10.

[153] A century before the Portuguese, in 1405, the Ming dynasty began a series of expeditions in the Indian Ocean led by Zheng He, a Muslim admiral. Unlike subsequent Europeans, the Chinese explorers did not plunder ports or kill local people. The number and size of ships in the Chinese fleet were larger than any European counterparts. In 1433, the Ming rulers of the time stopped the expeditions due to various reasons, including their anticommercialism. Paine 2013, 367–74; Maddison 2006, 241–3; Curtin 1984, 127. Mokyr (1990, 231) contrasts this Chinese experience with decentralized Western Europe, where no single government "could have stopped exploration."

indigenous people of Brazil and exploited their land and resources. Despite some Indian and Ottoman resistance, the Portuguese also established a maritime trade route between the Indian and Atlantic Oceans, which would later be used by Dutch and English merchants. This new route harmed the commercial interests of not only the Ottoman Empire but also its main partner in the Mediterranean trade: Venice.[154] Moreover, the flow of American silver to Eurasia led to inflation in the Ottoman economy between the late sixteenth and the early seventeenth century.[155]

In short, around the beginning of the sixteenth century, Western Europe had experienced multiple processes, including the Renaissance, the printing revolution, the Protestant Reformation, and geographical explorations. At that time, again according to Tilly, there were between 80 and 500 independent political units in Western Europe, based on varying definitions.[156] Charles V (r. 1519–56), a Catholic Habsburg, challenged this decentralization by ruling today's Spain, the Netherlands, Germany, half of Italy, and Austria. Nonetheless, even Charles could not dominate Western Europe.[157] If his rule had inaugurated a universal Catholic empire, this could have promoted conservatism in Western Europe as centralized empires did in the Muslim world.[158]

In Spain, the exclusionary policies of the Catholic monarchy led to both conservatism and economic failure despite the substantial wealth looted from the Americas.[159] The Spanish monarchy used the American bullion to sustain its unproductive rentier system.[160] The Spanish system was based on the alliance between the Catholic clergy and the aristocracy, in many ways similar to the ulema–state alliance in Muslim empires. With the support of the crown, the Catholic clergy used the Spanish Inquisition to eradicate heretics, particularly "crypto-Muslims" and "crypto-Jews," who were forced to convert to Catholicism but were suspected of maintaining their old beliefs and traditions.[161] The Spanish Inquisition began in the late fifteenth century and

---

[154] İnalcık 1994, 341, 353–4.
[155] Barkan 1975, 27; Kasaba 1988, 12; İnalcık 2000 [1973], 49; Akdağ 2009 [1963], 424–30.
[156] Tilly 1992, 45.   [157] Rady 2017, 26–31; Asch 2015, 363–7.
[158] For Braudel (1976, 669), the two dynasties were similar: "In the East the Ottomans; in the West the Habsburgs." In 1572, the Ottoman sultan sent a letter to the French king offering naval assistance and suggesting a joint attack against the Habsburg Empire by France, England, and the Netherlands. İnalcık 1994, 367.
[159] "[F]rom 1493 to 1800, 85 percent of the world's silver and over 70 percent of its gold came from the Americas." Barrett 1990, 224. Spain was the primary exploiter of these American resources, which included 1,700 tons of gold and 73,000 tons of silver. Maddison 2004, 36. See also Barrett 1990, 242–3.
[160] Adam Smith (1993 [1776], 118) criticized the Spaniards for being obsessed with America's bullion instead of focusing on commerce and division of labor: "Wealth ... [for Mongols] consisted in cattle, as according to Spaniards it consisted in gold and silver."
[161] Following the fall of Granada to the Catholics, Cardinal Ximenez, who would become the Grand Inquisitor of Spain, organized bonfires of Muslim books. Eighty thousand volumes were burnt. Mackensen 1935a, 83–4; Lerner 1998, 78.

continued over three centuries.[162] Given this oppression, a significant number of Muslims and Jews left Spain or were expelled, with negative consequences on the Spanish economy.[163] Furthermore, the Spanish monarchy overtaxed its people and often violated their property rights. As a result, Spain faced several economic crises starting in the late sixteenth century.[164]

Spain's intolerant imperial policies also led to the Dutch Revolt. During the reign of Philip II, the son of Charles V, the mostly Protestant population of the Netherlands revolted against the Spanish Empire, culminating in the establishment of an independent Dutch Republic in the late sixteenth century.[165] Unlike in Spain, in the Dutch Republic, merchants were the engine of a trade-based economy, as well as parliamentary politics.[166] Also unlike Spain, the Dutch Republic accommodated a certain level of religious diversity. In the seventeenth century, the Dutch Republic created a virtuous circle of achievements in commerce, philosophy and the natural sciences, the arts, and the military.[167]

The Netherlands hosted and produced several pioneering scholars. Although he was a French citizen, Descartes (1596–1650) spent more than two decades in the Netherlands. He was an eminent mathematician and has generally been regarded as the founder of rationalism. Another principal philosopher of rationalism, Spinoza (1632–77), who criticized Cartesian mind–body duality, also lived in the Netherlands.[168] A famous Dutch jurist of that period, Grotius (1583–1645), followed the opposite trajectory of Descartes: he fled from the Netherlands to France and lived there for more than a decade. Grotius wrote on natural law and has been regarded as the father of international law.[169]

The Dutch people reached the highest estimated literacy rate in the world between 1600 (45 percent) and 1800 (75 percent).[170] Book production also reflected the high literacy rate: in the first half of the eighteenth century, while its population was only 2 million, the Netherlands produced about 52 million books.[171] Dutch schooling rates were very high too; in the seventeenth century, it reached around 10 percent. In the same period, the Netherlands had a comparatively high university enrollment rate as well.[172] This human capital development became the basis of the Netherlands' economic growth and military power, which was disproportionate to its small population and territory.

[162] Arnold Angenendt (2011, 55) writes, "Between 1480 and 1530, the Spanish Inquisition had about 5,000 people executed for their dubious Christianity. From 1540 until 1750, there were 826 executions, also counting sex offences and not just cases of heresy."
[163] Braudel 1976, 790–7.   [164] North and Thomas 1973, 127–31; Rubin 2017, 172–84.
[165] Israel 1998, chs. 7–10.
[166] In the words of Braudel (1984, 205), "for the Dutch, commerce was king, and in Holland commercial interests effectively replaced *raison d'état.*"
[167] Israel 1998, chs. 14, 15, 23, 24, 26, 28, 34, 39.   [168] Israel 2001, chs. 2, 8, 13–16.
[169] Miller 2011.
[170] Van Zanden 2009, 129, 191. See also De Vries and Van der Woude 1997, 170.
[171] Van Zanden 2009, 192.
[172] De Vries and Van der Woude 1997, 170–1. See also Israel 1998, 899–902.

The Dutch East India Company was founded in the early seventeenth century and became the first corporation to issue shares to the public. The Company acted as the Dutch agent in colonizing Muslim lands in the Indonesian archipelago.[173] Similar to its Portuguese predecessor, the Dutch colonization was very violent.[174]

In the sixteenth and seventeenth centuries, England was another military and commercial rival of the Spanish Empire. Like their Dutch counterparts, the English bourgeoisie enjoyed increasing political influence. This influence was visible in the strengthening protection of property rights, including patents, in the English legal system.[175] The East India Company was founded almost simultaneously to its Dutch counterpart and played an important role in the expansion of English maritime trade.[176]

England also achieved educational, philosophical, and scientific progress. Cambridge and Oxford emerged as leading European universities. Bacon (1561–1626), an English champion of modern science and philosopher became one of the founders of empiricism.[177] Later, Locke (1632–1704) wrote the foundational text of empiricism, *An Essay Concerning Human Understanding*, where he refutes Descartes's notion of innate ideas. Instead, Locke argues that the source of knowledge is human experience through sensation and/or reflection.[178] English scholars also excelled in the natural sciences. Harvey (1578–1657) became the first physician to discern by experimentation the full blood circulation through the human body.[179] England also produced Newton (1643–1727), who arguably culminated the scientific revolution begun by Copernicus.[180]

In sum, the rise of Western Europe resulted from the overlapping processes of the Renaissance, the printing revolution, the Protestant Reformation, geographical discoveries, and the scientific revolution. During this period, the Muslim world neither produced comparable developments nor learned from European experiences. Western Europe had clearly surpassed the Muslim world in the natural sciences and philosophy by the early seventeenth century. In terms of economic growth, European and Muslim countries had substantial

---

[173] Israel 1998, 936–54; Curtin 1984, 152–4.   [174] Hefner 2000, 26–32; Maddison 2004, 60.

[175] The patent system was first enacted in Venice in the late fifteenth century, then spread to other European countries; it was most effectively institutionalized in England by the passing of Statute of Monopolies in 1624. Mokyr 1990, 79. See also Khan 2011, 207–8.

[176] Curtin 1984, 155–7.   [177] Bacon 2000 [1620]; Jardin 2000.

[178] Locke 1996 [1689b]. In 1671, Edward Pococke and his son (with the same name) published the Latin translation of Ibn Tufayl's *Hayy bin Yaqzan* with the title *Philosophus autodidactus* (*Self-Taught Philosopher*). According to Gül Russell (1994, esp. 224–31), Locke had close relationships with both Pocockes and it is likely that *Philosophus autodidactus* had an impact on Locke's metaphor of the tabula rasa, which depicts human mind at birth as a blank slate. See also Ben-Zaken 2010, esp. ch 4.

[179] Meyerhof 1935, 120.

[180] Israel 2001, ch. 27; Israel 2006, ch. 8; Daly 2014, 207–8; Eisenstein 2005 [1983], ch. 7.

internal variation, which makes it difficult to evaluate them as two groups until the early nineteenth century. According to Kıvanç Karaman and Pamuk, by the second half of the eighteenth century, GDP per capita in England and the Dutch Republic – the two economically most successful European cases – was approximately double that of the Ottoman Empire. However, GDP per capita in several other Western European countries was slightly more than that of the Ottoman Empire until the early nineteenth century.[181]

Two social classes played leading roles in developments in Western Europe. One was the bourgeoisie, as seen in the relations between the Medicis and the Renaissance, the German and Italian bourgeoisie and print-capitalism, and the Dutch and English bourgeoisie and the multidimensional rise of the Netherlands and England. The other was the intellectual class, which included university professors, independent scholars, and dissenting theologians. Together, these thinkers weakened the ideational dominance of the Catholic Church. Moreover, leading European scholars revolutionized the natural sciences by refuting Ptolemaic astronomy and Galenic anatomy/physiology. They also promoted rationalism and empiricism, which challenged Aristotelian epistemology. Thus, the intellectual class became the engine of the Renaissance, the Reformation, and the scientific revolution. In sum, the combined efforts of the bourgeoisie and the intellectuals enabled the rise of Western Europe.

The ruling elite and the Catholic clergy also made some contributions to Western European progress. Spanish rulers, for example, patronized geographical explorations. Spain, however, also shows that centralized state authority, which in that case pursued rentier policies and persecuted religious minorities, could be a reactionary force. Similarly, some members of the Catholic clergy, especially Aquinas of the thirteenth century, had been pivotal in advancing philosophical studies in Western Europe. Yet overall, the Catholic clergy played a reactionary role as seen in the case of the Inquisition. Therefore, the bourgeoisie and intellectuals generally had to confront the rulers and clergy while pursuing their progressive agendas in Western Europe.

ALTERNATIVE EXPLANATIONS OF THE RISE OF WESTERN EUROPE

My explanations of both the rise of Western Europe and the decline of the Muslim world are similarly based on class relations. The influence of the bourgeoisie and the intellectuals were the main pillars of economic and intellectual progress in Western Europe, whereas the undermining of these two classes by the ulema–state alliance led to economic and intellectual stagnation in Muslim societies. Several scholars have already stressed the importance of the

---

[181] Karaman and Pamuk 2010, 614. See also Van Zanden 2009, 241.

bourgeoisie in Western developments.[182] My argument adds the role of the intellectuals to this approach.

In the massive literature on the rise of Western Europe, two alternative explanations have been particularly influential. The first one can be defined as the anti-colonial approach. It is a broad research project featuring contributions from many scholars. According to this explanatory narrative, around 1500, Western Europe was economically marginalized given its geographical location. Necessity, therefore, led Europeans to search for a sea route to India. They accidentally discovered the Americas. Following this fortunate coincidence, Europeans colonized the New World and exploited its resources, as well as those of several Asian and African countries.[183] Nonetheless, until around 1800, there was no "divergence" yet between economically advanced parts of Western Europe and those of Asia.[184] Around that time, England combined the advantages of its colonies and accessible coal reserves, initiated the Industrial Revolution, and became a model for other Western European countries.[185] This is by and large how Western Europe eventually surpassed Asia in wealth.

Although I share some of "anti-colonial" scholars' criticisms of culturally or geographically deterministic explanations of the rise of the West,[186] I still have nine main disagreements with these scholars' broad narrative. First, immediately before the overseas explorations around 1500, Western Europe was no longer a minor actor in the world economy.[187] Second, it was mostly Spain and Portugal, not all of Western Europe, which was marginalized in existing commercial routes. Venice, by contrast, was effectively using them and, despite certain problems, collaborated with the Ottomans in intercontinental trade.[188] Third, necessity does not always lead to innovations or discoveries.[189] At least from the nineteenth century to the present, many Asian and African countries have had major crises and necessities without major innovations or

---

[182] Braudel 1982, 578–81, 594–6; Marx and Engels 1994 [1848], 160–1. Deirdre McCloskey (2010; 2016) argues that bourgeois ideas caused the rise of Western Europe. Joseph Needham (2004, xlv–xlvii, 229) famously asked "why modern science did not arise in China after so many centuries of technical leadership." For him, "the rise of the bourgeoisie" in Western Europe led to scientific development, and the absence of a comparable bourgeoisie explains why China did not achieve such a development.

[183] Marks 2007; Frank 1998; Frank 2015; Blaut 1993; Blaut 2000.

[184] Hobson 2004; Parthasarathi 2011; Goldstone 2008.   [185] Pomeranz 2000.

[186] An example of cultural determinism is Landes 1998. An example of geographical determinism is Diamond 1997.

[187] Van Zanden 2009, 22–5, 271–2. Angus Maddison (2006, 242) estimates that in 1500, China and India had almost the same size GDPs – the largest in the world. Western Europe was the third in the world with a GDP about two-thirds that of China and India (separately).

[188] İnalcık 1994, 315–19, 342–4.

[189] Mokyr (1990, 151) writes about technological innovations: "Statements such as 'necessity is the mother of invention' are clearly nonsense . . . Human appetites what they are, necessity is always there; the ability to satisfy it is not." The same is true for geographical explorations.

discoveries.[190] Fourth, even if Columbus had not unintentionally reached the Americas, another Iberian explorer would have reached it anyway, given that many Iberians before and after him frequently explored oceans and even circumnavigated the earth.[191] Fifth, in general, world-historical developments do not follow accidental trajectories; major transformations are results of long-term, complex processes.[192]

Sixth, although the exploitation of American resources enriched the countries of Western Europe, their economic growth began earlier than this exploitation.[193] Furthermore, the expropriation of American bullion did not sustain long-term economic development for that resource's main exploiter, Spain.[194] Similarly, European colonization of Africa and Asia also contributed to European economic growth through slavery and other means of exploitation, but the rise of Western Europe was too multifaceted and complex to be explained with reference to colonialism alone. Moreover, one should ask what made Western Europeans so powerful vis-à-vis others, particularly former powers like the Muslim and Chinese empires. I will elaborate the issue of colonialism in Chapter 7.

Seventh, several scholars have noted that the beginning of the Industrial Revolution in England was a gradual result of earlier economic, intellectual, and political developments, rather than an abrupt change.[195] Eighth, one should not exaggerate the role of English coal reserves in industrialization. Muslim countries had 60 percent of the world's oil reserves, but this wealth of natural resources did not lead to an economic or technological break-through. Finally, this explanatory narrative is too materialistic; it focuses on colonial exploitation and industrialization, as if the intellectual development was irrelevant to the rise of Western Europe. In reality, European educational, philosophical, and scientific achievements supported economic growth by promoting human capital and facilitating conditions for innovation.[196]

The second alternative explanation for the rise of Western Europe has been provided by scholars of the new institutionalist school. In *The Rise of the Western World*, Douglass North and Robert Thomas point to the protection of property rights as a crucial factor that would "create an incentive to channel individual

---

[190] About four centuries after Columbus and Vasco da Gama, the first Ottoman voyage to the Americas was accidentally made by two naval ships from Istanbul. The ships then left Brazil and completed their originally planned voyage to Basra by rounding Africa in 1866. Faik 2006 [1868].

[191] Iberian explorations could also be seen as a continuation of Italian merchants' long-distance voyages between the Mediterranean, North, and Baltic Seas starting in the fourteenth century. Paine 2013, 345.

[192] Braudel 1976, 678–81; Carr 1961, ch. 4; North 1990, 89.

[193] Van Zanden 2009, esp. 241, 258.   [194] Drelichman 2005.

[195] Van Zanden 2009, esp. 291–6; Mokyr 1990, ch. 4. In the words of Robert Allen (2009, 15), "[s]ince high wages and cheap energy were consequences of Britain's success in the global economy, the Industrial Revolution can be traced back to prior economic success."

[196] Van Zanden 2009, part III; Allen 2009, ch. 10; Mokyr 2010, chs. 2–5, 19; Jacob 1997.

economic effort." Without such protection, "few would risk private resources for
social gains."[197] North and Thomas explain not only the rise of Western Europe
but also the divergence between various Western European countries stemming
from differing regimes of property right protection in the sixteenth and particularly seventeenth centuries. The Spanish state deprived minorities – Jews and
Muslims – of their property beginning around 1492. This policy was "symptom-
atic of the insecurity of all property rights" in Spain. The more the Spanish crown
faced financial difficulties, the more it confiscated private properties. Consequently, "people were driven out of productive pursuits. As no property right
was secure, economic retardation was the inevitable consequence."[198] North and
Thomas contrast Spain with the opposite cases of the Netherlands and England,
where the protection of property rights led to economic growth.[199]

Later, North and Barry Weingast singled out the Glorious Revolution
(1688), which consolidated parliamentary limits on monarchical authority, as
a landmark event in the institutionalization of the protection of property rights
in England. In the subsequent decade, institutional reforms helped not only
private entrepreneurs but also the government, which "gained access to an
unprecedented level of funds" from lenders who perceived that the government
would "honor its agreements."[200] The path-dependent impact of the Glorious
Revolution enabled subsequent British economic achievement. Elsewhere,
North drew even broader conclusions: "The security of property rights and
the development of the public and private capital market were instrumental
factors not only in England's subsequent rapid economic development, but in
its political hegemony and ultimate dominance of the world."[201] Mancur
Olson developed a similar argument: "Individual rights to property and contract enforcement were probably more secure in Britain after 1689 than any-
where else, and it was in Britain, not very long after the Glorious Revolution,
that the Industrial Revolution began."[202]

This new institutionalist argument is largely complementary with my argument. Nonetheless, the two differ on an important point: the new institution-
alists overemphasize institutions (such as laws protecting property rights) at the
expense of human agency. By contrast, I stress the roles of human agents in the
making of institutions. In the British and Dutch cases, the bourgeoisie and
intellectuals played important roles in the formation of institutions. The bourgeoisie were powerful and shaped parliamentary politics, while the intellectuals
provided ideological legitimacy for the protection of property and other liberal
institutions. Laws in legal texts do not matter unless there are influential groups
of individuals who enforce them by political power and legitimize them by
ideologies. From the nineteenth century to the present, many Asian and African
countries have followed the British model and passed laws to ensure property

[197] North and Thomas 1973, 1, 3.   [198] North and Thomas 1973, 131.
[199] North and Thomas 1973, esp. 101, 156–7.   [200] North and Weingast 1989, 805.
[201] North 1990, 139.   [202] Olson 1993, 574. See also Acemoglu and Robinson 2012, 102–3.

rights. Yet due to the absence of influential bourgeois and intellectual classes to support them, these laws have by and large remained ineffective.

These are my criticisms about the two alternative explanations – the anti-colonial approach and the new institutionalism – of the rise of Western Europe. I use the same argument, which emphasizes the class relations, for the decline of the Muslim world. The next section critically evaluates alternative explanations of this issue.

ALTERNATIVE EXPLANATIONS OF THE DECLINE OF THE MUSLIM WORLD

I will examine three significant examples of works on the decline of the Muslim world in order to elaborate the ways in which they differ from my analysis. The first one is Lisa Blaydes and Eric Chaney's article, "The Feudal Revolution and Europe's Rise: Political Divergence of the Christian West and the Muslim World before 1500 CE" (2013). Blaydes and Chaney assess "political divergence" based on different levels of political stability. While measuring political stability, the authors provide comparative data about the durations of monarchs' rules. They argue that from 1100 to 1500, Western European monarchs remained in power, on average, longer than their Muslim counterparts. The shorter average tenure of Muslim monarchs suggests that Muslims had less stable polities than Europeans. For the authors, the average duration of a monarch's rule was tied to the presence or absence of slave soldiers. Slave soldiers shortened reigns, destabilized politics, and weakened civil society in the Muslim world, whereas the absence of slave soldiers ultimately enabled the rise of Western Europe.

I have four main reservations about this well-researched article. First, Blaydes and Chaney's focus on "political stability" explains very little about how Western Europe rose and surpassed the Muslim world. Both of these interrelated developments entailed complex processes, which included intellectual and socioeconomic dimensions. Political stability per se was not so crucial. The Ottoman Empire was politically stable – it was ruled by a single family for six centuries. Thus, political stability cannot explain the eventual "divergence" between the Ottomans and Western Europeans.

Second, Blaydes and Chaney's data show that the average duration of monarchs' rules was shorter in the Muslim world than in Western Europe. However, this finding does not necessarily indicate more political stability in the latter. In fact, most countries in the contemporary Middle East have experienced a dictator staying in power for decades; no one, however, would define the Middle East as politically more stable than Europe.[203]

---

[203] Blaydes and Chaney (2013, 18n45) try to address this essential problem in their analysis with just a footnote, which provides some arbitrary examples.

Third, the duration of a monarch's rule may be affected by various factors besides the presence or absence of slave soldiers. These factors include elite competition, economic conditions, and the perception of monarchs as sacred. Bloch explains that very few Western European monarchs, especially English and French kings, were murdered roughly between 1000 and 1300 as a result of their sacred status. He writes, "The kings of France, certainly from Philip I and probably from Robert the Pious, and the kings of England, from Henry I, were believed to posses the power to cure certain sickness by the touch of their hands." A smaller number of English and French kings therefore "died a violent death at the hand of their subjects," in contrast to larger numbers of Muslim monarchs and European vassals killed: "By comparison with the hecatombs of Islamic history, or with what the West itself could show in the number of great vassals murdered, and considering the general moral outlook of this age of violence, this number seems small indeed."[204]

Finally, Blaydes and Chaney argue that the presence of slave soldiers made Muslim monarchs absolute authorities, unlike European monarchs, who needed to negotiate with local notables. According to the authors, Muslim monarchs had shorter reigns despite being absolutist rulers because slave soldiers deposed them in several cases. If this explanation is true, then why did Muslim monarchs prefer to have slave soldiers for centuries? Moreover, the authors' depiction of slave soldiers as inherently detached from society is questionable. In the Ottoman case, the Janissary revolts incorporated members of the ulema and the people of Istanbul. In the words of Şerif Mardin, "the Janissaries were not confined to their barracks ... but mingled with the 'bazaar' population." Thus, their revolts often "had two dimensions, one military and the other civilian, and ... the two were supposed to work in tandem."[205]

Timur Kuran's *The Long Divergence* offers a much more complex account of the "divergence." In comparison to Blaydes and Chaney's focus on political stability and slave soldiers, Kuran analyzes long-term economic development and its institutional causes. Kuran argues that Islamic law (particularly regarding inheritance, partnership, and waqfs) inhibited economic development and led to the weakness of civil society in the Muslim world between the eleventh and eighteenth centuries. For him, Islamic law distributed inheritance among too many persons, which dissolved partnerships and hindered capital accumulation. Islamic law on partnership did not recognize impersonal entities; hence, it prevented the establishment of large corporations. Islamic waqfs were unable to adapt to changing socioeconomic conditions due to their inflexible rules; thus, the endowed properties were used in economically inefficient ways. According to Kuran, Muslim societies were stuck with these problematic laws,

---

[204] Bloch 2014 [1940], 401–2.
[205] Mardin 1988, 30. According to İnalcık (2000 [1973], 98), the depositions of five sultans from the mid-seventeenth to the early nineteenth century were caused by popular uprisings, which included the people of Istanbul, the Janissaries, and the shaykh al-Islam. In some cases, "the people of Istanbul rose" even "against the power of the Janissary junta."

which had worked relatively well in the Early Middle Ages but later hindered Muslim economic development for about a millennium. In the nineteenth century, Muslim countries began reforming these laws based on Western models, but it was too late to catch up with Western competitors in the international economic system.[206]

I agree with Kuran that institutional dynamism and efficiency helped Western actors surpass their Muslim competitors. Kuran's explanation of the ways in which Islamic law restricted the formation of big corporations is convincing.[207] As a related issue, some other scholars have stressed how credit and banking institutions emerged earlier in Muslim lands than they did in Western Europe; later, however, Muslim financial institutions stagnated.[208] Kuran's emphasis on the economic inefficiencies of Islamic waqfs is persuasive too.[209] Other scholars have also noted that Muslim waqfs were less flexible and effective than Western alternatives.[210]

Nevertheless, Kuran's comparison of Islamic and Western laws of inheritance leaves many questions unanswered. He seems to be criticizing Islamic law for distributing assets to too many inheritors – sons and daughters, father and mother, and even some other male and female relatives – in comparison to primogeniture in many European countries, which strongly favored the first-born son in inheritance and facilitated capital accumulation.[211] Empirically, Kuran does not sufficiently document such a causal relationship between Islamic inheritance law and the lack of private wealth accumulation.[212]

My main disagreement with Kuran pertains to his overemphasis on law at the expense of the ulema and the state. Kuran's central argument, articulated in his book's subtitle, *How Islamic Law Held Back the Middle East*, points to Islamic law as if it single-handedly shaped Muslim institutions for centuries. Yet

---

[206] Kuran 2011. See also Kuran 2004.

[207] "In seventeenth-century Istanbul, 77.1 percent of the partnerships mentioned in court records consisted of just two people. Only 7.6 percent had five or more members." Kuran 2011, 64–5.

[208] According to Abraham Udovitch (1975, 6–7), financial institutions emerged in the Muslim world in the eighth century – about four centuries before they did in Western Europe. Muslim financial institutions, however, remained mostly unchanged for long time, while their Western European counterparts transformed into "great commercial banking houses" between the fourteenth and sixteenth centuries.

[209] The spread of waqfs meant the "outflow of mercantile wealth from the profit-oriented private sector," further reducing "the likelihood of partnerships expanding in size and gaining complexity." Kuran 2011, 127. In the late Ottoman Empire, roughly 20 percent of agricultural lands belonged to waqfs. Hanioğlu 2008, 20. David Powers (1989, 537–8) estimates a higher percentage.

[210] Makdisi (1981, 289–90) compares static Muslim waqfs with dynamic Western alternatives: "Islam labored under the heavy 'dead hand' ('main morte') of mortmain; whereas the West was able to make use of all the benefits of the waqf, and make even this form of perpetuity dynamic through corporation." See also Arjomand 1999, 291.

[211] "Islam's relatively egalitarian inheritance system raised the costs of liquidating a partnership prematurely." Kuran 2011, 126; also 81–8.

[212] Normatively, Islamic law has generally been criticized for giving half-shares to females in inheritance; therefore, it sounds odd to present it as more problematic than primogeniture.

Kuran's book in fact contains a complex analysis that provides readers with data about the significance of the ulema and the state as well. In other words, his analysis includes many insights and data that are complementary to, or at least compatible with, my argument emphasizing the roles of the ulema and the state. I will clarify this issue with reference to five examples.

First, Kuran acknowledges that the ulema constructed Islamic law even by drawing from pre-Islamic traditions: "[T]he Muslim jurists who developed an Islamic law of partnership did not start from scratch. They built on established customs of Arabia, Mesopotamia, Persia, and Greece, and also Jewish and Christian traditions."[213] Second, Kuran recognizes the role of rulers in Muslim countries' legal systems. He writes that "from an early period onward the military was reorganized, sundry fines and tolls were imposed, the tax system was altered, and rules governing the inheritance of land were revised, all by decree and with only the flimsiest basis in Islamic law."[214] Third, Kuran notes how the absence of a strong merchant class was an important factor for the persistence of problematic aspects of Islamic partnership law: "[I]f some major constituency had pressured the Islamic court system to grant legal personhood to commercial organizations, religious obstacles could have been overcome."[215] These three examples stress the impact of class relations (strong ulema and rulers vis-à-vis weak merchants) on legal issues. Even Islamic law itself appears to be largely an effect of class relations, rather than being the independent cause of Muslims' economic conditions.

Fourth, in the case of the Ottomans, Kuran emphasizes the centralized state authority, rather than certain characteristics of Islamic law, when explaining the lack of autonomous guilds. Until the mid-fifteenth century, guilds gained autonomy, because "Anatolia was in turmoil, with weak statelets vying for authority in the face of frequently shifting boundaries – much as in western Europe during the half-millennium that saw the proliferation of the earliest religious and urban corporations." If the political turmoil had continued, the guilds might have developed "corporate features." Yet "the Ottomans managed to unite Anatolia," opted "to make guilds to serve state goals," and "saw no reason to grant them legal personhood."[216] Kuran also highlights the centralized state while explaining Ottoman waqfs. Many officials and merchants "sheltered wealth within waqfs" because property rights were not protected against state seizure.[217] In short, Kuran's explanations of both the absence of autonomous guilds and the mushrooming of waqfs in the Ottoman

[213] Kuran 2011, 49.   [214] Kuran 2011, 125.

[215] Kuran 2011, 125. Yet "Middle Eastern merchants had no means to establish ... permanent associations pursuing their collective interests." Kuran 2011, 271.

[216] Kuran 2011, 133. "[T]he independent and powerful position of the guilds in the thirteenth and fourteenth centuries weakened [later] under the centralist system of government of the Ottomans." İnalcık 1970, 216.

[217] Kuran 2011, 127. "Because waqfs were considered sacred, rulers were reluctant to confiscate their assets." Kuran 2004, 75.

Empire are, at least partially, based on the negative policies of the centralized state, rather than merely the nature of Islamic law.

Finally, Kuran examines the difference between a Quranic principle and the Muslim practice regarding contracts. A Quranic verse (2:282) orders: "Believers, when you contract a debt for a fixed period, put it in writing ... Do not fail to put your debts in writing, be they small or big, together with the day of payment." Nonetheless, Kuran notices that "a large majority of litigants who faced off in seventeenth-century Istanbul courts were doing business in violation" of this rule. "Even debt contracts, explicitly required to be documented, were left undocumented." He explains this attitude as primarily a result of the fact that "documentation carried the risk of transmitting information to officials prepared to grab resources wherever possible." "The oral legal culture" of Ottoman society, Kuran concludes, "was grounded, then, in the prevailing political and economic conditions. It did not stem from some essential element of Islamic doctrine."[218]

In sum, despite its subtitle and central argument emphasizing Islamic law per se, Kuran's book includes significant data and convincing analyses about the roles of particular class relations and state policies in the economic underdevelopment of the Muslim world. Thus, certain parts of Kuran's book agree with my argument that the ulema and the state were the principal factors that both made Islamic law ineffective and held back the Muslim world.

The third and last work I will discuss is Jared Rubin's *Rulers, Religion, and Riches: Why the West Got Rich and the Middle East Did Not.* There are many similarities between Rubin's central argument and mine. For Rubin, the Netherlands and England achieved economic progress because the "economic elite" became effective in their policy-making processes following the printing revolution and the Protestant Reformation. The Ottoman Empire, by contrast, remained economically stagnant because "religious authorities" rather than an economic elite provided legitimacy to the rulers and held an important seat in the political bargaining table. Ottoman religious authorities blocked progressive efforts, such as the establishment of printing presses. Spain was similar to the Ottoman Empire in terms of religious actors' political efficacy and the resulting economic stagnation.

Nonetheless, Rubin's analysis differs from my own in two important respects. First, according to Rubin, Islam has always provided "a unifying ideology" to religious and state actors, and thus the Ottoman pattern of class relations (politically favoring the ulema and undermining the merchants) was just a continuation of this robust ideology. Rubin argues that "the economic elite never had a place at the bargaining table because Middle Eastern rulers were strong enough, due to the legitimizing capacity of Islam, to exclude them."[219] Thus for Rubin, before the year 1000 too, religious rather than commercial actors shaped policy in Muslim states, but for some reason under

---

[218] Kuran 2011, 246–8. "In Venice written contracts became mandatory on matters of importance in 1394, in France in 1566, in Scotland in 1579, and in Belgium in 1611." Kuran 2011, 242.

[219] Rubin 2017, 17.

early medieval conditions this arrangement did not hinder economic progress.[220] I argue the opposite: in early Islamic history, merchants were an influential class, and that status was one of the reasons for Muslims' economic progress. Later, I stress, the marginalization of merchants harmed Muslim economies.

Second, although Rubin repeatedly insists that his argument does not essentialize Islam, in reality it does just that. Rubin asserts that "Christian doctrine" was essentially different and "was not as conducive to legitimizing political authority as Islamic doctrine was." He also writes, "These doctrinal differences are clear in the Bible and the Qur'an."[221] For him, "the capacity of the religious elite to legitimize political rule," which impeded economic development, "was stronger in Islam than in Catholicism, and minimal in Protestantism."[222] To support this claim, Rubin even quotes the fabricated hadith: "Muhammad himself claimed that, 'Islam and government are twin brothers. One cannot thrive without the other. Islam is the foundation, and government the guardian. What has no foundation, collapses; what has no guarding, perishes.'"[223] I have explained that this statement is a Sasanian maxim, not a hadith, and that it reflects the post-eleventh-century mentality of the ulema. Chapter 4 also documented that many leading Islamic scholars refused to be state servants until the eleventh century. The Ottoman model of the ulema–state alliance, therefore, represents neither a textual essence of Islam nor the entire Islamic history. Instead, it is a phenomenon constructed during a particular period of Islamic history. Rubin's portrayal of Christianity is problematic too. The Eastern Orthodox Church, for example, strongly legitimized and even accepted the superiority of political rulers in the Byzantine Empire, under so-called Caesaropapism. This point contradicts Rubin's argument that Christianity's historical origin rendered it less capable of legitimizing political rule compared with Islam.

I am not opposed to Rubin's usage of religious ideas as an explanatory variable. On the contrary, my criticism is that he does not examine such ideas in a sufficiently extensive and deep manner. Simply claiming an Islamic ideology of religion–state unity is insufficient. For this reason, I have explored changing Muslim ideas on religion–state relations from early Islamic history to the present. These ideas are not simply written in religious texts but are interpreted and articulated by scholars. In early Islamic history, an intellectual class – including philosophers, dissenting theologians, and Islamic scholars who refused to serve the state – played a crucial role in Muslims' intellectual achievement. Later, however, the ulema–state alliance undermined both intellectuals and merchants. This undermining came with a doctrinal transformation on many issues, including Islam's relations with the state. Regarding these issues, my analysis differs substantially from that of Rubin.

---

[220] Rubin 2017, 202–3, 209.   [221] Rubin 2017, 54; also 67.   [222] Rubin 2017, 205–6.

[223] Rubin (2017, 50) quotes this fabricated hadith from Lewis (1995, 149), who actually defines this statement as "a dictum often cited by Muslim authors, sometimes as a piece of old Persian wisdom, sometimes even as a saying of the Prophet." Rubin apparently disregarded Lewis's cautionary note.

CONCLUSION

In the early sixteenth century, three powerful Muslim empires – the Ottoman, the Savafid, and the Mughal – ruled large territories. Two centuries later, Muslim empires had lost their military dominance and faced complex political and socioeconomic crises. This chapter has argued that even during the period of military power, these empires had substantial intellectual and economic handicaps, which led to their eventual decline. Their common problem had to do with class relations: the ulema–state alliance prevented the emergence of independent scholars and marginalized the merchants. Intellectually and economically, Muslims lacked creativity and remained indifferent to European advancements, including the printing revolution and the scientific revolution.

In the Ottoman Empire, the ulema–state alliance was very elitist. The ulema and officials defined the rest of society as *reaya*, which can be translated as the "subjects" or the "flock." The emergence of civil society independent of the state was not possible in such a system. Moreover, the hierarchical nature of Ottoman socioeconomic structure hindered individual innovation. Unlike the Dutch and English states, the Ottoman state did not effectively protect property rights, another major disincentive for individual entrepreneurship and creativity. As a result, very few innovators, discoverers, or entrepreneurs emerged in the Ottoman Empire, as was the case in the Safavid and Mughal Empires and in contrast to much of Western Europe.

Western Europe underwent multiple processes of development between the fifteenth and seventeenth centuries. The intellectuals and the bourgeoisie played major roles in these interdependent developments. The Renaissance promoted interests in not only the human body and nature but also arts and philosophy. The printing revolution led to unprecedented increases in book production and literacy. Geographical discoveries expanded Europe's commercial capacity. Printing presses also contributed to the Protestant Reformation by disseminating texts criticizing the Catholic Church. The scientific revolution produced new knowledge and perspectives on human body and nature, and challenged established Aristotelian and Catholic notions. In the seventeenth century, the Netherlands and England exemplified the artistic, philosophical, commercial, scientific, and political aspects of the rise of Western Europe. European economic growth was certainly linked to the exploitation of American, African, and Asian resources and people. Nonetheless, focusing only on colonial exploitation and disregarding intellectual and institutional developments misses important aspects of the rise of Western Europe.

Chapter 7 will focus on the eighteenth and nineteenth centuries. It analyzes how European powers established either direct or indirect colonial rule across the Muslim world. The chapter will also examine how Muslim officials and intellectuals tried to respond to European challenges with institutional and intellectual reforms.

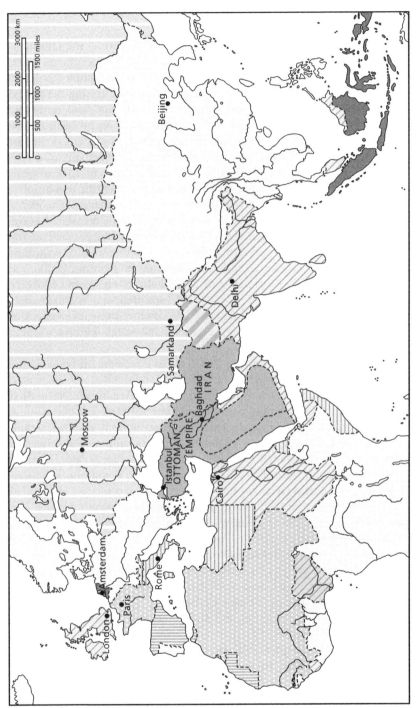

MAP 5 The European Colonization of the Muslim World (c. 1914)

7

Collapse

Western Colonialism and Muslim Reformists (Eighteenth to Nineteenth Centuries)

During and after the failed siege of Vienna in 1683, the Ottomans suffered defeats by multiple European forces. With the Treaty of Karlowitz (1699), the Empire lost substantial territories in Eastern Europe. In the first half of the eighteenth century, the Ottomans gained back some of these territories from Austria, Russia, and Venice, but during the second half of the eighteenth century, they were repeatedly vanquished by Russia. With the Treaty of Kucuk Kaynarca in 1774, the Ottoman Empire gave up Crimea, which made its subsequent occupation by Russia possible. With the treaty, Russia also gained protector status over Orthodox Christian subjects of the Ottoman Empire.[1] Following Napoleon's invasion of Egypt (1798–1801),[2] it became increasingly important for the Ottoman Empire to ally with some European powers against others. After the Ottoman armies' successive defeats by Mehmed Ali's Egyptian troops in the 1830s, the very survival of the Empire hinged in large part on the balance of power in Europe.

A loss of economic sovereignty followed military failure. The 1838 Treaty of Balta Limani, also known as the Anglo-Ottoman Treaty, provided certain advantages for British exports to the Ottoman Empire. According to Pamuk, it was no longer possible for the weak Ottoman Empire to reject the demands of Britain and other European powers. Nearly three decades later, the Empire was even forced to accept the foreigners' rights to purchase agricultural land and the foreign-owned Ottoman Bank's monopoly to print paper currency in its territory.[3] The capitulations the Ottoman Empire had previously signed with European countries also facilitated European domination of its economy.

---

[1] Crimea was the first Muslim-majority territory the Ottomans lost to a non-Muslim power. Kafadar 1997–8, 46; Ortaylı 1983, 128.
[2] See Laurens 1989.   [3] Pamuk 1987, 13, 19.

Moreover, as Turan Kayaoğlu points out, European states' extraterritorial jurisdiction in the Ottoman Empire's territory increasingly violated its sovereignty.[4]

In the late seventeenth and early eighteenth centuries Safavid Iran also experienced socioeconomic crises, as well as military challenges from the Ottomans, Mughals, Russians, Uzbeks, and Afghans, leading to its demise.[5] Following the end of the Safavid rule, Nader Shah (r. 1736–47), a military mastermind from a different tribe, emerged as the ruler of Iran.[6] He expanded Iranian territories at the expense of its neighbors. After Nader's death, however, his empire was partitioned into smaller, rival polities. Later, in 1794, the Qajar dynasty unified Iran again and managed to rule it (albeit with a weak state) until 1925.

In a similar vein, the Mughal Empire began to break down during and after the reign of its last great emperor, Aurangzeb (d. 1707). Some reasons for its decline included extravagant spending,[7] intolerant policies against the Hindu majority, Hindu revolts and secessions by the Rajputs and the Marathas, Iranian invasions led by Nader Shah, and Afghan raids led by Ahmad Shah Durrani.[8] Around 1764, the British East India Company colonized Bengal and subsequently other parts of India. Following the unsuccessful Indian Mutiny in 1857, the British Empire established direct colonial rule in India and formally terminated the (already merely symbolic) Mughal dynasty.

European colonization of Ottoman lands began with the French occupation of Algiers in 1830. Half a century later, France brought Tunisia under its colonial rule, which by then extended over almost all of West Africa, mostly populated by Muslims. In 1869, the Suez Canal was opened as a French-Egyptian enterprise. A few years later, Britain bought the Egyptian shares in the Canal. In 1882, Britain's gradual occupation of Egypt began. British colonization was also extended to Sudan and the Gulf. Iran was never directly colonized. Nonetheless, in the early twentieth century it was divided between British and Russian zones of influence. Russia at that time had already colonized several Muslim populations living in the Eurasian Steppe, Central Asia, and the Caucasus (see Map 5).

By the end of World War I, the entire Middle East was under direct or indirect control by Britain and France.[9] Following the armistice in 1918, British, French, and Italian troops entered Istanbul. Two years later, Britain

---

[4] Kayaoğlu 2010, 104–34.   [5] Matthee 2012, 222–41.

[6] Nader Shah brought together fifty-six leading Sunni and Shii ulema, including the mufti of Baghdad, to sign an agreement on certain compromises, such as not cursing the first three caliphs (by Shiis) and the recognition of the Jafari school as the fifth legitimate school of law (by Sunnis). Arjomand 1984, 215–16.

[7] "The Mogul ... courts were centers of conspicuous consumption on a scale which the Sun King at Versailles might have thought excessive." Kennedy 1987, 13.

[8] Dale 2010, 256–68.   [9] Provence 2017, ch. 2.

and its allies arrested Ottoman parliamentarians and occupied various official posts in the city. With these developments, the Ottoman sultan, who also claimed to be the caliph of Muslims, became a hostage, and for the second time in history (following the Mongol invasion of Baghdad), the heart of the caliphate was in the hands of non-Muslim forces.

The unprecedented extent of European colonization of the Muslim world – far surpassing the conquests of the Mongols and Crusaders in earlier centuries – depended on but was not limited to military force. Europeans also dominated through educational institutions, scientific knowledge, technology, and economic organizations. How did Europeans become so advanced and overtake Muslims on so many fronts? In this chapter, I will explore how Muslim rulers and intellectuals confronted and debated this question.

PRINTING PRESSES AND QURAN TRANSLATIONS

During the political crises in various Muslim countries, the ulema kept, if not strengthened, their influential position. Toward the end of the Safavid Empire, the higher-ranking ulema increased their political power. Muhammad Baqir Majlisi, the shaykh al-Islam of the capital Isfahan from 1687 to 1699, was a powerful player in Safavid politics. He organized persecution campaigns against Sufis and religious minorities.[10] Similarly, the Ottoman ulema became so powerful in the eighteenth century that they established a sort of aristocracy, with certain degrees and offices increasingly assigned to the sons of prominent ulema.[11]

The main source of the ulema's legitimacy was its monopoly over interpreting Islam, which they maintained through their control of madrasas. Printing presses could threaten this monopoly; therefore, the ulema opposed their establishment. Not a single book was printed by Muslims from 1455 (when the first European book was printed) to 1729 (when the first Ottoman book was printed). The ulema also opposed the translation of the Quran into vernacular languages. This opposition resulted in an extremely low (around 1 percent in 1800) literacy rate in Ottoman society,[12] whereas Western European

[10] Foran 1992, 293–4; Dale 2010, 250–1; Matthee 2012, 192, 201–2. According to Keddie (1972, 213), the Iranian ulema's sociopolitical authority expanded with the decline of state authority, especially under the Qajars.

[11] Zilfi 1988, 39–40, 74; Itzkowitz 1962, 91–3. Also in the eighteenth-century Ottoman Empire, the hereditary succession of Sufi shaykhs became widespread. Trimingham 1971, 73.

[12] Joseph Szyliowicz (1992, 253) estimates the literacy rate in the Ottoman Empire at 1 percent in 1800, 2 percent in 1868, 5 percent in 1876, and 10 percent in 1914. Carter Findley (1989, 52, 139) also estimates it increased from around 1 percent in 1800 to 5–10 percent in 1900. For slightly higher estimates, see Quataert 2005, 169–70. Kemal Karpat (1985, 221) provides higher rates for some Ottoman cities in 1895. Findley (1989, 139n17) depicts Karpat's rates as implausibly high. Issawi (1968, 385) estimates the literacy rates in Egypt at 7 percent in 1907 and in India at 7 percent in 1911.

countries attained much higher average literacy rates (31 percent by 1800),[13] thanks in part to the establishment of printing presses, access to the vernacular Bible and other texts, and diverse educational institutions.[14]

Nearly half a century after Gutenberg, the Jewish minority in Istanbul established the first printing press in Ottoman lands in order to print Hebrew texts. It would take two more centuries for a printing press to be established by Ottoman Muslims. It has been argued that there were 80–90,000 copyists in seventeenth-century Istanbul and they formed a powerful bloc in opposition to the printing press due to the economic threat it posed to them.[15] Considering the estimated population of Istanbul at the time was around 700,000,[16] this number is obviously misleading. But even if there had been strong scribal opposition to the printing press, it could not have delayed the establishment of presses for centuries. In the fifteenth-century Paris, the scribe guild strongly opposed the printing press, but "succeeded in delaying the introduction of printing" only twenty years.[17]

Another explanation is that the Arabic alphabet was simply more difficult to render into standardized type than the Latin alphabet. In the Arabic alphabet, each letter has different forms and linkages to other letters, depending on whether it is in the beginning, middle, or end of the word.[18] But this explanation for delayed Ottoman adoption of the printing press is not persuasive either. The difficulty of converting Arabic letters to set type did not prevent European publishers from printing books with Arabic script. Between the sixteenth and eighteenth centuries, European presses printed various titles in Arabic (and some in Persian and Turkish), including the Quran, the Bible, books by early Muslim philosophers, and grammars, and exported some of them to the Ottoman Empire.[19]

---

[13] According to the estimates of Buringh and Van Zanden (2009, 434), the average literacy rate in Western Europe increased from 12 percent by 1500 to 18 percent by 1600, 25 percent by 1700, and 31 percent by 1800.

[14] Hence, I disagree with Bloom (2001, 224), who argues that "the tardiness of the Muslim world to adopt printing was just a brief pause" and that it "was not crucial, primarily because Islamic society had already developed practical and effective means of reproducing and disseminating large numbers of texts."

[15] Bloom 2001, 222; Wilson 2014, 41. The source of this frequently cited data is Marsigli, a Habsburg scholar and official who traveled through the Ottoman Empire. Faroqhi 2000, 96.

[16] Chandler 1987, 20–1.

[17] Mokyr 1990, 179. See also Rubin 2017, 104. In many other cases, traditionalist producers opposed new technologies but could not delay their adoption for a long time. For example, in England, James Hargreaves invented the spinning jenny, which mechanized spinning, in 1764. In a vain attempt to protect their livelihood, a group of spinners broke into his house and destroyed his machine. Allen 2009, 191; Kiaulehn 1971, 26–28.

[18] Mahdi 1995, 1–4; Burke 2009, 179–80.

[19] Pedersen 1984 [1946], 131–3; Koloğlu 2008, 14–7. For Sultan Murad III's 1588 decree to permit European publishers to export non-Islamic books to the Ottoman Empire, see Jones 1994, 98–9.

The real reason for the Ottomans' delay in establishing a printing press was the ulema's opposition, which was rooted in their desire to preserve their monopoly over education and scholarship. Unlike Western European states, the Ottoman Empire did not have an influential merchant class who could profit from printing and therefore supported the establishment of printing presses. Anderson makes a similar argument about China: "[A]lthough printing was invented first in China, possibly 500 years before its appearance in Europe, it had no major, let alone revolutionary impact – precisely because of the absence of capitalism there."[20]

The sultan and officials were the only group in the Ottoman Empire that could lift the barriers put in place by the ulema. Following a series of wars with Austria and Venice, the Ottomans enjoyed a decade of peace in the 1720s. The grand vizier at the time, İbrahim Pasha, inaugurated the so-called Tulip Period, which witnessed artistic flourishing and early efforts at Westernization. İbrahim Pasha patronized the establishment of the first printing press for Muslims in Istanbul. The Ottoman emissary to France, Mehmed Çelebi, was also a key supporter of the press. His son, who would later become grand vizier, collaborated with İbrahim Muteferrika, a Hungarian convert and diplomat, on this initiative. In 1727, the printing of non-religious books was permitted by a decree of the sultan and a supportive fatwa of the shaykh al-Islam.[21]

In his petition to Ottoman authorities, Muteferrika explained the necessity of the printing press with reference to several reasons, which can be summarized in three main points. First, book writing and reading were in a bad shape in the Muslim world. This was a legacy of the Mongol invasion of Asia and the Iberian Catholics' invasion of Andalus, both of which destroyed many Muslim books. Second, compared with writing manuscripts, printing books would be less expensive, have longer-lasting ink, and entail fewer errors (in copying the text). Third, printed books would have novel features such as indexes and tables of contents.[22]

Muteferrika's press in Istanbul started printing books in 1729. By 1745, it had printed seventeen titles and an estimated 12,000 books.[23] From 1746 to 1802, Ottoman presses printed twenty-eight other titles. Hence, the total number of books they printed in the eighteenth century can be estimated to be less than 50,000. By contrast, in the same century, nearly 1 billion books were produced in Europe.[24] Between 1803 and 1875, the number of titles printed in Ottoman presses increased but remained relatively low: 2,855.[25]

---

[20] Anderson 1983, 44n21.
[21] For the texts of the decree and the fatwa, see "Firman of Ahmed III" 1995 [1727], 284–5.
[22] Müteferrika 1995 [1726], 286–92. See also Müteferrika 1990 [1732].
[23] Sabev 2006, 289–90. See also Gerçek 1939, 84–5.   [24] Buringh and Van Zanden 2009, 417.
[25] Baysal 1968, 57–74; Sabev 2006, 317. In 1875, there were 151 printing presses in the Ottoman Empire, 116 of which were in Istanbul. Baysal 1968, 55.

There were two major reasons for the limited impact of Ottoman presses in their first 150 years. One was the absence of a dynamic bourgeoisie who could have used the presses effectively. The other was the lack of a vibrant intellectual atmosphere with a demand for new books by a large number of readers. The case of Muteferrika illustrates both factors. Professionally, Muteferrika continued to work as a diplomat, so he could not focus on printing and selling books, as a merchant might do. Intellectually, Muteferrika had sufficient qualifications: a polymath, he updated and printed important books on geography, history, and languages. Nonetheless, the Ottoman state did not sufficiently appreciate his intellectual contributions and did not let him focus on his publications. Instead, the state kept using Muteferrika as a diplomat traveling long distances, as far as Poland,[26] which resulted in long hiatuses and inefficiencies in his publication process.

Muslim-run presses were established even later in other parts of the Muslim world: 1817 in Iran (Tabriz), 1819 in India (Lucknow), 1821 in Egypt (Cairo), 1844 in Russia (Kazan; lithographic), and 1853 in Indonesia (Surabaya; lithographic).[27] In Central Asia, which was once a brilliant center of scholarship, no printing press existed until the Russian invasion, which began in 1864.[28]

The belated establishment of printing presses in Muslim societies was associated with their illiteracy problem. It also led to a reversal between Muslims and Western Europeans in terms of the sizes of their library collections. In early Islamic history, there were far more books in Muslim libraries than Western European ones (see Chapter 4). In the late nineteenth century, however, data for the Ottoman Empire and France indicate the opposite. According to the first Ottoman statistical yearbook, written in 1897, there were 324 public libraries with the total of only 193,000 books (74,000 manuscripts, 49,000 printed books, and the rest unspecified).[29] By contrast, in France – the country with the largest library collection in Europe – there were 7,298,000 books in 505 libraries in 1880.[30]

Another associated problem was the delayed mass production of Quran translations, which left Muslims who did not read classical Arabic entirely dependent on the ulema for understanding their religion. In fact, early Muslims were very open to the idea of translating the Quran. Abu Hanifa (d. 767) is reported to have permitted recitation of a Persian translation of the Qur'an

---

[26] Erginbaş 2014, 53, 61–6.

[27] Albin 2007, 171–5; Beydilli 2003, 107–9; Proudfoot 1995, 216.

[28] Khalid 1994, 187. The rulers of Bukhara were particularly traditionalist and so opposed to this innovation that "the first press did not open there until 1917." Khalid 1994, 189. See also Fromkin 2001, 486.

[29] Güran 1997 [1897], 117.

[30] Cipolla 1969, 110. The Bibliothèque Nationale in Paris alone had about half a million books in 1860. Harris 1995, 133; Daly 2014, 157.

in daily prayers, regardless of whether the person had mastered Arabic.[31] The oldest extant Persian translation of the Quran was written in the tenth century in the interlinear form (between the lines of the Arabic text) as part of the Persian translation of Taberi's Arabic exegesis. Surviving "Eastern" Turkish and Anatolian Turkish translations of the Quran were also interlinear and written in the fourteenth and fifteenth centuries, although a reported (non-extant) translation is dated as early as the tenth century.[32]

In the 1730s, Shah Wali Allah, a leading Islamic scholar in India, wrote a Persian interlinear translation in Delhi. At that time, conservative Muslims' resistance to translating the Quran was so deep that even Wali Allah, despite his scholarly reputation, faced opposition.[33] In the case of Europe, the mass dissemination of Bible translations was made possible by the printing press.[34] In the Muslim world, the late adoption of the press delayed the wide circulation of Quran translations. Wali Allah's translation was finally printed in 1866.[35] The Ottoman ulema put extra barriers against the publication of a Turkish translation of the Quran. First, they prohibited the printing of Islamic books until 1803. Next, they blocked the printing of the Quran until 1873.[36] Finally, they prevented the printing of a complete Turkish translation of the Quran until the demise of the Empire.

Brett Wilson has examined an important effort in 1898 to work around the Ottoman ulema's barriers to printing a Turkish translation of the Quran. Şemseddin Sami (1850–1904), an Ottoman intellectual who compiled the first modern Turkish dictionary,[37] wrote a Quranic translation in Turkish. He submitted the manuscript to the Ministry of Education for approval. The ministry sent it to the shaykh al-Islam, whose approval was required for the publication of Islamic books. Shaykh al-Islam Mehmet Cemaleddin replied that Sami's work "translated the verses in a way that 'contradicted the explanations and interpretations' of the great Qur'anic commentators and could 'never' be published." The manuscript was eventually either destroyed or lost. Moreover, "Sami faced public censure and, possibly, some type of punishment for trans-lating the Qur'an into Turkish."[38] Because of the ulema's opposition, the printing of the first complete Turkish translation of the Quran became possible only in 1924, a year after the foundation of the Turkish Republic.[39]

---

[31] His two main students, Abu Yusuf and Shaybani, by contrast, made this permission contingent on the person not possessing mastery of Arabic. Zadeh 2012, 54–7.

[32] Togan 1964, 1–3, 13. See also Hamza 1976 [c. 1424].

[33] Later, one of Wali Allah's sons wrote an interlinear Urdu translation of the Quran. Zadeh 2012, 20. See also Rahman 1982, 40–1.

[34] Febvre and Martin 1997 [1958], 289, 294–5.   [35] Wilson 2014, 3.

[36] Baysal 1968, 79; Wilson 2014, 64; Sabev 2006, 329.   [37] Kushner 1977, 76–9.

[38] Wilson 2014, 108–9.

[39] The translator was Süleyman Tevfik – not a member of the ulema but a "people's writer" and translator of Arabic, English, and French texts. Wilson 2014, 162. See also Bein 2011, 118.

Although the late Ottoman ulema were still influential enough to prevent the translation of the Quran into Turkish, the ulema–state alliance was experiencing a profound crisis due to its failure to address Western challenges. The next section will explore these challenges.

WESTERN DOMINANCE

In the eighteenth and nineteenth centuries, the Netherlands's position in the world economy and politics declined, while Britain gained the leading position.[40] Britain's preeminence was associated with its pioneering role in the Industrial Revolution. British inventors of such important technologies as the steam engine and textile machine were private entrepreneurs rather than governmental agents.[41] These private inventions were combined with the British state's transportation and communication infrastructure, including the railroads, in addition to its usage of military and political power to exploit other countries' economic resources. As a result of this collaboration of private entrepreneurship and state power, Britain surpassed its competitors on the European continent and around the globe.

Additionally, Britain played a leading role in the spread of scientific societies. Together with the Paris Academy of Sciences (established in 1666), the Royal Society, which was founded in London in 1660, became a model for subsequent academic societies, including the Berlin Academy of Sciences (established in 1700). Between 1701 and 1793, seventy official and forty private scientific societies were established – all in Western Europe, except six in the United States and one in Russia.[42]

British philosophers joined with their French, Dutch, and German counterparts in contributing to the intellectual movement known as the Enlightenment.[43] These philosophers transformed European political thought. Hobbes, Locke, and Rousseau wrote on the state of nature and the theory of the social contract. Locke promoted limited government and religious toleration. Montesquieu elaborated the separation of powers. Smith articulated the dynamics of the market economy.[44]

---

[40] Israel 1998, part IV.
[41] Allen 2009, 259. Prominent British inventions included Thomas Newcomen's steam engine (1712), John Kay's flying shuttle (1733), James Watt's improvements to the steam engine (1765–88), and Samuel Crompton's spinning mule (1779). McNeill 1991 [1963], 692.
[42] McClellan 1985, 1.
[43] See Himmelfarb 2003. In the words of Immanuel Kant (2009 [1784]), "Enlightenment is man's emergence from his self-incurred immaturity. Immaturity is the inability to use one's own understanding without the guidance of another."
[44] Hobbes 1994 [1651]; Locke 1980 [1690]; Rousseau 1992 [1755]; Rousseau 2001 [1762]; Locke 1983 [1689]; Montesquieu 1990 [1748]; Smith 1993 [1776].

These ideas influenced leaders of the American (1775–83) and French (1789) revolutions.[45] In the American case, the bourgeoisie and intellectuals led the revolt against the British crown and designed the newly independent United States. They did not attack the clergy, except the Anglican Church, because other churches were independent from the British monarchy.[46] In the French Revolution, however, the bourgeoisie and intellectuals jointly attacked[47] both the aristocracy and its main ally, the Catholic clergy.[48] The United States became a model for many countries in terms of constitutionalism, religion–state separation, and democracy,[49] while post-revolutionary France became a model for republicanism and nationalism throughout Europe and other parts of the world.[50]

In sum, the intellectuals and bourgeoisie played leading roles in such complex processes as the Enlightenment, the American and French Revolutions, and the Industrial Revolution, which transformed Western European and North American (i.e., Western) societies and polities. These processes contributed to Western countries' intellectual vibrancy, political participation, economic strength, and military power. By contrast, Muslim countries lacked such dynamic intellectuals and merchants. They did not experience philosophical, political, or technological revolutions. Hence, they became politically and militarily weaker than their Western counterparts.

Western countries used their power to directly or indirectly colonize most parts of the world, including Muslim lands. Russia (starting in the 1690s) and Japan (starting in 1868) followed Western models and adopted certain Western institutions by state-led reforms. Like Western countries, they established colonial empires to exploit their neighbors' resources.

A major criticism I received while writing this book is that by emphasizing progressive aspects of the rise of the West, I might downplay the violence and destruction Western colonialism has entailed. I acknowledge that Western, Russian, and Japanese colonialisms were based on coercive domination and

---

[45] Locke influenced the American founders. His emphasis on "life, liberty, estate" was partially reflected in Thomas Jefferson's phrase, "life, liberty, and pursuit of happiness" in the Declaration of Independence. Locke 1980 [1690], 46, 66; Zuckert 2002, ch. 8; Bailyn 1967, ch. 2. The impact of Rousseau, particularly his concept of the general will, on French revolutionaries is visible in the Declaration of the Rights of Man and of the Citizen of 1789 (especially articles 1 and 6). Rousseau 1992 [1755], esp. 68–9, 143–5. See also Israel 2011, 924–33.

[46] Kuru 2009, 28–9, 74–83; Munoz 2009; Esbeck 2004, 1457–97; McConnell 1990, 1421–30.

[47] With some reservations, Moore (1966, 413) defines the French Revolution as a "bourgeois revolution." Theda Skocpol (1979, 176, 179) stresses that the Revolution's "political leadership came primarily from the ranks of professionals (especially lawyers), office holders, and intellectuals" and defines it "as much or more a bureaucratic ... and state-strengthening revolution as it was (in any sense) a bourgeois revolution."

[48] Kuru 2009, 136–41; Tocqueville 1983 [1858], 6–7, 151; Baubérot 2004, chs. 1 and 2; Baubérot and Milot 2011, part I; Gunn 2004, 432–51.

[49] See Tocqueville 2000 [1835].   [50] Hobsbawm 1996 [1962], 53–5.

had negative consequences for colonized societies.[51] Although they made some positive contributions, such as building transportation and communication infrastructure, colonizers generally damaged local institutions and promoted internal divisions in colonized societies.[52] Besides colonization, slavery was also an important component of Western economic development,[53] from plantations in British West Indies[54] to those in the southern United States. Western industrialization was also associated with the exploitation of the working class, including child labor.[55]

British colonialism was destructive for many parts of the Muslim world. It led to multiple disasters, such as the 1770 famine in Bengal.[56] British colonialism also caused the "deindustrialization" of India, turning that country into an exporter of raw materials and an importer of British textiles.[57] Britain's forced sale of opium in China made millions of Chinese addicted.[58] In general, French colonialism in Muslim lands was more culturally assimilationist than British colonialism.[59] The nature of Russian colonialism varied; in some periods, it was more culturally assimilationist toward Muslims than even French colonialism. Russia also pursued ethnic cleansing, in particular against Crimean Tatars and certain Caucasian Muslims.[60]

I have two main reasons for not focusing on these aspects of the rise of the West in my analysis. First, the history of Muslim societies also included

[51] Colonialism was a complex phenomenon. For two types of British colonialism, see Acemoglu et al. 2001. For differences between British and Spanish colonialism, see Mahoney 2010; Engerman and Sokoloff 2012.

[52] Some Western scholars justified colonization as the "white men's burden." See Cubberley 1948 [1920], 838–9. In contrast, J. H. Bernardin de Saint Pierre (1775, 105) wrote, "Whether coffee and sugar are really necessary to the happiness of Europe, is more than I can say, but I affirm – that these two vegetables have brought wretchedness and misery upon America and Africa. The former is depopulated, that Europeans may have a land to plant them in; and the latter, is stripped of its inhabitants, for hands to cultivate them."

[53] According to Herbert Klein (2010, 167, 215), the estimated number of Africans enslaved and mostly shipped to the Americas by Europeans between 1501 and 1866 was 12.5 million. Philip Curtin (2000, 7, 12) notes that before 1800, the number of African slaves arriving at the Americas was larger than that of European immigrants.

[54] In the seventeenth and eighteenth centuries, the British commercial network was based on a triangle of exchanges, which included exports from American colonies to Europe (sugar and other cash crops from the Caribbean, and timber and fish from North America), European exports to Africa (finished goods, especially textiles), and African slaves brought to the Americas. Marks 2007, 83. See also Findlay and O'Rourke 2007, 230–8.

[55] Beckert 2014, 98–120, 188–92; Hobsbawm 1996 [1962], ch. 11.

[56] Hodgson 1974c, 151. In British India in 1876–1902, the number of people who died from famine is estimated between 12 and 29 million. Parthasarathi 2011, 224. See also Davis 2001, esp. 7, 44, 111–12, 162–75.

[57] Parthasarathi 2011, esp. 13, 18, 252–4; Braudel 1984, 522.   [58] Marks 2007, 127, 137.

[59] Luizard 2006; Shepard 2006.

[60] Togan 1942–7, 276–344; Khalid 2007, ch. 2; McCarthy 1995, 15–45. German colonization was more limited in terms of time and space. On the brutality of German rule in Southwest Africa, see Ferguson 2011, 176–81.

occupation, exploitation, assimilation, slavery, and ethnic cleansing (e.g., the late Ottoman Empire against Armenians[61]). I do not elaborate them because it is very difficult to make a comparative analysis of the general human problem of violence, as I emphasized in Chapter 1. Second, this book is concerned with what made Western Europe – once a marginal corner of the world – so powerful that it could directly or indirectly colonize almost the entire rest of the world. Hence, colonialism can be only a part of my much broader analysis.

When European countries colonized various territories of the Ottoman Empire, their domination was not simply based on military power; instead, it had political, economic, and ideological dimensions. In the second half of the eighteenth century, the Ottomans suffered major defeats against Russia, which was supported by Austria and Britain. From a military point of view, these losses indicated that "European military organization, training, tactical notions, and weaponry had surpassed those of Ottomans."[62] From an economic perspective, these losses resulted from the expanding revenues of Russia and other European powers, which were increasingly able to invest in their militaries.[63] Around the year 1900, according to the estimates of Eric Zürcher, the Ottoman state's income (330 million Dutch guilders) was much smaller than those of Russia (2,113 million), France (1,831 million), Britain (1,680 million), and Austria-Hungary (1,321 million).[64]

Russia's large population also gave it a military advantage over the Ottomans. The estimated population of the Ottoman Empire was 26 million in 1800; it reached its zenith with 40 million in 1867; and it declined to 21 million in 1914, as a result of the Ottomans' low fertility rate and shrunken territory (reduced by half).[65] The population of the Russian Empire, by contrast, increased from 28 million in 1783 to 60 million in 1835 and 161 million in 1913 due to both its high fertility rate and territorial expansion.[66] Zürcher explains Ottoman military defeats by Russia in the late nineteenth century as a function of the increasing socioeconomic gap between the two empires: "In a

---

[61] Reynolds 2011, ch. 5; Quataert 2005, 186–91.

[62] Kafadar 1997–8, 41, 46. See also Cipolla 1970, 73–9, 107; Lieven 2001, 139.

[63] Karaman and Pamuk 2010, 610–12. According to one estimate, in 1789, state revenues of the Ottoman Empire were around 3.4 million pounds, whereas those of Britain were 16.8 million and France 24 million. McGowan 1994, 714.

[64] Zürcher 2010, 63. See also Hanioğlu 2008, 181n57. In 1913, the foreign trade of the Ottoman Empire (exports [$94 million] and imports [$179 million]) was much smaller than that of Russia (exports [$782 million] and imports [$707 million]). The comparison between Iran (exports [$38 million] and imports [$55 million]) and Britain (exports [$2.556 billion] and imports [$3.208 billion]) also shows the widening economic gap between Middle Eastern and European countries. Issawi 1968, 384.

[65] Quataert 1994, 777–9.

[66] Hingley 1991, 97–8. In 1913, other European powers also had larger populations than the Ottoman Empire: the British Empire 441 million (the United Kingdom: 10%), the French Empire 89 million (France: 46%), the German Empire 79 million (Germany: 84%), Austria-Hungary 52 million, and the Italian Empire 39 million (Italy: 95%). Osterhammel 2014, 119.

struggle with a country like Russia, which was seven times as rich, five times as populous, produced almost thirty times as much coal and had eleven times as big a rail network, who should be surprised at the outcome?"[67]

The socioeconomic, political, and military challenges facing the Ottomans continued until the Empire's demise. An important subset of Ottoman officials recognized these problems and tried to solve them through Westernization reforms in the nineteenth century. At that time, Egypt became semi-independent and pursued its own Westernization reforms. Related to these state-led efforts, reformist intellectuals across the Muslim world debated the proper course of action.

WESTERNIZATION REFORMS AND REFORMIST INTELLECTUALS

In the late eighteenth century, the earliest Ottoman Westernization reforms introduced new educational institutes to address what was seen as the existential threat to the empire: its declining military capacity.[68] The Janissaries were so opposed to military reform that they revolted and imprisoned the reformist sultan, Selim III. The new sultan, Mahmud II (r. 1808–39), waited until conditions were more favorable to implement reform. In 1826 the Janissaries revolted against Mahmud's initiative to modernize the army, but they failed to gain the support of other army units or the people of Istanbul. Troops loyal to Mahmud shelled the Janissaries' barracks with artillery, killing thousands. Mahmud abolished the institution of the Janissary corps altogether. As a result, the ulema, "who had so effectively opposed earlier reforming sultans through their coalition with the janissaries, had now lost their strong arm."[69]

By abolishing the Janissaries and sidelining the ulema, Mahmud and his court bureaucrats gained the control they needed to modernize the Ottoman state. They started the reforms by opening Western-style military colleges. Westernization of the Ottoman military implied that "the traditional links between the military and the religious institutions had been broken decisively."[70] In 1839, right after the death of Mahmud, the new sultan and the bureaucrats issued the Tanzimat Edict, which guaranteed the protection of all Ottoman subjects' "life, honor, and property."[71] The Edict set in motion a series of restoration policies, the so-called Tanzimat reforms. In 1844, a legal change abrogated capital punishment for apostasy from Islam.[72] In 1856, the Islahat Edict promised full equality and religious liberty to non-Muslim citizens,

---

[67] Zürcher 2010, 67.   [68] Ergin 1977, part I; Somel 2001, 15.
[69] Zürcher 2004, 41. With the elimination of the Janissaries, "the ulema lost a main source of leverage over the court and the bureaucracy." Hanioğlu 2008, 59.
[70] Berkes 1998 [1964], 111.
[71] Instead of "liberty" in Locke's phrase (life, liberty, estate [property]), the Edict uses the word "honor." "The Hatt-ı Şerif of Gülhane" 1975 [1839], 270.
[72] Zürcher 2004, 61.

in an effort to remove the protection of Christian minorities as a pretext for European powers' intervention in Ottoman domestic affairs.[73]

During this reform process, bureaucrats took over certain public positions previously held by the ulema. Developments in the education sector clearly reflected the downgrading of the ulema. The madrasas were so outdated and confined to religious studies that Ottoman reformers opted to establish entirely new colleges and schools based on Western models and specializing in such issues as the military, governance, diplomacy, medicine, and engineering. The ulema were still in charge of madrasas and some neighborhood schools, but they lost the monopoly over education.[74] French became a language of instruction in some Ottoman colleges and schools, which trained officers and civilian bureaucrats. Translations of books written in European languages also sharply increased.[75]

With the emergence of Western-style commercial courts and laws, the ulema's judicial and legislative functions were also restricted. The bureaucrats wanted to adopt French commercial and civil codes, while the ulema aimed to codify Islamic law for both realms. In an Imperial Council meeting, the Grand Vizier Mustafa Reshid Pasha, who served intermittently between 1846 and 1858, said that sharia had nothing to do with the legal reforms. The ulema present accused him of apostasy, and he was temporarily removed from office by the sultan. Nonetheless, he returned to office and succeeded in having an adaptation of French commercial code promulgated in 1850.[76]

Egypt also pursued its own Westernization reforms. Mehmed (Muhammad) Ali Pasha, an Ottoman officer of Albanian origin, was sent to Egypt right after Napoleon's invasion. A few years later, in 1805, he became governor of Egypt. In 1811, Mehmed Ali invited Mamluk commanders to a celebration in his citadel in Cairo and had them killed. He then ordered his army to destroy the remaining Mamluks, thus eradicating this centuries-old institution. Mehmed Ali also weakened the ulema by confiscating landed property of the foundations, which supported Al-Azhar and other mosques and madrasas.[77] Having eliminated old power holders, Mehmed Ali implemented Westernization reforms for the military, bureaucracy, taxation, medicine, and schooling. He

---

[73] "Islahat Fermanı" 1975 [1856]. See also Karpat 2001, 75–7.

[74] Berkes 1998 [1964], 99–128; Lewis 1968, 83–6.

[75] Ülken 2016 [1935], 243–55. The Ottoman state allowed the opening of Western-run schools, which were mostly missionary primary schools, due to both their high quality and Western countries' pressure. It is estimated that before the World War I, there were 530 French schools with 54,000 students, 273 American schools with 18,000 students, and 126 British schools with 10,000 students in the Ottoman Empire. There were also a smaller number of Russian, Italian, German, and Austrian schools. Ergün 1996, 390. See also Davison 1961, 291; Deringil 1999 ch. 5.

[76] Lewis 1968, 110–14. See also İnalcık 1964, 56–62; Berkes 1998 [1964], 160–7. Later, the Ottomans codified Islamic law into a civil code known as the Mecelle.

[77] Findley 1992, 125.

sent students to European countries for education. Taking advantage of Ottoman military weakness following the abolishment of the Janissaries, Mehmed Ali attacked Syria and then Anatolia. He defeated Ottoman troops, but European powers intervened to halt his conquest. In 1841, Mehmed Ali withdrew from Syria and Anatolia in exchange for the international recognition of his hereditary rule in Egypt as semi-independent from the Ottoman Empire.[78]

Westernizing reforms led to the emergence of a class of Western-educated intellectuals in both the Ottoman Empire and Egypt. Rifaa al-Tahtawi (1801–73) was one of the students the Egyptian government sent to Paris for education. On his return to Cairo, he became the director of the Language School and coordinated the translation of numerous works. He supervised the translation of nearly 2,000 texts from French, other European languages, and Turkish into Arabic.[79] In the Ottoman Empire, a group of young intellectuals and bureaucrats known as the Young Ottomans tried to synthesize Western and Islamic concepts to reform sociopolitical life.[80] One of their well-known members was Namık Kemal (1840–88), who promoted such notions as "motherland" and "freedom."[81] Ziya Pasha (c. 1829–80) expressed Young Ottoman views through poetry. In one of his famous poems, Ziya Pasha acknowledged the gap between Western and Muslim levels of (urban) development:

> I traveled through the land of infidels and saw cities and mansions,
> I explored the realm of Islam and saw total ruins.[82]

In another famous poem, he criticizes those who blame Islam for Muslims' lack of progress:

> Islam, they say, is a stumbling-block to the progress of the state,
> This story was not known before, and now it is the fashion.[83]

The Young Ottomans hoped to establish a constitutional monarchy. Abdulhamid II (r. 1876–1909) became sultan with their support, which he won by promising to share power with a parliament. The first Ottoman constitution was promulgated in 1876; a year later the Ottoman Parliament was inaugurated. Parliament had two branches: the Chamber of Deputies (consisting of elected representatives) and the Chamber of Notables (consisting of the sultan's appointees). In the first session, the Chamber of Deputies included

---

[78] Rogan 2009, ch. 3; Cleveland 2004, 65–74. Mehmed Ali's dynasty continued in Egypt until 1953.
[79] Newman 2004, 47–51.
[80] Mardin 2000 [1962], chs. 1–5; Ülken 1966, ch. 2; Türköne 1991, ch. 2.
[81] Kemal 1969 [1884]; Kemal 1962 [1910]; Mardin 2000 [1962], 283–336; Özkan 2012, 39–47.
[82] Paşa 1987 [1870], 281.   [83] Translated and quoted by Lewis 1968, 139.

119 representatives: 71 Muslims, 44 Christians, and 4 Jews.[84] The Chamber of Notables also reflected religious diversity. Thus, the Ottoman Parliament became the first truly multireligious parliament of a major country in the world. One year later, however, Abdulhamid closed parliament and ruled as an absolute monarch for more than three decades. Abdulhamid was suspicious of intellectuals; hence, he sent Namık Kemal into exile, where the latter died. It was also during Abdulhamid's rule that Şemseddin Sami, the abovementioned translator of the Quran, was put under house arrest until his death, probably due to his political associations. Under this oppressive regime, many Ottoman intellectuals moved to Paris, where they organized opposition to the sultan.[85]

Beyond Istanbul and Cairo, Muslim reformers emerged in other parts of the Muslim world too. In India, Syed Ahmad Khan (1817–98) promoted a rationalist interpretation of Islam compatible with modern sciences. His major legacy is Aligarh Muslim University.[86] Jamal al-Din al-Afghani (1838–97) also defended Muslims' adoption of rationalism and modern sciences. To spread his ideas, Afghani traveled through Afghanistan, Iran, India, Egypt, France, and the Ottoman Empire. Despite their shared emphasis on modern sciences, there was a major disagreement between Ahmad Khan and Afghani. Ahmad Khan sought friendly relations with the British and focused his efforts on improving (Indian) Muslim education. Afghani, however, was a pan-Islamist who advocated Muslim political unity against Western colonialism.[87] Among those who were inspired by Afghani, the most famous one was Islamic scholar and reformer Muhammad Abduh (1849–1905). Abduh served on the administrative board of Al-Azhar and proposed to reform aspects of that institution in line with Western universities, as well as incorporating Ibn Khaldun's *Muqaddimah* and works of rationalist Mutazili theologians into its curriculum.[88]

Like Ahmad Khan, İsmail Gaspıralı (1851–1914) lived under a colonial regime – in this case Russian rule in Crimea. He published a newspaper, *Tercüman*, with the goal of disseminating a common language for Turkic peoples. Trying to maintain good relations with the Russian rulers, Gaspıralı concentrated on modernizing education for Turkic youth while avoiding an anti-Russian discourse. He encouraged Muslim reformism and developed a new (*jadid*) method of primary school instruction. His ideas and teaching methods inspired a movement, Jadidism, which was very influential in Azerbaijan and Central Asia until its destruction under Stalin.[89]

---

[84] Hanioğlu 2008, 119. In 1867, the estimated population of the Ottoman Empire included 24 million Muslims and 15 million Christians. Karpat 1985, 25.

[85] Mardin 2000 [1962], 76–7; Kushner 1977, 16–7; Berkes 1998 [1964], ch. 9.

[86] Ahmad 1967, 31–56; Ahmed 2013, 30–72; Hassan 2009, 162–4; McAuliffe, 2015, 597–600.

[87] Keddie 1968.

[88] Rahman 1982, 49–77; Hourani 1983, ch. 6; McAuliffe, 2015, 531–9, 601–2.

[89] Gasprinskii 2002 [1901]; Devlet 1988; Khalid 1998, chs. 3–8. In Baku in May 1917, about 900 delegates representing Turkic Muslims in Russia organized a congress. They discussed, among other issues, the abrogation of patriarchal rules in Islamic law by prohibiting polygamy

Yusuf Akçura (1876–1935) was a prominent intellectual who was influenced by Gaspıralı. Similar to that of Afghani, the biography of Akçura reflects the increasing interconnectedness of Muslim intellectuals across the world in the late nineteenth century.[90] Akçura was born in a city in Russia, grew up in Istanbul, went to exile and was educated in Paris, wrote his famous essay "Three Types of Policy" in Kazan (again in Russia), and had it published in Cairo in 1904.[91] In the essay, Akçura explained the problems of Ottomanism (pursued by Tanzimat bureaucrats) and pan-Islamism (partially pursued by Abdulhamid). Contra these policies, he proposed pan-Turkism as an alternative policy for the Ottoman Empire.[92]

Akçura's Turkish nationalism gained importance after the Young Turk Revolution in 1908. The Young Turks included both intellectuals and military officers. Unlike the Young Ottomans with their Ottoman patriotism and Islamic constitutionalism, the Young Turks emphasized Turkish nationalism and secularism. One famously secularist Young Turk was Abdullah Cevdet (1869–1932), who translated and popularized European works of materialist philosophy. Cevdet declared that "[r]eligion is the science of the masses, whereas science is the religion of the elite."[93] In terms of Turkish nationalism, the leading ideologue of the Young Turks was Ziya Gökalp (1876–1924). Influenced by the sociology of Emile Durkheim, Gökalp stressed the importance of national culture in holding Turkish society together. He argued for the compatibility of Turkish culture, Islam (as a religion), and Western civilization.[94]

Nationalist and secularist ideas of late Ottoman intellectuals influenced the founders of the Turkish Republic (declared in 1923). Its first president, Mustafa Kemal (later, Atatürk) appointed Akçura as the president of Turkish History Association. Nonetheless, Mustafa Kemal was much more radical than Akçura and especially Gökalp in his opposition to the public role of Islam in the modern Turkish state. His assertive secularist views were closer to those of Cevdet.[95]

---

and acknowledging women's rights to choose husbands and to divorce. They also recognized women's right to vote. While the majority of the delegates supported these reforms, the traditionalist ulema and their supporters (constituting 25 percent of the delegates) rejected them. Ilgar 1990, 402, 420–8.

[90] Another example was Hayreddin (Khayr al-Din) Pasha (c. 1820–90), who was born in the Caucasus, received an elite education in Istanbul, spent four years in Paris, became a top bureaucrat and pursued (educational and constitutional) reforms in Tunis, and briefly served as the Ottoman grand vizier (again in Istanbul). Hayreddin Pasha advocated Westernization reforms, including a constitutional government, in order to solve Muslims' problems. He argued that such reforms were compatible with Islam. Khayr al-Din 1967 [1867].

[91] Georgeon 1986, esp. 20–30.   [92] Akçura 1976 [1904].   [93] Quoted in Hanioğlu 2011, 56.

[94] Gökalp 2007, 210; Gökalp 1976. See also Durkheim 1984 [1893]; Gökçek 2008, ch. 6.

[95] Georgeon 1986, 105–11; Kuru 2009, 220–2; Hanioğlu 2012, 38–50; Hanioğlu 2011, 52–67, 151–9.

To sum up, in the nineteenth century, Muslim lands experienced state-led Westernization reforms and produced many Western-educated intellectuals. The traditional ulema–state alliance weakened and in some cases disintegrated altogether. The reforms achieved some progress in the Ottoman Empire and Egypt, in terms of modernization of the military, the taxation system, medical conditions, and schooling. In colonized India and Russia, Muslim intellectuals also contributed to the education system of their communities. In particular, Ottoman reformists and intellectuals established a foundation for Turkish political mobilization during the Independence War (1919–22) against Greek, French, Italian, and British occupiers. This mobilization and the war were led initially by some representative congresses and eventually by the Turkish Parliament.[96]

Yet reformist and intellectual efforts during the nineteenth century ultimately failed to help Muslims "catch up with the West." Muslims in Turkey, Egypt and other Arab countries, Iran, India, and Russia entered the twentieth century with accumulated problems of political oppression and socioeconomic backwardness. Nineteenth-century Muslim reformism proved ineffective for five reasons, enumerated below.

First, although the ulema were largely sidelined and an independent intellectual class emerged, Muslims' class-based problems mostly persisted. Rulers and their bureaucrats filled the vacuum left by the ulema. The Ottoman Sultan Mahmud, Egypt's Mehmed Ali, and most of their successors were absolutist rulers who did not accept sharing power with other institutions or classes. Their Westernization reforms were by and large top-down projects that did not accommodate the concerns or interests of intellectuals or merchants.[97]

There were two major attempts to turn the Ottoman political system into a constitutional monarchy, both of which failed. In 1878, Abdulhamid, who could be defined as an Islamist, suspended parliament for good. In 1908, secularist Young Turks revolted and forced Abdulhamid to reopen parliament.[98] However, the Committee of Union and Progress (CUP),[99] the party of the Young Turks, eventually established an authoritarian regime. The CUP regime was led by the "three pashas" and continued until the end of World War

---

[96] Ahmet Demirel (1994, 614) stresses that during the Independence War, the Turkish Parliament in Ankara (elected in 1920) had a participatory decision-making process and an opposition group that checked Mustafa Kemal's power.

[97] See Timur 1986, 160–1.

[98] Due to the secession of Balkan nations, the percentage of Christians in the Ottoman population and 1908 parliament decreased. Yet there still existed substantial ethnic and religious diversity within parliament. Among the 288 representatives in the Chamber of Deputies, there were 234 Muslims (147 Turks, 60 Arabs, and 27 Albanians), 50 Christians (26 Greeks, 14 Armenians, and 10 Slavs), and 4 Jews. Ahmad 1969, 28. See also Kayalı 1997, 65–72. In 1897, the Ottoman population included 14.1 million Muslims and 4.9 million non-Muslims. Güran 1997 [1897], 20.

[99] Temo 1987 [1939].

I. Hence, Ottoman Westernization failed to produce a parliamentary and participatory political system.[100]

Second, authoritarian Muslim rulers controlled the economy without sufficiently encouraging the accumulation of private capital or the rise of a native bourgeoisie. In the Ottoman Empire, certain legal reforms promised to protect private property (the Tanzimat Edict of 1839)[101] and were designed to uphold private ownership of lands (the Land Law of 1858),[102] but in practice the state violation of private property and control over lands largely continued.[103] A bourgeois class flourished, but it was almost exclusively a product of European powers' support for non-Muslim merchants. According to one analysis, in 1912, although non-Muslims, including Greeks and Armenians, constituted only 19 percent of the Ottoman population, they comprised between 66 and 85 percent of major local traders.[104] This proportion was a result of the Ottoman state's centuries-old neglect of Muslim merchants, as well as its semi-colonized status at that time. Many Christian merchants among the Ottoman citizens turned into "European protégés" by becoming dual citizens of a European state. While these protégés were safeguarded against the arbitrariness of the Ottoman state policies, other Ottoman citizens remained vulnerable to state violations of their property. The protégés also paid lower taxes than regular citizens and were tried in consular courts instead of Ottoman ones.[105] Consequently, the Ottoman bureaucracy regarded the bourgeoisie, which consisted mostly of protégés, as more European than native.[106] This quasi-foreign identity mitigated the influence this bourgeoisie could exert on Ottoman politics.

Said Halim Pasha was one of the Muslim intellectuals who was aware of this problem. He was the grandson of Egypt's Mehmed Ali, a leading Young Turk, and Ottoman grand vizier (1913–16). In his book *Our Crises*, Said Halim Pasha lamented that in the Ottoman Empire, it was state servants rather than the aristocracy or the bourgeoisie that were the dominant class. For him, the state servants were inherently docile, obedient, and risk-averse. They were

[100] Tüccarzade Hilmi (Çığıraçan), a pioneering Muslim private book publisher and seller in Istanbul, wrote a book about the causes of the Ottoman decline. Among the causes, he emphasizes the authoritarian but ineffective state and the bigoted ulema (Çığıraçan 2010 [1912–13], esp. 32–3).

[101] The Edict promised to abolish confiscation: "[T]he innocent heirs of a criminal shall not be deprived of their hereditary rights as a result of the confiscation of the property of such a criminal." "The Hatt-ı Şerif of Gülhane" 1975 [1839], 270.

[102] İslamoğlu 2000, 26–42; Gerber 1987, ch. 5.

[103] Karpat 1968, 74, 81; Mardin 1979, 24, 31, 36; Çakmak 2014.   [104] Kuran 2011, 193.

[105] Issawi 1982, 89–90; Kuran 2011, 199. In 1882, in Galata, Istanbul's major commercial district, foreigners and protégés constituted 112,000 of the 237,000 residents. Kuran 2011, 201. For foreigners and protégés in İzmir, see Kasaba 1988, 70–3.

[106] See Göçek 1996, ch. 3.

afraid of taking initiative and responsibility. In Western Europe, by contrast, the aristocratic and bourgeois classes had independence and courage – necessary qualities to become entrepreneurial.[107]

Third, the Ottoman education reform was unapologetically elitist. As late as 1910–12, an Ottoman minister of education defined the policy as similar to the "Tuba tree." Tuba was perceived to be an otherworldly tree, whose roots were at the top and branches at the bottom. The minister implied that instead of prioritizing the roots (mass education in primary schools), they prioritized the branches (elite education in high schools and colleges). In fact, this metaphor conveyed the general nature of Ottoman education reforms. Ottoman policy-makers largely supported this prioritization based on their belief that the Empire urgently needed a bureaucratic elite to respond to the crises of the times. This policy undermined the elementary education of society at large.[108] The Ottoman education reform, therefore, was very different from the Japanese education reform, which began in 1868 with the Meiji Restoration and attached importance to mass elementary education.[109] By 1908, Japan had made six years of schooling free and compulsory, and had over 90 percent of eligible students enrolled in schools.[110]

Fourth, efforts at Westernization encountered political and religious resistance. In the Ottoman Empire, political resistance to Westernization was strongest under the rule of Abdulhamid, who pursued a policy of Islamic modernization. On the one hand, Abdulhamid attacked intellectuals, rejected their demand for parliamentarianism, and promoted certain ulema and Sufi shaykhs to use Islam and his title "caliph" as a source of legitimacy in domestic and international politics. On the other hand, he opened many modern schools and established railroads.[111] The main source of religious resistance was naturally the ulema. In the Ottoman Empire, the ulema were still part of the government in the late nineteenth century and had veto power on certain issues, such as the publication of the Turkish translation of the Quran. In Egypt, the ulema rejected Abduh's proposals to reform Al-Azhar.[112] In Central Asia and

---

[107] Paşa 2012 [1919], 62–3.
[108] Ergün 1996, 42–7; Frey 1964, 214–17. The Ottoman emphasis on higher education was not sufficient either. By 1900, the Ottomans had opened around a dozen colleges. Findley 1989, 154–63; İhsanoğlu 1990. In contrast, the number of colleges founded in the United States by that time was around 500. Cubberley 1948 [1920], 705. This was complementary with the American success in schooling and literacy. In 1870, the US literacy rate – 80 percent of the total population (and 89 percent of whites) – was highest in the world. Engerman and Sokoloff 2012, 29.
[109] Ward and Rustow 1964, 455. [110] Lockwood 1964, 138. [111] Karpat 2001, ch. 7.
[112] The shaykh of Al-Azhar at the time accused Abduh of being willing to "destroy the clear paths of religious instruction and to convert this great mosque into a school of philosophy and literature." The shaykh adds, "As for the worldly affairs and modern learning, they have nothing to do with Al-Azhar." Quoted in Rahman 1982, 68.

other Muslim lands under Russian rule, the ulema resisted the reform project of the Jadidists.[113]

There was also popular resistance to educational reforms. According to Selçuk Somel, the Ottoman public primary schools "were often not accepted by the Muslim population, whereas the traditional Quran schools, with the religious *hoca* as schoolmaster, continued to be respected by the people."[114] This popular resistance might have further encouraged the Ottoman policy-makers to prioritize elitist secular schools, rather than wrangling with the conservative masses over disagreements regarding primary education.

Fifth and finally, European colonization was a major impediment to the success of Muslims' reforms. Muslims in India and Russia were already under colonial rule, and Egypt gradually turned into a British colony in the late nineteenth century. Colonization restricted Muslims' freedom to flourish and engendered reactionary anti-Western ideologies among them. The Ottoman Empire increasingly lost its economic independence in the face of European encroachment. The Empire was collapsing under the pressure of Russian, French, British, and Italian occupations, as well as the secession of and attacks by Balkan nations.[115]

CONCLUSION

In the eighteenth and nineteenth centuries, Western Europe and North America experienced important transformations such as the Enlightenment, the American and French Revolutions, and the Industrial Revolution. The Muslim world, however, remained mostly stagnant in the eighteenth century. Muslim countries even failed to effectively use printing technologies until the nineteenth-century Westernization reforms. While Western European societies read millions of copies of Bible translations from the fifteenth century onward, printing a complete translation of the Quran remained taboo in Muslim societies until the twentieth century. With their intellectual and socioeconomic dynamism, Western countries developed their military technologies and organizations, and dominated the rest of the world. Only Russia and Japan caught up with Western levels of technological advance and organizational effectiveness, and both became colonial powers.

In a nutshell, this is how European powers, particularly Britain, France, and Russia, used their military, political, and technological advances to colonize most of the Muslim world. Certain rulers in the Ottoman Empire and Egypt

---

[113] Khalid 2007, chs. 2 and 3; Tuna 2015, 171–94.   [114] Somel 2001, 272.

[115] Again, a comparison with the successful Japanese modernization would be helpful: (1) unlike the Ottoman Empire's ulema, Japan did not have a religious class that put constraints on legal and educational modernization, and (2) unlike the collapsing Ottoman Empire, Japan did not experience foreign occupations and secessions. Findley 1989, 135; Kayaoğlu 2010, 118–21; Issawi 1983.

acknowledged this problem and undertook Westernization reforms in the nineteenth century. These reforms as well as colonial rule also led to the emergence of new, reformist intellectuals in various Muslim lands. Amid these developments, the traditional alliance between the ulema and the state weakened, even in those Muslim countries that maintained a certain level of independence from colonial powers, such as the Ottoman Empire and early nineteenth-century Egypt.

On the one hand, state-led reforms and intellectual movements contributed to Muslims' development of their bureaucracies and educational and medical institutions. On the other hand, these reforms and movements did not succeed in bringing Muslim societies to Western levels of political and socioeconomic development. Authoritarian rulers established absolutist regimes and consolidated state monopolies over the economy in the Ottoman Empire and Egypt. The lack of a native bourgeoisie prevented economic creativity and innovation. The Ottoman Empire took pioneering steps by opening a parliament twice, but it failed to establish a truly representative political system. Opposition from Islamist rulers and the ulema, as well as European powers' direct and indirect colonization, also hindered the success of political and socioeconomic reforms in the Muslim world.

Among Muslim countries, the Ottoman Empire can be evaluated as the "most likely case" for successful Westernization. The Ottomans were geographically in the most western part of the Muslim world. They inherited the capital city and a certain imperial legacy from the Byzantine Empire. Eastern European Christians constituted a large percentage of their population for a long time. Their bureaucratic elite included many formerly Christian converts. Together with Egypt's Mehmed Ali, who was also originally an Ottoman officer, the Ottoman Empire undertook Westernization reforms before any other Muslim country, and even before Japan and China. Thus, if Westernization reforms could not succeed in this most likely case, they were unlikely to succeed in another Muslim country. That is why the Ottoman experiment is crucial in the analysis of Westernization reforms in the Muslim world.

Despite the ulema's diminishing position in the Ottoman state, Ottoman Muslims largely continued to imagine the state and religion as twins and to jointly revere them. According to Mardin, even the Young Ottomans, who were much more Westernized than the Muslim masses, were still heirs to a historically constructed dual devotion to Islam and the state. This devotion was reflected in "the extremely common saying, '*Allah din-ü devlete zeval vermesin*' ('[May] God protect religion and the state')."[116] This communitarian and statist worldview continued to be a major factor in the absence of creative philosophers, explorers, innovators, and entrepreneurs in the Ottoman Empire. Although the ulema–state alliance was weakened by the abolishment of the

---

[116] Mardin 2000 [1962], 106.

Janissaries and institutional Westernization reforms, this alliance's cultural legacy endured for two main reasons. First, Ottoman intellectuals, including the secularists, remained mostly communitarian and statist and tended not to support individualism. Second, as already elaborated, in terms of intellectual debates and educational institutions, the Ottoman reforms were largely an elitist project, which had limited influence among the Muslim masses.

In sum, in the nineteenth century, the Muslim world inherited multiple intellectual, socioeconomic, and political problems from earlier centuries, as I elaborated in Part II. Despite efforts of reformist rulers and intellectuals, the Muslim world failed to solve most of these problems, which, as I explored in Part I, persisted into the twentieth century and continue to shape Muslim countries today.

Conclusion

COMPARATIVE HISTORICAL DEVELOPMENT

In Part II of this book I analyzed transformations in crucial periods of Muslim history in comparison to Western European history. This analysis has refuted the essentialist view that presents Muslim and Western cases as dichotomous, if not antagonistic, entities. This view not only misses the historical complexity of both cases but also reproduces stereotypes about them. Indeed, the Muslim and Western cases have had many similarities. The current differences between the two cases that seemingly justify the conventional comparative judgments between them are the result of complex historical processes and even reversals.

In terms of class relations, from the eighth to the eleventh century, Muslim societies had characteristics similar to what Western European societies would gain during the Renaissance – creative intellectuals and influential merchants.[1] During this period, most Islamic scholars avoided serving the state; they were funded by trade revenue and regarded interactions with the rulers as corrupting.

This arrangement began to change in the eleventh-century Seljuk Empire, which formed an ulema–state alliance. This formation was based on two main transformations. First, the military class came to dominate the economy and undermined merchants. Through the expansion of the *iqta* system, the land revenues were distributed to military and other officials. Second, with the establishment of Nizamiya madrasas, the Sunni orthodoxy was consolidated and entrenched, while Islamic scholars increasingly became state servants. This ideological and institutional transformation gradually eliminated philosophers and independent Islamic scholars.

Later, foreign attacks from Western Europe (Crusaders) and Inner Asia (Mongols) led many Muslims to seek refuge in the leadership of military and

---

[1] See Sabra 1996, 662; Collins 2000, 451.

religious elites. Eventually, the Seljuk model of ulema–state alliance was adapted and adopted by subsequent Muslim empires, especially the Ayyubids/ Mamluks, Ottomans, Safavids, and Mughals. Hence, the class relations that became dominant in the Muslim world during and after the eleventh century resembled those in the early medieval Europe: clerical and military elites dominated society and inhibited the flourishing of intellectuals and merchants.

Western Europe also began to experience a multidimensional and gradual transformation in the eleventh century, particularly on three issues. First, the separation between the Catholic Church and royal authorities was institutionalized, as neither side had proved capable of completely subduing the other. Second, class relations began to change, with merchants becoming increasingly influential. Third, universities started to be established, which would maintain an institutional basis for the flowering of intellectuals. New class relations ultimately became a source of economic and intellectual achievements during the Renaissance and in subsequent eras.

Changing class relations had important consequences for Muslims' and Western Europeans' comparative levels of scholarly, economic, and military development. Notwithstanding the risk of overgeneralizing and well aware of the criticisms on the horizon, I have summarized in Table C.1 my general

TABLE C.1 *Comparative Historical Development: Muslims and Western Europeans*

	Muslim supremacy	Comparable levels of development	Western European supremacy
Philosophy and natural sciences	c. 800 to 1198 (from the Baghdad Scholars to the death of Ibn Rushd)	1198 to c. 1610 (to Galileo and Kepler)	c. 1610 to present
Economy	c. 697 to 1252 (from the Umayyad gold coin to the first gold coin in Western Europe)	1252 to c. 1820 (to the Industrial Revolution [c. 1750 for Dutch and English economic supremacy])	c. 1820 to present
Military	711 to 1085/99 (from the Muslim conquest of Toledo to the Reconquista of Toledo/the Crusader conquest of Jerusalem)	1085/99 to 1764/74 (to the Battle of Buxar [the British defeat of the Mughals and their allies]/ the Kucuk Kaynarca Treaty [between the Ottomans and Russia])	1764/74 to present

Sources: Numerous sources cited in Part II, especially the following: Sarton 1927; Sayılı 1960; Shatzmiller 2011; Watson 1983; Bloch 2014 [1940]; Braudel 1982; Van Zanden 2009; Karaman and Pamuk 2010; İnalcık 1994; Hodgson 1974c.

understanding of the comparative historical development between Muslim and Western European societies.[2] I have designed the table with an eye toward preventing certain misunderstandings regarding my analysis. For example, while I argue that Muslim scholarly advances became slower after the eleventh century, I do not mean that Western Europe immediately exceeded Muslims on this front. As the table indicates, it was only in much later centuries that Western Europeans clearly surpassed Muslims in philosophy and the natural sciences.[3]

VIOLENCE, AUTHORITARIANISM, AND UNDERDEVELOPMENT

In Part I of this book I examined the low levels of political and socioeconomic development in most Muslim-majority countries in comparison to world averages. Especially in comparison to Western countries, levels of development in Muslim countries are undeniably low today. I critically evaluated arguments pointing to either Western colonialism or Islam as the main cause of these problems in the Muslim world. I argued instead that the ulema–state alliance has been the main cause of Muslims' problems. This alliance continued for centuries and left a legacy of authoritarianism and socioeconomic underdevelopment in the twentieth-century Muslim world.

Starting with Turkey's Atatürk in the 1920s, several secularist leaders either weakened or abolished the ulema–state alliance while establishing newly independent Muslim-majority states. Nonetheless, Muslim masses largely remained loyal to conservative ideas supporting a strong public role for the ulema. In a broader sense, three groups that I collectively call "Islamic actors" – the ulema, Islamists, and Sufi shaykhs[4] – have received substantial popular support even in

---

[2] My table is inspired by Needham's (2004, 28, 40) figure (no. 7), which provides a comparative historical analysis of Chinese and Western societies in six scientific fields.

[3] One may claim earlier dates for the beginning of Muslim military supremacy (642: Muslim victories against Sasanian and Byzantine Empires), Muslim scientific supremacy (c. 750: Jabir), Western scientific supremacy (1580: Tycho Brahe's observatory), and Western economic supremacy (the early eighteenth century). One may also extend the period of Muslim scientific supremacy (until 1274: the death of Tusi). I have tried to be conservative about the length of supremacy periods in all cases (picking the later alternative for the beginning of a supremacy and an earlier alternative for the end of it). One may argue that in the sixteenth century, the combined military power of the Ottomans, Safavids, and Mughals was superior to that of Western Europeans. I opted not to address this in the table, because no combined (Ottoman–Safavid–Mughal) Muslim military attack on Western Europe ever occurred. Moreover, although the Ottomans conquered European lands as far west as Hungary, their military supremacy over Western Europe was not clear in the sixteenth century – they failed in the siege of Vienna (1529), were defeated by a European armada at Lepanto (1571), and could not stop the Portuguese expansion in the Indian Ocean.

[4] The ulema are trained in Islamic studies in madrasas or their modern equivalents; the Islamists are political activists aiming to establish Islamic states; and the Sufi shaykhs are mystical leaders of Sufi orders.

countries where top-down secularization policies were implemented for decades, including Turkey and Tunisia. The repeated failures of secularist politicians in foreign policy, the economy, and social reforms contributed to this popularity. Moreover, many secularist leaders reproduced certain aspects of the historical ulema–state alliance while trying to legitimize their rules by using Islamic institutions, such as Turkey's Diyanet and Egypt's Al-Azhar. Finally, in several Muslim countries, the ulema–state alliance either has continued to exist (such as in Saudi Arabia) or been revived in a different form (such as in Iran).

My analysis particularly focused on three contemporary problems – violence, authoritarianism, and underdevelopment – which have constituted a vicious circle in the Muslim world. Although each of the three has its own causes, they are all interrelated. Regarding the problem of violence, there is no Muslim exceptionalism; violence has occurred in all parts of the world. The frequent Muslim terrorist activities are a relatively recent trend that began in the 1980s. This trend is related to the worldwide decline of socialism and the rise of religious political movements. Until the 1980s, the most visible actors engaging violence were socialist groups, even in the Middle East; later, Islamist groups replaced socialists in engaging in terrorism. Muslim countries have also had a large number of interstate and civil wars. These military conflicts and terrorism have multiple causes, including the colonial legacy, poverty, and authoritarian states, in particular.

Assessing the relationship between Islam and violence (in Chapter 1), I emphasized two points. First, we should examine various interpretations of Islam rather than analyzing Islam as a single, monolithic entity. A particular interpretation of Islam, Jihadi-Salafism, has promoted violence primarily because it is based on the idea that one single Quranic verse (about attacking polytheists in Mecca) abrogated more than a hundred other verses upholding peace, patience, toleration, and freedom of conscience. Second, although Jihadi-Salafis have been numerically marginal, their message has spread widely, because neither the ulema nor other Muslims have successfully promoted peace-promoting ideas as alternatives. The ulema did not effectively produce original alternatives, given their training, which prioritizes defending the tradition rather than reforming it. Other Muslims have also been unable to produce counterarguments to produce peace because the ulema have monopolized the production of legitimate Islamic discourses. Muslim intellectuals with no training in madrasas or their equivalents would have very limited legitimacy in the eyes of the Muslim community at large if they attempted to produce alternative interpretations of Islam.

Political leaders have obviously had the lion's share of responsibility for violence in the Muslim world. It is they who declare wars against other states, and their authoritarian policies at home lead some groups to take up arms against them. Moreover, their authoritarian concern to retain power at any cost has made many Muslim countries inward-looking and security-obsessed.

Electoral democracies constitute more than half of all countries in the world but less than one-fifth of the forty-nine Muslim-majority countries. Like violence, authoritarianism is a multifaceted problem with multiple ideological and economic causes. In the Muslim world, both Islamic and secularist actors have contributed to it. Close cooperation between the ulema and the state has secured a religious monopoly for the former and generated religious legitimacy for the latter. The ulema have hindered alternative interpretations of Islam, while the state has used religion to justify its crackdowns on political opponents.[5] Other Islamic actors have also had problematic relations with democratic principles. The Islamists aim to impose a set of religious laws over the state and society. Where they have taken power or emerged as an influential opposition, the Islamists have generally led states to be more authoritarian. The Sufi shaykhs have largely promoted spiritual and even social hierarchy; thus, their ideas and orders have contributed to authoritarianism. The secularists also have embraced and promoted various non-democratic ideologies in many Muslim countries.

Additionally, authoritarianism in the Muslim world has had a strong material basis. As a geological reality, Muslim countries have possessed 60 percent of the world's oil reserves. I elaborated in Chapter 2 how oil, gas, and other sources of rents have prolonged the dominance of non-productive political and religious elites in most Muslim countries. These rents have enabled the survival of many Islamist regimes, which are dominated by the ulema (such as Iran) or by an ulema–monarchy alliance (such as Saudi Arabia). In some other Muslim cases, the absence of oil revenues forced political authorities to reduce state control over the economy and society. But these politicians have generally continued to seek rents and ways of going back to statist socioeconomic policies. Even in Turkey, without oil rents and with European Union candidacy, Erdoğan has built a semi-rentier system by receiving international loans and selling Istanbul's lands in order to finance his statist and authoritarian regime based on a new form of ulema–state alliance.

Authoritarianism and rentierism have also been associated with the long-lasting socioeconomic underdevelopment in the Muslim world. The overwhelming majority of Muslim countries gained independence after 1940, having already suffered for centuries with problems of low literacy rates, ineffective school and college systems, an absence of competitive corporations, inadequate transportation and communication infrastructure, and technological handicaps. Muslim countries needed creative intellectuals and a productive bourgeoisie to

---

[5] Currently, the ulema's understanding of law as something a group of experts deduce from religious texts contradicts the democratic notion of a legislature, which adapts and transforms the law according to changing conditions and with popular participation. Historically, the only exception the ulema recognized with the authority to make laws were the sultans; more accurately, the ulema were forced to acknowledge the sultans' legislative authority given the latter's coercive capability.

address these problems. Yet the marginalized status of the intellectuals and bourgeoisie has persisted in Muslim societies during the twentieth century and onward. The following section summarizes my explanation of this persistence.

NO INTELLIGENTSIA/BOURGEOISIE, NO DEVELOPMENT

Muslim intellectuals and bourgeoisie have had limited influence in contemporary Muslim societies due to the limitations the ulema–state alliance has continued to put on them. Historically, the ulema declared some eminent philosophers and their followers as apostates to be killed. Contemporary ulema have not seriously grappled with this record and have left the issue of apostasy in Islamic law books unreformed, continuing to view apostasy as a punishable offense. Most ulema have not been directly responsible for the assassinations and executions of various intellectuals in such countries as Egypt and Sudan, but they have failed to challenge the ideological bases of these acts.

Moreover, the ulema have defended an inflexible epistemology, discouraging new ideas and delegitimizing Muslim intellectuals' efforts at reinterpreting Islam. The ulema's epistemology relies on the Quran, hadiths, consensus of the ulema, and analogical reasoning. As I have elaborated, although this formula of four hierarchical sources was initially constructed by Shafii as a jurisprudential methodology, its influence was later expanded by Ghazali and other leading ulema, particularly during and after the eleventh century, to the extent that it dominated theology and Sufism, and ultimately ordered even general Muslim knowledge.[6] In this literalist epistemological hierarchy, reason is the least important source of knowledge and is confined to drawing analogies based solely on the three other (and superior) sources. Early Muslims generally used the concepts of "reasoning" and "consensus" in much more emancipatory and egalitarian ways. Abu Hanifa stressed a jurist's reason-based decision as a key criterion for jurisprudential authority. Consensus was also understood as a broad concept referring to the agreement of the Muslim community at large. Later, however, the ulema restricted reasoning writ large to mere "analogical reasoning" and consensus of the entire community to the "consensus of the ulema." The powerful ulema have defended this hierarchical and exclusionary epistemology; they have undermined some exceptional ulema's attempts to make it more flexible by adding new criteria, such as the "higher objectives" of Islamic law.[7]

---

[6] See also the Introduction.

[7] A leading promoter of the five "higher objectives" of Islamic law was the eminent jurist Shatibi, who "found that the political, social, commercial and legal changes in Granada in [the] fourteenth century posed problems that could not be solved by the deductive method of *qiyas* [analogical reasoning]." Masud 1995, 253. If Shatibi could see the world today, he would be surprised to see Muslims still using analogical reasoning in their attempts to address the accumulated problems of the seven centuries after his death.

Despite their criticisms of the ulema, the Islamists have embraced the ulema's epistemology and thus acknowledged their authority to produce Islamic law. Similarly, although the Sufi shaykhs have had an additional criterion in their epistemology – so-called mystical knowledge – they have largely accepted the epistemology and authority of the ulema. In sum, this epistemology, which has sidelined reason and disregarded empirical experience, has constituted a basis for the shared anti-intellectualism of the ulema, Islamists, and Sufi shaykhs.[8]

One might assume that the secularists would support intellectuals given their own two-century-long struggle against Islamic actors, but this is not always the case. In most Muslim countries secularist leaders have been authoritarian, statist, and nationalist, not champions of intellectual freedom and exploration. These leaders and their parties have generally been opposed to individualism, critical thinking, and diversity – necessary conditions for the flourishing of intellectual life. In many Muslim countries, secularists established a cult of personality around their leader, which resembled Sufis' glorification of their shaykh as a "perfect man" or the Mahdi. The secularists sidelined the ulema and allowed bureaucrats to occupy the vacuum where the ulema once held power. In this regard, political secularization strengthened bureaucrats but did not substantially improve the status of the intellectuals or bourgeoisie.

In many Muslim countries, industrialists and businesspeople did emerge; but they have been too embedded within the state to constitute an independent bourgeoisie. Both the Islamic actors and secularists are responsible for the enduring weakness of the bourgeoisie. With few exceptions, the ulema have cooperated with and been coopted by officials rather than allying with the bourgeoisie. The Islamists have aimed to capture state power and to redesign society in a top-down manner; their totalitarian project leaves no room for an independent bourgeoisie. Likewise, the preaching of Sufi shaykhs has been too concerned with mysticism to promote a bourgeois work ethic. At the same time, secularist politicians have generally pursued statist economic policies, or at least a mixed economy combining a free market with state intervention. They have regarded an independent bourgeois class as a potential threat to their power. Many secularist leaders in such cases as Turkey, Iran, Egypt, Iraq, Syria, Algeria, Tunisia, Pakistan, and Indonesia had military backgrounds, which made it unlikely for them to truly appreciate the importance of the bourgeoisie for the economic and political development of their countries. In sum, lacking strong intellectual and bourgeois classes, twentieth-century Muslim countries were rarely able to solve the political and socioeconomic problems they inherited.

---

[8] Shii ulema have more emphasis on reason in their epistemology. Salafi Sunni ulema are critical of the consensus of the earlier ulema. Yet these differences have not made any of these groups of ulema pro-intellectual.

RECOMMENDATIONS

Throughout the twentieth century and onward, several Islamic actors and secularists have tried to solve the aforementioned problems in the Muslim world. Islamic actors have attributed these problems to Western colonialism and imperialism. Although the secularists have primarily blamed Islamic actors for these problems, they have also criticized the West. Both of these antagonistic groups have proposed state-centric political solutions; therefore, both have tried to capture the state completely and eliminate the other side.

I do not deny that Western colonialism and imperialism have destroyed local institutions and exploited natural resources in many Muslim countries. Nonetheless, focusing on the damage wrought by Western powers has distracted Muslims from addressing their own failures and reforming their ideas, policies, and institutions. Neither anti-Westernism nor the tug-of-war between Islamic actors and secularists will help Muslims solve their problems. Instead, both Islamic actors and secularists ought to address the problems of anti-intellectualism and state control over the economy.

Islam is not responsible for Muslims' problems, but certain quasi-Islamic theories are. Throughout this book I have demonstrated that the theory and practice of the ulema–state alliance, which was inspired by the Sasanian notion of religion–state brotherhood, has been a source of Muslims' multiple crises. Today Muslims need new perspectives on politics and government. The secularists in the twentieth century, and their reformist predecessors in the nineteenth century, accepted this necessity, though they have not been successful in producing philosophically deep and publicly convincing alternative political theories. The Islamic actors, by contrast, have largely continued to expect solutions from political theories written in the High and Late Middle Ages (1000–1500), by perceiving them as based on Islam's sacred and timeless principles. However, this view is historically inaccurate; high and late medieval Islamic political thought and the theory of the caliphate in particular were heavily influenced by the Sasanian tradition of governance as well as specific political conditions, particularly those of the eleventh century.

I have analyzed the views of Mawardi, Ghazali, and Ibn Taymiyya, authors of the most influential treatises on the theory of the caliphate (and sharia politics). Mawardi's ideal system rested on the rule by one man, the caliph, who holds executive, legislative, and judicial powers and then delegates his powers to viziers, governors, and judges. Since this ideal was not practical even in the eleventh century, Mawardi and Ghazali discussed the coexistence of the caliph with the sultan(s). More than two centuries later, Ibn Taymiyya made further compromises from the ideal one-man rule by prescribing joint governance by the rulers and the ulema.[9] These caliphate theories include no

---

[9] Al-Mawardi 1996 [1045–58]; al-Ghazali 1999 [1095], 234–44; al-Ghazali 2013 [1095], 229–40; Ibn Taymiyya 1994a [1309–14].

discussion of the perils of one-man rule, of mechanisms for holding rulers accountable, or possibilities of legitimate opposition. These unapologetically authoritarian (and patriarchal) theories are worth our attention only as historical texts and should not inform Muslims' political thought in the twenty-first century.[10] Defending these political theories keeps Islamic actors out of step with present realities and heightens secularists' anxieties about Islamic activism.[11]

My historical analysis may seem deterministic and pessimistic; in fact, it is neither. By explaining the ulema–state alliance as an eleventh-century construction, my analysis has indicated the possibility of change and the reasonableness of optimism. It has exposed the historical inaccuracy of seeing the ulema–state alliance as something essential to Islamic texts or permanent in Islamic history. Contemporary perceptions of Islam as a religion that necessarily rejects religion–state separation are mistaken. Hence, Muslims can redesign the relationship between their religion and their states in way that would promote intellectual and economic creativity. Moreover, my analysis has shown that there is a historical basis for such a reform. From the eighth to the tenth century, Islamic scholars were mostly funded by commerce and largely avoided serving the state. During this period, Muslim societies produced cutting-edge polymaths and influential merchants. Critically analyzing Muslim history may contribute to the construction of a new, democratic, and progressive relationship between Islam and the state today.

In order to solve the problems of violence, authoritarianism, and underdevelopment, as well as catch up to Western levels of development, Muslims should establish competitive and meritocratic systems. These will require substantial socioeconomic and political reform with ideological and institutional dimensions. For such a reform to take place, Muslims need creative intellectuals and an independent bourgeoisie, who can balance the power of the ulema and state authorities.

---

[10] In contrast, a contemporary translator of Mawardi's *Ordinances* presents it as "a refreshing antidote to the teaching of modernists." Yate 1996, 5.

[11] Even Muhammad Asad, an otherwise open-minded author, was misled by the idea of implementing the medieval caliphate theory in the modern world. He argues that the caliphate resembles the US presidential system, but he ignores central features of the latter, including term limits and separation of powers. His book concludes with a call for what amounts to a totalitarian Islamic state: "[T]he Muslim is not only legally but also morally bound always to subordinate his personal interests to the interests of the Islamic state as a whole, and this is pursuance of the principle that such a state is 'God's vice-gerent [caliph] on earth.'" Asad 1961, 61, 83.

Bibliography

Abattouy, Mohammed, Jürgen Renn, and Paul Weinig. 2001. "Transmission as Transformation: The Translation Movements in the Medieval East and West in a Comparative Perspective." *Science in Context* 14, 1–2: 1–12.

El-Abbadi, Mostafa. 1990. *The Life and Fate of the Ancient Library of Alexandria.* Paris: UNESCO/UNDP.

Abbès, Makram. 2015. "Essai sur les arts de gouverner en Islam." In Al-Mawardi, *De l'éthique du Prince et du gouvernement de l'État.* Translated into French and edited by Makram Abbès. Paris: Les Belles Lettres.

Abdel Razek, Ali. 2012 [1925]. *Islam and the Foundations of Political Power.* Translated by Maryam Loutfi. Edited by Abdou Filali-Ansary. Edinburgh: Edinburgh University Press.

Abdul-Jabbar, Ghassan. 2007. *Bukhari.* New York: Oxford University Press.

Abou El Fadl, Khaled. 2003. *The Place of Tolerance in Islam.* Boston: Beacon Press.

  2004. *Islam and the Challenge of Democracy.* Princeton: Princeton University Press.

  2009. *Rebellion and Violence in Islamic Law.* New York: Cambridge University Press.

  2014. *Reasoning with God: Reclaiming Shari'ah in the Modern Age.* New York: Rowman and Littlefield.

Abu-Lughod, Janet L. 1989. *Before European Hegemony: The World System A.D. 1250–1350.* New York: Oxford University Press.

Abu-Rabi', Ibrahim M. 1995. *Intellectual Origins of Islamic Resurgence in the Modern Arab World.* Albany: SUNY Press.

Abu Zaid [Zayd], Nasr Hamid. 2000. "Divine Attributes in the Qur'an: Some Poetic Aspects." In John Cooper, Ronald Nettler, and Mohamad Mahmoud, eds., *Islam and Modernity: Muslim Intellectuals Respond.* New York: I. B. Tauris.

  2004. *Voice of an Exile: Reflections on Islam.* Edited by Esther R. Nelson. Westport, CT: Praeger.

  2006. *Reformation of Islamic Thought: A Critical Historical Analysis.* Amsterdam: Amsterdam University Press.

Acemoglu, Daron, and James A. Robinson. 2009. *Economic Origins of Dictatorship and Democracy*. New York: Cambridge University Press.
    2012. *Why Nations Fail: The Origins of Power, Prosperity, and Poverty*. New York: Crown Business.
Acemoglu, Daron, Simon Johnson, and James A. Robinson. 2001. "The Colonial Origins of Comparative Development: An Empirical Investigation." *American Economic Review* 91, 5: 1369–401.
Adamson, Peter. 2016. *Philosophy in the Islamic World: A History of Philosophy without Any Gaps*. New York: Oxford University Press.
Adıvar, A. Adnan. 1982 [1939]. *Osmanlı Türklerinde İlim*. Istanbul: Remzi Kitabevi.
    1969. *Tarih Boyunca İlim ve Din*. Ankara: Remzi Kitabevi.
Adonis [Ali Ahmad Said Esber]. 2015. *Violence et islam. Entretiens avec Houria Abdelouahed*. Paris: Seuil.
El-Affendi, Abdelwahab. 2014. "Mahmoud Taha: Heresy and Martyrdom." *Critical Muslim* 12: 115–30.
Afsaruddin, Asma. 2008. *The First Muslims: History and Memory*. Oxford: Oneworld.
    2015. *Contemporary Issues in Islam*. Edinburgh: Edinburgh University Press.
Agoston, Gabor. 2005. *Guns for the Sultan: Military Power and the Weapons Industry in the Ottoman Empire*. New York: Cambridge University Press.
Ahmad, Aziz. 1967. *Islamic Modernism in India and Pakistan: 1857–1964*. London: Oxford University Press.
Ahmad, Barakat. 1979. *Muhammad and the Jews: A Re-Examination*. New Delhi: Vikas.
    1989. "Conversion from Islam." In C. E. Bosworth, Charles Issawi, Roger Savory, and A. L. Udovitch, eds., *The Islamic World from Classical to Modern Times: Essays in Honor of Bernard Lewis*. Princeton: Darwin Press.
Ahmad, Feroz. 1969. *The Young Turks: The Committee of Union and Progress in Turkish Politics, 1908–1914*. New York: Oxford University Press.
Ahmad, Irfan. 2009. "Genealogy of the Islamic State: Reflections on Maududi's Political Thought and Islamism." *Journal of the Royal Anthropological Institute* 15: 145–62.
Ahmad, Mumtaz. 1991. "Islamic Fundamentalism in South Asia: The Jamaat-i-Islami and the Tablighi Jamaat." In Martin E. Marty and R. Scott Appleby, eds., *Fundamentalisms Observed*. Chicago: University of Chicago Press.
Ahmed, Munir-ud Din. 1968. *Muslim Education and the Scholars' Social Status up to the 5th Century Muslim Era (11th Century Christian Era) in the Light of Ta'rikh Baghdad*. Zurich: Verlag "Der Islam."
Ahmed, Safdar. 2013. *Reform and Modernity in Islam: The Philosophical, Cultural and Political Discourses among Muslim Reformers*. New York: I. B. Tauris.
Ahmed, Shahab. 2003. "Review of Daphna Ephrat's *A Learned Society in a Period of Transition: The Sunni 'Ulama' of Eleventh-Century Baghdad*." *Journal of the American Oriental Society* 123, 1: 179–82.
    2015. *What Is Islam? The Importance of Being Islamic*. Princeton: Princeton University Press.
Ahmed-Ghosh, Huma, ed. 2015. *Asian Muslim Women: Globalization and Local Realities*. Albany: SUNY Press.
Ali, Kecia. 2006. *Sexual Ethics and Islam: Feminist Reflections on Qur'an, Hadith, and Jurisprudence*. Oxford: Oneworld Publications.

Akbulut, Zeynep. 2015a. "Veiling as Self-Disciplining: Muslim Women, Islamic Discourses, and the Headscarf Ban in Turkey." *Contemporary Islam* 9, 3: 433–53.

2015b. "The Headscarf Ban and Muslim Women's Rights Discourse in Turkey." In Huma Ahmed-Ghosh, ed., *Contesting Feminisms: Gender and Islam in Asia*. Albany: SUNY Press.

Akçura, Yusuf. 1976 [1904]. *Üç Tarz-ı Siyaset*. Ankara: Türk Tarih Kurumu.

Akdağ, Mustafa. 1971. *Türkiye'nin İktisadi ve İçtimai Tarihi: Vol. II, 1453–1559*. Ankara: Türk Tarih Kurumu Basımevi.

2009 [1963]. *Türk Halkının Dirlik ve Düzenlik Kavgası: Celali İsyanları*. İstanbul: Yapı Kredi Yayınları.

Akyol, Mustafa. 2011. *Islam without Extremes: A Muslim Case for Liberty*. New York: W. W. Norton.

Alam, Muzaffar. 2004. *The Languages of Political Islam: India, 1200–1800*. Chicago: University of Chicago Press.

2013. "A Muslim State in a Non-Muslim Context: The Mughal Case." In Mehrzad Boroujerdi, ed., *Mirror for the Muslim Prince: Islam and the Theory of Statecraft*. Syracuse: Syracuse University Press.

Alatas, Syed Faris. 2013. *Ibn Khaldun*. Oxford: Oxford University Press.

2014. *Applying Ibn Khaldun: The Recovery of a Lost Tradition in Sociology*. New York: Routledge.

Albin, Michael. 2007. "The Islamic Book." In Simon Eliot and Jonathan Rose, eds., *A Companion to the History of the Book*. Malden, MA: Blackwell.

Alexander, Amy C., and Christian Welzel. 2011. "Islam and Patriarchy: How Robust Is Muslim Support for Patriarchal Values?" *World Values Research* 4, 2: 40–70.

Alexseev, Mikhail A. 1997. *Without Warning: Threat Assessment, Intelligence, and Global Struggle*. London: Macmillan.

Algar, Hamid. 1982. "Introduction." In *The Path of God's Bondsmen from Origin to Return*. Translated from Persian and edited by Hamid Algar. New York: Caravan Books.

Ali, Souad T. 2009. *A Religion, Not a State: Ali 'Abd al-Raziq's Islamic Justification of Political Secularism*. Salt Lake City: University of Utah Press.

Ali, Syed Ameer. 2012 [1902]. *The Spirit of Islam or the Life and Teachings of Mohammed*. San Bernardino: Forgotten Books.

Allard, Michel. 1952–4. "Le rationalisme d'Averroès d'après une étude sur la creation." *Bulletin d'Études Orientales* (Damas) 14: 7–59.

Allen, Robert C. 2009. *The British Industrial Revolution in Global Perspective*. New York: Cambridge University Press.

Amin, Samir. 1976. *Unequal Development: An Essay on the Social Formations of Peripheral Capitalism*. New York: Monthly Review Press.

Aminrazavi, Mehdi. 2010a. "Fakhr al-Din Razi." In Seyyed Hossein Nasr and Mehdi Aminrazavi, eds., *An Anthology of Philosophy in Persia. Vol. 3: Philosophical Theology in the Middle Ages and Beyond*. New York: I. B. Tauris.

2010b. "Sa'd al-Din Taftazani." In Seyyed Hossein Nasr and Mehdi Aminrazavi, eds., *An Anthology of Philosophy in Persia. Vol. 3: Philosophical Theology in the Middle Ages and Beyond*. New York: I. B. Tauris.

Anderson, Benedict. 1983. *Imagined Communities: Reflections on the Origin and Spread of Nationalism*. New York: Verso.

Andrade, Tonio. 2016. *The Gunpowder Age: China, Military Innovation, and the Rise of the West in World History*. Princeton: Princeton University Press.

Angenendt, Arnold. 2011. "Christians between Tolerance and Violence in Europe." In Erik Eynikel and Angeliki Ziaka, eds., *Religion and Conflict: Essays on the Origins of Religious Conflicts and Resolution Approaches*. London: Harptree Publishing.

Angrist, Michele. 2012. "War, Resisting the West, and Women's Labor: Toward an Understanding of Arab Exceptionalism." *Politics and Gender* 8, 1: 51–82.

Anjum, Ovamir. 2012. *Politics, Law, and Community in Islamic Thought: The Taymiyyan Moment*. New York: Cambridge University Press.

Aquil, Raziuddin. 2008. "On Islam and *Kufr* in the Delhi Sultanate: Towards a Re-Interpretation of Ziya' al-Din Barani's *Fatawa-i Jahandari*." In Rajat Datta, ed., *Rethinking a Millennium: Perspectives on Indian History from the Eighth to the Eighteenth Century*. Delhi: Aakar Books.

Aquinas, Thomas. 1988 [1265–72]. *On Law, Morality, and Politics* (excerpts from *Summa Theologica*). Translated by Richard J. Regan. Edited by William P. Baumgarth and Richard J. Regan. Indianapolis: Hackett Publishing.

Aristotle. 1996a [c. 350 BCE]. *Nicomachean Ethics*. In Michael L. Morgan, ed., *Classics of Moral and Political Theory*. Translated from ancient Greek by Terence Irwin. Indianapolis: Hackett Publishing.

1996b [c. 350 BCE]. *The Politics*. In *The Politics and the Constitution of Athens*. Translated from ancient Greek by Benjamin Jowett and revised by Jonathan Barnes. Edited by Stephen Everson. New York: Cambridge University Press.

Arjomand, Said Amir. 1984. *The Shadow of God and the Hidden Imam: Religion, Political Order, and Societal Change in Shi'ite Iran from the Beginning to 1890*. Chicago: University of Chicago Press.

1988. *The Turban for the Crown: The Islamic Revolution in Iran*. New York: Oxford University Press.

1999. "The Law, Agency, and Policy in Medieval Islamic Society: Development of the Institutions of Learning from the Tenth to the Fifteenth Century." *Comparative Studies in Society and History* 41, 2: 263–93.

2010. "Legitimacy and Political Organisation: Caliphs, Kings, and Regimes." In Robert Irwin, ed., *The New Cambridge History of Islam. Vol. IV: Islamic Cultures and Societies to the End of the Eighteenth Century*. New York: Cambridge University Press.

2017. "Persianate Islam and Its Regional Spread." In Patrick Michel, Adam Possamai, and Bryan S. Turner, eds., *Religions, Nations, and Transnationalism in Multiple Modernities*. New York: Palgrave Macmillan.

Armstrong, Karen. 2014. *Fields of Blood: Religion and the History of Violence*. New York: Alfred A. Knopf.

Arslan, Ahmet. 1972. "Kemal Paşa-zade'nin 'Haşiya 'ala Tahafut al-Falasifa'si." *Araştırma: Ankara Üniversitesi Dil ve Tarih-Coğrafya Fakültesi Felsefe Bölümü Dergisi* 10: 19–45.

1999. *İslam Felsefesi Üzerine*. Ankara: Vadi Yayınları.

Asad, Muhammad. 1961. *The Principles of State and Government in Islam*. Berkeley: University of California Press.

1984. *The Message of the Qur'an*. Gibraltar: Dar al-Andalus.

Asad, Talal. 1993. *Genealogies of Religion: Discipline and Reasons of Power in Christianity and Islam*. Baltimore: Johns Hopkins University Press.

2003. *Formations of the Secular: Christianity, Islam, Modernity*. Stanford: Stanford University Press.

Asch, Ronald G. 2015. "Monarchy in Western and Central Europe." In Scott Hamish, ed., *The Oxford Handbook of Early Modern European History, 1350–1750. Vol. II: Cultures and Power*. New York: Oxford University Press.

Al-Ashari. 1953 [c. 935]. *Kitab al-Luma'* [*The Luminous Book*]. Translated by Richard J. McCarthy. In *The Theology of al-Ashari*. Beirut: Imprimerie catholique.

Ashtor, E[liyahu]. 1976. *A Social and Economic History of the Near East in the Middle Ages*. London: Collins.

1983. *Levant Trade in the Later Middle Ages*. Princeton: Princeton University Press.

Askari, Nasrin. 2016. *The Medieval Reception of the Shahnama as a Mirror for Princes*. Boston: Brill.

Aslan, Reza. 2005. *No God but God: The Origins, Evolution, and Future of Islam*. New York: Random House.

Atçıl, Abdurrahman. 2016. *Scholars and Sultans in Early Modern Ottoman Empire*. New York: Cambridge University Press.

Ayalon, David. 1956. *Gunpowder and Firearms in the Mamluk Kingdom: A Challenge to a Mediaeval Society*. London: Vallentine, Mitchell.

Ayoob, Mohammed. 2007. *The Many Faces of Political Islam: Religion and Politics in the Muslim*. Ann Arbor: University of Michigan Press.

Al-Azmeh, Aziz. 1997. *Muslim Kingship: Power and the Sacred in Muslim, Christian, and Pagan Polities*. New York: I. B. Tauris.

2014. "Abbasid Culture and the Universal History of Freethinking Humanism." *Critical Muslim* 12: 73–88.

Baali, Fuad. 1988. *Society, State, and Urbanism: Ibn Khaldun's Sociological Thought*. Albany: SUNY Press.

Bacık, Gökhan, and Ahmet Kuru. 2017. "Said Nursi'yi Eleştirel Okumak (1): İman ve Namaz Çözüm mü?" *Kitalar Arası*, December 20, https://kitalararasi.com/2017/12/20/said-nursiyi-elestirel-okumak-1-iman-ve-namaz-cozum-mu-gokhan-bacik-ve-ahmet-kuru/.

Bacon, Francis. 2000 [1620]. *The New Organon*. Edited by Lisa Jardine and Michael Silverthorne. New York: Cambridge University Press.

Badawi, Nesrine. 2014. "Sunni Islam: Classical Sources." In Gregory M. Reichberg and Henrik Syse, eds., *Religion, War, and Ethics: A Sourcebook of Textual Traditions*. New York: Cambridge University Press.

Baer, Marc David. 2007. *Honored by the Glory of Islam: Conversion and Conquest in Ottoman Europe*. New York: Oxford University Press.

Bagley, F[rank] R. C. 1964. "Introduction." In *Ghazali's Book of Counsel for Kings (Nasihat al-Muluk)*. Translated from Persian and edited by F. R. C. Bagley. New York: Oxford University Press.

Bailyn, Bernard. 1967. *The Ideological Origins of the American Revolution*. Cambridge, MA: Harvard University Press.

Bairoch, Paul. 1988. *Cities and Economic Development: From the Dawn of History to the Present*. Translated by Christopher Braider. Chicago: University of Chicago Press.

Banfield, Edward C., with Laura F. Banfield. 1958. *The Moral Basis of a Backward Society*. Glencoe, IL: Free Press.

Al-Banna, Gamal. 2001. *Vers une nouvelle jurisprudence islamique*. In *L'enseignement de Gamal al-Banna*. Translated into French, abridged, and edited by Mouna A. Akouri. Cairo: Dar al-Fikr al-Islami.

——— 2003. *Al-Islam Din wa Ummah wa Laysa Dinan wa Dawlah*. Cairo: Dar al-Fikr al-Islami.

Al-Banna, Hasan. 1978 [1938–45]. *Five Tracts of Hasan al-Banna' (1906–1949): A Selection of the Majmuat Rasa'il al-Imam al-Shahid Hasan al-Banna'*. Translated by Charles Wendell. Berkeley: University of California Press.

——— 1979 [1938–45]. *Majmu'at Rasa'il al-Imam al-Shahid Hasan al-Banna*. Beirut: Al-Mu'assasah al-Islamiyah lil-Țiba'ah wa-al-Sihafah wa-al-Nashr.

Banu Musa bin Shakir. 1979 [850]. *The Book of Ingenious Devices (Kitab al-Hiyal)*. Translated by Donald R. Hill. Boston: D. Reidel Publishing.

Barani, Ziauddin. 1961 [c. 1358–9]. *Fatawa-i Jahandari*. In *The Political Theory of the Delhi Sultanate*. Translated from Persian by Afsar Umar Salim Khan. Edited by Mohammad Habib. Delhi: Kitab Mahal.

Barkan, Ömer Lütfi. 1940. "Şark Ticaret Yolları Hakknda Notlar." *İstanbul Üniversitesi İktisat Fakültesi Mecmuası* 1, 4: 448–56.

——— 1975. "The Price Revolution of the Sixteenth Century: A Turning Point in the Economic History of the Near East." Translated by Justin McCarthy. *International Journal of Middle East Studies* 6, 1: 3–28.

Barkey, Karen. 2008. *Empire of Difference: The Ottomans in Comparative Perspective*. New York: Cambridge University Press.

——— 2012. "Rethinking Ottoman Management of Diversity: What Can We Learn for Modern Turkey?" In Ahmet T. Kuru and Alfred Stepan, eds., *Democracy, Islam, and Secularism in Turkey*. New York: Columbia University Press.

Barras, Amelie. 2014. *Refashioning Secularisms in France and Turkey: The Case of the Headscarf Ban*. New York: Routledge.

Barrett, Ward. 1990. "World Bullion Flows, 1450–1800." In James D. Tracy, ed., *The Rise of Merchant Empires: Long-Distance Trade in the Early Modern World, 1350–1750*. New York: Cambridge University Press.

Barro, Robert J., and Rachel M. McCleary. 2005. "Which Countries Have State Religions?" *The Quarterly Journal of Economics* 104, 4: 1331–70.

Barthold, W[ilhelm]. 1977 [1900]. *Turkestan Down to the Mongol Invasion*. Translated from Russian by T. Minorsky. London: E. J. W. Gibb Memorial Trust.

Bartlett, Robert. 1993. *The Making of Europe: Conquest, Colonization and Cultural Exchange, 950–1350*. Princeton: Princeton University Press.

Başkan, Birol. 2014. *From Religious Empires to Secular States: State Secularization in Turkey*. New York: Routledge.

Bates, Robert. 1981. *Markets and States in Tropical Africa: The Political Basis of Agricultural Policies*. Berkeley: University of California Press.

Baubérot, Jean. 2004. *Histoire de la laïcité en France*. Paris: PUF, Que sais-je?

Baubérot, Jean, and Micheline Milot. 2011. *Laïcités sans frontières*. Paris: Seuil.

Bayat, Asef. 2007. *Making Islam Democratic: Social Movements and the Post-Islamist Turn*. Stanford: Stanford University Press.

Baysal, Jale. 1968. *Müteferrika'dan Birinci Meşrutiyete Kadar: Osmanlı Türklerinin Bastıkları Kitaplar*. Istanbul: İstanbul Üniversitesi Edebiyat Fakültesi.

Beblawi, Hazem, and Giacomo Luciani, eds. 1987. *The Rentier State*. London: CroomHelm.

Becker, Sascha O., and Ludger Woessmann. 2009. "Was Weber Wrong? A Human Capital Theory of Protestant Economic History." *The Quarterly Journal of Economics* 124, 2: 531–96.

Beckert, Sven. 2014. *Empire of Cotton: A Global History*. New York: Vintage Books.

Beckett, Katharine Scarfe. 2003. *Anglo-Saxon Perceptions of the Islamic World*. New York: Cambridge University Press.

Bein, Amit. 2011. *Ottoman Ulema, Turkish Republic: Agents of Change and Guardians of Tradition*. Stanford: Stanford University Press.

Bellah, Robert N. 1991. "Islamic Tradition and the Problems of Modernization." In his *Beyond Belief: Essays on Religion in a Post-Traditionalist World*. Berkeley: University of California Press.

Bellin, Eva. 2004. "The Robustness of Authoritarianism in the Middle East: Exceptionalism in Comparative Perspective." *Comparative Politics* 36, 2: 139–57.

　　2012. "Reconsidering the Robustness of Authoritarianism in the Middle East: Lessons from the Arab Spring." *Comparative Politics* 44, 2: 127–49.

Belting, Hans. 2011. *Florence and Baghdad: Renaissance Art and Arab Science*. Translated from German by Deborah Luce Schneider. Cambridge, MA: Belknap Press of Harvard University Press.

Ben-Zaken, Avner. 2010. *Reading Hayy Ibn-Yaqzan: A Cross-Cultural History of Autodidacticism*. Baltimore: Johns Hopkins University Press.

Berger, Peter, ed. 1999. *The Desecularization of the World: Resurgent Religion and World Politics*. Grand Rapids, MI: Eerdmans.

Berkes, Niyazi 1998 [1964]. *The Development of Secularism in Turkey*. New York: Routledge.

Berkey, Jonathan Porter. 1992. *The Transmission of Knowledge in Medieval Cairo: A Social History of Islamic Education*. Princeton: Princeton University Press.

　　2003. *The Formation of Islam: Religion and Society in the Near East, 600–1800*. New York: Cambridge University Press.

Berman, L[awrence] V. 1968–9. "Review of E. I. J. Rosenthal's translation of *Averroes' Commentary on Plato's 'Republic.'*" *Oriens* 21–2: 436–9.

Bernier, François. 1891 [c. 1668]. *Travels in the Mogul Empire: A.D. 1656–1668*. Translated from French by Irving Brock. Edited by Archibald Constable. Westminster: Constable.

Bey, Kochi. 1972 [1631–40]. *Koçi Bey Risalesi*. Translated from Ottoman Turkish to modern Turkish by Zuhuri Danışman. Istanbul: Milli Eğitim Basımevi.

Bey, Seyyid. 1942 [1924]. "Hilafetin Mahiyeti Şer'iyesi." In *T. B. M. M. Kavanin Mecmuası*. Vol. II, Devre II, İçtima 1. Ankara: T. B. M. M. Matbaası.

　　1969 [1924]. *Hilafetin Mahiyeti Şer'iyesi: Türkiye Büyük Millet Meclisindeki Açıklamaları*. Edited by Suphi Menteş. Istanbul: Menteş Matbaası.

Beydilli, Kemal. 2003. "Matbaa." In Bekir Topaloğlu et al., eds., *Türkiye Diyanet Vakfı İslam Ansiklopedisi*. Vol. 28. Ankara: Türkiye Diyanet Vakfı.

Bier, Carole. 1993. "Piety and Power in Early Sasanian Art." In Eiko Matsushima, ed., *Official Cult and Popular Religion in the Ancient Near East*. Heidelberg: C. Winter.

Bilgin, Fevzi. 2011. *Political Liberalism in Muslim Societies*. New York: Routledge.

Al-Biruni. 1964 [1030]. *Alberuni's India: An Account of the Religion, Philosophy, Literature, Geography, Chronology, Astronomy, Customs, Laws and Astrology of India about A.D. 1030* [*Tarikh al-Hind*]. Translated by Edward C. Sachau. Abridged and edited by Ainslie T. Embree. New Delhi: S. Chand.

El-Bizri, Nader, ed. 2008. *Epistles of the Brethren of Purity: The Ikhwan al-Safa and Their Rasa'il. An Introduction*. New York: Oxford University Press.

Black, Antony. 2008. *The West and Islam Religion and Political Thought in World History*. New York: Oxford University Press.

　　2011. *The History of Islamic Political Thought: From the Prophet to the Present*. Edinburgh: Edinburgh University Press.

Blair, Sheila, and Jonathan Bloom. 1995. *The Art and Architecture of Islam: 1250–1800*. New Haven: Yale University Press.

Blaut, J[ames] M. 1993. *The Colonizer's Model of the World: Geographical Diffusionism and Eurocentric History*. New York: Guilford Press.

　　2000. *Eight Eurocentric Historians*. New York: Guilford Press.

Blaydes, Lisa, and Eric Chaney. 2013. "The Feudal Revolution and Europe's Rise: Political Divergence of the Christian West and the Muslim World before 1500 CE." *American Political Science Review* 107, 1: 16–34.

Bloch, Marc. 2014 [1940]. *Feudal Society*. Translated from French by L. A. Manyon. New York: Routledge.

Bloom, Jonathan. 2001. *Paper before Print: The History and Impact of Paper in the Islamic World*. New Haven: Yale University Press.

Bloom, Jonathan, and Sheila Blair. 2002. *Islam: A Thousand Years of Faith and Power*. New Haven: Yale University Press.

Boix, Carles. 2003. *Democracy and Redistribution*. New York: Cambridge University Press.

　　2011. "Democracy, Development, and the International System." *American Political Science Review* 105, 4: 809–28.

Boix, Carles, and Susan C. Stokes. 2003. "Endogenous Democratization." *World Politics* 55, 4: 517–49.

Bonadeo, Cecilia Martini. 2015. "'Abd al-Latif al-Baghdadi." In Edward N. Zalta, ed., *The Stanford Encyclopedia of Philosophy*, September 9, https://plato.stanford.edu/archives/fall2015/entries/al-baghdadi/.

Bonner, Michael. 2010. "The Waning of Empire: 861–945." In Chase F. Robinson, ed., *The New Cambridge History of Islam. Vol. 1: The Formation of the Islamic World. Sixth to Eleventh Centuries*. New York: Cambridge University Press.

Bons, Eberhard, and Erik Eynikel. 2011. "Holy War and Old Testament: Old Testament Traditions Connected to Religion and Violence." In Erik Eynikel and Angeliki Ziaka, eds., *Religion and Conflict: Essays on the Origins of Religious Conflicts and Resolution Approaches*. London: Harptree Publishing.

Borsch, Stuart J. 2005. *The Black Death in Egypt and England*. Austin: University of Texas Press.

Bosker, Maarten, Eltjo Buringh, and Jan Luiten van Zanden. 2008. "From Baghdad to London: The Dynamics of Urban Growth in Europe and the Arab World, 800–1800." Centre for Economic Policy Research, Discussion Paper 6833.

Bosworth, C. E. 1968. "The Political and Dynastic History of the Iranian World (A.D. 1000–1217)." In J. A. Boyle, ed., *The Cambridge History of Iran. Vol. V: The Saljuq and Mongol Periods*. New York: Cambridge University Press.

Botticini, Maristella, and Zvi Eckstein. 2012. *The Chosen Few: How Education Shaped Jewish History, 70–1492*. Princeton: Princeton University Press.

Boulakia, Jean David C. 1971. "Ibn Khaldun: A Fourteenth-Century Economist." *Journal of Political Economy* 79, 5: 1105–18.

Boyce, M. 1968. "Introduction." In *The Letter of Tansar*. Translated and edited by M. Boyce. Rome: Istituto Italiano per il Medio ed Estremo Oriente.

BP. 2011. "Statistical Review of World Energy 2011," June, www.bp.com/statisticalreview.

Brague, Remi. 1993. "Note sur la traduction arabe de la Politique, derechef, qu'elle n'existe pas." In Pierre Aubenque and Alonso Tordesillas, eds., *Aristote politique: Etudes sur la Politique d'Aristote*. Paris: Presses universitaires de France.

Braude, Benjamin, and Bernard Lewis. 1982. "Introduction." In Benjamin Braude and Bernard Lewis, eds., *Christians and Jews in the Ottoman Empire: The Functioning of a Plural Society*. Vol. I. New York: Holmes and Meier Publishers.

Braudel, Fernand. 1976. *The Mediterranean and the Mediterranean World in the Age of Philip II*. Vol. II. Translated from French by Sian Reynolds. New York: Harper and Row.

   1981. *Civilization and Capitalism, 15th–18th Century*. Vol. 1: *The Structures of Everyday Life*. Translated from French by Sian Reynolds. New York: Harper and Row.

   1982. *Civilization and Capitalism, 15th–18th Century*. Vol. 2: *The Wheels of Commerce*. Translated from French by Sian Reynolds. New York: Harper and Row.

   1984. *Civilization and Capitalism, 15th–18th Century*. Vol. 3: *The Perspective of the World*. Translated from French by Sian Reynolds. New York: Harper and Row.

   1993. *A History of Civilizations*. Translated from French by Richard Mayne. New York: Allen Lane, Penguin Press.

Brentjes, Sonja. 2011. "The Prison of Categories: 'Decline' and Its Company." In Felicitas Opwis and David Reisman, eds., *Islamic Philosophy, Science, Culture, and Religion Studies in Honor of Dimitri Gutas*. Leiden: Brill.

Brentjes, Sonja, with Robert G. Morrison. 2010. "The Sciences in Islamic Societies (750–1800)." In Robert Irwin, ed., *The New Cambridge History of Islam*. Vol. 4: *Islamic Cultures and Societies to the End of the Eighteenth Century*. New York: Cambridge University Press.

Briggs, Martin S. 2005 [1931]. "Architecture." In Sir Thomas Arnold and Alfred Guillaume, eds., *The Legacy of Islam*. New Delhi: Aravali Books International.

Britannica. 2018. "Great Books of the Western World," https://britannicashop.britannica.co.uk/epages/Store.sf/Shops/Britannicashop/Products/ENC_BOOK_0123.html.

Broadie, Alexander. 1996. "Maimonides." In Seyyed Hossein Nasr and Oliver Leaman, eds., *History of Islamic Philosophy*. New York: Routledge.

Brotton, Jerry. 2002. *The Renaissance Bazaar: From the Silk Road to Michelangelo*. New York: Oxford University Press.

Brown, Jonathan. 2013. "Scripture in the Modern Muslim World: The Quran and Hadith." In Jeffrey T. Kenney and Ebrahim Moosa, eds., *Islam in the Modern World*. New York: Routledge.

Brownlee, Jason. 2012. *Democracy Prevention: The Politics of the U.S.-Egyptian Alliance*. New York: Cambridge University Press.

Bryson. 2013 [c. 1st century]. *Management of the Estate*. Translated by Simon Swain. In Simon Swain, *Economy, Family, and Society from Rome to Islam: A Critical Edition, English Translation, and Study of Bryson's* Management of the Estate. New York: Cambridge University Press.

Buehler, Michael. 2016. *The Politics of Shari'a Law: Islamist Activists and the State in Democratizing Indonesia*. New York: Cambridge University Press.

Bulliet, Richard W. 1972. *The Patricians of Nishapur: A Study in Medieval Islamic Social History*. Cambridge, MA: Harvard University Press.

1979. *Conversion to Islam in the Medieval Period: An Essay in Quantitative History*. Cambridge, MA: Harvard University Press.

1990. *The Camel and the Wheel*. New York: Columbia University Press.

1995a. *Islam: The View from the Edge*. New York: Columbia University Press.

1995b. "Review of Peter Christensen's *The Decline of Iranshahr: Irrigation and Environments in the History of the Middle East, 500 B.C. to A.D. 1500*." *International Journal of Middle East Studies* 27, 4: 519–20.

2009. *Cotton, Climate, and Camels: A Moment in World History*. New York: Columbia University Press.

Burak, Guy. 2015. *The Second Formation of Islamic Law: The Hanafi School in the Early Modern Ottoman Empire*. New York: Cambridge University Press.

Buringh, Eltjo, and Jan Luiten van Zanden. 2009. "Charting the 'Rise of the West': Manuscripts and Printed Books in Europe. A Long-Term Perspective from the Sixth through Eighteenth Centuries." *The Journal of Economic History* 69, 2: 409–45.

Burke, Edmund III. 2009. "Islam at the Center: Technological Complexes and the Roots of Modernity." *Journal of World History* 20, 2: 165–86.

Burnett, Charles. 2009. *Arabic into Latin in the Middle Ages*. Burlington, VT: Ashgate, Variorum.

Burton, John. 1990. *The Sources of Islamic Law: Islamic Theories of Abrogation*. Edinburgh: Edinburgh University Press.

Butterworth, Charles E. 2001. "Biographical Sketch of Averroes (1126–1198)." In *Decisive Treatise and Epistle Dedicatory*. Translated and edited by Charles E. Butterworth. Provo, UT: Brigham Young University Press.

Büttgen, Philippe, Alain de Libera, Marwan Rashed, and Irène Rosier-Catach. 2009. *Les Grecs, les Arabes et nous: Enquête sur l'islamophobie savant*. Paris: Fayard.

Butzer, Karl W., Juan F. Mateu, Elisabeth K. Butzer, and Pavel Kraus. 1985. "Irrigation Agrosystems in Eastern Spain: Roman or Islamic Origins?" *Annals of the Association of American Geographers* 75, 4: 479–509.

Cahen, Claude. 1953. "L'évolution de l'iqta du IXe au XIIIe siècle: Contribution à une histoire comparée des sociétés médiévales." *Annales. Économies, Sociétés, Civilisations* 8, 1: 25– 52.

1962. "A propos et autour d' 'Ein arabisches Handbuch der Handelswissenschaft.'" *Oriens* 15: 160–71.

Çakmak, Diren. 2014. *Osmanlı İmparatorluğu'nun Kapitalistleşme Tecrübesi ve Telif Haklarının Gelişimi*. Istanbul: Libra Kitap.

Cammett, Melani, Ishac Diwan, Alan Richards, and John Waterbury. 2015. *A Political Economy of the Middle East*. Boulder, CO: Westview Press.

Cantarino, Vincente. 2007. "Dante and Islam: History and Analysis of a Controversy (1965)." *Dante Studies* 125: 37–55.

Capoccia, Giovanni, and R. Daniel Kelemen. 2007. "The Study of Critical Junctures: Theory, Narrative, and Counterfactuals in Historical Institutionalism." *World Politics* 59, 3: 341–69.

Cardoso, Fernando Henrique, and Enzo Faletto. 1979. *Dependency and Development in Latin America*. Translated from Spanish by Marjory Mattingly Urquidi. Berkeley: University of California Press.

Carr, Edward Hallett. 1961. *What Is History?* New York: Vintage Books.

Carter, Jimmy. 2006. *Palestine: Peace Not Apartheid*. New York: Simon and Schuster.

Casale, Giancarlo. 2010. *The Ottoman Age of Exploration*. New York: Oxford University Press.

Casanova, Jose. 1994. *Public Religions in the Modern World*. Chicago: University of Chicago Press.

Cavanaugh, William T. 2009. *The Myth of Religious Violence: Secular Ideology and Roots of Modern Conflict*. New York: Oxford University Press.

Çelebi, Katip. 1982 [c. 1652]. *Bozuklukların Düzeltilmesinde Tutulacak Yollar (Düsturu'l-Amel li-Islahi'l-Halel)*. Translated from Ottoman Turkish to modern Turkish by Ali Can. Ankara: Kültür ve Turizm Bakanlığı Yayınları.

———. 2007 [c. 1653]. *Keşfü'z-Zunun an Esami'l-Kütübi ve'l-Fünun (Kitapların ve İlimlerin İsimlerinden Şüphelerin Giderilmesi)*. Translated into Turkish by Rüştü Balcı. Istanbul: Tarih Vakfı Yurt Yayınları.

———. 2008 [1654]. *Cihannüma: 360 Yıllık Bir Öykü (A 360 Year Old Story)*. Translated from Turkish by Füsun Savcı. Edited by Bülent Özükan. Istanbul: Boyut.

———. 2007 [1656a]. *Deniz Savaşları Hakkında Büyüklere Armağan (Tuhfetü'l-Kibar fi Esfari'l-Bihar)*. Translated from Ottoman Turkish to modern Turkish by Orhan Şaik Gökyay. Istanbul: Kabalcı.

———. 2008 [1656b]. *Mizanü'l-Hakk fi İhtiyari'l-Ehakk (En Doğruyu Seçmek İçin Hak Terazisi)*. Translated from Ottoman Turkish to modern Turkish by Orhan Şaik Gökyay. Istanbul: Kabalcı Yayınevi.

Central Intelligence Agency. 2014. "The World Factbook: Independence," www.cia .gov/library/publications/the-world-factbook/fields/2088.html.

Chamberlain, Michael. 1994. *Knowledge and Social Practice in Medieval Damascus, 1190–1350*. New York: Cambridge University Press.

Chandler, Tertius. 1987. *Four Thousand Years of Urban Growth: An Historical Census*. Lewiston, NY: Edwin Mellen Press.

Chaney, Eric. 2012. "Democratic Change in the Arab World, Past and Present." *Brookings Papers on Economic Activity* 1: 363–400.

Charfi, Abdelmajid. 2004. *L'islam entre le message et l'histoire*. Paris: Albin Michel.

Charrad, Mounira M. 2001. *States and Women's Rights: The Making of Postcolonial Tunisia, Algeria, and Morocco*. Berkeley: University of California Press.

Chaudhuri, K[irti] N. 1990. *Asia Before Europe: Economy and Civilisation of the Indian Ocean from the Rise of Islam to 1750*. New York: Cambridge University Press.

Chayes, Sarah. 2015. *Thieves of State: Why Corruption Threatens Global Security*. New York: W. W. Norton.

Cheddadi, Abdesselam. 2006. *Ibn Khaldûn: L'homme et le théoricien de la civilisation*. Paris: Gallimard.

Chirot, Daniel. 1994. *How Societies Change*. Thousand Oaks, CA: Pine Forge Press.

Chittick, William C. 1989. *Ibn al-'Arabi's Metaphysics of Imagination: The Sufi Path of Knowledge.* Albany: SUNY Press.

Christensen, Peter. 1993. *The Decline of Iranshahr: Irrigation and Environments in the History of the Middle East, 500 B.C. to A.D. 1500.* Translated from Danish by Steven Sampson. Odense: Museum Tusculanum Press.

Çığıraçan, Tüccarzade İbrahim Hilmi. 2010 [1912–3]. *Osmanlı Devletinin Çöküş Nedenleri.* Edited by Başak Ocak. Istanbul: Libra Kitapçılık.

Cipolla, Carlo M. 1969. *Literacy and Development in the West.* London: Penguin Books.

   1970. *European Culture and Overseas Expansion.* Middlesex: Penguin Books.

Çizakça, Murat. 2011. *Islamic Capitalism and Finance: Origins, Evolution, and the Future.* Northampton, MA: Edward Elgar.

Cizre, Ümit. 2017. "Fear and Loathing in Turkey: The Backstory to Erdoğan's Referendum." *Middle East Research and Information Project*, April 26, https://www.merip.org/mero/mero042617.

Cleveland, William L. 2004. *A History of the Modern Middle East.* Boulder: Westview Press.

Cohen, Hayyim J. 1970. "The Economic Background and the Secular Occupations of Muslim Jurisprudents and Traditionists in the Classical Period of Islam (Until the Middle of the Eleventh Century)." *Journal of the Economic and Social History of the Orient* 13, 1: 16–61.

Cole, Juan. 2002. "Review of Bernard Lewis' *What Went Wrong: Western Impact and Middle Eastern Response.*" *Global Dialogue* 4, 4; www.juancole.com/2018/05/bernard-western-response.html.

Collier, David. 1991. "The Comparative Method: Two Decades of Change." In Dankwart A. Rustow and Kenneth Paul, eds., *Comparative Dynamics: Global Research Perspectives.* New York: Harper Collins.

Collier, Paul. 2007. *The Bottom Billion: Why the Poorest Countries Are Failing and What Can Be Done About It.* New York: Oxford University Press.

Collier, Paul, and Anke Hoeffler. 2004. "Greed and Grievance in Civil Wars." *Oxford Economic Papers* 56: 563–95.

Collins, Randall. 2000. *The Sociology of Philosophies: A Global Theory of Intellectual Change.* Cambridge, MA: Harvard University Press.

Cook, Michael. 1997. "The Opponents of the Writing of Tradition in Early Islam." *Arabica* 44, 4: 437–530.

   2000. *Commanding Right and Forbidding Wrong in Islamic Thought.* New York: Cambridge University Press.

   2014. *Ancient Religion, Modern Politics: The Islamic Case in Comparative Perspective.* Princeton: Princeton University Press.

Cooley, Alexander. 2008. *Base Politics: Democratic Change and the U.S. Military Overseas.* Ithaca, NY: Cornell University Press.

Corbin, Henry. 1986. *Histoire de la philosophie islamique.* Paris: Gallimard.

Cosandey, David. 1997. *Le secret de l'Occident: Vers une théorie générale du progress scientifique.* Paris: Champs-Flammarion.

Crone, Patricia. 1987. "Did al-Ghazali Write a Mirror for Princes? On the Authorship of *Nasihat al-muluk.*" *Jerusalem Studies in Islam and Arabic* 10: 167–91.

   2004. *Medieval Islamic Political Thought.* Edinburgh: Edinburgh University Press.

Crone, Patricia, and Martin Hinds. 1986. *God's Caliph: Religious Authority in the First Centuries of Islam*. New York: Cambridge University Press.

Cubberley, Ellwood P. 1948 [1920]. *The History of Education: Educational Practice and Progress Considered as a Phase of the Development and Spread of Western Civilization*. Boston: Houghton Mifflin.

Curtin, Philip D. 1984. *Cross-Cultural Trade in World History*. New York: Cambridge University Press.

2000. *The World and the West: The European Challenge and the Overseas Response in the Age of Empire*. New York: Cambridge University Press.

Dabashi, Hamid. 1996a. "Khawajah Nasir al-Din Tusi: The Philosopher/Vizier and the Intellectual Climate of His Times." In Seyyed Hossein Nasr and Oliver Leaman, eds., *History of Islamic Philosophy*. New York: Routledge.

1996b. "Mir Damad and the Founding of the 'School of Isfahan'." In Seyyed Hossein Nasr and Oliver Leaman, eds., *History of Islamic Philosophy*. New York: Routledge.

Dagli, Caner K. 2015. "Conquest and Conversion, War and Peace in the Quran." In Seyyed Hossein Nasr, Caner K. Dagli, Maria Massi Dakake, Joseph B. Lumbard, and Mohammed Rustom, eds., *The Study Quran: A New Translation and Commentary*. New York: HarperOne.

Dale, Stephen F. 2010. *The Muslim Empires of the Ottomans, Safavids, and Mughals*. New York: Cambridge University Press.

2015. *The Orange Trees of Marrakesh: Ibn Khaldun and the Science of Man*. Cambridge, MA: Harvard University Press.

Dallal, Ahmad. 1999. "Science, Medicine, and Technology." In John L. Esposito, ed., *The Oxford History of Islam*. New York: Oxford University Press.

2010. *Islam, Science, and the Challenge of History*. New Haven: Yale University Press.

Daly, Jonathan. 2014. *The Rise of Western Power: A Comparative History of Western Civilization*. New York: Bloomsbury.

Darling, Linda T. 2013. *A History of Social Justice and Political Power in the Middle East: The Circle of Justice from Mesopotamia to Globalization*. New York: Routledge.

Davis, Mike. 2001. *Late Victorian Holocausts: El Nino Famines and the Making of the Third World*. New York: Verso.

Davison, Roderic H. 1961. "Westernized Education in Ottoman Turkey." *Middle East Journal* 15, 3: 289–301.

Dawani, Jalaladdin. 1839 [c. 1477]. *Practical Philosophy of the Muhammadan People: Exhibited in Its Professed Connexion with the European, So as to Render Either an Introduction to the Other. Being a Translation of the* Akhlak-i Jalaly, *the Most Esteemed Ethical Work of Middle Asia*. Translated from Persian with notes by W. F. Thompson. London: Forgotten Books.

1939 [c. 1477]. The English Translation of *Akhlak-i Jalali*: A Code of Morality in Persian. Translated by S. H. Deen. Lahore: Sh. Mubarak Ali.

[Daya], Najm al-Din Razi. 1982 [1223]. *The Path of God's Bondsmen from Origin to Return (Mersad al-'Ebad men al-Mabda'ela'l-Ma'ad)*. Translated from Persian and edited by Hamid Algar. New York: Caravan Books.

De Long, J. Bradford, and Andrei Shleifer. 1993. "Princes and Merchants: European City Growth before the Industrial Revolution." *Journal of Law and Economics* 36, 2: 671–702.

De Vries, Jan, and Ad van der Woude. 1997. *The First Modern Economy: Success, Failure, and Perseverance of the Dutch Economy, 1500–1815*. New York: Cambridge University Press.

Demirel, Ahmet. 1994. *Birinci Meclis'te Muhalefet: İkinci Grup*. Istanbul: İletişim.

Denny, Frederick M. 2004. "Islam and Peacebuilding: Continuities and Transitions." In Harold Coward and Gordon S. Smith, eds., *Religion and Peacebuilding*. Albany: State University of New York Press.

Deringil, Selim. 1999. *The Well-Protected Domains: Ideology and the Legitimation of Power in the Ottoman Empire 1876–1909*. New York: I. B. Tauris.

Devlet, Nadir. 1988. *İsmail Bey Gaspıralı*. Ankara: Kültür Bakanlığı Yayınları.

Dhanani, Alnoor. 2007. "Jurjani: 'Ali ibn Muhammad ibn 'Ali al-Husayni al-Jurjani (al-Sayyid al-Sharif)." In Thomas Hockey, ed., *The Biographical Encyclopedia of Astronomers*. New York: Springer.

Diamond, Jared. 1997. *Guns, Germs, and Steel: The Fates of Human Societies*. New York: W. W. Norton.

Diamond, Larry. 2010. "Why Are There No Arab Democracies?" *Journal of Democracy* 21, 1: 93–104.

Dignas, Beate, and Engelbert Winter. 2007. *Rome and Persia in Late Antiquity: Neighbours and Rivals*. New York: Cambridge University Press.

Al-Dimashqi, Abu al-Fadl. 1995a [c. 11th century]. *Kitab al-Ishara ila Mahasin al-Tijara*. Edited by Youssef Seddik and Yassine Essid. Tunis: Edition Media Com.

——— 1995b [c. 11th century]. *Eloge du commerce [Kitab al-Ishara fi Mahasin al-Tijara]*. Translated into French by Youssef Seddik. Edited by Yassine Essid. Tunis: Edition Media Com.

Diner, Dan. 2009. *Lost in the Sacred: Why the Muslim World Stood Still*. Translated from German by Steven Rendall. Princeton: Princeton University Press.

Diouf, Mamadou. 2013. *Tolerance, Democracy, and Sufis in Senegal*. New York: Columbia University Press.

Dixon, Jeffrey. 2009. "What Causes Civil Wars? Integrating Quantitative Research Findings." *International Studies Review* 11, 4: 707–35.

Djaït, Hichem. 1989. *La grande discorde: Religion et politique dans l'islam des origins*. Paris: Gallimard.

Dodge, Bayard. 1970. "Introduction." In *The Fihrist of al-Nadim: A Tenth-Century Survey of Muslim Culture*. Vols. I and II. Translated and edited by Bayard Dodge. New York: Columbia University Press.

Dols, Michael W. 1977. *The Black Death in the Middle East*. Princeton: Princeton University Press.

Donner, Fred M. 1991. "The Sources of Islamic Concepts of War." In John Kelsay and James Turner Johnson, eds., *Just War and Jihad: Historical and Theoretical Perspectives on War and Peace in Western and Islamic Traditions*. New York: Greenwood Press.

Doyle, Michael W. 1983. "Kant, Liberal Legacies, and Foreign Affairs." *Philosophy and Public Affairs* 12, 3: 205–35.

Drelichman, Mauricio. 2005. "The Curse of Moctezuma: American Silver and the Dutch Disease." *Explorations in Economic History* 42: 349–80.

Duby, Georges. 1980. *The Three Orders: Feudal Society Imagined*. Translated from French by Arthur Goldhammer. Chicago: University of Chicago Press.

Duchesne, Ricardo. 2011. *The Uniqueness of Western Civilization*. Boston: Brill.

Dunn, Ross E. 1986. *The Adventures of Ibn Battuta: A Muslim Traveler of the 14th Century*. Berkeley: University of California Press.

Dunning, Thad. 2008. *Crude Democracy: Natural Resource Wealth and Political Regimes*. New York: Cambridge University Press.

Dupouey, Patrick. 1998. *Machiavel: Le Prince. Texte intégral, notes et commentaires*. Paris: Les intégrals de Philo/Nathan.

Durkheim, Emile. 1984 [1893]. *The Division of Labor in Society*. Translated by W. D. Halls. New York: Free Press.

Easterlin, Richard A. 1981. "Why Isn't the Whole World Developed?" *Journal of Economic History* 41, 1: 1–17.

Eaton, Richard M. 1993. *The Rise of Islam and the Bengal Frontier, 1204–1760*. Berkeley: University of California Press.

Economist Intelligence Unit. 2011. "Country Reports," http://country.eiu.com/AllCountries.aspx.

Edwards, Jeremy, and Sheilagh Ogilvie. 2012. "Contract Enforcement, Institutions, and Social Capital: The Maghribi Traders Reappraised." *Economic History Review* 65, 2: 421–44.

Edwards, Mark U. 1994. *Printing, Propaganda, and Martin Luther*. Berkeley: University of California Press.

Eisenstein, Elizabeth L. 2005 [1983]. *The Printing Revolution in Early Modern Europe*. New York: Cambridge University Press.

Ekelund, Robert B., Robert D. Tollison, Gary M. Anderson, Robert F. Hébert, and Aubrey B. Davidson. 1996. *Sacred Trust: The Medieval Church as an Economic Firm*. New York: Oxford University Press.

Elbadawi, Ibrahim, Samir Makdisi, and Gary Milante. 2010. "Explaining the Arab Democracy Deficit: The Role of Oil and Conflicts." In Ibrahim Elbadawi and Samir Makdisi, eds., *Democracy in the Arab World: Explaining the Deficit*. New York: Routledge.

Elias, Norbert. 2000 [1939]. *The Civilizing Process*. Translated from German by Edmund Jephcott. Malden, MA: Blackwell.

Ellenblum, Ronnie. 2012. *The Collapse of the Eastern Mediterranean: Climate Change and the Decline of the East, 950–1072*. New York: Cambridge University Press.

Ellethy, Yaser. 2011. "Quran and Islamic Tradition Connected to Religion and Violence? The Absent Texts." In Erik Eynikel and Angeliki Ziaka, eds., *Religion and Conflict: Essays on the Origins of Religious Conflicts and Resolution Approaches*. London: Harptree Publishing.

⸺ 2015. *Islam, Context, Pluralism, and Democracy: Classical and Modern Interpretations*. New York: Routledge.

Embree, Ainslie T. 1971. "Introduction." In *Alberuni's India: An Account of the Religion, Philosophy, Literature, Geography, Chronology, Astronomy, Customs, Laws and Astrology of India about A.D. 1030*. Abridged and edited by Ainslie T. Embree. New Delhi: S. Chand.

Emre, Yunus. 2102 [c. 1321]. *Divan: Seçmeler*. Edited by Mustafa Tatcı. Ankara: Diyanet İşleri Başkanlığı.

Endress, Gerhard. 2006. "Reading Avicenna in the Madrasa: Intellectual Genealogies and Chains of Transmission of Philosophy and the Sciences in the Islamic East."

In James E. Montgomery, ed., *Arabic Theology, Arabic Philosophy: From the Many to the One: Essays in Celebration of Richard M. Frank.* Leuven: Peeters.

Engerman, Stanley L., and Kenneth L. Sokoloff. 2012. *Economic Development in the Americas since 1500.* New York: Cambridge University Press.

Ephrat, Daphna. 2000. *A Learned Society in a Period of Transition: The Sunni 'Ulama' of Eleventh-Century Baghdad.* Albany: SUNY Press.

Ergin, Osman. 1977. *Türkiye Maarif Tarihi. Cild 2.* Istanbul: Eser Matbaası.

Erginbaş, Vefa. 2014. "Enlightenment in the Ottoman Context: İbrahim Müteferrika and His Intellectual Landscape." In Geoffrey Roper, ed., *Historical Aspects of Printing and Publishing in Languages of the Middle East.* Boston: Brill.

Ergün, Mustafa. 1996. *İkinci Meşrutiyet Devrinde Eğitim Hareketleri (1908–1914).* Ankara: Ocak Yayınları.

Erünsal, İsmail E. 2014. *Osmanlı Kültür Tarihinin Bilinmiyenleri.* Istanbul: Timaş Yayınları.

Esbeck, Carl H. 2004. "Dissent and Disestablishment: The Church–State Settlement in the Early American Republic." *BYU Law Review* 4: 1385–492.

Esposito, John L. 2015. "Islam and Political Violence." *Religions* 6, 3: 1067–81.

Esposito, John L., Tamara Sonn, and John O. Voll. 2016. *Islam and Democracy after the Arab Spring.* New York: Oxford University Press.

Essid, Yassine. 1995. *A Critique of the Origins of Islamic Economic Thought.* Leiden: Brill.

Ettinghausen, Richard, Oleg Grabar, and Marilyn Jenkins-Madina. 2001. *Islamic Art and Architecture 650–1250.* New Haven: Yale University.

Euben, Roxanne L., and Muhammad Qasim Zaman. 2009. "Introduction." In Roxanne L. Euben and Muhammad Qasim Zaman, eds., *Princeton Readings in Islamist Thought: Texts and Contexts from al-Banna to Bin Laden.* Princeton: Princeton University Press.

Evans, Peter. 1995. *Embedded Autonomy: States and Industrial Transformation.* Princeton: Princeton University Press.

Evans, Peter B., Dietrich Rueschemeyer, and Theda Skocpol. 1985. *Bringing the State Back In.* New York: Cambridge University Press.

Fadel, Mohammad. 2011. "A Tragedy of Politics or an Apolitical Tragedy?" *Journal of the American Oriental Society* 131, 1: 109–27.

Faik, Mühendis. 2006 [1868]. *Türk Denizcilerin İlk Amerika Seferi (Seyahatname-i Bahr-i Muhit).* Edited by N. Ahmet Özalp. Istanbul: Kitabevi.

Fakhry, Majid. 1988. "The Devolution of the Perfect State: Plato, Ibn Rushd, and Ibn Khaldun." In George N. Atiyeh and Ibrahim M. Oweiss, eds., *Arab Civilization: Challenges and Responses.* Albany: SUNY Press.

    1991. *Ethical Theories in Islam.* Leiden: Brill.

    2001. *Averroes (Ibn Rushd): His Life, Works and Influence.* Oxford: Oneworld.

    2004. *A History of Islamic Philosophy.* New York: Columbia University Press.

Falagas, Matthew E., Effie A. Zarkadoulia, and George Samonis. 2006. "Arab Science in the Golden Age (750–1258 C.E.) and Today." *The FASEB Journal* 20, 10: 1581–6.

Fancy, Nahyan. 2013. *Science and Religion in Mamluk Egypt: Ibn al-Nafis, Pulmonary Transit and Bodily Resurrection.* New York: Routledge.

Fanon, Frantz. 2004 [1961]. *The Wretched of the Earth.* New York: Grove Press.

Al-Farabi. 2005 [c. 930]. *The Book of Letters* [*Kitab al-Huruf*]. Abridged, translated, and edited by Muhammad Ali Khalidi. In *Medieval Islamic Philosophical Writings.* New York: Cambridge University Press.

1985 [c. 940]. *Al-Farabi on the Perfect State (Abu Nasr al-Farabi's Mabadi Ara Ahl al-Madina al-Fadila)*. Translated with notes by Richard Walzer. New York: Oxford University Press.

1963 [c. 941–9]. *The Political Regime [Al-Siyasat al-Madaniyyah]*. Partially translated by Fauzi M. Najjar. In Ralph Lerner and Muhsin Mahdi, eds., *Medieval Political Philosophy: A Sourcebook*. New York: Free Press.

Faroqhi, Suraiya. 2000. *Subjects of the Sultan: Culture and Daily Life in the Ottoman Empire*. Translated from German by Martin Bott. New York: I. B. Tauris.

Fatoohi, Louay. 2013. *Abrogation in the Qur'an and Islamic Law*. New York: Routledge.

Fazlıoğlu, İhsan. 2003. "Osmanlı Felsefe-Biliminin Arkaplanı: Semerkand Matematik-Astronomi Okulu." *Divan: İlmi Araştırmalar* 14: 1–66.

Fearon, James D., and David D. Laitin. 2003. "Ethnicity, Insurgency, and Civil War." *American Political Science Review* 97, 1: 75–90.

Febvre, Lucien, and Henri-Jean Martin. 1997 [1958]. *The Coming of the Book: The Impact of Printing 1450–1800*. Translated by David Gerard. New York: Verso.

Ferguson, Niall. 2011. *Civilization: The West and the Rest*. New York: Penguin Books.

Filali-Ansary, Abdou. 2002. *L'islam est-il hostile à la laïcité?* Paris: Sindbad, Actes Sud.

2003. *Réformer l'islam? Une introduction aux débats contemporains*. Paris: La Découverte.

Findlay, Ronald, and Kevin H. O'Rourke. 2007. *Power and Plenty: Trade, War, and the World Economy in the Second Millenium*. Princeton: Princeton University Press.

Findley, Carter Vaughn. 1989. *Ottoman Civil Officialdom: A Social History*. Princeton: Princeton University Press.

1992. "Knowledge and Education." In Cyril E. Black and L. Carl Brown, eds., *Modernization in the Middle East: The Ottoman Empire and Its Afro-Asian Successors*. Princeton: Darwin Press.

"Firman of Ahmed III." 1995 [1727]. In "Appendix: Ottoman Imperial Documents Relating to the History of Books and Printing." Translated from Ottoman Turkish by Christopher M. Murphy. In George N. Atiyeh, ed., *The Book in the Islamic World: The Written Word and Communication in the Middle East*. Albany: SUNY Press.

Fischel, Walter J. 1967. *Ibn Khaldun in Egypt: His Public Functions and His Historical Research (1382–1406)*. Berkeley: University of California Press.

Fish, M. Steven. 2002. "Islam and Authoritarianism." *World Politics* 55, 1: 4–37.

2011. *Are Muslims Distinctive? A Look at the Evidence*. New York: Oxford University Press.

Fish, M. Steven, Francesca R. Jensenius, and Katherine E. Michel. 2010. "Islam and Large-Scale Political Violence: Is There a Connection?" *Comparative Political Studies* 43, 11: 1327–62.

Fleischer, Cornell. 1983. "Royal Authority, Dynastic Cyclism, and 'Ibn Khaldunism' in Sixteenth-Century Ottoman Letters." *Journal of Asian and African Studies* 18, 3–4: 198–220.

Flynn, Dennis O., and Arturo Giráldez. 1995. "Born with a 'Silver Spoon': The Origin of World Trade in 1571." *Journal of World History* 6, 2: 201–21.

Foran, John. 1992. "The Long Fall of the Safavid Dynasty: Moving beyond the Standard Views." *International Journal of Middle East Studies* 24, 2: 281–304.

Fox, Jonathan. 2004. "Religion and State Failure: An Examination of the Extent and Magnitude of Religious Conflict from 1950 to 1996." *International Political Science Review* 25, 1: 55–76.

    2008. *A World Survey of Religion and the State.* New York: Cambridge University Press.

Frank, Andre Gunder. 1998. *ReORIENT: Global Economy in the Asian Age.* Berkeley: University of California Press.

    2015. *ReOrienting the 19th Century: Global Economy in the Continuing Asian Age.* Edited by Robert A. Denemark. Boulder: Paradigm Publishers.

Freedom House. 1973–2018. "Country and Territory Ratings and Statuses, 1973–2018," https://freedomhouse.org/content/freedom-world-data-and-resources.

    2013. "Freedom in the World 2013," May 1, www.freedomhouse.org/sites/default/files/FIW%202013%20Booklet.pdf.

    2018. "List of Electoral Democracies 2018," June 18, https://freedomhouse.org/report-types/freedom-world.

Freeman, Charles. 2005. *The Closing of the Western Mind: The Rise of Faith and the Fall of Reason.* New York: Vintage Books.

Frey, Frederick W. 1964. "Education: Turkey." In Robert E. Ward and Dankwart A. Rustow, eds., *Political Modernization in Japan and Turkey.* Princeton: Princeton University Press.

Fromherz, Allen James. 2010. *Ibn Khaldun: Life and Times.* Edinburgh: Edinburgh University Press.

Fromkin, David. 2001. *A Peace to End All Peace: The Fall of the Ottoman Empire and the Creation of the Modern Middle East.* New York: Henry Holt and Company.

Frye, Richard N. 2005. "Commentary on the Translation." In Richard N. Frye, ed., *Ibn Fadlan's Journey to Russia: A Tenth-Century Traveler from Baghdad to the Volga River.* Princeton: Markus Wiener Publishers.

Fukuyama, Francis. 1995. *Trust: The Social Virtues and the Creation of Prosperity.* New York: Free Press.

    2011. *The Origins of Political Order: From Prehuman Times to the French Revolution.* New York: Farrar, Straus and Giroux.

    2014. *Political Order and Political Decay: From the Industrial Revolution to the Globalization of Democracy.* New York: Farrar, Straus and Giroux.

Gabrieli, Francesco. 1969. *Arab Historians of the Crusades.* Translated from Italian by E. J. Costello. Berkeley: University of California Press.

Galeano, Eduardo. 1973. *Open Veins of Latin America: Five Centuries of the Pillage of a Continent.* Translated from Spanish by Cedric Belfrage. New York: Monthly Review Press.

Garden, Kenneth. 2014. *The First Islamic Reviver: Abu Hamid al-Ghazali and His Revival of the Religious Sciences.* New York: Oxford University Press.

Gasprinskii, Ismail Bey. 2002 [1901]. "First Steps toward Civilizing the Russian Muslims." Translated from Tatar by Edward J. Lazzerini. In Charles Kurzman, ed., *Modernist Islam: 1840–1940.* New York: Oxford University Press.

Gaudiosi, Monica M. 1988. "The Influence of the Islamic Law of Waqf on the Development of the Trust in England: The Case of Merton College." *University of Pennsylvania Law Review* 136, 4: 1231–61.

Gazali. 2014 [1095]. *Filozofların Tutarsızlığı* [*Tahafut al-Falasifa*]. Translated into Turkish by Hüseyin Sarıoğlu and Mahmut Kaya. Istanbul: Klasik Yayınları.

1974a [c. 1097]. *Ihyau 'Ulumi'd-Din*. Vol. I. Translated into Turkish by Ahmed Serdaroğlu. Istanbul: Bedir Yayınevi.

1974b [c. 1097]. *Ihyau 'Ulumi'd-Din*. Vol. II. Translated into Turkish by Ahmed Serdaroğlu. Istanbul: Bedir Yayınevi.

Geertz, Clifford. 1975. "Mysteries of Islam: Review of Marshall G. S. Hodgson's *The Venture of Islam: Conscience and History in a World Civilization.*" *New York Review of Books* 22, 20: 18–26.

Gellner, Ernest. 1983. *Muslim Society*. Cambridge: Cambridge University Press.

Genç, Mehmet. 2000. *Osmanlı İmparatorluğu'nda Devlet ve Ekonomi*. Istanbul: Ötüken.

George, Alexander L., and Andrew Bennett. 2005. *Case Studies and Theory Development in the Social Sciences*. Cambridge, MA: MIT Press.

Georgeon, François. 1986. *Türk Milliyetçiliğinin Kökenleri: Yusuf Akçura (1876–1935)*. Translated from French to Turkish by Alev Er. Ankara: Yurt Yayınları.

Gerber, Haim. 1987. *The Social Origins of the Modern Middle East*. Boulder: Lynne Rienner.

Gerçek, Selim Nüzhet. 1939. *Türk Matbaacılığı I: Müteferrika Matbaası*. Istanbul: Devlet Basımevi.

Gerges, Fawaz A. 2005. *The Far Enemy: Why Jihad Went Global*. New York: Cambridge University Press.

Al-Ghazali. 1999 [1095]. *The Infamies of the Batinites and the Virtues of the Mustazhirites (Fada'ih al-Batiniyya wa Fada'il al-Mustazhiriyya)*. Partially translated and edited by Richard J. McCarthy. In *Freedom and Fulfillment. Deliverance from Error: Five Key Texts Including His Spiritual Autobiography, al-Munqidh min al-Dalal*. Louisville, KY: Fons Vitae.

2000 [1095]. *The Incoherence of the Philosophers* [*Tahafut al-Falasifa*]. Translated by Michael E. Marmura. Provo, UT: Brigham Young University Press.

2013 [1095]. *Moderation in Belief (Al-Iqtisad fi al-I'tiqad)*. Translated by Aladdin M. Yaqub. Chicago: University of Chicago Press.

1962 [c. 1097]. *The Book of Knowledge* [*Kitab al-Ilm*. Book I of *The Revival of the Religious Sciences*]. Translated by Nabih Amin Faris. New Delhi: Islamic Book Service.

1963 [c. 1097]. *Ihya Ulum-id-Din. The Revival of Religious Learnings*. Vol. II. Abridged and translated by Alhaj Maulana Fazlul Karim. Lahore: Book House.

1984 [c. 1097]. *Book on the Etiquette of Marriage* [*Kitab Adab al-Nikah*. Book XII of the *Revival of the Religious Sciences*]. Translated by Madelain Farah. In Madelain Farah, *Marriage and Externality in Islam: A Translation of al-Ghazali's Book on the Etiquette of Marriage from the Ihya'*. Salt Lake City: University of Utah Press.

2000 [c. 1097]. *On the Manners Relating to Eating. Kitab Adab al-Akl. Book XI of the Revival of the Religious Sciences. Ihya' 'Ulum al-Din*. Translated by D. Johnson-Davies. Cambridge: Islamic Texts Society.

2014 [c. 1097]. *On the Lawful and Unlawful. Kitab al-Halal wa'l-Haram. Book XIV of the Revival of the Religious Sciences. Ihya' 'Ulum al-Din*. Translated by Yusuf T. Delorenzo. Cambridge: Islamic Texts Society.

2015 [c. 1097]. *Kitab al-'Ilm: The Book of Knowledge. Book I of the Ihya' 'Ulum al-Din: The Revival of the Religious Sciences*. Translated and edited by Kenneth Honerkamp. Louisville: Fons Vitae.

1998 [c. 1098–1105]. *The Niche of Lights* [*Mishkat al-Anwar*]. Translated by David Buchman. Provo, UT: Brigham Young University Press.

2002 [c. 1105]. *The Decisive Criterion for Distinguishing Islam from Masked Infidelity (Faysal al-Tafriqa bayna al-Islam wa al-Zandaqa).* Translated and edited by Sherman A. Jackson. In *On the Boundaries of Theological Tolerance in Islam: Abu Hamid al-Ghazali's Faysal al-Tafriqa.* Karachi: Oxford University Press.

1964 [c. 1107]. *Book of Counsel for Kings (Nasihat al-Muluk).* Translated from Persian and edited by F. R. C. Bagley. New York: Oxford University Press.

1953 [c. 1108]. *Deliverance from Error* [*Al-Munqidh min al-Dalal*]. Translated by W. Montgomery Watt. In *The Faith and Practice of Al-Ghazali.* London: George Allen and Unwin.

1999 [c. 1108]. *Deliverance from Error.* Translated and edited by Richard J. McCarthy. In *Freedom and Fulfillment. Deliverance from Error: Five Key Texts Including His Spiritual Autobiography, al-Munqidh min al-Dalal.* Louisville, KY: Fons Vitae.

Ghazanfar, S. M., and A. Azim Islahi. 2003. "Explorations in Medieval Arab-Islamic Economic Thought: Some Aspects of Ibn Taimiyah's Economics." In S. M. Ghazanfar, ed., *Medieval Islamic Economic Thought: Filling the "Great Gap" in European Economics.* New York: Routledge.

Ghobadzadeh, Naser. 2014. *Religious Secularity: A Theological Challenge to the Islamic State.* New York: Oxford University Press.

Gibb, H[amilton] A. R. 1933. "The Islamic Background of Ibn Khaldun's Political Theory." *Bulletin of the School of Oriental and African Studies* 7, 1: 23–31.

Gibbon, Edward. 2000 [1776–88]. *The History of the Decline and Fall of the Roman Empire: Abridged Edition.* Abridged by David Womersley. London: Penguin Classics.

Gill, Anthony. 1998. *Rendering unto Caesar: The Catholic Church and State in Latin America.* Chicago: University of Chicago Press.

Glaeser, Edward L., Rafael La Porta, Florencio Lopez-De-Silanes, and Andrei Shleifer. 2004. "Do Institutions Cause Growth?" *Journal of Economic Growth* 9, 3: 271–303.

Gleditsch, Nils Petter, and Ida Rudolfsen. 2016. "Are Muslim Countries More Prone to Violence?" *Research and Politics* 3, 2: 1–9.

Glick, Thomas F. 2005. *Islamic and Christian Spain in the Early Middle Ages.* Boston: Brill.

Göçek, Müge. 1996. *Rise of Bourgeoisie, Demise of Empire: Ottoman Westernization and Social Change.* New York: Oxford University Press.

Goddard, Hugh. 2000. *A History of Christian-Muslim Relations.* Chicago: New Amsterdam Books.

Goitein, S[helomo] D. 1964. "The Commercial Mail Service in Medieval Islam." *Journal of the American Oriental Society* 84, 2: 118–24.

1966a. "The Rise of the Middle-Eastern Bourgeoisie in Early Islamic Times." In S. D. Goitein, *Studies in Islamic History and Institutions.* Leiden: Brill.

1966b. "The Mentality of the Middle Class in Medieval Islam." In S. D. Goitein, *Studies in Islamic History and Institutions.* Leiden: Brill.

Gökalp, Ziya. 1976 [1918]. *Türkleşmek, İslamlaşmak, Muasırlaşmak.* Istanbul: Devlet Kitapları.

2007 [1923]. "Türkçülüğün Esasları." In his *Kitaplar*. Vol. 1. Istanbul: Yapı Kredi.

Gökçek, Mustafa. 2008. "A Kazan Tatar Contribution to the Late Ottoman Debates on Nationalism and Islam: The Life and Works of Halim Sabit Sjbay." PhD dissertation. University of Wisconsin, Madison.

Goldberg, Ellis. 1991. "Smashing Idols and the State: The Protestant Ethic and Egyptian Sunni Radicalism." *Comparative Studies in Society and History* 33, 1: 3–35.

Goldin, Claudia, and Lawrence F. Katz. 2009. *The Race between Education and Technology*. Cambridge, MA: Belknap Press of Harvard University Press.

Goldstone, Jack. 2006. "Knowledge – Not Capitalism, Faith, or Reason – Was the Key to 'The Rise of the West.'" *Historically Speaking* 7, 4: 6–10.

2008. *Why Europe? The Rise of the West in World History, 1500–1800*. New York: McGraw-Hill.

Goldziher, Ignaz. 1981 [1916]. "The Attitude of Orthodox Islam toward the 'Ancient Sciences.'" Translated from German by Marlin L. Swartz. In Marlin L. Swartz, ed., *Studies on Islam*. New York: Oxford University Press.

Göle, Nilüfer. 1996. *The Forbidden Modern: Civilization and Veiling*. Ann Arbor: University of Michigan Press.

Goodman, Lenn E. 1996. "Ibn Tufayl." In Seyyed Hossein Nasr and Oliver Leaman, eds., *History of Islamic Philosophy*. New York: Routledge.

2003. *Islamic Humanism*. New York: Oxford University Press.

Goodrich, Thomas D. 1990. "Preface" and "Introduction." In Thomas D. Goodrich, ed., *The Ottoman Turks and the New World: A Study of* Tarih-i Hind-i Garbi *and Sixteenth-Century Ottoman Americana*. Wiesbaden: Otto Harrassowitz.

Goody, Jack. 2006. *The Theft of History*. New York: Cambridge University Press.

2010. *The Eurasian Miracle*. Malden, MA: Polity.

Gouguenheim, Sylvain. 2008. *Aristote au mont Saint-Michel: Les racines grecques de l'Europe chrétienne*. Paris: Éditions du Seuil.

Grabar, Oleg. 1987. *The Formation of Islamic Art*. Revised and enlarged edition. New Haven: Yale University Press.

Gran, Peter. 1979. *Islamic Roots of Capitalism: Egypt, 1760–1840*. Austin: University of Texas Press.

Grant, Edward. 1996. *The Foundations of Modern Science in the Middle Ages: Their Religious, Institutional, and Intellectual Contexts*. New York: Cambridge University Press.

Grant, Jonathan A. 1999. "Rethinking the Ottoman 'Decline': Military Technology Diffusion in the Ottoman Empire, Fifteenth to Eighteenth Centuries." *Journal of World History* 10, 1: 179–201.

Green, Nile. 2012. *Sufism: A Global History*. Malden, MA: Wiley-Blackwell.

Greif, Avner. 1994. "Cultural Beliefs and the Organization of Society: A Historical and Theoretical Reflection on Collectivist and Individualist Societies." *The Journal of Political Economy* 102, 5: 912–50.

2006. *Institutions and the Path to the Modern Economy: Lessons from Medieval Trade*. New York: Cambridge University Press.

2012. "The Maghribi Traders: A Reappraisal?" *Economic History Review* 65, 2: 445–69.

Griffel, Frank. 2007. "Apostasy." In Marc Gaborieau et al., eds., *Encyclopedia of Islam, Three*. Vol. I. Leiden: Brill.

2009. *Al-Ghazali's Philosophical Theology*. New York: Oxford University Press.

Grote, Rainer, and Tilmann Röder, eds. 2012. *Constitutionalism in Islamic Countries: Between Upheaval and Continuity*. Oxford: Oxford University Press.

Guillaume, Alfred. 2005 [1931]. "Philosophy and Theology." In Sir Thomas Arnold and Alfred Guillaume, eds., *The Legacy of Islam*. New Delhi: Aravali Books International.

Günaltay, Şemsettin. 1987 [1938]. "İslam Dünyasının İnhitatı Sebebi Selçuk İstilası mıdır? (Ve Gazali'nin Tenkidi)." In İsmail Kara, ed., *Türkiye'de İslamcılık Düşüncesi: Metinler/Kişiler II*. Istanbul: Risale Yayınları.

Güngör, Erol. 1981. *İslamın Bugünkü Meseleleri*. Istanbul: Ötüken Neşriyat.

1982. *İslam Tasavvufunun Meseleleri*. Istanbul: Ötüken Neşriyat.

Gunn, T. Jeremy. 2004. "Religious Freedom and Laïcité: A Comparison of the United States and France." *Brigham Young University Law Review* 24, 2: 419–506.

Gupta, Dipak K. 2008. *Understanding Terrorism and Political Violence: The Life Cycle of Birth, Growth, Transformation, and Demise*. New York: Routledge.

Güran, Tevfik, ed. 1997 [1897]. *Osmanlı Devleti'nin İlk İstatistik Yıllığı, 1897*. Ankara: T. C. Başbakanlık Devlet İstatistik Enstitüsü.

Gürbüz, Mustafa. 2016. *Rival Kurdish Movements in Turkey: Transforming Ethnic Conflict*. Amsterdam: Amsterdam University Press.

Gutas, Dimitri. 1998. *Greek Thought, Arabic Culture: The Graeco-Arabic Translation Movement in Baghdad and Early 'Abbasid Society (2nd–4th/8th–10th Centuries)*. New York: Routledge.

2012. "Farabi: Biography." In *Encyclopedia Iranica*, January 24, www.iranicaonline .org/articles/farabi-i.

2014. *Orientations of Avicenna's Philosophy: Essays on His Life, Method, Heritage*. Burlington, VT: Ashgate, Variorum.

Hacib, Yusuf Has. 1974 [1070]. *Kutadgu Bilig*. Translated from Karakhanid Turkish to modern Turkish by Reşid Rahmeti Arat. Ankara: Türk Tarih Kurumu.

Hafez, Mohammed M. 2003. *Why Muslims Rebel: Repression and Resistance in the Islamic World*. Boulder: Lynne Rienner Publishers.

Hall, John A. 1992. *Powers and Liberties: The Causes and Consequences of the Rise of the West*. New York: Penguin Books.

Hall, Robert E., and Charles I. Jones. 1999. "Why Do Some Countries Produce So Much More Output per Worker than Others?" *The Quarterly Journal of Economics* 114, 1: 83–116.

Hallaq, Wael B. 1993. "Introduction." In *Ibn Taymiyya against the Greek Logicians*. Translated and edited by Wael B. Hallaq. Oxford: Clarendon Press.

1997. *A History of Islamic Legal Theories: An Introduction to Sunni Usul al-Fiqh*. New York: Cambridge University Press.

2009. *Shari'a: Theory, Practice, Transformations*. New York: Cambridge University Press.

Halm, Heinz. 1997. *Shi'a Islam: From Religion to Revolution*. Translated by Allison Brown. Princeton: Markus Wiener Publishers.

Hamid, Shadi. 2014. *Temptations of Power: Islamists and Illiberal Democracy in the Middle East*. New York: Oxford University Press.

Hamza, Muhammed bin. 1976 [1424]. *XV. Yüzyıl Başlarında Yapılmış "Satır-Arası" Kur'an Tercümesi*. Edited by Ahmet Topaloğlu. Istanbul: Kültür Bakanlığı Yayınları.

Hanioğlu, M. Şükrü. 2008. *A Brief History of the Late Ottoman Empire*. Princeton: Princeton University Press.

———. 2011. *Atatürk: An Intellectual Biography*. Princeton: Princeton University Press.

———. 2012. "The Historical Roots of Kemalism." In Ahmet T. Kuru and Alfred Stepan, eds., *Democracy, Islam, and Secularism in Turkey*. New York: Columbia University Press.

Hanne, Eric J. 2007. *Putting the Caliph in His Place: Power, Authority, and the Late Abbasid Caliphate*. Madison, NJ: Farleigh Dickinson University Press.

Hanson, Hamza Yusuf. 2015. "Foreword." In *Kitab al-'Ilm: The Book of Knowledge. Book 1 of the Ihya' 'Ulum al-Din: The Revival of the Religious Sciences*. Translated and edited by Kenneth Honerkamp. Louisville: Fons Vitae.

Hanson, Stephen E. 2010. *Post-Imperial Democracies: Ideology and Party Formation in Third Republic France, Weimar Germany, and Post-Soviet Russia*. New York: Cambridge University Press.

Hanushek, Erik A., and Ludger Woessmann. 2008. "The Role of Cognitive Skills in Economic Development." *Journal of Economic Literature* 46, 3: 607–68.

Haqqani, Husain. 2005. *Pakistan: Between Mosque and Military*. Washington, DC: Carnegie Endowment for International Peace.

Haque, Amber. 2004. "Psychology from Islamic Perspective: Contributions of Early Muslim Scholars and Challenges to Contemporary Muslim Psychologists." *Journal of Religion and Health* 43, 4: 357–77.

Harborn, Lotta, and Peter Wallensteen. 2010. "Armed Conflicts, 1946–2009." *Journal of Peace Research* 47, 4: 501–9.

Harhash, Nadia I. 2016. "Debating Gender: A Study of Medieval and Contemporary Discussions in Islam." MA thesis. Free University of Berlin, Institute of Islamic Studies.

Harris, Michael H. 1995. *History of Libraries in the Western World*. London: Scarecrow Press.

Harrison, Lawrence E. 1985. *Under-Development Is a State of Mind: The Latin American Case*. Boston: University Press of America.

Hashemi, Nader. 2009. *Islam, Secularism, and Liberal Democracy: Toward a Democratic Theory for Muslim Societies*. New York: Oxford University Press.

Hashemi, Nader, and Danny Postel, eds. 2017. *Sectarianization: Mapping the New Politics of the Middle East*. New York: Oxford University Press.

Al-Hassan, Ahmad Y. 2001. "Transmission of Islamic Science to the West." In A. Y. al-Hassan, Maqbul Ahmed, and A. Z. Iskandar, eds., *The Different Aspects of Islamic Culture. Vol. IV: Science and Technology in Islam. Part I: The Exact and Natural Sciences*. Paris: UNESCO Publishing.

Al-Hassan, Ahmad Y., and Donald R. Hill. 1986. *Islamic Technology: An Illustrated History*. New York: Cambridge University Press.

Hassan, Riffat. 2009. "Islamic Modernist and Reformist Discourse in South Asia." In Shireen T. Hunter, ed., *Reformist Voices of Islam: Mediating Islam and Modernity*. Armonk, NY: M. E. Sharpe.

"The Hatt-ı Şerif of Gülhane." 1975 [1839]. Translated by J. C. Hurewitz. In J. C. Hurewitz, ed., *The Middle East and North Africa in World Politics: A Documentary Record*. Vol. 1. New Haven: Yale University Press.

Hefner Robert W. 2000. *Civil Islam: Muslims and Democratization in Indonesia*. Princeton: Princeton University Press.

2009. "Introduction: The Politics and Cultures of Islamic Education in Southeast Asia." In Robert W. Hefner, ed., *Making Modern Muslims: The Politics of Islamic Education in Southeast Asia*. Honolulu: University of Hawai'i Press.

    ed. 2011. *Shari'a Politics: Islamic Law and Society in the Modern World*. Bloomington: Indiana University Press.

    ed. 2016. *Shari'a Law and Modern Muslim Ethics*. Bloomington: Indiana University Press.

Hegre, Havard, Tanja Ellingsen, Scott Gates, and Nils Petter Gleditsch. 2001. "Toward a Democratic Civil Peace? Democracy, Political Change, and Civil War, 1816–1992." *American Political Science Review* 95, 1: 33–48.

Herb, Michael. 2005. "No Representation without Taxation? Rents, Development, and Democracy." *Comparative Politics* 37, 3: 297–317.

Hegre, Havard, Tanja Ellingsen, Scott Gates, and Nils Petter Gleditsch. 2009. "A Nation of Bureaucrats: Political Participation and Economic Diversification in Kuwait and the United Arab Emirates." *International Journal of Middle East Studies* 41, 3: 375–95.

Hess, Andrew C. 1968. "The Moriscos: An Ottoman Fifth Column in Sixteenth-Century Spain." *American Historical Review* 74, 1: 1–25.

    1972. "The Battle of Lepanto and Its Place in Mediterranean History." *Past and Present* 57: 53–73.

    1974. "Piri Reis and the Ottoman Response to the Voyages of Discovery." *Terrae Incognitae* 6, 1: 19–37.

Hibbard, Scott W. 2010. *Religious Politics and Secular States: Egypt, India, and the United States*. Baltimore: Johns Hopkins University Press.

Al-Hibri, Azizah Y. 1997. "Islam, Law and Custom: Redefining Muslim Women's Rights." *American University International Law Review* 12, 1: 1–44.

El-Hibri, Tayeb. 2002. "Review of Daphna Ephrat's *A Learned Society in a Period of Transition: The Sunni 'Ulama' in Eleventh-Century Baghdad*." *International Journal of Middle East Studies* 34, 4: 736–38.

Hill, Donald D. 1994. "Arabic Fine Technology and Its Influence on European Mechanical Engineering." In Dionisius A. Agius and Richard Hitchcock, eds., *The Arab Influence in Medieval Europe*. Reading: Ithaca Press.

Hillenbrand, Carole. 1988. "Islamic Orthodoxy or Realpolitik? Al-Ghazali's View on Government." *Journal of British Institute of Persian Studies* 26, 1: 81–94.

Hilmi, Şehbenderzade Filibeli Ahmed. 2011 [1911]. *İslam Tarihi*. Edited by Hüseyin Rahmi Yananlı. Istanbul: Huzrur Yayınevi.

Himmelfarb, Gertrude. 2003. *The Roads to Modernity: The British, French, and American Enlightenments*. New York: Vintage Books.

Hingley, Ronald. 1991. *Russia: A Concise History*. London: Thames and Hudson.

Hirschler, Konrad. 2016. *Medieval Damascus: Plurality and Diversity in an Arabic Library. The Ashrafiya Library Catalogue*. Edinburgh: Edinburgh University Press.

Hobbes, Thomas. 1994 [1651]. *Leviathan*. Edited by Edwin Curley. Indianapolis: Hackett Publishing.

Hobsbawm, Eric. 1996 [1962]. *The Age of Revolution, 1789–1848*. New York: Vintage Books.

    1987. *The Age of Empire, 1875–1914*. New York: Pantheon Books.

Hobson, John M. 2004. *The Eastern Origins of Western Civilisation*. New York: Cambridge University Press.

Hodgson, Marshall G. S. 1974a. *The Venture of Islam: Conscience and History in a World Civilization. Vol. 1: The Classical Age of Islam.* Chicago: University of Chicago Press.

   1974b. *The Venture of Islam: Conscience and History in a World Civilization. Vol. 2: The Expansion of Islam in the Middle Periods.* Chicago: University of Chicago Press.

   1974c. *The Venture of Islam: Conscience and History in a World Civilization. Vol. 3: The Gunpowder Empires and Modern Times.* Chicago: University of Chicago Press.

   1993. *Rethinking World History: Essays on Europe, Islam, and World History.* Edited by Edmund Burke III. New York: Cambridge University Press.

Homans, George C. 1962. "Review of Lynn White, Jr.'s *Medieval Technology and Social Change.*" *American Journal of Sociology* 68, 3: 396–7.

Hoodbhoy, Pervez. 1991. *Islam and Science: Religious Orthodoxy and the Battle for Rationality.* London: Zed Books.

   2007. "Science and the Islamic World: The Quest for Rapprochement." *Physics Today* 60, 8: 49–55.

Hourani, Albert. 1983. *Arabic Thought in the Liberal Age, 1789–1939.* New York: Cambridge University Press.

   1991. *A History of the Arab Peoples.* Cambridge, MA: Harvard University Press.

Hourani, George F. 1995 [1951]. *Arab Seafaring: In the Indian Ocean in Ancient and Early Medieval Times.* Princeton: Princeton University Press.

   1961. "Introduction." *Averroes on the Harmony of Religion and Philosophy.* London: E. J. W. Gibb Memorial Trust.

   1984. "A Revised Chronology of Ghazali's Writings." *Journal of the American Oriental Society* 104, 2: 289–302.

Hudson, Michael. 2009. "The United States in the Middle East." In Louise Fawcett, ed., *International Relations of the Middle East.* New York: Oxford University Press.

Huff, Toby E. 2011. *Intellectual Curiosity and the Scientific Revolution: A Global Perspective.* New York: Cambridge University Press.

Human Rights Watch. 2012. "The Government Could Have Stopped This: Sectarian Violence and Ensuing Abuses in Burma's Arakan State," August, www.hrw.org/sites/default/files/reports/burma0812webwcover.pdf.

Humphreys, Macartan. 2005. "Natural Resources, Conflict, and Conflict Resolution: Uncovering the Mechanisms." *Journal of Conflict Resolution* 49, 4: 508–37.

Hung, Ho-fung. 2015. *The China Boom: Why China Will Not Rule the World.* New York: Columbia University Press.

Hunke, Sigrid. 1984 [1960]. *Le Soleil d'Allah brille sur l'Occident: Notre héritage arabe.* Translated from German to French by Georges de Lalène. Paris: Editions Albin Michel.

Huntington, Samuel P. 1984. "Will More Countries Become Democratic?" *Political Science Quarterly* 99, 2: 193–218.

   1991. *The Third Wave: Democratization in the Late Twentieth Century.* Norman: Oklahoma University Press.

   1993. "The Clash of Civilizations?" *Foreign Affairs* 72, 3: 22–49.

Hussin, Iza. 2016. *The Politics of Islamic Law: Local Elites, Colonial Authority, and the Making of the Muslim State.* Chicago: University of Chicago Press.

Ibn Battuta. 2002 [1355]. *The Travels of Ibn Battutah* [*Al-Rihla*]. Translated by Hamilton Gibb and C. F. Beckingham. Abridged by Tim Mackintosh-Smith. London: Picador.

Ibn Fadlan, Ahmad. 1995 [922]. *İbn Fazlan Seyahatnamesi.* Translated into Turkish by Ramazan Şeşen. Istanbul: Bedir Yayınevi.

2005 [922]. "Translation of His Travels." Translated and edited by Richard N. Frye. In *Ibn Fadlan's Journey to Russia: A Tenth-Century Traveler from Baghdad to the Volga River.* Princeton: Markus Wiener Publishers.

Ibn Khaldun. 1967 [1377]. *The Muqaddimah: An Introduction to History.* Vols. I–III. Translated by Frantz Rosenthal. New York: Pantheon Books.

2005 [1377]. *The Muqaddimah: An Introduction to History.* Translated by Frantz Rosenthal. Abridged and edited by N. J. Dawood. Princeton: Princeton University Press.

1952 [1405]. *Autobiography* [*Al-Ta'rif*]. Partially translated by Walter J. Fischel. In Walter J. Fischel, *Ibn Khaldun and Tamerlane.* Berkeley: University of California Press.

1980 [1405]. *Le Voyage d'Occident et d'Orient: Autobiographie* [*Al-Ta'rif bi Ibn Khaldun wa Rihlatuhu Gharban wa Sharqan*]. Translated into French by Abdesselam Cheddadi. Paris: Sindbad.

Ibn al-Nafis. 1968 [1268–77]. *The Theologus Autodidactus of Ibn al-Nafis* [*Al-Risalah al-Kamiliyah fi al-Sirah al-Nabawiyah*]. Translated and edited by Max Meyerhof and Joseph Schacht. Oxford: Clarendon Press.

Ibn Rushd. 2001a [c. 1179]. *Kitab Fasl al-Maqal wa Taqrir ma bayn al-Shari'a wa al-Hikma min al-Ittisal* and *Risalat al-Ihda'* (*Damima*). Edited by Charles E. Butterworth. In *Decisive Treatise and Epistle Dedicatory.* Provo, UT: Brigham Young University Press.

2001b [c. 1179]. *Decisive Treatise* [*Fasl al-Maqal*] *and Epistle Dedicatory* [*Risalat al-Ihda'*]. Translated and edited by Charles E. Butterworth. Provo, UT: Brigham Young University Press.

2001c [1179–80]. *Faith and Reason in Islam: Averroes' Exposition of Religious Arguments.* [*Al-Kashf 'an Manahij al-'Adilla fi 'Aqaid al-Milla*]. Translated by Ibrahim Najjar. Oxford: Oneworld.

1954 [1180]. *Averroes' Tahafut Al-Tahafut (The Incoherence of the Incoherence).* Vols. I and II. Translated and edited by Simon van den Bergh. London: E. J. W. Gibb Memorial Trust.

1974 [c. 1194]. *Epitome of Plato's "Republic."* Translated and edited by Ralph Lerner. In *Averroes on Plato's "Republic."* Ithaca, NY: Cornell University Press.

Ibn Sina. 2005 [c. 1020]. "On the Soul" [from *The Book of Salvation* (*Kitab al-Najat*)]. Translated and edited by Muhammad Ali Khalidi. In *Medieval Islamic Philosophical Writings.* New York: Cambridge University Press.

1974 [c. 1037]. *Autobiography.* Translated and edited by William E. Gohlman. In *The Life of Ibn Sina: A Critical Edition and Annotated Translation.* Albany: SUNY Press.

Ibn Taymiyya, Abu al-Abbas Ahmad. 1994a [1309–14]. *Al-Siyasah al-Shar'iyah fi Islah al-Ra'i wa al-Ra'iyah* [*Sharia-based Governance in Reforming Both the Ruler and His Flock*]. Algiers: Editions ENAG.

1994b [1309–14]. *Le traité du droit public (Al-Siyasah al-shar'iyah fi islah al-ra'i wa al-ra'iyah).* Translated into French by Henri Laoust. Algiers: Editions ENAG.

1966 [1309–14]. *Ibn Taimiyya on Public and Private Law in Islam or Public Policy in Islamic Jurisprudence* [*Al-Siyasah al-shar'iyah fi islah al-ra'i wa al-ra'iyah*]. Translated by Omar A. Farrukh. Beirut: Khayats.

Ibn Tufayl. 2005 [c. 1175]. *Hayy ibn Yaqzan*. Translated, abridged, and edited by Muhammad Ali Khalidi. In *Medieval Islamic Philosophical Writings*. New York: Cambridge University Press.

Ibrahim, Mahmood. 1994. "Religious Inquisition as Social Policy: The Persecution of the *Zanadiqa* in the Early Abbasid Caliphate." *Arab Studies Quarterly* 16, 2: 53–72.

İhsanoğlu, Ekmeleddin. 1990. "Darulfünun Tarihçesine Giriş: İlk İki Teşebbüs." *Belleten* 210: 699–738.

Ilgar, İhsan. 1990. *Rusya'da Birinci Müslüman Kongresi Tutanakları*. Ankara: Kültür Bakanlığı Yayınları.

Imber, Colin. 1997. *Ebu's-su'ud: The Islamic Legal Tradition*. Stanford: Stanford University Press.

———. 2009. *The Ottoman Empire*. New York: Palgrave Macmillan.

İnalcık, Halil. 1964. "The Nature of Traditional Society." In Robert E. Ward and Dankwart A. Rustow, eds., *Political Modernization in Japan and Turkey*. Princeton: Princeton University Press.

———. 1970. "The Ottoman Economic Mind and Aspects of the Ottoman Economy." In M. A. Cook, ed., *Studies in the Economic History of the Middle East: From the Rise of Islam to the Present Day*. New York: Oxford University Press.

———. 2000 [1973]. *The Ottoman Empire: The Classic Age, 1300–1600*. Translated by Norman Itzkowitz and Colin Imber. London: Phoenix.

———. 1994. "The Ottoman State: Economy and Society, 1300–1600." In Halil İnalcık with Donald Quataert, eds., *An Economic and Social History of the Ottoman Empire*. *Vol. I: 1300–1600*. New York: Cambridge University Press.

———. 2000. "Timar." In P. J. Bearman et al., eds., *The Encyclopedia of Islam. New Edition*. Vol. X. Leiden: Brill.

Inglehart, Ronald, and Pippa Norris. 2003. "The True Clash of Civilizations." *Foreign Policy* 135: 62–70.

International Monetary Fund. 2007–11. "Country Information: Article IV Staff Reports," www.imf.org/external/country/index.htm.

Iqbal, Muhammad. 2013 [1930]. *The Reconstruction of Religious Thought in Islam*. Stanford: Stanford University Press.

Irwin, Robert. 2006. *Dangerous Knowledge: Orientalism and Its Discontents*. Woodstock, NY: Overlook Press.

"Islahat Fermanı." 1975 [1856]. Translated by J. C. Hurewitz. In J. C. Hurewitz, ed., *The Middle East and North Africa in World Politics: A Documentary Record*. Vol. 1. New Haven: Yale University Press.

İslamoğlu, Huri. 2000. "Property as a Contested Domain: A Reevaluation of the Ottoman Land Code of 1858." In Roger Owen, ed., *New Perspectives on Property and Land in the Middle East*. Cambridge, MA: Harvard Middle Eastern Monographs.

Ismail, Raihan. 2016. *Saudi Clerics and Shi'a Islam*. New York: Oxford University Press.

Ispahani, Farahnaz. 2017. *Purifying the Land of the Pure: A History of Pakistan's Religious Minorities*. New York: Oxford University Press.

Israel, Jonathan I. 1998. *The Dutch Republic: Its Rise, Greatness, and Fall, 1477–1806*. New York: Oxford University Press.

2001. *Radical Enlightenment: Philosophy and the Making of Modernity 1650–1750*. New York: Oxford University Press.

2006. *Enlightenment Contested: Philosophy, Modernity, and the Emancipation of Man 1670–1752*. New York: Oxford University Press.

2011. *Democratic Enlightenment: Philosophy, Revolution, and Human Rights, 1750–1790*. New York: Oxford University Press.

Issawi, Charles. 1968. "Asymmetrical Development and Transport in Egypt, 1800–1914." In William R. Polk and Richard L. Chambers, eds., *Beginnings of Modernization in the Middle East*. Chicago: University of Chicago Press.

1980. "Europe, the Middle East and the Shift in Power: Reflections on a Theme by Marshall Hodgson." *Comparative Studies in Society and History* 22, 4: 487–504.

1982. *An Economic History of the Middle East and North Africa*. New York: Columbia University Press.

1983. "Why Japan?" In Ibrahim Ibrahim, ed., *Arab Resources: The Transformation of a Society*. London: CroomHelm.

Itzkowitz, Norman. 1962. "Eighteenth Century Ottoman Realities." *Studia Islamica* 16: 73–94.

Al-Jabri, Mohammed Abed. 2011 [1984]. *The Formation of Arab Reason: Text, Tradition, and the Construction of Modernity in the Arab World*. Translated by the Centre for Arab Unity Studies. New York: I. B. Tauris.

1995. *Introduction à la critique de la raison arabe*. Translated into French by Ahmed Mahfoud and Marc Geoffroy. Paris: Éditions la Découverte.

Jackson, Sherman A. 2002a. "Jihad and the Modern World." *Islamic Law and Culture* 7, 1: 1–26.

2002b. "Introduction." In *On the Boundaries of Theological Tolerance in Islam: Abu Hamid al-Ghazali's Faysal al-Tafriqa*. Translated and edited by Sherman A. Jackson. Karachi: Oxford University Press.

2011. "Liberal/Progressive, Modern, and Modernized Islam: Muslim Americans and the American State." In Mehran Kamrava, ed., *Innovation in Islam: Traditions and Contributions*. Berkeley: University of California Press.

Jacob, Margaret C. 1997. *Scientific Culture and the Making of the Industrial West*. New York: Oxford University Press.

Jaffer, Tariq. 2014. *Razi: Master of Qur'anic Interpretation and Theological Reasoning*. New York: Oxford University Press.

Jahiz. 1969. [c. 862]. *The Life and Works of Jahiz: Translations of Selected Texts*. Translated into French and edited by Charles Pellat. Translated from French by D. M. Hawke. Berkeley: University of California Press.

Jamal, Amaney. 2012. *Of Empires and Citizens: Pro-American Democracy or No Democracy at All?* Princeton: Princeton University Press.

Jansen, Yolande. 2011. "Postsecularism, Piety and Fanaticism: Reflections on Saba Mahmood's and Jürgen Habermas' Critiques of Secularism." *Philosophy and Social Criticism* 37, 9: 977–98.

Jardin, Lisa. 2000. "Introduction." In Lisa Jardine and Michael Silverthorne, eds., *The New Organon*. New York: Cambridge University Press.

Jones, Eric. 2003 [1981]. *The European Miracle: Environments, Economies and Geo-politics in the History of Europe and Asia.* New York: Cambridge University Press.

Jones, Robert. 1994. "The Medici Oriental Press (Rome 1584–1614) and the Impact of Its Arabic Publications on Northern Europe." In G. A. Russell, ed., *The "Arabick" Interest of the Natural Philosophers in Seventeenth-Century England.* New York: Brill.

Joseph, George Gheverghese. 2000. *The Crest of the Peacock: Non-European Roots of Mathematics.* Princeton: Princeton University Press.

Juergensmeyer, Mark. 2007. *Global Rebellion: Religious Challenges to the Secular State, from Christian Militias to al Qaeda.* Berkeley: University of California Press.

2017. *Terror in the Mind of God: The Global Rise of Religious Violence.* Berkeley: University of California Press.

Kadivar, Mohsen. 2006. "Freedom of Religion and Belief in Islam." In Mehran Kamrava, ed., *The New Voices of Islam: Reforming Politics and Modernity – A Reader.* Berkeley: University of California Press.

2013. "Routinizing the Iranian Revolution." In Jeffrey T. Kenney and Ebrahim Moosa, eds., *Islam in the Modern World.* New York: Routledge.

Kadri, Sadakat. 2012. *Heaven on Earth: A Journey through Shari'a Law from the Deserts of Ancient Arabia to the Streets of the Modern Muslim World.* New York: Farrar, Straus and Giroux.

Kafadar, Cemal. 1995. *Between Two Worlds: The Construction of the Ottoman State.* Berkeley: University of California Press.

1997–8. "The Question of Ottoman Decline." *Harvard Middle East and Islamic Review* 4, 1–2: 30–75.

Kalyvas, Stathis N. 1996. *The Rise of Christian Democracy in Europe.* Ithaca, NY: Cornell University Press.

Kamali, Mohammad Hashim. 2003. *Principles of Islamic Jurisprudence.* Cambridge: Islamic Texts Society.

Kant, Immanuel. 2009 [1784]. "An Answer to the Question: What Is Enlightenment?" In *An Answer to the Question: What Is Enlightenment?* Translated by H. B. Nisbet. New York: Penguin Books.

Kaplan, Sam. 2002. "Din-u Devlet All over Again? The Politics of Military Secularism and Religious Militarism in Turkey following the 1980 Coup." *International Journal of Middle East Studies* 34, 1: 113–27.

Karakaya, Süveyda. 2013. "Religion and Conflict: What Explains the Puzzling Case of 'Islamic Violence' and Islamist Party Moderation?" PhD dissertation. University of Tennessee, Knoxville.

Karaman, Hayrettin. 1990. "Islam'da Din ve Devlet İlişkisi." *Yeni Türkiye* 13: 13–23.

Karaman, K. Kıvanç, and Şevket Pamuk. 2010. "Ottoman State Finances in European Perspective, 1500–1914." *The Journal of Economic History* 70, 3: 593–629.

Karamustafa, Ahmet T. 2007. *Sufism: The Formative Period.* Edinburgh: Edinburgh University Press.

Karpat, Kemal. 1968. "The Land Regime, Social Structure, and Modernization in the Ottoman Empire." In William R. Polk and Richard L. Chambers, eds., *Beginnings of Modernization in the Middle East.* Chicago: University of Chicago Press.

1985. *Ottoman Population 1830–1914: Demographic and Social Characteristics.* Madison: University of Wisconsin Press.

2001. *The Politization of Islam: Reconcstructing Identity, State, Faith, and Community in the Late Ottoman State.* New York: Oxford University Press.

Kasaba, Reşat. 1988. *The Ottoman Empire and the World Economy: The Nineteenth Century.* Albany: SUNY Press.

Kaşgarlı, Mahmud. 1986 [1077]. *Divanü Lugati't Türk.* Vols. I–III. Translated from Karakhanid Turkish to modern Turkish by Besim Atalay. Ankara: Türk Dil Kurumu Yayınları.

Kassab, Elizabeth Suzanne. 2009. *Contemporary Arab Thought: Cultural Critique in Comparative Perspective.* New York: Columbia University Press.

Kau, Justin. 2018. "Greater Books," www.greaterbooks.com.

Kaufmann, Daniel, Aart Kraay, and Pablo Zoido-Lobaton. 1999. "Governance Matters." World Bank Development Research Group, Policy Research Working Paper 2196: 1–60.

Kayalı, Hasan. 1997. *Arabs and Young Turks: Ottomanism, Arabism, and Islamism in the Ottoman Empire, 1908–1918.* Berkeley: University of California Press.

Kayaoğlu, Turan. 2010. *Legal Imperialism: Sovereignty and Extraterritoriality in Japan, the Ottoman Empire, and China.* New York: Cambridge University Press.

2015. *The Organization of Islamic Cooperation: Politics, Problems, and Potential.* New York: Routledge.

Kazancıgil, Aykut. 1999. *Osmanlılarda Bilim ve Teknoloji.* Istanbul: Gazeteciler ve Yazarlar Vakfı Yayınları.

Keddie, Nikki R. 1968. *An Islamic Response to Imperialism: Political and Religious Writings of Sayyid Jamal ad-Din al-Afghani.* Berkeley: University of California Press.

1972. "The Roots of the Ulama's Power in Modern Iran." In Nikki R. Keddie, ed., *Scholars, Saints, and Sufis: Muslim Religious Institutions in the Middle East since 1500.* Berkeley: University of California Press.

1984. "Material Culture and Geography: Toward a Holistic Comparative History of the Middle East." *Comparative Studies in Society and History* 26, 4: 709–35.

Kemal, Namık. 1969 [1884]. *Celaleddin Harzemşah.* Edited by Hüseyin Ayan. Istanbul: Hareket Yayınları.

1962 [1910]. *Renan Müdafaanamesi: İslamiyet ve Maarif.* Edited by M. Fuad Köprülü. Ankara: Milli Kültür.

Kemal, Rahimuddin, and Salim Kemal. 1996. "Shah Waliullah." In Seyyed Hossein Nasr and Oliver Leaman, eds., *History of Islamic Philosophy.* New York: Routledge.

Kennedy, Hugh. 2002. *Mongols, Huns, and Vikings: Nomads at War.* London: Cassell.

2005. *When Baghdad Ruled the Muslim World: The Rise and Fall of Islam's Greatest Dynasty.* Cambridge, MA: Da Capo Press.

2007. *The Great Arab Conquests: How the Spread of Islam Changed the World We Live In.* Philadelphia: De Capo Press.

Kennedy, Paul. 1987. *The Rise and Fall of the Great Powers.* New York: Vintage Books.

Khalaf-Allah, Muhammad. 1998 [1973]. "Legislative Authority." Translated by Joseph Massad. In Charles Kurzman, ed., *Liberal Islam: A Sourcebook.* New York: Oxford University Press.

Khalid, Adeeb. 1994. "Printing, Publishing, and Reform in Tsarist Central Asia." *International Journal of Middle East Studies* 26, 2: 187–200.

1998. *The Politics of Muslim Cultural Reform: Jadidism in Central Asia.* Berkeley: University of California Press.

2007. *Islam after Communism: Religion and Politics in Central Asia.* Berkeley: University of California Press.

Khalidi, Muhammad Ali. 2005. "Introduction." In *Medieval Islamic Philosophical Writings.* Translated and edited by Muhammad Ali Khalidi. New York: Cambridge University Press.

Khalidi, Rashid. 2004. *Resurrecting Empire: Western Footprints and America's Perilous Path in the Middle East.* Boston: Beacon Press.

Al-Khalili, Jim. 2011. *The House of Wisdom: How Arabic Science Saved Ancient Knowledge and Gave Us the Renaissance.* New York: Penguin Books.

Khan, B. Zorina. 2011. "Premium Inventions: Patents and Prizes as Incentive Mechanisms in Britain and the United States, 1750–1930." In Dora L. Costa and Naomi R. Lamoreaux, eds., *Understanding Long-Run Economic Growth: Geography, Institutions, and the Knowledge Economy.* Chicago: University of Chicago Press.

Khayr al-Din (al-Tunisi). 1967 [1867]. *The Surest Path to Knowledge Concerning the Condition of Countries.* Translated and edited by Leone Carl Brown. In *The Surest Path: The Political Treatise of a Nineteenth-Century Muslim Statesman.* Cambridge, MA: Harvard University Press.

Khomeini, Ruhollah. 1981 [1970]. "Islamic Government." In *Islam and Revolution: Writings and Declarations of Imam Khomeini.* Translated from Persian by Hamid Algar. Berkeley: Mizan Press.

Kiaulehn, Walther. 1971. *Demir Melekler: Makinenin Doğuşu, Tarihi ve Kudreti.* Tranlated from German to Turkish by Hayrullah Örs. Istanbul: Remzi Kitabevi.

Kilgour, Frederick G. 1998. *The Evolution of the Book.* New York: Oxford University Press.

Kılınç, Ramazan. 2019. *Alien Citizens: State and Religious Minorities in Turkey and France.* New York: Cambridge University Press.

Kınalızade, Ali Çelebi. 2012 [1565]. *Ahlak-ı Ala'i.* Edited by Mustafa Koç. Istanbul: Klasik.

King, David A. 1993. *Astronomy in the Service of Islam.* Brookfield, VT: Ashgate, Variorum.

1999. *World-Maps for Finding the Direction and Distance to Mecca: Innovation and Tradition in Islamic Science.* Leiden: Brill.

2004. *In Synchrony with the Heavens: Studies in Astronomical Timekeeping and Instrumentation in Medieval Islamic Civilization.* Vol. 1: *The Call of the Muezzin.* Leiden: Brill.

Klein, Herbert S. 2010. *The Atlantic Slave Trade.* New York: Cambridge University Press.

Knysh, Alexander D. 1999. *Ibn 'Arabi in the Later Islamic Tradition: The Making of a Polemical Image in Medieval Islam.* Albany: SUNY Press.

Kohli, Atul. 2004. *State-Directed Development: Political Power and Industrialization in the Global Periphery.* New York: Cambridge University Press.

Koloğlu, Orhan. 2008. "Türk Matbaacılığının Piri Olarak İbrahim Müteferrika." In Katip Çelebi, *Cihannüma: 360 Yıllık Bir Öykü (A 360 Year Old Story).* Edited by Bülent Özükan. Istanbul: Boyut Yayıncılık.

Köprülü, Fuad. 1976 [1919]. *Türk Edebiyatında İlk Mutasavvıflar.* Ankara: Diyanet İşleri Başkanlığı Yayınları.

Kopstein, Jeffrey S., and David A. Reilly. 2000. "Geographic Diffusion and the Transformation of the Postcommunist World." *World Politics* 53, 1: 1–37.

Kraemer, Joel L. 1992. *Humanism in the Renaissance of Islam: The Cultural Revival during the Buyid Age.* New York: Brill.

Kraus, Paul. 1986 [1942]. *Jabir ibn Hayyan: Contribution à l'histoire des idées scientifiques dans l'Islam. Jabir et la science grecque.* Paris: Les Belles Lettres.

Kubicek, Paul. 2015. *Political Islam and Democracy in the Muslim World.* New York: Lynne Rienner.

Küng, Hans. 2007. *Islam: Past, Present, and Future.* Translated from German by John Bowden. Oxford: Oneworld.

Künkler, Mirjam, and Alfred Stepan, eds. 2013. *Democracy and Islam in Indonesia.* New York: Columbia University Press.

Kuran, Timur. 2004. "Why the Middle East Is Economically Underdeveloped: Historical Mechanisms of Institutional Stagnation." *The Journal of Economic Perspectives* 18, 3: 71–90.

   2011. *The Long Divergence: How Islamic Law Held Back the Middle East.* Princeton: Princeton University Press.

Kuru, Ahmet T. 2002. "Between the State and Cultural Zones: Nation Building in Turkmenistan." *Central Asian Survey* 21, 1: 71–90.

   2009. *Secularism and State Policies toward Religion: The United States, France, and Turkey.* New York: Cambridge University Press.

   2011. "Review of Brian J. Grim and Roger Finke's *The Price of Freedom Denied.*" *Middle East Policy* 18: 172–5.

   2014. "Authoritarianism and Democracy in Muslim Countries: Rentier States and Regional Diffusion." *Political Science Quarterly* 129, 3: 399–427.

   2015. "Turkey's Failed Policy toward the Arab Spring: Three Levels of Analysis." *Mediterranean Quarterly* 26, 3: 94–116.

   2017. "Islam, Democracy, and Secularism in Turkey: Analyzing the Failure." *Montreal Review*, December, www.themontrealreview.com/2009/Islam-And-Dem ocracy-In-Turkey.php.

Kuru, Ahmet T., and Alfred Stepan. 2012. "*Laïcité* as an 'Ideal Type' and a Continuum: Comparing Turkey, France, and Senegal." In Ahmet T. Kuru and Alfred Stepan, eds., *Democracy, Islam, and Secularism in Turkey.* New York: Columbia University Press.

Kurucan, Ahmet. 2006. "İslam Hukukunda Düşünce Özgürlüğü." PhD dissertation. Atatürk University, Erzurum (Turkey).

Kurzman, Charles. 1996. "Structural Opportunity and Perceived Opportunity in Social-Movement Theory: The Iranian Revolution of 1979." *American Sociological Review* 61, 1: 153–70.

   ed. 1998. *Liberal Islam: A Sourcebook.* New York: Oxford University Press.

Kushner, David. 1977. *The Rise of Turkish Nationalism, 1876–1908.* London: Frank Cass.

Lacoste, Yves. 1998 [1966]. *Ibn Khaldoun: Naissance de l'Histoire, passé du tiers monde.* Paris: La Découverte.

Laffer, Arthur B. 2004. "The Laffer Curve: Past, Present, and Future." *Backgrounder* 1765: 1–16.

Lahlali, El Mustapha. 2010. "The Review of Moustapha Safaouan's *Why Are the Arabs Not Free? The Politics of Writing*." *Discourse and Society* 21, 2: 240–1.

Lakhdhar, Latifa. 2013. *De quoi demain sera-t-il fait? Le monde arabo-musulman fait sa révolution*. Tunis: Nirvana.

Lambton, Ann K. S. 1962. "The Merchant in Medieval Islam." In S. H. Taqizadeh, ed., *A Locust's Leg: Studies in Honour of S. H. Taqizadeh*. London: Percy Lund, Humphries.

  1965. "Reflections on the *Iqta'*." In George Makdisi, ed., *Arabic and Islamic Studies in Honor of Hamilton A. R. Gibb*. Cambridge, MA: Harvard University Press.

  1981. *State and Government in Medieval Islam. An Introduction to the Study of Islamic Political Theory: The Jurists*. New York: Oxford University Press.

  1988. *Continuity and Change in Medieval Persia*. Albany: SUNY Press.

  1991. *Landlord and Peasant in Persia: A Study of Land Tenure and Land Revenue Administration*. New York: I. B. Tauris.

Landes, David S. 1998. *The Wealth and Poverty of Nations: Why Some Are So Rich and Some So Poor*. New York: W. W. Norton.

Lane, Rose Wilder. 2014 [1943]. *The Discovery of Freedom: Man's Struggle against Authority*. N.p.: CreateSpace.

Laoust, Henri. 1939. *Essai sur les doctrines sociales et politiques de Taki-d-Din Ahmad b. Taimiya, canoniste ḥanbalite, né à Harrān en 661/1262, mort à Damas en 728/1328*. Cairo: L'Institut français d'archéologie orientale.

  1970. *La politique de Gazali*. Paris: Librairie Orientaliste Paul Geuthner.

  1971. "Ibn Taymiyya." In B[ernard] Lewis et al., eds., *The Encyclopedia of Islam, New Edition*. Vol. III. Leiden: Brill.

Lapidus, Ira M. 1975. "The Separation of State and Religion in the Development of Early Islamic Society." *International Journal of Middle East Studies* 6, 4: 363–85.

  1984. *Muslim Cities in the Later Middle Ages*. New York: Cambridge University Press.

  1996. "State and Religion in Islamic Societies." *Past and Present* 151, 1: 3–27.

  1999. "Sultanates and Gunpowder Empires." In John L. Esposito, ed., *The Oxford History of Islam*. New York: Oxford University Press.

  2002. *A History of Islamic Societies*. New York: Cambridge University Press.

Laroui, Abdallah. 1974. *La crise des intellectuels arabes: Traditionalisme ou historicisme?* Paris: Librairie François Maspero.

Laurens, Henry. 1989. *L'Expédition d'Égypte, 1798–1801*. Paris: Armand Colin.

Lauzière, Henri. 2016. *The Making of Salafism: Islamic Reform in the Twentieth Century*. New York: Columbia University Press.

Lawrence, Bruce B. 2014. "Al-Biruni: Against the Grain." *Critical Muslim* 12: 61–72.

Laycock, Stuart. 2012. *All the Countries We've Ever Invaded: And the Few We Never Got Round To*. Stroud: History Press.

Layne, Christopher. 1994. "Kant or Cant." *International Security* 19, 2: 5–49.

Leaman, Oliver. 1988. *Averroes and His Philosophy*. Oxford: Clarendon Press.

  1996. "Ibn Miskawayh." In Seyyed Hossein Nasr and Oliver Leaman, eds., *History of Islamic Philosophy*. New York: Routledge.

Lerner, Fred. 1998. *The Story of Libraries: From the Invention of Writing to the Computer Age*. New York: Continuum.

Lerner, Hanna. 2014. "Critical Junctures, Religion, and Personal Status Regulations in Israel and India." *Law and Social Inquiry* 39, 2: 387–415.

Lerner, Ralph. 1974. "Preface" and "Introduction." In *Averroes on Plato's "Republic."* Translated and edited by Ralph Lerner. Ithaca, NY: Cornell University Press.

The Letter of Tansar. 1968 [n.a.]. Translated and edited by M. Boyce. Rome: Istituto Italiano per il Medio ed Estremo Oriente.

Levene, Mark. 2005. *Genocide in the Age of the Nation-State. Vol. II: The Rise of the West and the Coming of the Genocide.* New York: I. B. Tauris.

Levitsky, Steven, and Lucan A. Way. 2010. *Competitive Authoritarianism: Hybrid Regimes after the Cold War.* New York: Cambridge University Press.

Lewicka, Paulina. 2003. "When a Shared Meal Is Formalized: Observations on Arabic 'Table Manners' Manuals of the Middle Ages." *Studia Arabistyczne i Islamistyczne* 11: 96–107.

Lewis, Archibald R. 1988. *Nomads and Crusaders, A.D. 1000–1368.* Bloomington: Indiana University Press.

Lewis, Bernard. 1968. *The Emergence of Modern Turkey.* London: Oxford University Press.

1970. "The Arabs in Eclipse." In Carlo M. Cipolla, ed., *The Economic Decline of Empires.* London: Methuen.

2001 [1982]. *The Muslim Discovery of Europe.* New York: W. W. Norton.

1990. "The Roots of Muslim Rage." *The Atlantic Monthly* 266: 47–60.

1994. "Why Turkey Is the Only Muslim Democracy." *Middle East Quarterly* 1, 1: 41–9.

1995. *The Middle East: A Brief History of the Last 2,000 Years.* New York: Scribner.

2003. *What Went Wrong? The Clash between Islam and Modernity in the Middle East.* New York: Perennial.

2004. *The Crisis of Islam: Holy War and Unholy Terror.* New York: Random House.

2008. "The Arab Destruction of the Library of Alexandria: Anatomy of a Myth." In Mostafa El-Abbadi and Omnia Fathallah, eds., *What Happened to the Ancient Library of Alexandria?* Boston: Brill.

2010. *Faith and Power: Religion and Politics in the Middle East.* New York: Oxford University Press.

Lewis, David Levering. 2009. *God's Crucible: Islam and the Making of Europe, 570–1215.* New York: W. W. Norton.

Lieven, Dominic. 2001. *Empire: The Russian Empire and Its Rivals.* New Haven: Yale University Press.

Lin, Justin Yifu. 1995. "The Needham Puzzle: Why the Industrial Revolution Did Not Originate in China." *Economic Development and Cultural Change* 43, 2: 269–92.

Lindberg, David C. 1976. *Theories of Vision from Al-Kindi to Kepler.* Chicago: University of Chicago Press.

2007. *The Beginnings of Western Science: The European Scientific Tradition in Philosophical, Religious, and Institutional Context, Prehistory to A.D. 1450.* Chicago: University of Chicago Press.

Lindner, Rudi Paul. 1983. *Nomads and Ottomans in Medieval Anatolia.* Bloomington: Indiana University Press.

Lingwood, Chad G. 2013. *Politics, Poetry, and Sufism in Medieval Iran: New Perspectives on Jami's Salaman va Absal.* Boston: Brill.

Linz, Juan, and Alfred Stepan. 1996. *Problems of Democratic Transition and Consolidation: Southern Europe, South America, and Post-Communist Europe.* Baltimore: Johns Hopkins University Press.

Lipset, Seymour Martin. 1959. "Some Social Requisites of Democracy: Economic Development and Political Legitimacy." *American Political Science Review* 53, 1: 69–105.

Locke, John. 1983 [1689a]. *A Letter Concerning Toleration.* Edited by James H. Tully. Indianapolis: Hackett Publishing.

   1996 [1689b]. *An Essay Concerning Human Understanding.* Abridged and edited by Kenneth P. Winkler. Indianapolis: Hackett Publishing.

   1980 [1690]. *Second Treatise of Government.* Edited by C. P. Macpherson. Indianapolis: Hackett Publishing.

Lockwood, William W. 1964. "Economic and Political Modernization: Japan." In Robert E. Ward and Dankward E. Rustow, eds., *Political Modernization in Japan and Turkey.* Princeton: Princeton University Press.

Logan, F. Donald. 2013. *A History of the Church in the Middle Ages.* New York: Routledge.

Lombard, Denys. 2000. "The Malay Sultanate as a Socio-Economic Model." In Denys Lombard and Jean Aubin, eds., *Asian Merchants and Businessmen in the Indian Ocean and the China Sea.* Delhi: Oxford University Press.

Lombard, Maurice. 1975. *The Golden Age of Islam.* Translated from French by Joan Spencer. New York: American Elsevier Publishing.

Luciani, Giacomo. 1987. "Allocation vs. Production States: A Theoretical Framework." In Hazem Beblawi and Giacomo Luciani, eds., *The Rentier State.* London: CroomHelm.

Luizard, Pierre-Jean, ed. 2006. *Le choc colonial et l'islam: Les politiques religieuses des puissances coloniales en terres d'islam.* Paris: La Découverte.

Lust, Ellen. 2011. "Missing the Third Wave: Islam, Institutions, and Democracy in the Middle East." *Studies in Comparative International Development* 46, 2: 163–90.

Lyons, Jonathan. 2010. *The House of Wisdom: How the Arabs Transformed Western Civilization.* New York: Bloomsbury Press.

Maalouf, Amin. 1984. *The Crusades through Arab Eyes.* Translated from French by Jon Rothschild. New York: Schocken Books.

Machiavelli, Niccolo. 1996 [c. 1513]. *The Prince.* In Michael L. Morgan, ed., *Classics of Moral and Political Theory.* Translated from Italian by David Wootton. Indianapolis: Hackett Publishing.

Mack, Rosamond E. 2002. *Bazaar to Piazza: Islamic Trade and Italian Art, 1300–1600.* Berkeley: University of California Press.

Mackensen, Ruth Stellhorn. 1935a. "Moslem Libraries and Sectarian Propaganda." *American Journal of Semitic Languages and Literatures* 51, 2: 83–113.

   1935b. "Background of the History of Moslem Libraries." *American Journal of Semitic Languages and Literatures* 51, 2: 114–25.

Mackintosh-Smith, Tim. 2002. "Foreword." In *The Travels of Ibn Battutah* [*Al-Rihla*]. Abridged and edited by Tim Mackintosh-Smith. London: Picador.

Maçoudi. 1863 [947]. *Les prairies d'or* [*Muruj al-Dhahab*]. Vol. II. Arabic-French text edited and translated by C. Barbier de Meynard and Pavet de Courteille. Paris: L'imprimerie imperial.

Madden, Thomas F. 2013. *The Concise History of the Crusades.* New York: Rowman and Littlefield.

Maddison, Angus. 2004. *Growth and Interaction in the World Economy: The Roots of Modernity.* Washington, DC: AEI Press.

2006. "China in the World Economy: 1300–2030." *International Journal of Business* 11, 3: 239–54.

Madelung, Wilfred. 1985. "The Spread of Maturidism and the Turks." In Wilfred Madelung, *Religious Schools and Sects in Medieval Islam.* London: Variorum Reprints.

Madjid, Nurcholish. 2003. *The True Face of Islam: Essays on Islam and Modernity in Indonesia.* Ciputat: Voice Center Indonesia.

Mahdi, Muhsin. 1964. *Ibn Khaldun's Philosophy of History: A Study in the Philosophic Foundation of the Science of Culture.* Chicago: University of Chicago Press.

1987. "Alfarabi." In Leo Strauss and Joseph Cropsey, eds., *History of Political Philosophy.* Chicago: University of Chicago Press.

1995. "From the Manuscript Age to the Age of Printed Books." In George N. Atiyeh, ed., *The Book in the Islamic World: The Written Word and Communication in the Middle East.* Albany: SUNY Press.

Mahmood, Saba. 2006. "Secularism, Hermeneutics and Empire: The Politics of Islamic Reformation." *Public Culture* 18, 2: 323–47.

Mahmoud, Mohamed. 2000. "Mahmud Muhammad Taha's Second Message of Islam and His Modernist Project." In John Cooper, Ronald Nettler, and Mohamad Mahmoud, eds., *Islam and Modernity: Muslim Intellectuals Respond.* New York: I. B. Tauris.

Mahoney, James. 2001. *The Legacies of Liberalism: Path Dependence and Political Regimes in Central America.* Baltimore: Johns Hopkins University Press.

2010. *Colonialism and Postcolonial Development: Spanish America in Comparative Perspective.* New York: Cambridge University Press.

Mahoney, James, and Dietrich Rueschemeyer. 2003. *Comparative Historical Analysis in the Social Sciences.* New York: Cambridge University Press.

Makdisi, George. 1970. "Madrasa and University in the Middle Ages." *Studia Islamica* 32: 255–64.

1981. *The Rise of Colleges: Institutions of Learning in Islam and the West.* Edinburgh: Edinburgh University Press.

Mamdani, Mahmood. 2005. *Good Muslim, Bad Muslim.* New York: Three Rivers Press.

Manz, Beatrice Forbes. 1989. *The Rise and Rule of Tamerlane.* New York: Cambridge University Press.

March, Andrew. 2011. *Islam and Liberal Citizenship: The Search for an Overlapping Consensus.* New York: Oxford University Press.

Mardin, Şerif. 2000 [1962]. *The Genesis of Young Ottoman Thought: A Study in the Modernization of Turkish Political Ideas.* Syracuse: Syracuse University Press.

1969. "Power, Civil Society and Culture in the Ottoman Empire." *Comparative Studies in Society and History* 11, 3: 258–81.

1979. "Turkey: The Transformation of an Economic Code." In Ergun Özbudun and Aydın Ulusan, eds., *The Political Economy of Income Distribution in Turkey.* New York: Holmes and Meier Publishers.

1988. "Freedom in an Ottoman Perspective." In Metin Heper and Ahmet Evin, eds., *State, Democracy, and the Military: Turkey in the 1980s*. Berlin: Walter de Gruyter.

Marenbon, John. 1996. "Medieval Christian and Jewish Europe." In Seyyed Hossein Nasr and Oliver Leaman, eds., *History of Islamic Philosophy*. New York: Routledge.

Marks, Monica. 2018. "Cross-Ideological Coalition Building in Tunisia's Democratic Transition." In Alfred Stepan, ed., *Democratic Transition in the Muslim World: A Global Perspective*. New York: Columbia University Press.

Marks, Robert B. 2007. *The Origins of the Modern World: A Global and Ecological Narrative from the Fifteenth to the Twentieth-First Century*. New York: Rowman and Littlefield.

Marlow, Louise. 1997. *Hierarchy and Egalitarianism in Islamic Thought*. New York: Cambridge University Press.

2016. *Council for Kings: Wisdom and Politics in Tenth-Century Iran*. Vol. I: *The* Nasihat Al-Muluk *of Pseudo-Mawardi. Contexts and Themes*. Edinburgh: Edinburgh University Press.

Martin, Henri-Jean. 1994. *The History and Power of Writing*. Translated by Lydia G. Cochrane. Chicago: University of Chicago Press.

Marx, Anthony W. 2003. *Faith in Nation: Exclusionary Origins of Nationalism*. New York: Oxford University Press.

Marx, Karl. 1991 [1861–3]. *Economic Manuscript of 1861–63* ["Division of Labour and Mechanical Workshop. Tool and Machinery"]. In Karl Marx and Friedrick Engels, *Collected Works*. Vol. 33. New York: International Publishers.

Marx, Karl, and Friedrich Engels. 1994 [1848]. "The Communist Manifesto." In Lawrence H. Simon, ed., *Karl Marx: Selected Writings*. Indianapolis: Hackett Publishing.

Masoud, Tarek. 2014. *Counting Islam: Religion, Class, and Elections in Egypt*. New York: Cambridge University Press.

Masoud, Tarek, Amaney Jamal, and Elizabeth Nugent. 2016. "Using the Qur'an to Empower Arab Women? Theory and Experimental Evidence from Egypt." *Comparative Political Studies* 49, 12: 1555–98.

Masud, Muhammad Khalid. 1995. *Shatibi's Philosophy of Islamic Law*. Islamabad: Islamic Research Institute.

Masudi. 1989 [947]. *The Meadows of Gold [Muruj al-Dhahab]: The Abbasids*. Partially translated by Paul Lunde and Caroline Stone. New York: Kegan Paul International.

Matthee, Rudi. 2012. *Persia in Crisis: Safavid Decline and the Fall of Isfahan*. New York: I. B. Tauris.

Mattson, Ingrid. 2000–1. "Review of *Al-Ahkam al-Sultaniyyah: The Laws of Islamic Governance* and *The Ordinances of Government: A Translation of Al-Ahkam al-Sultaniyya w'al-Wilayat al-Diniyya*." *Journal of Law and Religion* 15, 1–2: 399–403.

Maududi, Sayyid Abul A'la. 1960. *The Islamic Law and Constitution*. Translated from Urdu and edited by Khurshid Ahmad. Lahore: Islamic Publications.

Al-Mawardi. 2015 [1032–40]. *De l'éthique du Prince et du gouvernement de l'État* [*Ahlaq al-Malik wa Siyasat al-Mulk*]. Translated into French and edited by Makram Abbès. Paris: Les Belles Lettres.

1996 [1045–58]. *The Ordinances of Government: A Translation of Al-Ahkam al-Sultaniyya w'al-Wilayat al-Diniyya*. Translated by Wafaa H. Wahba. London: Garnet Publishing.

Mayer, Ann Elizabeth. 1995. "War and Peace in the Islamic Tradition and International Law." In John Kelsay and James Turner Johnson, eds., *Just War and Jihad: Historical and Theoretical Perspectives on War and Peace in Western and Islamic Traditions*. New York: Greenwood Press.

Mazrui, Ali A. 2007. "Human History as Divine Revelation: A Dialogue." In John J. Donohue and John L. Esposito, eds., *Islam in Transition: Muslim Perspectives*. New York: Oxford University Press.

McAuliffe, Jane Dammen. 1990. "Fakhr al-Din al-Razi on *ayat al-jizyah and ayat al-sayf*." In Michael Gervers and Ramzi Jibran Bikhazi, eds., *Conversion and Continuity: Indigenous Christian Communities in Islamic Lands, Eighth to Eighteenth Centuries*. Toronto: Pontifical Institute of Mediaeval Studies.

    2015. *The Norton Anthology of World Religions: Islam*. New York: W. W. Norton.

McCarthy, Justin. 1995. *Death and Exile: The Ethnic Cleansing of Ottoman Muslims, 1821–1922*. Princeton: Darwin Press.

McCarthy, Richard J. 1999. "Introduction." In Richard J. McCarthy, ed., *Freedom and Fulfillment. Deliverance from Error: Five Key Texts Including His Spiritual Autobiography, al-Munqidh min al-Dalal*. Louisville, KY: Fons Vitae.

McClellan, James E. III. 1985. *Science Reorganized: Scientific Societies in the Eighteenth Century*. New York: Columbia University Press.

McCloskey, Deirdre N. 2010. *Bourgeois Dignity: Why Economics Can't Explain the Modern World*. Chicago: University of Chicago Press.

    2016. *Bourgeois Equality: How Ideas, Not Capital or Institutions, Enriched the World*. Chicago: University of Chicago University Press.

McConnell, Michael W. 1990. "The Origins and Historical Understanding of Free Exercise of Religion." *Harvard Law Review* 103, 7: 1409–517.

McGowan, Bruce. 1994. "The Age of the Ayans, 1699–1812." In Halil İnalcık with Donald Quataert, eds., *An Economic and Social History of the Ottoman Empire. Vol. II: 1600–1914*. Cambridge: Cambridge University Press.

McIntosh, Gregory. 2000. *The Piri Reis Map of 1513*. Atlanta: University of Georgia Press.

McNeill, William H. 1991 [1963]. *The Rise of the West: A History of the Human Community*. Chicago: University of Chicago Press.

Mearsheimer, John J., and Stephen M. Walt. 2007. *The Israel Lobby and U.S. Foreign Policy*. New York: Farrar, Straus and Giroux.

Melchert, Christopher. 2006. *Ahmad ibn Hanbal*. Oxford: Oneworld.

Menchik, Jeremy. 2016. *Islam and Democracy in Indonesia: Tolerance without Liberalism*. New York: Cambridge University Press.

Menocal, Maria Rosa. 2002. *The Ornament of the World: How Muslims, Jews, and Christians Created a Culture of Tolerance in Medieval Spain*. New York: Little, Brown.

Meriç, Cemil. 1996. *Umrandan Uygarlığa*. Istanbul: İletişim.

Mernissi, Fatima. 1993. *The Forgotten Queens of Islam*. Translated by Mary Jo Lakeland. Minneapolis: University of Minnesota Press.

Meyerhof, Max. 2005 [1931]. "Science and Medicine." In Sir Thomas Arnold and Alfred Guillaume, eds., *The Legacy of Islam*. New Delhi: Aravali Books International.

    1935. "Ibn An-Nafîs (XIIIth Cent.) and His Theory of the Lesser Circulation." *Isis* 23, 1: 100–20.

Meyerhof, Max, and Joseph Schacht. 1968. "Introduction." In *The Theologus Auto-didactus of Ibn al-Nafis*. Translated, abridged, and edited by Max Meyerhof and Joseph Schacht. Oxford: Clarendon Press.

Mez, Adam. 1937. *The Renaissance of Islam*. Translated from German by Salahuddin Khuda Bakhsh and D. S. Margoliouth. Patna: Jubilee Printing and Publishing House.

Migdal, Joel S. 1988. *Strong Societies and Weak States: State–Society Relations and State Capabilities in the Third World*. New York: Cambridge University Press.

——— 2001. *State in Society: Studying How State and Societies Transform and Constitute One Another*. Cambridge: Cambridge University Press.

——— 2014. *Shifting Sands: The United States in the Middle East*. New York: Columbia University Press.

Miller, Jon. 2011. "Hugo Grotius." In Edward N. Zalta, ed., *The Stanford Encyclopedia of Philosophy*, July 28, https://plato.stanford.edu/archives/spr2014/entries/grotius.

Mir-Hosseini, Ziba. 2006. "Muslim Women's Quest for Equality: Between Islamic Law and Feminism." *Critical Inquiry* 32, 4: 629–45.

Miskawayh. 1968 [c. 1030]. *The Refinement of Character: A Translation from the Arabic of Ahmad ibn Muhammad Miskawayh's* Tahdhib al-Akhlaq. Translated by Constantine K. Zurayk. Beirut: American University of Beirut.

Mitha, Farouk. 2001. *Al-Ghazali and the Ismailis: A Debate on Reason and Authority in Medieval Islam*. London: I. B. Tauris.

Moghadem, Valentine M., and Namrata Mitra. 2013. "Women and Gender in the Muslim World." In Jeffrey T. Kenney and Ebrahim Moosa, eds., *Islam in the Modern World*. New York: Routledge.

Moin, Azfar A. 2012. *The Millennial Sovereign: Sacred Kingship and Sainthood in Islam*. New York: Columbia University Press.

Mokyr, Joel. 1990. *The Lever of Riches: Technological Creativity and Economic Progress*. New York: Oxford University Press.

——— 2006. "Christianity and the Rise of the West: Rodney Stark and the Defeat of Reason." *Historically Speaking* 7, 4: 12–4.

——— 2010. *The Enlightened Economy: An Economic History of Britain, 1700–1850*. New Haven: Yale University Press.

——— 2016. *A Culture of Growth: The Origins of the Modern Economy*. Princeton: Princeton University Press.

Momen, Moojan. 1985. *An Introduction to Shi'i Islam: The History and Doctrines of Twelver Shi'ism*. New Haven: Yale University Press.

Montesquieu. 1990 [1748]. *The Spirit of the Laws*. In *Selected Political Writings*. Abridged and translated from French by Melvin Richter. Indianapolis: Hackett Publishing.

Moore, Barrington. 1966. *Social Origins of Dictatorship and Democracy: Lord and Peasant in the Making of the Modern World*. Boston: Beacon Press.

Moosa, Ebrahim. 2003. "The Debts and Burdens of Critical Islam." In Omid Safi, ed., *Progressive Muslims: On Justice, Gender, and Pluralism*. Oxford: Oneworld.

——— 2005. *Ghazali and the Poetics of Imagination*. Chapel Hill: University of North Carolina Press.

——— 2014. "Muslim Political Theology: Defamation, Apostasy, and Anathema." In Christopher S. Grenda, Chris Beneke, and David Nash, eds., *Profane: Sacrilegious Expression in a Multicultural Age*. Berkeley: University of California Press.

2015. *What Is a Madrasa?* Chapel Hill: University of North Carolina Press.

Morony, Michael G. 1984. *Iraq after the Muslim Conquest*. Princeton: Princeton University Press.

  1999. "Review of Peter Christensen's *The Decline of Iranshahr: Irrigation and Environments in the History of the Middle East, 500 B.C. to A.D. 1500.*" *Iranian Studies* 32, 3: 421–3.

Morrison, Kevin M. 2009. "Oil, Nontax Revenue, and the Redistributional Foundations of Regime Stability." *International Organization* 63, 1: 107–38.

Morrison, Robert G. 2007. *Islam and Science: The Intellectual Career of Nizam al-Din Nisaburi*. New York: Routledge.

Mottahedeh, Roy P. 1980. *Loyalty and Leadership in an Early Islamic Society*. Princeton: Princeton University Press.

Mouline, Nabil. 2014. *The Clerics of Islam: Religious Authority and Political Power in Saudi Arabia*. Translated from French by Ethan S. Rundell. New Haven: Yale University Press.

Mousseau, Michael. 2011. "Urban Poverty and Support for Islamist Terror: Survey Results of Muslims in Fourteen Countries." *Journal of Peace Research* 48, 1: 35–47.

Moustafa, Tamir. 2000. "Conflict and Cooperation between the State and Religious Institutions in Contemporary Egypt." *International Journal of Middle East Studies* 32, 1: 3–22.

  2007. *The Struggle for Constitutional Power: Law, Politics, and Economic Development in Egypt*. New York: Cambridge University Press.

Munoz, Vincent Phillip. 2009. *God and the Founders: Madison, Washington, and Jefferson*. New York: Cambridge University Press.

Müteferrika, İbrahim. 1995 [1726]. "The Usefulness of Printing." In "Appendix: Ottoman Imperial Documents Relating to the History of Books and Printing." Translated from Ottoman Turkish by Christopher M. Murphy. In George N. Atiyeh, ed., *The Book in the Islamic World: The Written Word and Communication in the Middle East*. Albany: SUNY Press.

  1990 [1732]. *Milletlerin Düzeninde İlmi Usuller (Usul'ül-Hikem fi Nizam'il-Ümem)*. Edited by Ömer Okutan. Istanbul: Milli Eğitim Bakanlığı Yayınları.

Al-Nadim. 1970 [987]. *The Fihrist of al-Nadim: A Tenth-Century Survey of Muslim Culture*. Vols. I and II. Translated and edited by Bayard Dodge. New York: Columbia University Press.

Nadwi, Mohammad Akram. 2010. *Abu Hanifah: His Life, Legal Method and Legacy*. Oxford: Kube and Interface Publications.

An-Na'im, Abdullahi Ahmed. 2008. *Islam and the Secular State: Negotiating the Future of Shari'a*. Cambridge, MA: Harvard University Press.

Najjar, Fauzi M. 1996. "The Debate on Islam and Secularism in Egypt." *Arab Studies Quarterly* 18, 2: 1–21.

Nasr, Seyyed Hossein. 1976. *Islamic Science: An Illustrated Study*. London: World of Islam Festival Publishing.

Nasr, Seyyed Hossein, Caner K. Dagli, Maria Massi Dakake, Joseph B. Lumbard, and Mohammed Rustom, eds. 2015. *The Study Quran: A New Translation and Commentary*. New York: HarperOne.

Nasr, Seyyed Vali Reza. 1996. *Mawdudi and the Making of Islamic Revivalism*. New York: Oxford University Press.

The National Counterterrorism Center. 2012. "2011 Report on Terrorism," March 12, https://fas.org/irp/threat/nctc2011.pdf.

Nawas, John. 2013. "The Ulama as Autonomous Bearers of Religious Authority: Explaining Western Europe's Current Identity Problem with Islam." In Monique Bernards and Marjo Buitelaar, eds., *Negotiating Autonomy and Authority in Muslim Contexts*. Leuven: Peeters.

Needham, Joseph. 2004. *Science and Civilisation in China. Vol. 7, Part 2: General Conclusions and Reflections*. New York: Cambridge University Press.

Newman, Andrew J. 2001. "Fayd al-Kashani and the Rejection of the Clergy/State Alliance: Friday Prayer as Politics in the Safavid Period." In Linda S. Walbridge, ed., *The Most Learned of the Shi'a: The Institution of the Marja'Taqlid*. New York: Oxford University Press.

Newman, Daniel L. 2004. "Introduction." In Rifa'a Rafi' al-Tahtawi, *An Imam in Paris: Account of a Stay in France by an Egyptian Cleric (1826–1831)*. Translated and edited by Daniel L. Newman. London: Saqi.

Nisbet, Robert. 1980. *History of the Idea of Progress*. New York. Basic Books.

Nizam al-Mulk. 1978 [1086–91]. *The Book of Government or Rules for Kings. The Siyar al-Muluk or Siyasat-nama of Nizam al-Mulk*. Translated from Persian by Hubert Darke. Boston: Routledge and Kegan Paul.

North, Douglass C. 1990. *Institutions, Institutional Change and Economic Performance*. New York: Cambridge University Press.

1991. "Institutions." *The Journal of Economic Perspectives* 5, 1: 97–112.

North, Douglass C., and Robert Paul Thomas. 1973. *The Rise of the Western World: A New Economic History*. New York: Cambridge University Press.

North, Douglass C., and Barry R. Weingast. 1989. "Constitutions and Commitment: The Evolution of Institutions Governing Public Choice in Seventeenth-Century England." *The Journal of Economic History* 49, 4: 803–32.

Nursi, Bediüzzaman Said. 1996 [1929–34]. "Mektubat." In his *Risale-i Nur Külliyatı*. Istanbul: Nesil Yayıncılık.

Nusseibeh, Sari. 2016. *The Story of Reason in Islam*. Stanford: Stanford University Press.

Al-Nuwayri, Shibab al-Din. 2016 [c. 1333]. *The Ultimate Ambition in the Arts of Erudition [Nihayat al-Arab fi Funun al-Adab]: A Compendium of Knowledge from the Classical Islamic World*. Abridged and translated by Elias Muhanna. New York: Penguin Classics.

OECD. 2012. "PISA 2012 Results in Focus," www.oecd.org/pisa/keyfindings/pisa-2012-results-overview.pdf.

Ohlander, Erik S. 2008. *Sufism in an Age of Transition: 'Umar al-Suhrawardi and the Rise of the Islamic Mystical Brotherhoods*. Boston: Brill.

Okumuş, Ejder. 2008. *Osmanlı'nın Gözüyle İbn Haldun*. Istanbul: İz Yayıncılık.

Olson, Mancur. 1993. "Dictatorship, Democracy, and Development." *American Political Science Review* 87, 3: 567–76.

Opwis, Felicitas. 2010. *Maslaha and the Purpose of the Law: Islamic Discourse on Legal Change from the 4th/10th to 8th/14th Century*. Boston: Brill.

Ormsby, Eric. 2007. *Ghazali: The Revival of Islam*. Oxford: Oneworld.

Ortaylı, İlber. 1983. *İmparatorluğun En Uzun Yüzyılı*. Istanbul: Hil.

Osman, Ghada. 2011. *A Journey in Islamic Thought: The Life of Fathi Osman*. New York: I. B. Tauris.

Osterhammel, Jürgen. 2014. *The Transformation of the World: A Global History of the Nineteenth Century.* Translated from German by Patrick Camiller. Princeton: Princeton University Press.

Owen, Roger, and Şevket Pamuk. 1999. *A History of Middle East Economies in the Twentieth Century.* Cambridge, MA: Harvard University Press.

Özbudun, Ergun. 2012. "Secularism in Islamic Countries: Turkey as a Model." In Rainer Grote and Tilmann Röder, eds., *Constitutionalism in Islamic Countries: Between Upheaval and Continuity.* Oxford: Oxford University Press.

Özervarlı, M. Sait. 2015a. "Arbitrating between al-Ghazali and the Philosophers: The *Tahafut* Commentaries in the Ottoman Intellectual Context." In Georges Tamer, ed., *Islam and Rationality: The Impact of al-Ghazali.* Vol. I. Boston: Brill.

2015b. "Ottoman Perceptions of al-Ghazali's Works and Discussions on His Historical Role in Its Late Period." In Frank Griffel, ed., *Islam and Rationality: The Impact of al-Ghazali.* Vol. 2. Boston: Brill.

Özkan, Behlül. 2012. *From the Abode of Islam to the Turkish Vatan: The Making of a National Homeland in Turkey.* New Haven: Yale University Press.

Öztürk, Ahmet Erdi. 2016. "Turkey's Diyanet under AKP Rule: From Protector to Imposer of State Ideology?" *Southeast European and Black Sea Studies* 16, 4: 619–35.

Packer, George. 2006. "The Moderate Martyr: A Radically Peaceful Vision of Islam." *The New Yorker*, September 11.

Paine, Lincoln. 2013. *The Sea and Civilization: A Maritime History of the World.* New York: Vintage Books.

Palacios, Miguel Asin. 2008 [1919]. *Islam and the Divine Comedy.* Abridged and translated from Spanish by Harold Sutherland. New York: Routledge.

Pamuk, Şevket. 1987. *The Ottoman Empire and European Capitalism, 1820–1913: Trade, Investment, and Production.* New York: Cambridge University Press.

2004. "Institutional Change and the Longevity of the Ottoman Empire, 1500–1800." *Journal of Interdisciplinary History* 35, 2: 225–47.

Pape, Robert A. 2003. "The Strategic Logic of Suicide Terrorism." *American Political Science Review* 97, 3: 343–61.

Parens, Joshua. 1995. *Metaphysics as Rhetoric: Alfarabi's Summary of Plato's "Laws."* Albany: SUNY Press.

Parker, Geoffrey. 1996. *The Military Revolution: Military Innovation and the Rise of the West, 1500–1800.* New York: Cambridge University Press.

Parthasarathi, Prasannan. 2011. *Why Europe Grew Rich and Asia Did Not: Global Economic Divergence, 1600–1850.* New York: Cambridge University Press.

Paşa, Said Halim. 2012 [1919]. *Buhranlarımız ve Son Eserleri.* Edited by M. Ertuğrul Düzdağ. İstanbul: İz Yayıncılık.

Paşa, Ziya. 1987 [1870]. "Gazeliyyat." In Önder Göçgün, ed., *Ziya Paşa'nın Hayatı, Eserleri, Edebi Şahsiyeti ve Bütün Şiirleri.* Ankara: Kültür ve Turizm Bakanlığı Yayınları.

Pedersen, Johannes. 1984 [1946]. *The Arabic Book.* Translated from Danish by Geoffrey French. Princeton: Princeton University Press.

Perliger, Arie. 2015. "Comparative Framework for Understanding Jewish and Christian Violent Fundamentalism." *Religions* 6, 3: 1033–47.

Perlo-Freeman, Elisabeth Sköns, Carina Solmirano, and Helén Wilandh. 2013. "Stockholm International Peace Research Institute Fact Sheet: Trends in World Military Expenditure, 2012," April, http://books.sipri.org/files/FS/SIPRIFS1304.pdf.

Pew Research Center. 2009. "Mapping the Global Muslim Population: A Report on the Size and Distribution of the World's Muslim Population," October 1, www.pew forum.org/files/2009/10/Muslimpopulation.pdf.

2012. "Laws Penalizing Blasphemy, Apostasy and Defamation of Religion Are Widespread," November 21, www.pewforum.org/2012/11/21/laws-penalizing-blas phemy-apostasy-and-defamation-of-religion-are-widespread/#_ftn1.

2013. "The World's Muslims: Religion, Politics, and Society," April 30, www.pew forum.org/files/2013/04/worlds-muslims-religion-politics-society-full-report.pdf.

Philpott, Daniel. 2007. "Explaining the Political Ambivalence of Religion." *American Political Science Review* 101, 3: 505–25.

2019. *Religious Freedom in Islam: The Fate of a Universal Human Right in the Muslim World Today*. New York: Oxford University Press.

Pickthall, Mohammed Marmaduke. 2017 [1930]. *The Meaning of the Glorious Quran*. Revised by Jane McAuliffe. In Jane McAuliffe, ed., *The Qur'an*. New York: W. W. Norton.

Pierson, Paul. 2000. "Increasing Returns, Path Dependence, and the Study of Politics." *American Political Science Review* 94, 2: 251–67.

Piketty, Thomas. 2014. *Capital in the Twenty-First Century*. Translated by Arthur Goldhammer. Cambridge, MA: Harvard University Press.

Pines, S[holomo]. 1957. "English Summaries: Notes on Averroes' Political Philosophy." *Iyyun* 8: 126–8.

1975. "Aristotle's *Politics* in Arabic Philosophy." *Israel Oriental Studies* 5: 150–60.

Plato. 1945 [c. 380 BCE]. *The Republic*. Translated from ancient Greek by Francis MacDonald Conford. New York: Oxford University Press.

Platteau, Jean-Philippe. 2017. *Islam Instrumentalized: Religion and Politics in Historical Perspective*. New York: Cambridge University Press.

Polity. 2010. "Polity IV: Country Reports 2010," December, www.systemicpeace.org/ polity/polity06.htm.

Pomeranz, Kenneth. 2000. *The Great Divergence: China, Europe, and the Making of the Modern World Economy*. Princeton: Princeton University Press.

Pormann, Peter E., and Emilie Savage-Smith. 2007. *Medieval Islamic Medicine*. Washington, DC: Georgetown University Press.

Powers, David S. 1989. "Orientalism, Colonialism, and Legal History: The Attack on Muslim Family Endowments in Algeria and India." *Comparative Studies in Society and History* 31, 3: 535–71.

Prince, Chris. 2002. "The Historical Context of Arabic Translation, Learning, and the Libraries of Medieval Andalusia." *Library History* 18, 2: 73–87.

Proudfoot, I[an]. 1995. "Early Muslim Printing in Southeast Asia." *Libri* (Copenhagen) 45, 3–4: 216–23.

Provence, Michael. 2017. *The Last Ottoman Generation and the Making of the Modern Middle East*. New York: Cambridge University Press.

Przeworski, Adam, and Fernando Limongi. 1997. "Modernization: Theories and Facts." *World Politics* 49, 2: 155–83.

Przeworski, Adam, Michael E. Alvarez, Jose Antonio Cheibub, and Fernando Limongi. 2000. *Democracy and Development: Political Institutions and Well-Being in the World, 1950–1990*. New York: Cambridge University Press.

Putnam, Robert D. 1993. *Making Democracy Work: Civic Traditions in Modern Italy.* Princeton: Princeton University Press.

Qadhi, Abu Ammar Yasir. 1999. *An Introduction to the Sciences of the Qur'an.* Birmingham: Al-Hidaayah Publishing.

Al-Qaradawi, Yusuf. 2007 [2003]. "Suicide Bombers Are Martyrs." In John J. Donohue and John L. Esposito, eds., *Islam in Transition: Muslim Perspectives.* New York: Oxford University Press.

Quandt, William B. 2005. *Peace Process: American Diplomacy and the Arab-Israeli Conflict since 1967.* Washington, DC: Brookings Institution.

Quataert, Donald. 1994. "The Age of Reforms, 1812–1914." In Halil İnalcık with Donald Quataert, eds., *An Economic and Social History of the Ottoman Empire. Vol. II: 1600–1914.* Cambridge: Cambridge University Press.

2005. *The Ottoman Empire, 1700–1922.* New York: Cambridge University Press.

Quraishi, Asifa. 1997. "Her Honor: An Islamic Critique of the Rape Laws of Pakistan from a Woman-Sensitive Perspective." *Michigan Journal of International Law* 18, 2: 287–320.

Qutb, Sayyid. 2002 [1964]. *Milestones.* (Anonymous translation.) New Delhi: Islamic Book Service.

Radhan, Luay. 2014. *Muslims against the Islamic State: Arab Critics and Supporters of Ali Abdarraziq's Islamic Laicism.* New York: PL Academic Research.

Rady, Martyn. 2017. *The Habsburg Empire: A Very Short Introduction.* New York: Oxford University Press.

Ragab, Ahmed. 2015. *The Medieval Islamic Hospital: Medicine, Religion, and Charity.* New York: Cambridge University Press.

Ragep, F. Jamil. 2007a. "Copernicus and His Islamic Predecessors: Some Historical Remarks." *History of Science* 45, 1: 65–81.

2007b. "Shirazi: Qutb al-Din Mahmud ibn Mas'ud Muslih al-Shirazi." In Thomas Hockey et al., eds., *The Biographical Encyclopedia of Astronomers.* New York: Springer.

Rahim, Lily Zubaidah. 2013. *Muslim Secular Democracy: Voices from Within.* New York: Palgrave Macmillan.

Rahman, Fazlur. 1965. *Islamic Methodology in History.* Karachi: Central Institute of Islamic Research.

1968. *Islam.* New York: Anchor Books.

1982. *Islam and Modernity: Transformation of an Intellectual Tradition.* Chicago: University of Chicago Press.

2000. *Revival and Reform in Islam: A Study of Islamic Fundamentalism.* Edited by Ebrahim Moosa. Oxford: Oneworld.

Ramadan, Tariq. 2003. *Western Muslims and The Future of Islam.* New York: Oxford University Press.

2009. *Radical Reform: Islamic Ethics and Liberation.* New York: Oxford University Press.

Al-Rasheed, Madawi. 2002. *A History of Saudi Arabia.* New York: Cambridge University Press.

Rashid, Ahmed. 2002. *Jihad: The Rise of Militant Islam in Central Asia.* New Haven: Yale University Press.

Raymond, Andre. 1979–80. "The Ottoman Conquest and the Development of the Great Arab Towns." *International Journal of Turkish Studies* 1, 1: 84–101.

Al-Raysuni, Ahmad. 2005. *Imam al-Shatibi's Theory of the Higher Objectives and Intents of Islamic Law.* Translated by Nancy Roberts. Washington, DC: International Institute of Islamic Thought.

Regan, Patrick M., and Daniel Norton Greed. 2005. "Greed, Grievance, and Mobilization in Civil Wars." *Journal of Conflict Resolution* 49, 3: 319–36.

Reid, Anthony. 1993a. *Southeast Asia in the Age of Commerce 1450–1680. Vol. II: Expansion and Crisis.* New Haven: Yale University Press.

    1993b. "Islamization and Christianization in Southeast Asia: The Critical Phase, 1550–1650." In Anthony Reid, ed., *Southeast Asia in the Early Modern Era: Trade, Power, and Belief.* Ithaca, NY: Cornell University Press.

Reis, Piri. 2013 [1521]. *Kitab-ı Bahriye.* In *Piri Reis: The Book of Bahriye.* Translated from Ottoman Turkish by E. Ökte and T. Duran. Edited by Bülent Özükan. Istanbul: Boyut.

Renan, Ernest. 1882 [1852]. *Averroès et l'averroïsme: Essai historique.* Paris: Calmann-Lévy.

    1883. *L'Islamisme et la science: Conférence faite à la Sorbonne, le 20 mars 1883.* Paris: Calmann Levy.

Revenue Watch. 2011. "Extractive Industries Transparency Initiative Report Summaries," http://data.revenuewatch.org/eiti/all.php?i%5B%5D1/40&i%5B%5D1/411&þSubmitþ1/4Submit.

Reynolds, Michael A. 2011. *Shattering Empires: The Clash and Collapse of the Ottoman and Russian Empires, 1908–1918.* New York: Cambridge University Press.

Robinson, Francis. 1997. "Ottomans–Safavids–Mughals: Shared Knowledge and Connective Systems." *Journal of Islamic Studies* 8, 2: 151–84.

Robinson, Glenn. 2004. "Hamas as Social Movement." In Quintan Wiktorowicz, ed., *Islamic Activism: A Social Movement Theory Approach.* Bloomington: Indiana University Press.

Rodinson, Maxime. 2004 [1966]. *Islam and Capitalism.* Translated from French by Brian Pearce. San Francisco: Saqi Essentials.

Rogan, Eugene. 2004. "Arab Books and Human Development." *Arab Studies Quarterly* 26, 2: 67–79.

    2009. *The Arabs: A History.* New York: Basic Books.

Rosenthal, Erwin I. J. 1958. *Political Thought in Medieval Islam: An Introductory Outline.* Cambridge University Press.

    1966. "Introduction" and "Notes." In *Averroes' Commentary on Plato's Republic.* Translated and edited by E. I. J. Rosenthal. New York: Cambridge University Press.

Ross, Michael L. 2001. "Does Oil Hinder Democracy?" *World Politics* 53, 3: 325–61.

    2008. "Oil, Islam, and Women." *American Political Science Review* 102, 1: 107–23.

    2012. *The Oil Curse: How Petroleum Wealth Shapes the Development of Nations.* Princeton: Princeton University Press.

Rossabi, Morris. 1990. "The 'Decline' of the Central Asian Caravan Trade." In James D. Tracy, ed., *The Rise of Merchant Empires: Long-Distance Trade in the Early Modern World, 1350–1750.* New York: Cambridge University Press.

El-Rouayheb, Khaled. 2010. *Relational Syllogisms and the History of Arabic Logic, 900–1900.* Leiden: Brill.

    2015. *Islamic Intellectual History in the Seventeenth Century: Scholarly Currents in the Ottoman Empire and the Maghreb.* New York: Cambridge University Press.

Rousseau, Jean-Jacques. 1992 [1755]. *Discourse on the Origin of Inequality.* Translated by Donald A. Cress. Indianapolis: Hackett Publishing.
    2001 [1762]. *Du contrat social.* Paris: GF Flammarion.
Rowley, Charles, and Nathanael Smith. 2009. "Islam's Democracy Paradox: Muslims Claim to Like Democracy, So Why Do They Have So Little?" *Public Choice* 139, 3: 273–99.
Roy, Olivier. 1996. *The Failure of Political Islam.* Cambridge, MA: Harvard University Press.
Rubin, Jared. 2017. *Rulers, Religion, and Riches: Why the West Got Rich and the Middle East Did Not.* New York: Cambridge University Press.
Rudolph, Ulrich. 2015. *Al-Maturidi and the Development of Sunni Theology in Samarqand.* Translated from German by Rodrigo Adem. Boston: Brill.
    2016. *Semerkant'ta Ehl-i Sünnet Kelamı: Maturidi.* Translated from German to Turkish by Özcan Taşçı. Istanbul: Litera Yayıncılık.
Rumi. 2004 [1258–73]. *The Mathnawi of Jalalu'ddin Rumi.* Vols. I–VI. Translated from Persian by Reynold A. Nicholson. Konya: Konya Metropolitan Municipality.
Runciman, Steven. 1951. *A History of the Crusades. Vol. I: The First Crusade and the Foundation of the Kingdom of Jerusalem.* Cambridge: Cambridge University Press.
    1954. *A History of the Crusades. Vol. III: The Kingdom of Acre and the Later Crusades.* Cambridge: Cambridge University Press.
    1959. "Muslim Influences on the Development of European Civilization." *Şarkiyat Mecmuası* 3: 13–24.
Russell, G[ül] A. 1994. "The Impact of the *Philosophus autodidactus*: Pocockes, John Locke, and the Society of Friends." In G. A. Russell, ed., *The "Arabick" Interest of the Natural Philosophers in Seventeenth-Century England.* New York: Brill.
Russett, Bruce. 1993. *Grasping the Democratic Peace: Principles for a Post–Cold War World.* Princeton: Princeton University Press.
Saadi. 2013 [c. 1258]. *Advice to the Kings [Nasihat al-Muluk].* Translated from Persian by Alireza Shomali and Mehrzad Boroujerdi. In Shomali and Boroujerdi, "Sa'di's Treatise on Advice to the Kings." In Mehrzad Boroujerdi, ed., *Mirror for the Muslim Prince: Islam and the Theory of Statecraft.* Syracuse: Syracuse University Press.
Sabev, Orlin. 2006. *İbrahim Müteferrika ya da İlk Osmanlı Matbaa Serüveni (1726–1746): Yeniden Değerlendirme.* Istanbul: Yeditepe Yayınevi.
Sabra, A[bdelhamid] I. 1987. "The Appropriation and Subsequent Naturalization of Greek Science in Medieval Islam: A Preliminary Statement." *History of Science* 25, 3: 223–43.
    1996. "Situating Arabic Science: Locality versus Essence." *Isis* 87, 4: 654–70.
Es-Sabuni, Nureddin [Ahmad ibn Mahmud]. 1995 [c. 1184]. *Matüridiyye Akaidi [al-Bidaya fi Usul al-Din].* Translated into Turkish by Bekir Topaloğlu. Ankara: Diyanet İşleri Başkanlığı.
Sachedina, Abdulaziz. 2001. *The Islamic Roots of Democratic Pluralism.* New York: Oxford University Press.
Saeed, Abdullah, and Hassan Saeed. 2004. *Freedom of Religion, Apostasy and Islam.* New York: Routledge.
Saeed, Sadia. 2016. *Politics of Desecularization: Law and the Minority Question in Pakistan.* New York: Cambridge University Press.

Safaouan, Moustapha. 2010. *Why Are the Arabs Not Free? The Politics of Writing.* Oxford: Blackwell Publishing.

Safi, Omid. 2006. *The Politics of Knowledge in Premodern Islam: Negotiating Ideology and Religious Inquiry.* Chapel Hill: University of North Carolina Press.

Şahin, Zeynep. 2011. "The Political Representation of Kurdish, Kemalist, and Conservative Muslim Women in Turkey (1990–2010)." PhD dissertation. University of Southern California, Los Angeles.

Said, Edward W. 1979. *Orientalism.* New York: Vintage Books.

Said, Yazeed. 2013. *Ghazali's Politics in Context.* New York: Routledge.

Saint Pierre, J. H. Bernardin de. 1775. *A Voyage to the Isle of Mauritius, the Isle of Bourbon, and the Cape of Good Hope: With Observations and Reflections upon Nature and Mankind.* Translation from French by John Parish. London: W. Griffin.

Salame, Ghassan. 1990. "'Strong' and 'Weak' States: A Qualified Return to the *Muqaddimah.*" In Giacomo Luciani, ed., *The Arab State.* Berkeley: University of California Press.

Saliba, George. 2007. *Islamic Science and the Making of the European Renaissance.* Cambridge, MA: MIT Press.

Salt, Jeremy. 2009. *The Unmaking of the Middle East: A History of Western Disorder in Arab Lands.* Berkeley: University of California Press.

Sardar, Ziauddin. 2013. "Return to Al-Andulus." *Critical Muslim* 6: 3–23.

2014. *Mecca: The Sacred City.* London: Bloomsbury.

Sarton, George. 1927. *Introduction to the History of Science. Vol. I: From Homer to Omar Khayyam.* Baltimore: Williams and Wilkins.

1931. *Introduction to the History of Science. Vol. II: From Rabbi Ben Ezra to Roger Bacon.* Baltimore: Williams and Wilkins.

1947. *Introduction to the History of Science. Vol. III: Science and Learning in the Fourteenth Century.* Baltimore: Williams and Wilkins.

Sartori, Giovanni. 1970. "Concept Misformation in Comparative Politics." *American Political Science Review* 64, 4: 1033–53.

Saunders, J[ohn] J. 1963. "The Problem of Islamic Decadence." *Cahiers d'histoire mondiale. Journal of World History* 7, 3: 701–20.

1966. "The Review of Muhsin Mahdi's *Ibn Khaldûn's Philosophy of History.*" *History and Theory* 5, 3: 342–7.

1977. *Muslims and Mongols: Essays on Medieval Asia.* Edited by G. W. Rice. Christchurch: University of Canterbury.

Savage-Smith, Emilie. 1995. "Attitudes toward Dissection in Medieval Islam." *Journal of the History of Medicine and Allied Sciences* 50, 1: 67–110.

Sayar, Ahmed Güner. 1986. *Osmanlı İktisat Düşüncesinin Çağdaşlaşması: Klasik Dönem'den II. Abdülhamid'e.* Istanbul: Der Yayınları.

Sayılı, Aydın. 1960. *The Observatory in Islam and Its Place in the General History of the Observatory.* Ankara: Türk Tarih Kurumu Basımevi.

Schacht, Joseph. 1964. *An Introduction to Islamic Law.* Oxford: Clarendon Press.

Schimmel, Annemarie. 1975. *Mystical Dimensions of Islam.* Chapel Hill: University of North Carolina Press.

Schwarz, Michael. 2002. "Review of Frank Griffel's *Apostasie und Toleranz.*" *Jerusalem Studies in Arabic and Islam* 27: 591–601.

Scott, James C. 1998. *Seeing Like a State: How Certain Schemes to Improve the Human Condition Have Failed.* New Haven: Yale University Press.

Sen, Amartya. 1999. *Development as Freedom.* New York: Alfred A. Knopf.

Sen, S[amarendra] N. 1971a. "A Survey of Source Materials." In D. M. Bose, S. N. Sen, and B. V. Subbarayappa, eds., *A Concise History of Science in India.* New Delhi: Indian National Science Academy.

1971b. "Astronomy." In D. M. Bose, S. N. Sen, and B. V. Subbarayappa, eds., *A Concise History of Science in India.* New Delhi: Indian National Science Academy.

Sezgin, Fuat. 2011a. *Science and Technology in Islam. Vol. I: Introduction to the History of Arabic-Islamic Sciences.* Translated from German by Renate Sarma and Sreeramula R. Sarma. Frankfurt: Institute for the History of Arabic-Islamic Science.

2011b. *Science and Technology in Islam. Vol. II: Catalogue of the Instruments: Astronomy.* Translated from German by Renate Sarma and Sreeramula R. Sarma. Frankfurt: Institute for the History of Arabic-Islamic Science.

2011c. *Science and Technology in Islam. Vol. III: Catalogue of the Instruments: Geography, Navigation, Clocks, Geometry, and Optics.* Translated from German by Renate Sarma and Sreeramula R. Sarma. Frankfurt: Institute for the History of Arabic-Islamic Science.

Sezgin, Yüksel. 2013. *Human Rights under State-Enforced Religious Family Laws in Israel, Egypt and India.* New York: Cambridge University Press.

Shahrastani, Muhammad b. 'Abd al-Karim. 1984 [c. 1127–8]. *Muslim Sects and Divisions. The Section on Muslim Sects in* Kitab al-Milal wa'l-Nihal. Translated by A. K. Kazi and J. G. Flynn. Boston: Kegan Paul International.

1986 [c. 1127–8]. *Livre des religions et des sects. Vol. I [Kitab al-Milal wa'l-Nihal].* Translated into French by Daniel Gimaret and Guy Monnot. Paris: Peeters, UNESCO.

Shaltut, Mahmud. 2005 [1948]. "A Modernist Interpretation of Jihad: Mahmud Shaltut's Treatise *Koran and Fighting.*" Translated and abridged by Rudolph Peters. In Rudolph Peters, ed., *Jihad in Classical and Modern Islam: A Reader.* Princeton: Markus Wiener Publishers.

Shatzmiller, Maya. 1993. *Labour in the Medieval Islamic World.* Leiden: Brill.

2000. "Tidjara." In P. J. Bearman et al., eds., *The Encyclopedia of Islam, New Edition.* Vol. X. Leiden: Brill.

2011. "Economic Performance and Economic Growth in the Early Islamic World." *Journal of the Economic and Social History of the Orient* 54, 2: 132–84.

2013. "Review of Ronnie Ellenblum's *The Collapse of the Eastern Mediterranean. Climate Change and the Decline of the East 950–1072.*" *Der Islam* 90, 1: 192–5.

Shaykhutdinov, Renat. 2011. "Education for Peace: Protest Strategies of Ethnic Resistance Movements." *Journal of Peace Education* 8, 2: 143–55.

Shepard, Todd. 2006. *The Invention of Decolonization: The Algerian War and the Remaking of France.* Ithaca, NY: Cornell University Press.

Skocpol, Theda. 1979. *States and Social Revolutions: A Comparative Analysis of France, Russia, and China.* New York: Cambridge University Press.

Sloterdijk, Peter. 2012. *Rage and Time: A Psychopolitical Investigation.* Translated from German by Mario Wenning. New York: Columbia University Press.

Smith, Adam. 1993 [1776]. *An Inquiry into the Nature and Causes of the Wealth of Nations*. Abridged and edited by Laurence Dickey. Indianapolis: Hackett Publishing.

Smith, Anthony D. 1993. *National Identity*. Reno: University of Nevada Press.

Smith, Christian. 2003. "Introduction: Rethinking the Secularization of American Public Life." In Christian Smith, ed., *The Secular Revolution: Power, Interests, and Conflict in the Secularization of American Public Life*. Berkeley: University of California Press.

Smith, John Masson Jr. 1975. "Mongol Manpower and Persian Population." *Journal of the Economic and Social History of the Orient* 18, 3: 271–99.

Solingen, Etel. 2007. "Pax Asiatica versus Bella Levantina: The Foundations of War and Peace in East Asia and the Middle East." *American Political Science Review* 101, 4: 757–80.

Somel, Selçuk Akşin. 2001. *The Modernization of Public Education in the Ottoman Empire, 1839–1908: Islamization, Autocracy, and Discipline*. Leiden: Brill.

Sorli, Mirjam E., Nils Petter Gleditsch, and Havard Strand. 2005. "Why Is There So Much Conflict in the Middle East?" *Journal of Conflict Resolution* 49, 1: 141–65.

Soroush, Abdolkarim. 2000. *Reason, Freedom and Democracy in Iran: Essential Writings of Abdolkarim Soroush*. Translated from Persian and edited by Mahmoud Sadri and Ahmad Sadri. New York: Oxford University Press.

Soucek, Svat. 1994. "Piri Reis and Ottoman Discovery of the Great Discoveries." *Studia Islamica* 79: 121–42.

2000. *A History of Inner Asia*. New York: Cambridge University Press.

Southern, R[ichard] W. 1970. *Western Society and the Church in the Middle Ages*. New York: Penguin Books.

Spellberg, D. A. 1994. *Politics, Gender, and the Islamic Past: The Legacy of 'A'isha bint Abi Bakr*. New York: Columbia University Press.

Spengler, Joseph J. 1964. "Economic Thought of Islam: Ibn Khaldun." *Comparative Studies in Society and History* 6, 3: 268–306.

Spruyt, Hendrik. 1994. *The Sovereign State and Its Competitors*. Princeton: Princeton University Press.

Stahnke, Tad, and Robert C. Blitt. 2005. "The Religion–State Relationship and the Right to Freedom of Religion or Belief: A Comparative Textual Analysis of the Constitutions of Predominantly Muslim Countries." *Georgetown Journal of International Law* 36, 4: 947–1078.

Stark, Rodney. 2005. *The Victory of Reason: How Christianity Led to Freedom, Capitalism, and Western Success*. New York: Random House.

Starr, S. Frederick. 2009. "Rediscovering Central Asia." *The Wilson Quarterly* 33, 2: 33–43.

2013. *Lost Enlightenment: Central Asia's Golden Age from the Arab Conquest to Tamerlane*. Princeton: Princeton University Press.

Stepan, Alfred. 2001. *Arguing Comparative Politics*. New York: Oxford University Press.

2012. "Rituals of Respect: Sufis and Secularists in Senegal in Comparative Perspective." *Comparative Politics* 44, 4: 379–401.

Stepan, Alfred, with Graeme B. Robertson. 2003. "An 'Arab' More than 'Muslim' Electoral Gap." *Journal of Democracy* 14, 3: 30–44.

2004. "Arab, Not Muslim, Exceptionalism." *Journal of Democracy* 15, 4: 140–6.

Stephens, John D., Dietrich Rueschemeyer, and Evelyne Huber Stephens. 1992. *Capitalist Development and Democracy*. Chicago: University of Chicago Press.

Subtelny, Maria Eva, and Anas B. Khalidov. 1995. "The Curriculum of Islamic Higher Learning in Timurid Iran in the Light of the Sunni Revival under Shah-Rukh." *Journal of the American Oriental Society* 115, 2: 210–36.

Swain, Simon. 2013. *Economy, Family, and Society from Rome to Islam: A Critical Edition, English Translation, and Study of Bryson's Management of the Estate*. New York: Cambridge University Press.

Szyliowicz, Joseph S. 1992. "Functionalist Perspectives on Technology: The Case of Printing Press in the Ottoman Empire." In Ekmeleddin İhsanoğlu, ed., *Transfer of Modern Science and Technology to the Muslim World*. Istanbul: Research Centre for Islamic History, Art and Culture.

Tabak, Faruk. 2008. *The Waning of the Mediterranean, 1550–1870: A Geohistorical Approach*. Baltimore: Johns Hopkins University Press.

Al-Tabari. 1996 [c. 915]. *The History of al-Tabari (Ta'rikh al-Rusul wa'l-Muluk). Vol. XVII: The First Civil War; Vol. XVIII: Between Civil Wars. The Caliphate of Mu'awiyah; Vol. XIX: The Caliphate of Yazid b. Mu'awiyah*. Translated by G. R. Hawting, Michael G Morony, and I. K. A. Howard. Albany: SUNY Press.

Tabatabai, Javad. 2013. "An Anomaly in the History of Persian Political Thought." In Mehrzad Boroujerdi, ed., *Mirror for the Muslim Prince: Islam and the Theory of Statecraft*. Syracuse: Syracuse University Press.

Tabbaa, Yasser. 1997. *Constructions of Power and Piety in Medieval Aleppo*. University Park: Pennsylvania State University Press.

Taha, Mahmoud Mohamed. 1987. *The Second Message of Islam*. Translated by Abdullahi Ahmed AnNa'im. Syracuse: Syracuse University Press.

Takiyüddin. 1966 [1556]. *Mekanik Saat Konstrüksüyonuna Dair En Parlak Yıldızlar*. Translated into Turkish and edited by Sevim Tekeli. In *16'ıncı Asırda Osmanlılarda Saat ve Takiyüddin'in "Mekanik Saat Konstrüksüyonuna Dair En Parlak Yıldızlar" Adlı Eseri*. Ankara: Ankara Üniversitesi Basımevi.

Talbi, M[ohamed]. 1971. "Ibn Khaldun." In Bernard Lewis et al., eds., *Encyclopedia of Islam, New Edition*. Vol. III. Leiden: Brill.

Tarih-i Hind-i Garbi. 1990 [1580]. Translated from Ottoman Turkish by Thomas D. Goodrich. In *The Ottoman Turks and the New World: A Study of* Tarih-i Hind-i Garbi *and Sixteenth-Century Ottoman Americana*. Wiesbaden: Otto Harrassowitz.

Teicher, J[acob] L. 1960. "Review of E. I. J. Rosenthal's translation of *Averroes' Commentary on Plato's 'Republic.'" Journal of Semitic Studies* 5: 176–95.

Tekeli, Sevim. 1966. "Giriş." In Sevim Tekeli, ed., *16'ıncı Asırda Osmanlılarda Saat ve Takiyüddin'in "Mekanik Saat Konstrüksüyonuna Dair En Parlak Yıldızlar" Adlı Eseri*. Ankara: Ankara Üniversitesi Basımevi.

1985. *İlk Japon Haritasını Çizen Türk Kasgarlı Mahmud ve Kristof Kolomb'un Haritasına Dayanarak En Eski Amerika Haritasını Çizen Türk Amiralı Piri Reis*. Ankara: Atatürk Kültür Merkezi.

Temo, İbrahim. 1987 [1939]. *İbrahim Temo'nun İttihad ve Terakki Anıları*. Istanbul: Arba.

Tessler, Mark. 2015. *Islam and Politics in the Middle East: Explaining the Views of Ordinary Citizens*. Bloomington: Indiana University Press.

"Le Testament d'Ardasir." 1966 [n.a.]. Arabic-French text edited and translated by M. Grignaschi. In "Quelques spécimens de la littérature sassanide conservés dans les bibliothèqes d'Istanbul." *Journal Asiatique* 254: 46–90.

Tezcan, Baki. 2010. *The Second Ottoman Empire: Political and Social Transformation in the Early Modern World*. New York: Cambridge University Press.

Tezcür, Güneş Murat. 2016. "Ordinary People, Extraordinary Risks: Participation in an Ethnic Rebellion." *American Political Science Review* 110, 2: 247–64.

Thelen, Kathleen. 2000. "Timing and Temporality in the Analysis of Institutional Evolution and Change." *Studies in American Political Development* 14, 1: 101–8.

Tierney, Brian. 1988. *The Crisis of Church and State: 1050–1300*. Toronto: University of Toronto Press.

Tilly, Charles. 1992. *Coercion, Capital, and European States: AD 990–1992*. Cambridge, MA: Blackwell.

Timur, Taner. 1979. *Osmanlı Toplumsal Düzeni: Kuruluş ve Yükseliş Dönemi*. Ankara: Turhan Kitabevi.

1986. *Osmanlı Kimliği*. Istanbul: Hil Yayın.

Tocqueville, Alexis de. 2000 [1835]. *Democracy in America*. Translated by George Lawrence. Edited by J. P. Mayer. New York: Perennial Classics.

1983 [1858]. *The Old Regime and the French Revolution*. Translated by Stuart Gilbert. New York: Anchor Books.

Toft, Monica Duffy. 2007. "Getting Religion? The Puzzling Case of Islam and Civil War." *International Security* 31, 4: 97–131.

Togan, Zeki Velidi. 1942–7. *Bugünkü Türkili (Türkistan) ve Yakın Tarihi*. Istanbul: Arkadaş, İbrahim Horoz ve Güven Basımevleri.

1964. "The Earliest Translation of the Qur'an into Turkish." *İslam Tetkikleri Enstitüsü Dergisi/Review of the Institute of Islamic Studies* 4: 1–19.

Transparency International. 2013. "2013 Corruption Perception Index," http://cpi .transparency.org/cpi2013/.

Trimingham, J. Spencer. 1971. *The Sufi Orders in Islam*. New York: Oxford University Press.

Tsui, Kevin. 2011. "More Oil, Less Democracy: Evidence from Worldwide Crude Oil Discoveries." *The Economic Journal* 121, 551: 89–115.

Tuna, Mustafa. 2015. *Imperial Russia's Muslims: Islam, Empire, and European Modernity, 1788–1914*. New York: Cambridge University Press.

Türker, Muhabat. 1956. *Üç Tehafüt Bakımından Felsefe ve Din Münasebeti*. Ankara: Ankara Üniversitesi DTCF Yayınları.

Türköne, Mümtazer. 1991. *Siyasi İdeoloji Olarak İslamcılığın Doğuşu*. İstanbul: İletişim.

Turner, Bryan S. 1974. *Weber and Islam: A Critical Study*. Boston: Routledge.

2013a. "Introduction to Section I: Classical Approaches – Understanding Islam." In Bryan S. Turner and Kamaludeen Mohamed Nasir, eds., *The Sociology of Islam: Collected Essays of Bryan S. Turner*. Burlington, VT: Ashgate.

2013b. "State, Science and Economy in Traditional Societies: Some Problems in Weberian Sociology of Science." In Bryan S. Turner and Kamaludeen Mohamed Nasir, eds., *The Sociology of Islam: Collected Essays of Bryan S. Turner*. Burlington, VT: Ashgate.

Turner, Howard R. 1995. *Science in Medieval Islam: An Illustrated Introduction*. Austin: University of Texas Press.

Tusi, Nasr al-Din. 1964 [c. 1235]. *The Nasirean Ethics [Akhlaq-i Nasiri]*. Translated from Persian with notes by G. M. Wickens. London: George Allen and Unwin.

Tyerman, Christopher. 2006. *God's War: A New History of the Crusades*. Cambridge, MA: Belknap Press of Harvard University Press.

Udovitch, Abraham L. 1975. "Reflections on the Institutions of Credits and Banking in the Medieval Islamic Near East." *Studia Islamica* 41: 5–21.

 1979. "Bankers without Banks: Commerce, Banking, and Society in the Islamic World of the Middle Ages." In Fredi Chiappelli, ed., *The Dawn of Modern Banking*. New Haven: Yale University Press.

Ulfelder, Jay. 2007. "Natural-Resource Wealth and the Survival of Autocracy." *Comparative Political Studies* 40, 8: 995–1018.

Ülgener, Sabri. 1981. *İktisadi Çözülmenin Ahlak ve Zihniyet Dünyası*. Istanbul: Der Yayınları.

Ülken, Hilmi Ziya. 2016 [1935]. *Uyanış Devirlerinde Tercümenin Rolü*. Istanbul: Türkiye İş Bankası Kültür Yayınları.

 1966. *Türkiye'de Çağdaş Düşünce Tarihi*. Istanbul: Ülken Yayınları.

Unat, Faik Reşit. 1964. *Türkiye Eğitim Sisteminin Gelişmesine Tarihi Bir Bakış*. Ankara: Milli Eğitim Basımevi.

United Nations. 2016. "National Accounts Main Aggregates Database: GNI (at Current Prices) in US Dollars: All Countries for All Years," http://unstats.un.org/unsd/snaama/dnllist.asp.

United Nations Development Programme. 2011. "Human Development Index 2011," http://hdr.undp.org/en/media/HDR_2011_EN_Table1.pdf.

United Nations Development Programme (and Arab Fund for Economic and Social Development). 2002. *Arab Human Development Report 2002: Creating Opportunities for Future Generations*. Jordan: UNDP Regional Bureau for Arab States.

United Nations Statistics Division. 2013. "Social Indicators: Education, Literacy," http://unstats.un.org/unsd/demographic/products/socind/.

United States Census Bureau 2010. "International Data Base (2010)," www.census.gov/data-tools/demo/idb/informationGateway.php.

Ünver, A. Süheyl. 1969. *İstanbul Rasathanesi*. Ankara: Türk Tarih Kurumu Yayınları.

Urdal, Henrik. 2004. "The Devil in the Demographics: The Effect of Youth Bulges on Domestic Armed Conflict, 1950–2000." *World Bank, Social Development Papers: Conflict Prevention and Reconstruction* 14: 1–23.

US Department of State. 2015. "International Religious Freedom Report for 2014," October 14, www.state.gov/j/drl/rls/irf/2015religiousfreedom/index.htm#wrapper.

Uzunçarşılı, İsmail Hakkı. 1983. *Osmanlı Tarihi. II. Cild*. Ankara: Türk Tarih Kurumu Yayınları.

Van den Bergh, Simon. 1954. "Introduction" and "Notes." In *Averroes' Tahafut Al-Tahafut (The Incoherence of the Incoherence)*. Vols. I and II. Translated and edited by Simon van den Bergh. London: E. J. W. Gibb Memorial Trust.

Van Zanden, Jan Luiten. 2009. *The Long Road to the Industrial Revolution: The European Economy in a Global Perspective, 1000–1800*. Leiden: Brill.

Van Zanden, Jan Luiten, Eltjo Buringh, and Maarten Bosker. 2012. "The Rise and Decline of European Parliaments, 1188–1789." *The Economic History Review* 65, 3: 835–61.

Vasalou, Sophia. 2016. *Ibn Taymiyya's Theological Ethics*. New York: Oxford University Press.

Vikor, Knut S. 2005. *Between God and the Sultan: A History of Islamic Law*. New York: Oxford University Press.

Wadud, Amina. 1999. *Qur'an and Woman: Rereading the Sacred Text from a Woman's Perspective*. New York: Oxford University Press.

Wahba, Wafaa H. 1996. "Translator's Introduction." In *The Ordinances of Government: A Translation of Al-Ahkam al-Sultaniyya w'al-Wilayat al-Diniyya*. Translated by Wafaa H. Wahba. London: Garnet Publishing.

Waines, David. 1977. "The Third Century Internal Crisis of the Abbasids." *Journal of the Economic and Social History of the Orient* 20, 3: 282–306.

Waldner, David. 1999. *State Building and Late Development*. Ithaca, NY: Cornell University Press.

Wallerstein, Immanuel. 2004. *World-Systems Analysis: An Introduction*. Durham: Duke University Press.

Walzer, Michael. 1983. *Spheres of Justice: A Defense of Pluralism and Equality*. New York: Basic Books.

Ward, Robert E., and Dankwart A. Rustow. 1964. "Conclusion." In Robert E. Ward and Dankwart A. Rustow, eds., *Political Modernization in Japan and Turkey*. Princeton: Princeton University Press.

Watson, Andrew M. 1983. *Agricultural Innovation in the Early Islamic World: The Diffusion of Crops and Farming Techniques, 700–1100*. New York: Cambridge University Press.

Watt, W. Montgomery. 1953. "Introduction." In *The Faith and Practice of Al-Ghazali*. London: George Allen and Unwin.

1972. *The Influence of Islam on Medieval Europe*. Edinburgh: Edinburgh University Press.

1973. *The Formative Period of Islamic Thought*. Edinburgh: Edinburgh University Press.

Weaver, Henry Grady. 2014 [1947]. *The Mainspring of Human Progress*. Eastford, CT: Martino Fine Books.

Weber, Max. 1998 [1905]. *The Protestant Ethic and the Spirit of Capitalism*. Translated from German by Talcott Parsons. Los Angeles: Roxbury Publishing.

1946 [1919]. "Politics as a Vocation." In *From Max Weber: Essays in Sociology*. Translated from German and edited by H. H. Gerth and C. Wright Mills. New York: Oxford University Press.

1964 [1920]. *The Sociology of Religion*. Translated from German by Ephraim Fischoff. Boston: Beacon Press.

1978 [1922]. *Economy and Society: An Outline of Interpretive Sociology*. Translated from German by Ephraim Fischoff et al. Edited by Guenther Roth and Claus Wittich. Berkeley: University of California Press.

Weiss, Bernard G. 1998. *The Spirit of Islamic Law*. Athens: University of Georgia Press.

Wellisch, Hans H. 1986. "The First Arab Bibliography: *Fihrist al-'Ulum*." *Occasional Papers, University of Illinois* 175: 1–42.

West, John B. 2008. "Ibn al-Nafis, the Pulmonary Circulation, and the Islamic Golden Age." *Journal of Applied Physiology* 105: 1877–80.

White, Lynn Jr. 1962. *Medieval Technology and Social Change*. New York: Oxford University Press.

1963. "What Accelerated Technological Progress in the Western Middle Ages?" In A. C. Crombie, ed., *Scientific Change: Historical Studies in the Intellectual, Social*

and Technical Conditions for Scientific Discovery and Technical Invention, from
Antiquity to the Present. New York: Basic Books.

Wiet, Gaston. 1953. "L'Empire néo-byzantin des Omeyyades et l'Empire néosassanide
des Abbassides." *Cahiers d'histoire mondiale. Journal of World History*: 63–71.

——. 1971. *Baghdad: Metropolis of the Abbasid Caliphate*. Translated from French by
Seymour Feiler. Norman: University of Oklahoma Press.

Wiktorowicz, Quintan, ed. 2004. *Islamic Activism: A Social Movement Theory*
Approach. Bloomington: Indiana University Press.

——. 2010. "A Genealogy of Radical Islam." In Frederik Volpi, ed., *Political Islam:*
A Critical Reader. New York: Routledge.

Wilson, M. Brett. 2014. *Translating the Qur'an in an Age of Nationalism: Print Culture*
and Modern Islam in Turkey. New York: Oxford University Press.

Wittek, Paul. 1936. "Deux chapitres de l'histoire des Turcs de Roum." *Byzantion* 11:
285–319.

——. 1938. "De la défaite d'Ankara à la prise de Constantinople." *Revue des études*
islamiques 12: 1–34.

Wolfson, Harry A. 1963. "Revised Plan for the Publication of a Corpus Commentar-
iorum Averrios in Aristotelem." *Speculum* 38, 1: 88–104.

Wood, Philip. 2015. "Christians in the Middle East, 600–1000: Conquest, Competition
and Conversion." In A. C. S. Peacock, Bruno De Nicola, and Sara Nur Yıldız, eds.,
Islam and Christianity in Medieval Anatolia. Burlington, VT: Ashgate.

World Bank. 2010. "World Development Indicators: GNI per Capita (PPP), 2010,"
http://data.worldbank.org/indicator/NY.GNP.PCAP.PP.CD.

——. 2014a. "Indicators: Mortality Rate, under-5 (per 1,000 Live Births), 2014," http://
data.worldbank.org/indicator/SH.DYN.MORT.

——. 2014b. "Worldwide Governance Indicators," http://info.worldbank.org/governance/
wgi/index.aspx#home.

World Values Survey. 2004–8. www.worldvaluessurvey.org/.

Worthen, Shana. 2009. "The Influence of Lynn White, Jr.'s *Medieval Technology and*
Social Change." *History Compass* 7, 4: 1201–17.

Yalpani, Mohamed, and Akbar Heydari. 2005. "Quantity over Quality: A Voice from
the Third World." *Chemistry and Biodiversity* 2, 6: 730–7.

Yaqub, Alaadin M. 2013. "Translator's Introduction." In *Moderation in Belief*
(Al-Iqtisad fi al-I'tiqad). Translated by Aladdin M. Yaqub. Chicago: University of
Chicago Press.

Yate, Asadullah. 1996. "Foreword." In Abu'l Hassan al-Mawardi, *Al-Ahkam*
as-Sultaniyyah: The Laws of Islamic Governance. Translated and edited by
Asadullah Yate. London: Ta-Ha Publishers.

Yıldırım, Rıza. 2008. "Turkomans between Two Empires: The Origins of the Qizilbash
Identity in Anatolia (1447–1514)." PhD dissertation. Bilkent University.

Yılmaz, İhsan. 2005. *Muslim Laws, Politics and Society in Modern Nation States:*
Dynamic Legal Pluralisms in England, Turkey and Pakistan. Burlington, VT:
Ashgate.

Yom, Sean L. 2015. *From Resilience to Revolution: How Foreign Interventions Desta-*
bilize the Middle East. New York: Columbia University Press.

Zadeh, Travis. 2012. *The Vernacular Qur'an: Translation and the Rise of Persian*
Exegesis. New York: Oxford University Press.

Zaman, Muhammad Qasim. 1997. *Religion and Politics under the Early 'Abbasids: The Emergence of the Proto-Sunni Elite*. Leiden: Brill.

———. 2002. *The Ulama in Contemporary Islam: Custodians of Change*. Princeton: Princeton University Press.

———. 2005. "Pluralism, Democracy, and the 'Ulama." In Robert W. Hefner, ed., *Remaking Muslim Politics: Pluralism, Contestation, Democratization*. Princeton: Princeton University Press.

———. 2011. "Pakistan: Shari'a and the State." In Robert W. Hefner, ed., *Shari'a Politics: Islamic Law and Society in the Modern World*. Bloomington: Indiana University Press.

———. 2012. *Modern Islamic Thought in a Radical Age: Religious Authority and Internal Criticism*. New York: Cambridge University Press.

Zaret, David. 2000. *Origins of Democratic Culture: Printing, Petitions, and the Public Sphere in Early-Modern England*. Princeton: Princeton University Press.

Zeghal, Malika. 1996. *Gardiens de l'islam: Les oulémas d'Al Azhar dans l'Egypte contemporaine*. Paris: Presses de la Fondation nationale des sciences politiques.

———. 1999. "Religion and Politics in Egypt: The Ulema of al-Azhar, Radical Islam, and the State (1952–94)." *International Journal of Middle East Studies* 31, 4: 371–99.

Ziai, Hossein. 1996a. "Shihab al-Din Suhrawardi: Founder of the Illuminationist School." In Seyyed Hossein Nasr and Oliver Leaman, eds., *History of Islamic Philosophy*. New York: Routledge.

———. 1996b. "Mulla Sadra: His Life and Works." In Seyyed Hossein Nasr and Oliver Leaman, eds., *History of Islamic Philosophy*. New York: Routledge.

Zilfi, Madeline C. 1988. *The Politics of Piety: The Ottoman Ulema in the Postclassical Age (1600–1800)*. Minneapolis: Bibliotheca Islamica.

Ziolkowski, Jan M. 2007. "Introduction [to special issue on Dante and Islam]." *Dante Studies* 125: 1–34.

Zubaida, Sami. 1972. "Economic and Political Activism in Islam." *Economy and Society* 1, 3: 308–38.

Zuckert, Michael P. 2002. *Launching Liberalism on Lockean Political Philosophy*. Lawrence: University Press of Kansas.

Zürcher, Eric J. 2004. *Turkey: A Modern History*. New York: I. B. Tauris.

———. 2010. *The Young Turk Legacy and Nation Building: From the Ottoman Empire to Atatürk's Turkey*. London: I. B. Tauris.

Index

Made in the USA
Las Vegas, NV
22 August 2024

94251842R00177